PRAISE FOR *THE MENU*

"Braving the pique of local restaurateurs with its **deft, unblushing prose,** *The Menu* has stormed in to the sound of spilled milk and falling idols. **Murumba and Goldstein are good friends to the honest diner—they call it as they see it,** forks at the ready...the local dining scene will never be the same."
> –T. Susan Chang,
> Food & Travel Correspondent,
> *Boston Globe*

"A **clever and engaging** culinary tour."
> –Tim Zagat, Co-Founder,
> *Zagat Survey*

"**Exceptionally experienced restaurantgoers...**Goldstein and Murumba are **knowledgeable and enthusiastic** about eating well. Whether you are looking for a **cheap meal** or an **exquisite dining experience**, these two Yale Law graduates can tell you exactly where to go to find the best eats in town. **The menu is endless.**"
> –*Yale Daily News*

"*The Menu* is the **perfect field guide** to great eats in New Haven—and **not-so-great eats, too.**"
> –Tom Gogola, Managing Editor,
> *New Haven Advocate*

"What a great guide book! Immensely useful, written with panache, respectful of the city's great 'Roadfood' as well as its 'fine-dining' establishments, it is truly one of the most compelling restaurant guides we've seen."
—Jane and Michael Stern,
Authors, *Roadfood*

"Frank and colorful."
—*Yale Law Report*

"Don't assume that Goldstein and Murumba are food snobs...it's just that they're not afraid to speak up when a restaurant's reputation exceeds reality."
—*Daily Hampshire Gazette*

"Dining's dynamic duo."
—*PLAY Magazine*

"*The Menu* is not just a useful book; it's a pleasure to read. The only people who won't find it a pleasure are the owners of some of the really bad restaurants it warns us about."
—David Ball, Professor Emeritus of French and Comparative Literature, Smith College

"Scathing and scintillating."
—*New Haven Register*

the menu™

by robin goldstein
with clare murumba

WWW.NEWHAVENMENU.COM

ABOUT THE AUTHORS

ROBIN GOLDSTEIN, the food critic for the *New Haven Advocate*, is a graduate of Harvard College and the Yale Law School. Robin also holds a certificate in cooking from the French Culinary Institute in New York City. He has written for more than 25 travel guides spanning North America, South America, and Europe, including *Fodor's Italy, Fodor's Rome, Fodor's Venice, Fodor's Mexico, Fodor's Argentina, Fodor's Chile, UpClose Italy, Let's Go: Mexico, Let's Go: Ecuador,* and *Let's Go: Spain and Portugal.* Robin is also a food correspondent for the Fodor's Travel Wire, and has written on food and restaurants for *El Clarín* in Buenos Aires, the largest newspaper in Latin America. Robin is admitted to the Massachusetts Bar, and has worked for the law firm Allen & Overy in London, and the management consulting firm McKinsey & Company in New York City. He has also lived in Genoa, Italy; he currently resides in New Haven.

CLARE MURUMBA is a graduate of Harvard College and the Yale Law School. Clare has also studied cooking at the French Culinary Institute in New York City, and has written on food for the *New Haven Advocate.* Clare has split allegiances between three continents and their cuisines: she was born in the fruit mecca of Kampala, Uganda, and grew up in the food town of Melbourne, Australia, before moving to the United States at age 18. Clare is admitted to the New York Bar; she has worked for the investment banking firm Goldman, Sachs & Company, and now practices law with Cleary, Gottlieb, Steen & Hamilton in New York City, where she currently lives.

ROBIN and **CLARE** are co-authors of the first edition of *The Menu: New Haven* (Off the Map Press, 2003), and of *The Menu: Northampton, Amherst, and the Five-College Area* (Off the Map Press, 2004).

the menu

new haven area restaurant guide

second edition

www.newhavenmenu.com

off the map PRESS

SECOND EDITION, 2006

Printed in Canada

ISBN 0-9740143-2-X

FOR ROSIE,
MATTHEW,
AND LUKE,

WITH THE HOPE
THAT THEY
WILL ALL LOVE
RAW FISH
SOMEDAY

THE MENU: NEW HAVEN
SECOND EDITION

ASSOCIATE EDITORS

Jamie Kaiser   Coco Krumme

CONTRIBUTING EDITORS

Kate Carman   Xin Dong
Barry Goldstein   Rosie Goldstein
Samantha Lazarus   Duncan Levin
Benjamin Lima   David Menschel
Corey Rossman   Hal Stubbs
Lu Stubbs   Susan Stubbs
Christie Yang

CONTENTS

ACKNOWLEDGMENTS

We would first like to acknowledge our Associate Editors, Jamie Kaiser and Coco Krumme, for their painstaking research, eloquent writing, and incisive editing; and our Contributing Editors, all of whom contributed considerable resources on a volunteer basis. Special thanks go to Christie Yang, our sales and marketing intern; to Tom Gogola, Mark Oppenheimer, and Josh Mamis at the *Advocate*, for reining us in; and to David Menschel, our first—and still our biggest—supporter.

We are incredibly appreciative of the financial and structural support of Nick Shalek and YES over the past year. We are also deeply indebted to Bruce Alexander and Michael Morand at Yale University's Office of New Haven and State Affairs; to Barbara Lamb and Henry Fernandez with the City of New Haven; to Ian Solomon at the Yale Law School, Anne Coyle at the Yale School of Management, and Peter Salovey at Yale College; to Patricia Barnes and the Yale Law School's COAP program; and to Sean Dunn and Chris Fasanella for their generous cartographical assistance.

We also owe a debt of gratitude to Sonia Baghdady at WTNH, Jonathan Cooper and Jane Rushmore of *PLAY Magazine*, Cari Tuna of the *Yale Daily News*, and Christina Barber-Just of the *Daily Hampshire Gazette*; and to John and Cornelia Rogers, the legendary masters of Berkeley College, who have been the most gracious hosts imaginable.

Thanks also to Claire Stanford and Chris LaConte for their hard work; to Frank Marco at Wiggin & Dana for sage advice; to Shana and Olaf Schneider at the Young Professionals organization for their vast generosity and enthusiasm; to Rebecca Sherman, Mary Miller, and the rest of the the spectacular Arts & Ideas Festival staff; to Eva Geertz at Atticus; and to Erast Markiw and Larry Gal at the Yale Bookstore.

We appreciate the invaluable contributions of friend and wise man Steve Maslow; of our agents Janis Donnaud and Jonathan Russo; and of Justin Kestler, Matt Lombardi, Peter Osnos, Elizabeth Varet, Thomas Lehrman, Kate Carman, Blair Wallace, Greg Cohn, and John Leibovitz. Special thanks to Jane and Michael Stern, Tim Zagat, Eric Asimov, and our board of advisers, as well as partners-in-eating Ben Lima, Rick Grossman, Aliza Judd, Caroline Richardson, and Jacob Katz, and we thank Elizabeth Morrison, our perennial last-minute savior.

As always, we are supremely thankful to Sam and Keren Murumba and to Barry Goldstein and Sue Stubbs, for their endless font of support, editing, advice, and delicious cooking, and to Lu and Hal Stubbs, for their countless hours of painstaking edits, boundless energyy, and patience. Thanks also to Rosie Goldstein for her discriminating opinions on linguine with clams, and to the immortal Frank Tasty, without whom this project would have been a mere dream.

PREFACE

Welcome to the Second Edition of *The Menu*. We have been thrilled with the response to the first edition, and we are now even more delighted to introduce you to 120 more places to eat—many newly opened, and many others just newly added to the book—bringing the total number of establishments in *The Menu* to 268.

In the minds of the uninitiated, the number 268 might come as a bit of a shock. To some outsiders, New Haven can still conjure up images of postindustrial urban decay rather than culinary excellence. But that image of New Haven no longer reflects reality. Over the past decade, buoyed by the prosperity of the late 1990s and a plummeting crime rate, the Elm City has experienced a renaissance. It has become a haven for young professionals, for struggling artists, for people who are fed up with the high rents of New York and the cultural malaise of the ever-sprawling Connecticut suburbs. At the same time, the city has also become a magnet for suburban residents looking for a night on the town. New Haven's renewed appeal—as a place to visit and as a place in which to live—both reflects and stimulates the further growth of its cultural offerings and the revitalization of its urban spaces. The more people come, the more the distance shrinks between the city that New Haven is and the city that it could be.

The signs are everywhere. Witness the restoration of Ninth Square, the old business district that largely had been deserted, and the dramatic refashioning of Broadway into the main Yale student shopping and eating district. Savor the lively International Festival of Arts and Ideas in June, and the eclectic artisans displaying their wares at a market along Chapel Street on autumn weekends. Appreciate the transformation of an abandoned back alley behind the Taft into an urban arcade—an alley that now links College Street and the Shubert Theater to a whole new group of restaurants, bars, and shops along a once-deserted stretch of Temple Street, expanding even further the reach of downtown's economic boom. Take in the grandeur of the apartments springing up on every corner of the Town Green and its surrounding blocks. And marvel at the proliferation of nightclubs along Crown Street, the new nerve center where twentysomethings throughout Connecticut flock to find love—at least for a night.

In short, aside from Boston, New Haven is now the most cosmopolitan and culturally vibrant city on the eastern seaboard north of New York City. This revitalization has been accompanied by a dramatic increase in the number of creative high-end restaurants offering sophisticated dishes in sleek, urbane surroundings. Many are inspired by New York trends: the Nuevo Latino of Roomba; the haute Malaysian of Bentara; the Asian-inflected New American of Zinc; the gleaming postmodern microbrewery-pizzeria aesthetic of Bar; the Eritrean-Mediterranean fusion of Caffè Adulis.

At New Haven's new generation of downtown hotspots, one can sip six kinds of '-atinis; eat dishes that are infused, encrusted, or tea-smoked, served with chutnies, essences, or reductions; and pair it all with hard-to-find Super-Tuscans. But then there are the restaurants that are truly charting their own culinary territory; witness the emergence of Ibiza, New Haven's renowned temple to cutting-edge Spanish cuisine whose chef, Luis Bollo, is perhaps the first non-pizza-maker to draw people from New York *to* New Haven just to taste his food.

At the same time, the city has witnessed an equally impressive proliferation of more modestly priced ethnic restaurants, which reflect a new wave of immigration to New Haven: multiple good Indian offerings; four good-value Thai places within a one-block radius along Chapel Street; spectacular Jamaican and Mexican in some of the city's traditionally less prosperous neighborhoods; and an increasing array of reliable sushi chefs, most prominently at the sparkling new Miso in Ninth Square. These additions to New Haven's culinary mix now complement the Italian strip along Wooster Street, whose odes to the cooking of immigrants from the area around Naples still thrive even as they serve as a testament to the settlement trends of an earlier era.

These restaurants remind us that New Haven's cultural diversity is part of what makes it such a vital place. The opening of a downtown branch of the soul food restaurant Sandra's, whose original Congress Avenue location lies far from Yale and the Green, was a symbolic leap forward. Sandra's (along with urban developer Bruce Alexander and his colleagues at Yale's Office of New Haven and State Affairs, who enabled the project) recognized that downtown New Haven's vibrancy had created a vast new market space for cultural and culinary intermingling among the city's diverse populations.

And yet, despite all of the new competition, many of the culinary institutions of earlier eras continue to thrive. This lies in stark contrast with the brand of gentrification that has occurred in cities like Cambridge, where much of the culinary old guard has been displaced by shifting demographics and skyrocketing rent prices. In New Haven, although property values have seen a similar increase, many of the most beloved eating establishments are still old classics. Some, like Yankee Doodle, Sally's, Frank Pepe's, and Louis' Lunch, have become part of local folklore and even American legend (many claim, for instance, that Louis' invented the hamburger). These places have managed to attract a generation of new devotees even as they stubbornly, and comfortably, hew to quirky old traditions (don't ask for ketchup at Louis' or a reservation at Sally's). And what's not to like? They serve unpretentious, excellent food, from recipes perfected over generations, at rock-bottom prices.

So we hope you're hungry. With something for every palate and every price range, there has never been a better time to eat in and around New Haven.

—David Menschel and Reiko Hillyer

INTRODUCTION: USING *THE MENU*

THE RATING SYSTEM

Welcome to the Second Edition. After meticulous research, endless eating, and copious data collection (all three with the help of our intrepid Associate Editors), we have re-rated all establishments and redesigned our numerical system to make it more simple and useful. All ratings are now on a 10-point scale, and they culminate in an overall rating and value rating that are also out of 10.

	weight
Food	60%
Atmosphere	30%
Attitude	10%
Overall out of 10	

Ratings

Price

Value out of 10

Food (1-10): This rating is strictly a measure of whether the food on offer is appetizing or objectionable, insipid or delicious. Don't be surprised to find a greasy spoon outscoring a historic, upscale, sit-down establishment, for one simple reason: the food just tastes better. Bear with us on this one. Close your eyes, open your mind (and your mouth), and give everything a chance. This metric is weighted to be by far the biggest component of the overall score. (Coffeeshops and bars with only very basic food offerings are ineligible for this rating; they shouldn't be penalized for what they don't really attempt.)

Atmosphere (1-10): The bottom line: does being here make us happy? The most emphatic "yes" inspires the highest ratings. This is not to be translated as "décor." We don't give out points for tablecloths, silverware, or fine china. We reward warm lighting, comfortable accomodations, a well-executed theme, and a sense of place. (Establishments that center their operations on take-out are ineligible for this rating, out of fairness to their focus.) The dim glow of candles and dark wood at your local dive might just garner more accolades than the proliferation of restaurant accoutrements at an over-bright, upmarket bistro. This is the democratization of restaurant reviews—or perhaps a nonviolent revolution: in our less humble moments we fancy ourselves the Subcomandante Marcos of the food-review world. Viva.

Attitude (1-10): Most guides call this "service," but we beg to differ. In our view, being served has limited appeal, but being treated with a good attitude goes a long way. The real question is this: when you see the waitstaff approaching your table, are you (a) delighted, (b) reasonably content, (c) filled with dread, or (d) exhausted, because you've been standing on your chair with flags, engaged in unsubtle semaphore for twenty minutes, just trying to get a dinner menu? High-end restaurants and take-out joints are all in the running—even if you're just dashing in to pick up your order, it is still worth knowing whether you'll love or loathe the prospect of interacting with the people who stand between you and your meal.

Overall (1-10): A restaurant's overall rating is calculated by taking a weighted average of the scores for food (60%), atmosphere (30%), and attitude (10%). The numbers might be lower than you expect—there's no grade inflation here. Let yourself get used to our system, and don't be summarily scared off by something in the 5s or 6s. Anything over 8 is highly recommended, and only four establishments in the entire book finish at 9 or above. For take-out spots without atmosphere ratings and coffeeshops without food ratings, we take weighted averages of the other two components to compute the overall rating. We use the following plain-English translations for these overall results:

9-10: Truly special; one of our favorite places in town
8-9: Very good; highly recommended
7-8: Good; recommended
6-7: Above average; recommended, but with some reservations
5-6: No better than average; not particularly recommended
4-5: Below average, with significant problems; not recommended
3-4: Bad; a place to avoid
1-3: Very bad; a place to avoid at all costs

Price: This dollar value is a guide to how much, on average, you should expect to spend per person on a full dinner at the restaurant, including tax and tip, but not including beer, wine, or other alcoholic drinks. For simple, informal places, we go by what the average person might buy, which is often just a sandwich or the like; at more elaborate restaurants, we usually figure in the cost of an appetizer and/or dessert course, depending on what people are likely to order. Only places that serve meals are eligible; this excludes ice cream shops and such. Keep in mind that, at the higher-end restaurants, you will generally spend considerably less than the quoted price if you go for lunch.

Value (1-10): This is a metric that expresses the relationship between the average price of a meal and all the other factors that we rate. We use a mathematical formula and bell curve to derive the value rating from those other scores. The distribution of value ratings is similar to that of overall ratings. The formula gives a measured sense of relative value between otherwise disparate establishments.

GEOGRAPHY 101

Back in the day, New Haven was laid out neatly in nine squares. These days, things are a little more haphazard, although if you look carefully at a map of the city you can see the original shape of the nine-square layout; the Ninth Square neighborhood still pays homage to this nomenclature. To make things easier for everybody, we have established our own subdivisions of the city. They are sections based on compass orientations and well-known neighborhood names. For locals, some of these will be familiar. Others are somewhat arbitrary, but, we hope, inherently intuitive.

In *The Menu*, we have provided exact street addresses for each establishment that we list. For specific directions, since we don't know where you're coming from, we advise that you consult the wonderful new Google Maps (maps.google.com), Mapquest, or one of the other Web-based mapping systems, all of which which tend to work quite well in the New Haven area. We have included a map of the most central neighborhoods in downtown New Haven, which is on pages 4-5, following this page. Our New Haven neighborhood subdivisions are as follows (each is listed with its northern, southern, eastern, and western bounding streets in parentheses):

Theater District (borders: Chapel St., George St., Church St., York St.): In downtown New Haven there are two major intersecting thoroughfares: Chapel Street, which runs roughly east-west, and Church Street, which runs roughly north-south. In this book, the part of town south of Chapel and west of Church is referred to as the Theater District, named for the landmark Shubert Theater and the old Palace Theater on College between Chapel and Crown. Still the cultural and entertainment center of New Haven, this area also includes the Taft apartment complex; the Yale Art Gallery and Center for British Art; a raft of eating establishments, stores, and coffee shops, especially near the intersection of College and Crown; and the new proliferation of restaurants and bars on Temple. Some of the best-known restaurants and bars in town can be found here, and the entertainment venues on Crown Street are the center of New Haven's lively night scene.

Upper Chapel Area (borders: Edgewood St., North Frontage St., York St., Howe St.): This part of town was once beyond the purvey of the college area, but has lately become truly a part of the Yale-New Haven mix. The southern part of this area, toward George Street and Route 34, is more representative of the old neighborhood than the new. The eastern border of the Upper Chapel Area is York Street, which runs north-south through the middle of the downtown area. West of York, the center of this neighborhood is the completely revitalized Howe Street, which is home to a bevy of affordable restaurants, including almost all of the Thai and Indian restaurants in town. To the north, the Upper Chapel Area gives way to the Broadway area.

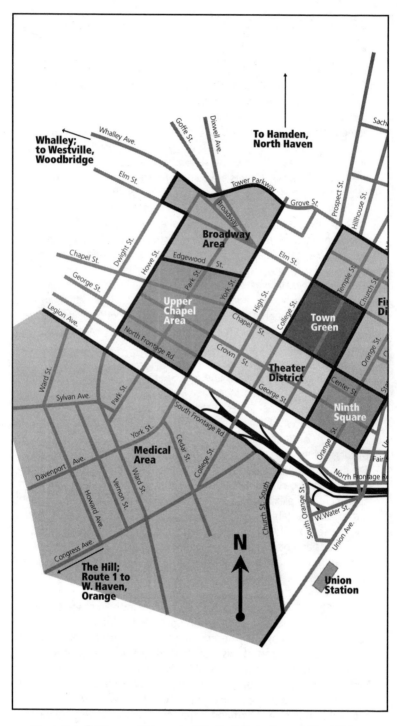

Central New Haven Neighborhoods: West

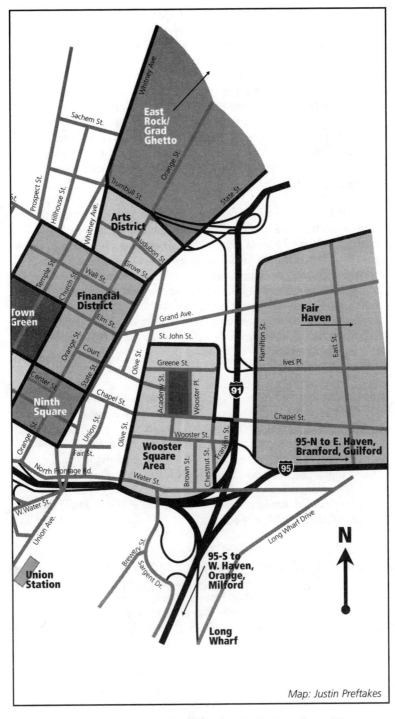

Map: Justin Preftakes

Central New Haven Neighborhoods: East

Broadway Area (borders: Tower Pkwy., Edgewood St., York St., Dwight St.): In some cities, Broadway goes on for miles. In New Haven, if you blink you might miss it. This brief thoroughfare begins at the intersection of York and Elm, and ends where Whalley and Dixwell Avenues begin. For such a small tract of town, the Broadway district has more than its share of stores and places to eat, in part due to revitalization efforts led by Yale University over the past decade. As a result, many of the establishments in the Broadway area cater specifically to students, whether they're bustling cafés, cheap lunch joints, all-night pizza places, or dive bars. For this guide, the Broadway Area extends north beyond Broadway proper to include York Street between Elm and Grove.

Financial District (borders: Grove St., Chapel St., State St., College St.): North of Ninth Square, and north and east of the Green, is New Haven's downtown business, government, financial, and academic center. This is no concrete jungle; while a few blocks of civic buildings, courthouses and office complexes mark the center of administration for the city, the Yale College campus sits just to the west and north (the campus itself has few commercial eating establishments). The neighborhood is characterized by a lot of good, quick, cheap lunchtime delis. Since "downtown" would be too broad an appellation, and "central business district" a bit grandiose, we have designated this part of town the Financial District.

Arts District (borders: Trumbull St., Grove St., State St., Whitney Ave.): Officially, the Arts District (so named by the City of New Haven) is on Audubon Street. Along with Broadway and Ninth Square, this area represents one of the City's most proactive development efforts. We're thankful for their work; while the name of the neighborhood might still be a bit premature, Audubon is indeed host to the Neighborhood Music School and a few art galleries, and the area has a pleasant feel. The neighborhood has its northern end at Trumbull Street, where the East Rock/Grad Ghetto area begins.

East Rock/Grad Ghetto (borders: East Rock, Trumbull St., State St., Whitney Ave.): The affectionate, Yale-centric "Grad Ghetto" misnomer has become one common term for the part of town that stretches north of Trumbull Street toward East Rock Park, where the bustle of downtown offices and shops gives way to wide streets, gracious multi-family houses, and expansive green lawns. More suburban than urban, the Grad Ghetto has earned its name for the many graduate students that tend to gravitate towards the shared houses and apartments in this part of town. Although the uninitiated may find this area to be a confusing maze of quiet, tree-lined streets that end abruptly or make unexpected turns, most of the relevant locations are on or just off the broad main streets like Orange and State. This subdivision also includes the area known as Science Hill.

Ninth Square (borders: Chapel St., George St., State St., Church St.): East of the Theater District and south of the Financial District is Ninth Square, the southeastern-most of the old nine squares of New Haven. Once a desolate part of town, Ninth Square is now a cultural mecca, including a prominent art gallery, a great live music space, and some of the city's hippest and most creative restaurants. Ninth Square ends at the railroad tracks just east of State Street; a couple of blocks away, on the other side of the tracks, is Wooster Square. For *The Menu*, the northern border of this district is Chapel Street, although local parlance defines the area a little less precisely.

Wooster Square Area (borders: St. John St., Water St., Chestnut St., Olive St.): This is a quiet, residential quadrant due east beyond State Street and across the train tracks; it's characterized by gracious old brownstones and plenty of greenery. Historically an Italian neighborhood, this part of town—especially Wooster Street—is home to many of New Haven's favorite pizza places and Italian restaurants, even though a lot of the old residents, many of whom came over from the Naples area at the beginning of the 20th century as a result of a grand recruitment effort by the Winchester Rifle company, have long since moved to the suburbs. The City-designated Historic Wooster Square district begins at Olive Street and centers around Wooster Street, but continues down to Water Street.

Fair Haven (borders: Middletown Ave., Chapel St., Quinnipiac Ave., State St.): A lively part of New Haven more modest and old-school than the downtown neighborhoods, Fair Haven, which is reached by continuing on Grand Avenue east of the train tracks and under the I-91 overpass, is little known to many downtown residents, who will need a car to reach it. Fair Haven is home to many of New Haven's more recent immigrant communities, particularly the Hispanic community, and thus also home to some of the best and most authentic Mexican and Latin American food in town. The western edge of Fair Haven, north of Wooster Square, also has some old Italian-American immigrant culture. To the east, the neighborhood continues to the Quinnipiac River, which is home to a couple of picturesque riverbank restaurants.

Long Wharf (borders: Water St., Church St. South, I-95, Union Ave.): The arrival of IKEA has jolted this long-underdeveloped area down toward New Haven Harbor, an area south of Wooster Square that is also home to the Long Wharf Theater and the Connecticut Limo terminal. You'll need wheels to get there from downtown.

Medical Area/The Hill (borders: South Frontage Rd., New Haven Harbor, Church Street South, the Boulevard): While there still aren't many restaurants in this redeveloping area of New Haven, it's home to some good, local food. The district also extends south to Bayview Park by the New Haven Harbor, where you can dine with beautiful waterfront views.

Whalley (borders: Fitch St., Dwight St., Whalley Ave.): This no-man's-land section of Whalley Ave. between the Broadway Area and Westville is not really connected to any other specific 'hood, and it's home to a vibrant mix of inexpensive ethnic restaurants, from Jamaican to kosher to soul food, including some of New Haven's best-kept secrets. Don't let yourself be guilty of tunnel vision when shuttling between downtown and Westville.

Westville (borders: Woodbridge town line, Fitch St., Fountain St., West Rock Park): Home to Southern Connecticut State University and a cute little assortment of shops and restaurants along a particular stretch of Whalley Avenue that lies about 2 miles northwest of the Broadway area and downtown, this is one of New Haven's most atmospheric little neighborhoods, and it's up-and-coming as a food destination, too. Continuing along Whalley past the Wilbur Cross Parkway, you'll reach Amity Road and the town of **Woodbridge**, which we also cover.

Other cities: Other cities' neighborhood designations are simply the cities themselves, and are more straightforward. The book covers the following cities:

North: To the north, **Hamden** and **North Haven** can be reached either by taking I-91 North (exits 9-12), or by heading north from downtown New Haven on Whitney Avenue or State Street. To reach **Derby**, head west from downtown New Haven on Derby Avenue (Route 34).

East: To the east of New Haven along the shoreline, reachable on I-95 North, are **East Haven** (exits 50-52), **Branford** (exits 53-56), and **Guilford** (exits 57-59).

West: To the west of New Haven on I-95 South lie **West Haven** (exits 43-44), **Orange** (exits 41-42), and **Milford** (exits 39-40). West Haven and Orange are also easily accessible from downtown New Haven by following Congress Avenue southwest through the Hill neighborhood, where it runs into Route 1 and heads into West Haven and then Orange.

THE LISTING SYSTEM

CUISINE CATEGORIES

Every establishment in *The Menu* is associated with one or more cuisine categories. Restaurants focusing on foreign culinary traditions are simply designated by country or region. These include **African, Chinese, French, Greek, Indian, Irish, Italian, Jamaican, Japanese, Korean, Latin American** (which includes Puerto Rican, Cuban, Central American, South American, and Nuevo Latino, but not Mexican), **Malaysian, Mexican, Middle Eastern, Spanish, Swedish, Thai, Turkish,** and **Vietnamese.**

As for American cuisine, since there's so much of it, we've filtered things more finely into the following 12 subdivisions:

Baked goods: The emphasis here is on breads and pastries, whether sweet or savory, ideally homemade, that accompany coffee or stand alone as dessert or a snack. Think croissants, muffins, bagels, and cake.

Bar Food: This is one of America's proudest indigenous food traditions. Buffalo wings, burgers, fries, nachos, and beer are the essentials, although grilled chicken, fried mozzarella, and jalapeño poppers are close on their heels.

Light American: This is the typical modern American lunch menu, with deli sandwiches, salads, and sometimes a bit of fusion (perhaps a dose of curry or chipotle), and generally a selection of breads and cheeses. This designation ranges from standard deli fare to the food from a more upscale panini or gourmet-salad purveyor.

New American: These restaurants, usually pricey, feature elaborate plating, construction cuisine, fusion influences (often, but not necessarily, from the Pacific Rim), and an adjectival yet minimalist menu. It's the sort of preparation that has come to permeate upscale big-city restaurant menus in the past decade or so.

Pizza: The pizza category includes ever-popular pizza by the slice, whole pies for delivery, and elaborate brick-oven pizza to be eaten in.

Seafood: This designates places specializing in fish or shellfish (although these restaurants often serve meat as well).

Short-order American: This refers to places that serve a menu full of diner food and casual classics that are cooked on a big griddle— hamburgers, bacon, egg, and cheese, and so forth—along with fries, basic salads, soups, and the like. You know the drill.

Southern: This category includes barbecue (ribs, pulled pork, brisket, and so on), fried chicken, fried fish, and other soul food—cornbread, mac and cheese, slaw, collards, and so on.

Steakhouse: The name says it all. Deeply steak-focused, even if there's seafood and chicken on the menu too.

Sweets: This is the catch-all American dessert category. It includes ice cream and all manner of candy. This designation is reserved for places that are focused only on desserts, candy, or sweet things.

Traditional American: Meat-and-potatoes classics are the norm here, along with more elaborate preparations: crab cakes, pot roasts, baked scrod, lobster, and other New England classics. This is restaurant food with few concessions to postmodernity.

Tex-Mex: This is distinct from Mexican in the sense that this cuisine is influenced more by Texas than by Mexico. It's your basic, cheesy, satisfying north-of-the-border fare: burritos, chimichangas, fajitas, chile con queso, and so on. Don't forget the margaritas.

ESTABLISHMENT TYPE

These classifications make it possible to learn, at a glance, whether an establishment is appropriate for a particular mood or occasion.

Bar and grill: This categorization refers to a bar that also has a kitchen, and regularly serves meals, generally with waiter service.

Café: For our purposes, this means a place that feels primarily focused on vending coffee, tea, and perhaps some pastries or ice cream—often a great place for studying, chatting, or whiling away the afternoon—but food service might well be a mere afterthought.

Casual restaurant: Expect full waiter service but a generally laid-back atmosphere without too much fuss. Good examples include pizzerias, simple Italian-American places, and most area Indian and Thai eateries.

Counter service: At these places, you order at a counter, and generally pick up your food there as well (although it might be brought out to you). Most customers eat in. As a rule, this label means that there is no table service to speak of once you're seated. This includes many sandwich shops, lunch spots, famous burger joints, and fish shacks.

Diner: This category is characterized by basic booths and a choice of counter or table service. Generally, there's a formulaic menu and a casual waitstaff. Ideally, the structure is a former train car. Around here, though, it rarely is.

Fast-food chain: This is your classic regional or national chain offering a standardized menu, typically centering on sandwiches, with food that's partially prepared well in advance so that you can munch within minutes. Drive-through windows proliferate.

Specialty grocery: Comprising a new category in *The Menu: Second Edition*, New Haven's specialty food stores are well known for their authentic imported Italian products, gourmet cheeses, olive oils, fresh produce, good meats, and so on, and also for prepared food that can be taken to go, or sometimes eaten at one of a couple of tables there.

Take-out: The establishment, and hopefully the food, is geared toward consumption elsewhere. The majority of customers at these places do not eat in. Seating is generally, but not always, minimal; more important, though, is the typical customer behavior. Late-night pizzerias, falafel windows, and food carts would be classic examples.

Upmarket Restaurant: This is the most elaborate sort of dining experience. Attentive and professional service, elegant place settings, and a wine list of some description are all par for the course. The food is usually about presentation as well as preparation. Note that the designation reflects style and ambition, but not necessarily quality and execution.

SPECIAL FEATURES

Breakfast: Although plenty of restaurants serve lunch and dinner, breakfast can be harder to come by. These places are open for business bright and early, and have a specific breakfast menu.

Brunch: In our book, it's a leisurely weekend meal (usually Sunday) that includes classic breakfast and lunch options, sometimes in a buffet. To qualify as serving brunch in our book, a restaurant must have a brunch menu that's distinct from the usual lunch menu.

Date-friendly: If you asked your most socially accomplished friend where to go for a date, these are places that he or she might mention. Some of these establishments are romantic, others are just plain fun. It's all about the vibe. None of them are uncomfortable or awkward.

Delivery: Free to your door, usually requiring a minimum purchase (typically in the seven-to-10-dollar range). Tipping is expected; most places have a geographical limit of their own town.

Outdoor dining: This is a seasonal denomination. When the weather's warm, these are places to be. This can mean anything from a couple of sidewalk tables to a sprawling beer garden.

Wireless internet: It's gotta be free. Sorry, Starbucks.

Vegetarian-friendly: There are, of course, the "vegetarian restaurants" that see meatlessness as a category of cuisine unto itself. But they are by no means the beginning and end of vegetarian dining in the area. There are many places that offer delicious meatless options, and typically don't advertise themselves as vegetarian. For those places, our "Vegetarian-friendly" special-feature designation bears witness to the fact that you can forsake meat and still have a broad range of dining options. This feature indicates that vegetarians will not feel constrained by the menu. Clare's seven years as a vegetarian (though she's now been an omnivore for six) deeply inform these choices.

OTHER PRACTICAL INFORMATION

. For each establishment, *The Menu* lists an address, telephone number, and web site (if available); which credit cards are accepted (we only query Visa, MasterCard, and American Express); weekly hours of operation; and whether, in our estimation, reservations are essential or advisable for dinner. As for the bar, "full" indicates that the establishment is licensed to serve hard liquor and, thus, mixed drinks and cocktails in addition to wine and beer. "Wine and beer" is another type of license; such places might serve just wine, or just beer, or both. There's also a handful of "BYO" restaurants, where you can bring your own wine or beer. We're fans of this concept—it can be a great opportunity to drink that nice bottle that's been sitting around the house, waiting for a good occasion.

Whatever food you're looking for, you'll find it in our handy set of lists, beginning on p. 17.

Easily track down the best place for Jamaican food (p. 28), seafood (p. 30), or vegetarian food (p. 51). Discover where you can BYO (p. 40), sit outdoors (p. 39), eat well on the cheap (p. 22), or get lucky (p. 38). Quickly find the area's top ice cream (p. 27), top soul food (p. 24), or top brunch (p.26). Locate the best meal in Branford (p.35)—or the best meal at 2:30am (p. 49).

RELENTLESSLY OPINIONATED

The Menu is relentlessly opinionated, as our moniker proclaims. One of our Contributing Editors calls it "in-your-face" restaurant reviewing. The *New Haven Register* called it "scathing." And some people have suggested that this style of reviewing is rude to the restaurants. But we consider it rude for restaurants to serve tasteless food at high prices, or to subject patrons to a disaffected attitude.

We think that too many restaurant critics have not deigned to embrace the art of simple criticism, thus giving readers the ultimate raw deal. For how is one to choose between two places if both are portrayed in dizzying, worshipful prose? And how frustrating is it to find out that at least one of them was a waste of your time and money? If you're celebrating a special occasion, as one often does by dining out, the sting of disappointment after a bad meal is that much more acute. What's *definitely* rude—and costly—is for an unsuspecting patron to dine on the strength of a sugar-coated review, only to discover the truth the hard way, with friends or date in tow. In short, our duty is to our readers, not to the restaurants.

We do not accept advertising from restaurants, and although we are occasionally recognized, we never identify ourselves when we dine. We also consult our Contributing Editors, combing their entire body of experiences to broaden our personal perspective on each restaurant, and assuring that our experiences were representative. Our goal is to save you the cost, disappointment, and possible discomfort of a bland, overpriced meal—and to point you preemptively in the direction of something better. Helping you choose, every time you eat out, is what makes this endeavor worthwhile for us. And so, within these pages, we tell you exactly what we'd tell a good friend if she called us up and asked what we *really* thought of a place.

This unapologetic approach may take a moment to get used to. But in the end, we believe opinionated commentary to be the highest possible compliment to the local dining scene. That is to say, the food here is definitely worth talking about. New Haven has arrived, and it deserves a serious restaurant guide.

We don't expect you to agree with everything we say—sometimes, we don't even agree with each other—but we do hope you can appreciate our conviction that, in food writing, opinion is better expressed openly than buried between the lines. We believe that, over the course of a *Menu* full of reviews, we will earn your trust. And whether you concur or dissent, we would love to hear from you; we'd like nothing better than to inspire more relentlessly opinionated diners in New Haven. Visit us at **www.newhavenmenu.com** to post your own opinions, or your thoughts on ours.

QUIRKS

"Mains"

You won't find the word "entrée" in *The Menu*. This universally used misnomer is inherently ambiguous, and particularly confusing to foreigners. In French, and in much of the English-speaking world outside America, it means "starter" or "appetizer." We're not sure how "entrée" came to mean a main course in the United States, but in this book we simply say "main course," or "main," if that's what we mean.

Overcooked

As you might have noticed, we prefer our meat (and certain kinds of fish) very rare. Specifically, our reviews often comment on whether or not establishments are willing to serve a dish as rare as we request it. Although we understand that there are many people who like their meat more cooked than we do, our complaint isn't with restaurants that serve meat medium or medium-well by default; it's with restaurants that refuse to serve meat rare *even upon emphatic request*. Still, people who like their meat cooked medium or more should take our comments with a grain of salt—and skip the following paragraph.

With very few exceptions, New Haven-area restaurants tend to cook meat at least one notch above the requested doneness. Be vigilant and serious about ordering rare, and don't be shy about sending things back, because this is the only way that area restaurants will eventually get the message. If you like medium rare, ask for it rare. And if you like it rare, look your server in the eye and add a "very" or two. Likewise for fish; restaurants around here rarely ask how you'd like your tuna or salmon grilled—you generally have to volunteer the information. In this case, being assertive can pay gustatory dividends.

Undersalted

In these pages, we complain often—some will say too often—about undersalted dishes. As a matter of chemistry, a certain amount of salt is necessary to bring out the complexity of flavor in most savory flavors: meats, fishes, soups, sauces, and so on. If you don't believe us, try this experiment, suggested by Italian food guru Marcella Hazan: pour two half-glasses of red wine, dump some salt into one of them, swirl them both around, and smell both glasses. The salt really brings out the bouquet (you won't want to drink it, though...). Undersalting is the most common way that a generally well-executed dish can fall completely flat. This problem can be corrected with the salt shaker on the table for many dishes, but it's too late to rescue some, including anything deep-fried.

For whatever reasons, undersalting seems to be an epidemic at restaurants in New Haven. Perhaps restaurants have decided that it is better to undersalt, which can be corrected at the table, than to oversalt, which cannot. We disagree with this philosophy. A customer who wants his or her dish undersalted should ask for it that way, and the request should be accommodated graciously. But we think that by default, a dish should come to the table properly seasoned and ready to eat, not left in the final stages of preparation. Forcing the customer to finish that process is as absurd, to us, as plopping a salad down in front of a customer with a carrot and a peeler.

For there is no such thing as salting "to taste" in the professional kitchen. Most good chefs around the world would agree that proper seasoning is a matter of necessity, not opinion. At a recent seminar with famed chef and Madison resident Jacques Pepin, an audience member asked him whether or not the classic French recipe that he was preparing would "work" with less salt. Responded Pepin: "If you have dietary restrictions, then let me know, and I will underseason your food—at your own risk. But I'm your chef, not your doctor." Amen.

The fine print
This entire book is a work of opinion, and should be understood as such. Any and all judgments rendered upon restaurants within these pages, regardless of tense, are intended as statements of pure opinion. Facts have been thoroughly checked with the restaurants in person and via telephone; we have gone to the utmost lengths to ensure that every fact is correct, and that every ingredient in every dish is properly referenced. Any factual errors that nonetheless remain are purely unintentional. That said, menus and plates change so frequently at restaurants that any printed book, however new, cannot help but be a bit behind the times. Check in with us at **www.newhavenmenu.com** for the latest updates, restaurant news, discussion boards, and more.

Feedback
The heart and soul of this endeavor is our firm belief that the world of restaurant reviewing can only be improved by opening outspoken channels of communication between restaurants and their customers. We hope that the honest articulation of our opinions and dining experiences will encourage you to do the same—if you have a bad meal, or a great one, *tell the restaurant.* Tell them what was right and what was wrong. It can only help. And tell us; we've set up an interactive space, **www.newhavenmenu.com**, for readers to express agreement or dissent of any sort. The commentary found on this site is (within limits) unedited and unadulterated. It doesn't require registration, and you can even post anonymously. Please, read some reviews, go try some restaurants, and then log on and let us know what you think. We look forward to hearing from you.

About Off the Map Press
Off the Map Press is a lean, independent publishing house dedicated to providing useful information in an engaging format. Off the Map Press publishes relentlessly opinionated, irreverent, and comprehensive guides to dining in smaller and midsize American cities and college towns. Look for other Off the Map Press titles, including *The Menu: Northampton, Amherst, and the Five-College Area.* For all of the latest information, or to buy any of these titles, please visit us at www.offthemappress.com.

LISTS

TOP 50 OVERALL

Rank			Location	Cuisine	Type	Price
1	Le Petit Café	9.6	Branford	French	Upmarket	$45
2	Ibiza	9.3	Theater District	Spanish	Upmarket	$44
3	Union League Café	9.2	Theater District	French	Upmarket	$46
4	Roomba	9.0	Theater District	Latin American	Upmarket	$52
5	East Japanese	8.8	Milford	Japanese	Upmarket	$32
6	Bentara	8.7	Ninth Square	Malaysian	Upmarket	$34
7	Carmen Anthony	8.7	Arts District	Steakhouse	Upmarket	$50
8	Jeffrey's	8.7	Milford	New American	Upmarket	$44
9	Stone House	8.6	Guilford	Seafood	Upmarket	$38
10	Zinc	8.5	Theater District	New American	Upmarket	$45
11	Bar (Brü Room)	8.5	Theater District	Pizza	Bar and grill	$15
12	Caffé Adulis	8.4	Theater District	African	Upmarket	$28
13	Modern Apizza	8.4	East Rock/Grad Ghetto	Pizza	Casual	$13
14	Sally's Apizza	8.3	Wooster Square Area	Pizza	Casual	$14
15	Soul de Cuba	8.3	Theater District	Latin American	Upmarket	$22
16	Trevethan's	8.3	East Rock/Grad Ghetto	New American	Upmarket	$36
17	Nini's Bistro	8.3	Ninth Square	New American	Upmarket	$35
18	Wild Ginger	8.3	Orange	Japanese	Upmarket	$33
19	Mother's	8.3	Medical Area/The Hill	Jamaican	Take-out	$12
20	Foe	8.2	Branford	New American	Upmarket	$35
21	Pacifico	8.2	Theater District	Latin American	Upmarket	$38
22	Bella Rosa Café	8.2	Westville	Light American	Casual	$17
23	Stillwater Bistro	8.2	Fair Haven	New American	Upmarket	$31
24	Roseland Apizza	8.2	Derby	Pizza	Casual	$32
25	Lou's Big Top	8.2	Westville	Short-order	Take-out	$7
26	Swagat	8.1	West Haven	Indian	Casual	$7
27	The Place	8.1	Guilford	Seafood	Casual	$19
28	Central Steakhouse	8.0	Ninth Square	Steakhouse	Upmarket	$51
29	Yankee Doodle	8.0	Broadway Area	Short-order	Diner	$6
30	L'Orcio	8.0	East Rock/Grad Ghetto	Italian	Upmarket	$33
31	Golden Seafood	8.0	Westville	Chinese	Casual	$22
32	Stony Creek Market	8.0	Branford	Light American	Counter	$12
33	Tenderloin's	8.0	Branford	Steakhouse	Upmarket	$39
34	Christopher Martin's	8.0	East Rock/Grad Ghetto	Bar food	Bar and grill	$17
35	Frank Pepe's	7.9	Wooster Square Area	Pizza	Casual	$14
36	Martin's Amer. Café	7.9	Guilford	New American	Upmarket	$39
37	Daiko (Jerry-San's)	7.9	West Haven	Japanese	Casual	$22
38	Caribbean Connection	7.9	Whalley	Jamaican	Take-out	$9
39	Hama	7.8	Hamden	Japanese	Casual	$18
40	Pot-au-Pho	7.8	Arts District	Vietnamese	Casual	$9
41	Avellino's Trattoria	7.8	Ninth Square	Italian	Upmarket	$31
42	La Piazza	7.7	Broadway Area	Italian	Casual	$27
43	Som Siam	7.7	Guilford	Thai	Casual	$22
44	Sandra's	7.7	Arts District, The Hill	Southern	Casual	$21
45	Anna Liffey's	7.7	Arts District	Irish	Bar and grill	$21
46	Darbar India	7.7	Branford	Indian	Upmarket	$20
47	Su Casa	7.7	Branford	Tex-Mex	Casual	$22
48	Geppi's	7.7	Fair Haven	Italian	Casual	$29
49	Louis' Lunch	7.7	Theater District	Short-order	Counter	$7
50	China Great Wall	7.7	Arts District	Chinese	Take-out	$5

TOP 50 FOOD

Rank			Location	Cuisine	Type	Price
1	Ibiza	9.8	Theater District	Spanish	Upmarket	$44
2	Sally's Apizza	9.6	Wooster Square Area	Pizza	Casual	$14
3	Roomba	9.5	Theater District	Latin American	Upmarket	$52
4	Le Petit Café	9.4	Branford	French	Upmarket	$45
5	East Japanese	9.4	Milford	Japanese	Upmarket	$32
6	Union League Café	9.3	Theater District	French	Upmarket	$46
7	Bar (Brü Room)	9.2	Theater District	Pizza	Bar and grill	$15
8	Modern Apizza	9.1	East Rock/Grad Ghetto	Pizza	Casual	$13
9	Zinc	9.0	Theater District	New American	Upmarket	$45
10	Carmen Anthony	8.9	Arts District	Steakhouse	Upmarket	$50
11	Stone House	8.8	Guilford	Seafood	Upmarket	$38
12	Jeffrey's	8.8	Milford	New American	Upmarket	$44
13	Wild Ginger	8.7	Orange	Japanese	Upmarket	$33
14	Taquería Mexicana	8.6	West Haven	Mexican	Counter	$6
15	Frank Pepe's	8.5	Wooster Square Area	Pizza	Casual	$14
16	Bentara	8.5	Ninth Square	Malaysian	Upmarket	$34
17	Swagat	8.5	West Haven	Indian	Casual	$7
18	Mother's	8.4	Medical Area/The Hill	Jamaican	Take-out	$12
19	Roseland Apizza	8.4	Derby	Pizza	Casual	$32
20	Foe	8.3	Branford	New American	Upmarket	$35
21	Trevethan's	8.3	East Rock/Grad Ghetto	New American	Upmarket	$36
22	Bella Rosa Café	8.3	Westville	Light American	Casual	$17
23	Lou's Big Top	8.3	Westville	Short-order	Take-out	$7
24	Caribbean Connection	8.3	Whalley	Jamaican	Take-out	$9
25	Central Steakhouse	8.2	Ninth Square	Steakhouse	Upmarket	$51
26	Som Siam	8.2	Guilford	Thai	Casual	$22
27	Yankee Doodle	8.2	Broadway Area	Short-order	Diner	$6
28	Gastronomique	8.1	Theater District	French	Take-out	$17
29	Golden Seafood	8.1	Westville	Chinese	Casual	$22
30	Dayton St. Apizza	8.1	Westville	Pizza	Take-out	$13
31	Hama	8.1	Hamden	Japanese	Casual	$18
32	Pot-au-Pho	8.0	Arts District	Vietnamese	Casual	$9
33	Darbar India	8.0	Branford	Indian	Upmarket	$20
34	Daiko (Jerry-San's)	8.0	West Haven	Japanese	Casual	$22
35	China Great Wall	8.0	Arts District	Chinese	Take-out	$5
36	Tenderloin's	8.0	Branford	Steakhouse	Upmarket	$39
37	Soul de Cuba	7.9	Theater District	Latin American	Upmarket	$22
39	Warong Selera	7.9	West Haven	Malaysian	Counter	$11
40	Royal Palace	7.8	Ninth Square	Chinese	Upmarket	$22
41	L'Orcio	7.8	East Rock/Grad Ghetto	Italian	Upmarket	$33
42	Martin's Amer. Café	7.8	Guilford	New American	Upmarket	$39
43	Tropical Delights	7.8	Westville	Jamaican	Take-out	$8
38	Avellino's Trattoria	7.8	Ninth Square	Italian	Upmarket	$31
44	Caffé Adulis	7.7	Theater District	African	Upmarket	$28
45	Pacifico	7.7	Theater District	Latin American	Upmarket	$38
46	Louis' Lunch	7.7	Theater District	Short-order	Counter	$7
47	Adriana's	7.7	Fair Haven	Italian	Upmarket	$24
48	El Charro	7.7	Fair Haven	Mexican	Casual	$12
49	Inka	7.6	East Haven	Latin American	Casual	$20
50	Sandra's	7.6	Arts District, The Hill	Southern	Casual	$21

TOP 40 ATMOSPHERE

<u>LISTED IN ORDER OF ATMOSPHERE RATING OUT OF 10</u>

Rank			Location	Cuisine	Type	Price
1	Le Petit Café	10	Branford	French	Upmarket	$45
2	Roomba	10	Theater District	Latin American	Upmarket	$52
3	The Place	10	Guilford	Seafood	Casual	$19
4	Bentara	9.5	Ninth Square	Malaysian	Upmarket	$34
5	Soul de Cuba	9.5	Theater District	Latin American	Upmarket	$22
6	Pacifico	9.5	Theater District	Latin American	Upmarket	$38
7	Skappo	9.5	Ninth Square	Italian	Upmarket	$29
8	Nini's Bistro	9.5	Ninth Square	New American	Upmarket	$35
9	Lenny's	9.5	Branford	Seafood	Casual	$25
10	Stillwater Bistro	9.5	Fair Haven	New American	Upmarket	$31
11	Atticus	9.5	Upper Chapel Area	Light American	Café	$9
12	Caffé Adulis	9.5	Theater District	African	Upmarket	$28
13	Union League Café	9.0	Theater District	French	Upmarket	$46
14	Stony Creek Market	9.0	Branford	Light American	Counter	$12
15	Bar (Brü Room)	9.0	Theater District	Pizza	Bar and grill	$15
16	Louis' Lunch	9.0	Theater District	Short-order	Counter	$7
17	Mory's	9.0	Broadway Area	Traditional Amer.	Upmarket	$28
18	Scoozzi	9.0	Upper Chapel Area	Italian	Upmarket	$37
19	Tony & Lucille's	9.0	Wooster Square Area	Italian	Casual	$29
20	Anna Liffey's	9.0	Arts District	Irish	Bar and grill	$21
21	Anchor	9.0	Theater District	Traditional Amer.	Bar and grill	$11
22	Su Casa	9.0	Branford	Tex-Mex	Casual	$22
23	Book Trader Café	9.0	Upper Chapel Area	Light American	Counter	$7
24	Blue Pearl	9.0	Financial District	New American	Upmarket	$32
25	Thai Taste	9.0	Upper Chapel Area	Thai	Casual	$21
26	Koffee?	9.0	Arts District	Baked goods	Café	$7
27	Rusty Scupper	9.0	Long Wharf	Seafood	Upmarket	$37
28	Bottega Lounge	9.0	Theater District	Italian	Casual	$32
29	Miya's	9.0	Upper Chapel Area	Japanese	Upmarket	$31
30	Café Nine	9.0	Ninth Square	Bar Food	Bar and grill	$9
31	Rainbow Gardens	8.5	Milford	New American	Upmarket	$24
32	L'Orcio	8.5	East Rock/Grad Ghetto	Italian	Upmarket	$33
33	Ibiza	8.5	Theater District	Spanish	Upmarket	$44
34	Hot Tomato's	8.5	Theater District	New American	Upmarket	$39
35	Bella Rosa Café	8.5	Westville	Light American	Casual	$17
36	Claire's	8.5	Theater District	Light American	Casual	$15
37	Sandra's	8.5	Arts District, The Hill	Southern	Casual	$21
38	La Piazza	8.5	Broadway Area	Italian	Casual	$27
39	Sage	8.5	Medical Area/The Hill	Traditional Amer.	Upmarket	$37
40	Jalapeño Heaven	8.5	Branford	Tex-Mex	Casual	$23

TOP 10 ATTITUDE (RATING OUT OF 10)

1	Skappo	10	Ninth Square	Italian	Upmarket	$29
2	Amato's	10	East Rock/Grad Ghetto	Pizza	Casual	$18
3	Som Siam	10	Guilford	Thai	Casual	$22
4	Le Petit Café	10	Branford	French	Upmarket	$45
5	Geppi's	10	Fair Haven	Italian	Casual	$29
6	Jeffrey's	10	Milford	New American	Upmarket	$44
7	Nini's Bistro	9	Ninth Square	New American	Upmarket	$35
8	Café Espresso	9	East Rock/Grad Ghetto	Light American	Café	$10
9	Pot-au-Pho	9	Arts District	Vietnamese	Casual	$9
10	Funki Munki	9	Theater District	Light American	Take-out	$7

TOP 50 VALUE

<u>LISTED IN ORDER OF VALUE RATING OUT OF 10</u>

OVERALL RATING

Rank				Location	Cuisine	Type	Price
1	Lou's Big Top	10.0	8.2	Westville	Short-order	Take-out	$7
2	Roomba Burrito Cart	9.9	7.6	Broadway Area	Tex-Mex	Take-out	$6
3	Yankee Doodle	9.9	8.0	Broadway Area	Short-order	Diner	$6
4	China Great Wall	9.8	7.7	Arts District	Chinese	Take-out	$5
5	Swagat	9.8	8.1	West Haven	Indian	Casual	$7
6	Louis' Lunch	9.7	7.7	Theater District	Short-order	Counter	$7
7	Glenwood Drive-In	9.7	7.5	Hamden	Short-order	Counter	$5
8	Jasmine Thai Cart	9.6	7.2	Financial District	American	Take-out	$5
9	Book Trader Café	9.6	7.6	Upper Chapel Area	Light Amer.	Counter	$7
10	Caribbean Connect.	9.5	7.9	Whalley	Jamaican	Take-out	$9
11	Modern Apizza	9.5	8.4	E. Rock/Grad Ghetto	Pizza	Casual	$13
12	Funki Munki	9.4	7.5	Theater District	Light Amer.	Take-out	$7
13	Zoi's on Orange	9.4	7.7	Arts District	Light Amer.	Counter	$8
14	Mother's	9.4	8.3	Medical Area/The Hill	Jamaican	Take-out	$12
15	Pot-au-Pho	9.3	7.8	Arts District	Vietnamese	Casual	$9
16	Bar (Brü Room)	9.3	8.5	Theater District	Pizza	Bar and grill	$15
17	Sally's Apizza	9.2	8.3	Wooster Square Area	Pizza	Casual	$14
18	Taquería Mexicana	9.2	7.1	West Haven	Mexican	Counter	$6
19	Vito's Deli	9.2	7.1	Ninth Square	Light Amer.	Take-out	$6
20	Stony Creek Market	9.0	8.0	Branford	Light Amer.	Counter	$12
21	Scarpellino's	8.9	7.0	Theater District	Italian	Take-out	$6
22	Atticus	8.8	7.5	Upper Chapel Area	Light Amer.	Café	$9
23	El Coquí	8.8	7.1	Fair Haven	Latin Amer.	Take-out	$7
24	Peppercorns	8.7	7.4	Westville	Light Amer.	Counter	$9
25	Tropical Delights	8.7	7.2	Westville	Jamaican	Take-out	$8
26	Bella Rosa Café	8.6	8.2	Westville	Light Amer.	Casual	$17
27	Frank Pepe's	8.6	7.9	Wooster Square Area	Pizza	Casual	$14
28	The Pantry	8.5	7.4	E. Rock/Grad Ghetto	Light Amer.	Casual	$10
29	Le Petit Café	8.4	9.6	Branford	French	Upmarket	$45
30	Christopher Martin's	8.3	8.0	E. Rock/Grad Ghetto	Bar food	Bar and grill	$17
31	Mediterranea	8.3	7.1	Financial District	Middle E.	Counter	$9
32	The Place	8.2	8.1	Guilford	Seafood	Casual	$19
33	Soul de Cuba	8.2	8.3	Theater District	Latin Amer.	Upmarket	$22
34	Café George	8.2	6.9	Theater District	Light Amer.	Counter	$8
35	Café Espresso	8.2	7.2	E. Rock/Grad Ghetto	Light Amer.	Café	$10
36	East Japanese	8.1	8.8	Milford	Japanese	Upmarket	$32
37	Ibiza	8.1	9.3	Theater District	Spanish	Upmarket	$44
38	Warong Selera	8.1	7.2	West Haven	Malaysian	Counter	$11
39	Dayton St. Apizza	8.0	7.4	Westville	Pizza	Take-out	$13
40	Moka	8.0	6.8	Financial District	Light Amer.	Café	$8
41	Hama	8.0	7.8	Hamden	Japanese	Casual	$18
42	Caribbean Fam. Pot	7.9	7.0	Medical Area/The Hill	Jamaican	Take-out	$10
43	Union League Café	7.9	9.2	Theater District	French	Upmarket	$46
44	Bentara	7.9	8.7	Ninth Square	Malaysian	Upmarket	$34
45	Rudy's Restaurant	7.9	6.7	Broadway Area	Light Amer.	Bar and grill	$8
46	Caffé Adulis	7.9	8.4	Theater District	African	Upmarket	$28
47	Golden Seafood	7.9	8.0	Westville	Chinese	Casual	$22
48	Alpha Delta Pizza	7.8	6.5	Broadway Area	Pizza	Take-out	$7
49	Daiko (Jerry-San's)	7.7	7.9	West Haven	Japanese	Casual	$22
50	Gastronomique	7.6	7.4	Theater District	French	Take-out	$17

BY CUISINE

LISTED IN ORDER OF FOOD RATING OUT OF 10

African

		Location	Type	Price
7.7	Caffé Adulis	Theater District	Upmarket	$28
5.6	Lalibela	Theater District	Casual	$21

American (subcategories: Bar food, Light American, New American, Short-order American, Southern/soul food, Steakhouses, Traditional American)

Bar food

7.6	Christopher Martin's	East Rock/Grad Ghetto	Bar and grill	$17
7.1	Anna Liffey's	Arts District	Bar and grill	$21
6.5	Pancho's Cantina	Westville	Bar and grill	$22
6.4	The Playwright	Hamden	Bar and grill	$22
6.1	Donovan's Reef	Branford	Bar and grill	$25
6.0	Richter's	Theater District	Bar and grill	$13
6.0	J.P. Dempsey's	East Rock/Grad Ghetto	Bar and grill	$22
6.0	Delaney's	Westville	Bar and grill	$21
5.8	Sidebar	Financial District	Casual	$22
5.7	TK's American Café	Theater District	Bar and grill	$13
5.7	Archie Moore's	East Rock/Grad Ghetto	Bar and grill	$15
5.6	SBC	Branford	Bar and grill	$23
5.5	Aunt Chilada's	Hamden	Casual	$27
5.5	Humphrey's East	East Rock/Grad Ghetto	Bar and grill	$16
5.1	The Playwright	Theater District	Bar and grill	$28
5.0	Café Nine	Ninth Square	Bar and grill	$9
3.9	Chili's	Hamden	Casual	$23
3.5	Sullivan's	Upper Chapel Area	Bar and grill	$17
1.2	Viva Zapata	Upper Chapel Area	Bar and grill	$18

Light American

8.3	Bella Rosa Café	Westville	Casual	$17
7.6	Stony Creek Market	Branford	Counter	$12
7.5	The Pantry	East Rock/Grad Ghetto	Casual	$10
7.5	Peppercorns	Westville	Counter	$9
7.4	Zoi's on Orange	Arts District	Counter	$8
7.2	Vito's Deli	Ninth Square	Take-out	$6
7.0	Café George	Theater District	Counter	$8
7.0	Book Trader Café	Upper Chapel Area	Counter	$7
6.8	Funki Munki	Theater District	Take-out	$7
6.7	Alpha Delta Pizza	Broadway Area	Take-out	$7
6.7	Café Espresso	East Rock/Grad Ghetto	Café	$10
6.5	Judies	Arts District	Counter	$9
6.4	Atticus	Upper Chapel Area	Café	$9
6.3	Katz's Restaurant	Woodbridge	Casual	$16
6.3	Rudy's Restaurant	Broadway Area	Bar and grill	$8
6.2	Moka	Financial District	Café	$8
6.0	Edge of the Woods	Whalley	Take-out	$13
5.9	Koffee Too?	Broadway Area	Café	$8
5.9	Yorkside Pizza	Broadway Area	Casual	$14
5.7	Rainbow Café	Theater District	Casual	$18
5.6	Chestnut Fine Foods	East Rock/Grad Ghetto	Counter	$12
5.5	Katz's 2 Go	Financial District	Take-out	$9
5.3	Alpine Restaurant	Financial District	Counter	$6
5.3	Celtica	Theater District	Counter	$10
5.3	Woodland Coffee	Ninth Square	Café	$8
5.0	Chap's Grille	Upper Chapel Area	Counter	$11

Light American *continued*

		Type	Price
4.9	Naples	Financial District	Counter	$8
4.9	Oolongs Tea Bar	Theater District	Café	-
4.9	Xando Cosí	Broadway Area	Casual	$15
4.9	Café Java	Financial District	Counter	$8
4.5	Stella's	Whalley	Take-out	$9
4.3	Breakaway Deli	Arts District	Counter	$6
4.0	Corner Deli	Financial District	Counter	$6
4.0	Bruegger's	Arts District	Fast-food chain	$6
3.9	Sweet Relief	Arts District	Counter	$7
3.6	Gourmet Heaven	Broadway Area, Arts Dist.	Take-out	$8
3.5	Subway	Theater District	Fast-food chain	$6
3.2	Town Pizza	Arts District	Casual	$8
3.1	Claire's	Theater District	Casual	$15
2.8	Dunkin' Donuts	Theater District	Fast-food chain	$7
2.4	Au Bon Pain	Broadway Area	Fast-food chain	$9

New American

9.0	Zinc	Theater District	Upmarket	$45
8.8	Jeffrey's	Milford	Upmarket	$44
8.3	Trevethan's	East Rock/Grad Ghetto	Upmarket	$36
8.3	Foe	Branford	Upmarket	$35
7.8	Martin's American Café	Guilford	Upmarket	$39
7.5	Nini's Bistro	Ninth Square	Upmarket	$35
7.4	Stillwater Bistro	Fair Haven	Upmarket	$31
7.3	Citrus	Milford	Upmarket	$39
7.1	Nikkita	Theater District	Bar and grill	$25
6.8	Rainbow Gardens	Milford	Upmarket	$24
6.3	Hot Tomato's	Theater District	Upmarket	$39
5.1	Blue Pearl	Financial District	Upmarket	$32

Short-order American

8.3	Lou's Big Top	Westville	Take-out	$7
8.2	Yankee Doodle	Broadway Area	Diner	$6
7.7	Louis' Lunch	Theater District	Counter	$7
7.5	Glenwood Drive-In	Hamden	Counter	$5
6.4	Roberto's	Financial District	Diner	$9
5.9	Contois Tavern	East Rock/Grad Ghetto	Bar and grill	$6
5.8	Athenian Diner	Westville	Diner	$18
5.7	Clark's Dairy	Arts District	Diner	$10
5.6	Educated Burgher	Broadway Area	Counter	$7
5.6	Copper Kitchen	Theater District	Diner	$11
5.0	Parthenon Diner	Branford	Diner	$17
5.0	McDonald's	Whalley	Fast-food chain	$6
4.8	Joe's Hubba Hubba	Financial District	Counter	$7
4.6	A One	Broadway Area	Counter	$6
4.4	Cody's Diner	Wooster Square Area	Diner	$10
3.3	Patricia's	Broadway Area	Diner	$6
3.0	Burger King	Whalley	Fast-food chain	$6

Southern/Soul Food/BBQ

7.6	Sandra's	Arts District, The Hill	Casual	$21
6.9	Uncle Willie's BBQ	Orange	Casual	$16
6.4	Southern Hospitality	Whalley	Take-out	$10
6.4	The Rib House	East Haven	Casual	$21
5.3	Popeye's	Whalley	Fast-food chain	$7
4.0	KFC	Whalley	Fast-food chain	$7

Steakhouses

8.9	Carmen Anthony	Arts District	Upmarket	$50
8.2	Central Steakhouse	Ninth Square	Upmarket	$51
8.0	Tenderloin's	Branford	Upmarket	$39
7.2	Chuck's Steak House	West Haven	Upmarket	$22
6.6	Polo Grille	Financial District	Upmarket	$42
5.2	Maxwell's	Orange	Upmarket	$27

Traditional American

		Type	Price
8.9 Carmen Anthony	Arts District	Upmarket	$50
8.8 Stone House	Guilford	Upmarket	$38
8.2 Central Steakhouse	Ninth Square	Upmarket	$51
8.0 Tenderloin's	Branford	Upmarket	$39
7.2 Chuck's Steak House	West Haven	Upmarket	$22
7.1 Temple Grill	Theater District	Bar and grill	$26
7.0 Scribner's	Milford	Upmarket	$32
6.7 Sage	Medical Area/The Hill	Upmarket	$37
6.6 Lenny's	Branford	Casual	$25
6.1 Donovan's Reef	Branford	Bar and grill	$25
6.0 Delaney's	Westville	Bar and grill	$21
6.0 168 York St. Café	Upper Chapel Area	Casual	$13
6.0 Jimmies	West Haven	Casual	$22
6.0 Mory's	Broadway Area	Upmarket	$28
5.7 Anchor	Theater District	Bar and grill	$11
5.2 Maxwell's	Orange	Upmarket	$27
5.1 Brown Stone House	Hamden	Casual	$8
5.0 500 Blake St. Café	Westville	Upmarket	$32
4.7 Templeton's	Theater District	Upmarket	$36
4.1 John Davenport's	Theater District	Upmarket	$40
3.8 Olde Blue	Upper Chapel Area	Upmarket	$26
2.2 Colonial Tymes	Hamden	Upmarket	$32

Baked goods

6.5 Judies	Arts District	Counter	$9
6.4 Atticus	Upper Chapel Area	Café	$9
5.9 Koffee Too?	Broadway Area	Café	$8
5.6 Chestnut Fine Foods	East Rock/Grad Ghetto	Counter	$12
5.3 Woodland Coffee	Ninth Square	Café	$8
4.9 Xando Cosí	Broadway Area	Casual	$15
4.5 Stella's	Whalley	Take-out	$9
4.5 Libby's Pastry	Wooster Square Area	Take-out	-
2.8 Dunkin' Donuts	Theater District	Fast-food chain	$7

Breakfast

8.4 Mother's	Medical Area/The Hill	Take-out	$12
8.3 Bella Rosa Café	Westville	Casual	$17
8.3 Caribbean Connection	Whalley	Take-out	$9
8.2 Yankee Doodle	Broadway Area	Diner	$6
8.1 Gastronomique	Theater District	Take-out	$17
7.8 Martin's American Café	Guilford	Upmrket	$39
7.6 Stony Creek Market	Branford	Counter	$12
7.5 The Pantry	East Rock/Grad Ghetto	Casual	$10
7.5 Peppercorns	Westville	Counter	$9
7.4 Gusto Italiano	Arts District	Counter	$11
7.4 Zoi's on Orange	Arts District	Counter	$8
7.2 Vito's Deli	Ninth Square	Take-out	$6
7.0 Scarpellino's	Theater District	Take-out	$6
7.0 Book Trader Café	Upper Chapel Area	Counter	$7
7.0 Café George	Theater District	Counter	$8
6.9 Uncle Willie's BBQ	Orange	Casual	$16
6.7 Café Espresso	East Rock/Grad Ghetto	Café	$10
6.5 Judies	Arts District	Counter	$9
6.4 Atticus	Upper Chapel Area	Café	$9
6.4 Roberto's	Financial District	Diner	$9
6.2 Moka	Financial District	Café	$8
6.0 Edge of the Woods	Whalley	Take-out	$13
5.9 Koffee Too?	Broadway Area	Café	$8
5.8 Athenian Diner	Westville	Diner	$18
5.7 Clark's Dairy	Arts District	Diner	$10
5.6 Copper Kitchen	Theater District	Diner	$11
5.6 Educated Burgher	Broadway Area	Counter	$7

	Breakfast *continued*	Location	Type	Price
5.6	Chestnut Fine Foods	East Rock/Grad Ghetto	Counter	$12
5.5	Caffé Bottega	Theater District	Bar and grill	$33
5.3	Woodland Coffee	Ninth Square	Café	$8
5.3	Alpine Restaurant	Financial District	Counter	$6
5.1	Brown Stone House	Hamden	Casual	$8
5.1	IKEA Restaurant	Long Wharf	Counter	$6
5.0	Chap's Grille	Upper Chapel Area	Counter	$11
5.0	McDonald's	Whalley	Fast-food chain	$6
5.0	Parthenon Diner	Branford	Diner	$17
4.9	Oolongs Tea Bar	Theater District	Café	-
4.9	Xando Cosí	Broadway Area	Casual	$15
4.9	Naples	Financial District	Counter	$8
4.9	Café Java	Financial District	Counter	$8
4.8	Joe's Hubba Hubba	Financial District	Counter	$7
4.7	Templeton's	Theater District	Upmarket	$36
4.6	A One	Broadway Area	Counter	$6
4.5	Stella's	Whalley	Take-out	$9
4.4	Cody's Diner	Wooster Square Area	Diner	$10
4.3	Breakaway Deli	Arts District	Counter	$6
4.1	John Davenport's	Theater District	Upmarket	$40
4.0	Corner Deli	Financial District	Counter	$6
4.0	Bruegger's	Arts District	Fast-food chain	$6
3.9	Sweet Relief	Arts District	Counter	$7
3.8	Olde Blue	Upper Chapel Area	Upmarket	$26
3.6	Gourmet Heaven	Broadway Area, Arts District	Take-out	$8
3.5	Subway	Theater District	Fast-food chain	$6
3.3	Patricia's	Broadway Area	Diner	$6
3.1	Claire's	Theater District	Casual	$15
3.0	Burger King	Whalley	Fast-food chain	$6
2.8	Dunkin' Donuts	Theater District	Fast-food chain	$7
2.4	Au Bon Pain	Broadway Area	Fast-food chain	$9
NR	Dolce Java	Upper Chapel Area	Café	-
NR	Koffee?	Arts District	Café	$7
NR	Lulu's	East Rock/Grad Ghetto	Café	-
NR	Nica's Market	East Rock/Grad Ghetto	Specialty grocery	-
NR	Romeo & Cesare's	East Rock/Grad Ghetto	Specialty grocery	-
NR	Starbucks	Theater District	Café	-
NR	Willoughby's	Financial District	Café	-

Brunch

8.8	Stone House	Guilford	Upmarket	$38
8.3	Bella Rosa Café	Westville	Casual	$17
8.1	Gastronomique	Theater District	Take-out	$17
7.8	Martin's American Café	Guilford	Upmarket	$39
7.6	Stony Creek Market	Branford	Counter	$12
7.6	Sandra's	Arts District, The Hill	Casual	$24
7.5	The Pantry	East Rock/Grad Ghetto	Casual	$10
7.4	Stillwater Bistro	Fair Haven	Upmarket	$31
7.2	Quattro's	Guilford	Upmarket	$32
7.1	Anna Liffey's	Arts District	Bar and grill	$21
7.0	East Buffet	Hamden	Casual	$16
6.9	Peroles Restaurant	Hamden	Casual	$18
6.8	Rainbow Gardens	Milford	Upmarket	$24
6.7	Sage	Medical Area/The Hill	Upmarket	$37
6.7	Scoozzi	Upper Chapel Area	Upmarket	$37
6.5	Royal India	Broadway Area	Casual	$18
6.4	The Playwright	Hamden	Bar and grill	$22
6.3	Katz's Restaurant	Woodbridge	Casual	$16
6.3	Zaroka	Upper Chapel Area	Upmarket	$24
6.1	Donovan's Reef	Branford	Bar and grill	$25
6.0	168 York St. Café	Upper Chapel Area	Casual	$13
6.0	Richter's	Theater District	Bar and grill	$13

	Brunch *continued*	Location	Type	Price
5.8	Avra Grille	Branford	Upmarket	$30
5.8	Tandoor	Upper Chapel Area	Casual	$20
5.7	Rainbow Café	Theater District	Casual	$18
5.1	The Playwright	Theater District	Bar and grill	$28
5.0	Café Nine	Ninth Square	Bar and grill	$9
5.0	500 Blake St. Café	Westville	Upmarket	$32
4.7	Templeton's	Theater District	Upmarket	$36
4.5	Stella's European Bakery	Whalley	Take-out	$9
4.1	Rusty Scupper	Long Wharf	Upmarket	$37
4.1	John Davenport's	Theater District	Upmarket	$40
3.8	Olde Blue	Upper Chapel Area	Upmarket	$26
2.2	Colonial Tymes	Hamden	Upmarket	$32

Chinese

8.1	Golden Seafood	Westville	Casual	$22
8.0	China Great Wall	Arts District	Take-out	$5
7.8	Royal Palace	Ninth Square	Upmarket	$22
7.0	East Buffet	Hamden	Casual	$16
6.2	House of Chao	Westville	Casual	$12
6.1	China Pavilion	Orange	Upmarket	$21
4.1	Hunan Café	Upper Chapel Area	Counter	$9
3.4	Main Garden	Broadway Area	Take-out	$9
3.4	China King	Theater District	Take-out	$8
2.8	Gourmet Heaven*	Broadway Area, Arts District	Take-out	$8
1.8	Ivy Noodle	Broadway Area	Casual	$8
1.7	Corner Deli*	Financial District	Counter	$6

*Food ratings in this list reflect only the Chinese food.

French

9.4	Le Petit Café	Branford	Upmarket	$45
9.3	Union League Café	Theater District	Upmarket	$46
8.1	Gastronomique	Theater District	Take-out	$17

Greek

6.7	Alpha Delta Pizza	Broadway Area	Take-out	$7
5.9	Yorkside Pizza	Broadway Area	Casual	$14
5.8	Avra Grille	Branford	Upmarket	$30
5.8	Athenian Diner	Westville	Diner	$18
5.0	Parthenon Diner	Branford	Diner	$17

Ice Cream

8.1	Wentworth's	Hamden	Take-out	-
8.0	Caffé Bottega**	Theater District	Bar and grill	-
7.6	Dolce Java**	Upper Chapel	Café	-
6.4	Ashley's Ice Cream	Broadway Area	Take-out	-
6.0	Chapel Sweet Shoppe**	Theater District	Take-out	-
5.4	Cold Stone Creamery	Theater District	Take-out	-
5.2	Tasti D-Lite**	Theater District	Take-out	-

**Food ratings in this list reflect only the ice cream and ice cream derivatives.

Indian

8.5	Swagat	West Haven	Casual	$7
8.0	Darbar India	Branford	Upmarket	$20
6.5	Royal India	Broadway Area	Casual	$18
6.3	Zaroka	Upper Chapel Area	Upmarket	$24
5.9	India Palace	Upper Chapel Area	Casual	$18
5.8	Tandoor	Upper Chapel Area	Casual	$20

Irish

		Location	Type	Price
7.1	Anna Liffey's	Arts District	Bar and grill	$21
6.4	The Playwright	Hamden	Bar and grill	$22
5.3	Celtica	Theater District	Counter	$10
5.1	The Playwright	Theater District	Bar and grill	$28
3.5	Sullivan's	Upper Chapel Area	Bar and grill	$17

Italian

7.8	L'Orcio	East Rock/Grad Ghetto	Upmarket	$33
7.8	Avellino's Trattoria	Ninth Square	Upmarket	$31
7.7	Adriana's	Fair Haven	Upmarket	$24
7.5	Tre Scalini	Wooster Square Area	Upmarket	$32
7.4	Billy's Pasta Così	Branford	Upmarket	$30
7.4	Gusto Italiano	Arts District	Counter	$11
7.3	La Piazza	Broadway Area	Casual	$27
7.2	Geppi's	Fair Haven	Casual	$29
7.2	Quattro's	Guilford	Upmarket	$32
7.1	Consiglio's	Wooster Square Area	Upmarket	$41
7.1	Luce	Hamden	Upmarket	$36
7.1	Portofino	East Rock/Grad Ghetto	Upmarket	$27
7.0	Scarpellino's	Theater District	Take-out	$6
6.9	Pazza Cucina	Woodbridge	Upmarket	$36
6.8	Assaggio	Branford	Upmarket	$33
6.8	Basta!	Theater District	Upmarket	$51
6.7	Scoozzi	Upper Chapel Area	Upmarket	$37
6.6	Polo Grille	Financial District	Upmarket	$42
6.5	Caffé Bravo	East Rock/Grad Ghetto	Casual	$28
6.4	Est Est Est	Upper Chapel Area	Counter	$8
6.3	Hot Tomato's	Theater District	Upmarket	$39
6.2	Bottega Lounge	Theater District	Casual	$32
6.1	Amato's	East Rock/Grad Ghetto	Casual	$18
5.8	Sidebar	Financial District	Casual	$22
5.8	Avra Grille	Branford	Upmarket	$30
5.8	Tony & Lucille's	Wooster Square Area	Casual	$29
5.7	Perrotti's	Wooster Square Area	Casual	$24
5.5	Caffé Bottega	Theater District	Bar and grill	$33
5.3	Gennaro's	Theater District	Upmarket	$38
5.2	Skappo	Ninth Square	Upmarket	$29
4.7	Abate Apizza	Wooster Square Area	Casual	$24
4.3	Quattro's	Theater District	Upmarket	$33
3.8	Brazi's	Long Wharf	Casual	$22
3.6	Yalie's Pizza	Upper Chapel Area	Take-out	$6

Italian specialty grocery stores

NR	Liuzzi's Cheese	North Haven	Specialty grocery	-
NR	Nica's Market	East Rock/Grad Ghetto	Specialty grocery	-
NR	Romeo & Cesare's	East Rock/Grad Ghetto	Specialty grocery	-

Jamaican

8.4	Mother's	Medical Area/The Hill	Take-out	$12
8.3	Caribbean Connection	Whalley	Take-out	$9
7.8	Tropical Delights	Westville	Take-out	$8
7.0	Caribbean Family Pot	Medical Area/The Hill	Take-out	$10

Japanese

9.4	East Japanese	Milford	Upmarket	$32
8.7	Wild Ginger	Orange	Upmarket	$33
8.1	Hama	Hamden	Casual	$18
8.0	Daiko (Jerry-San's)	West Haven	Casual	$22
7.2	Kampai	Branford	Upmarket	$28

Japanese *continued*	*Location*	*Type*	*Price*
7.1 Miso	Ninth Square	Upmarket	$25
6.9 Kiraku	Fair Haven	Upmarket	$31
6.9 Akasaka	Westville	Upmarket	$25
6.8 Kumo	Hamden	Upmarket	$28
6.0 Miya's	Upper Chapel Area	Upmarket	$31
3.1 Samurai	Theater District	Upmarket	$26
2.6 Haya	East Rock/Grad Ghetto	Casual	$22

Korean

7.6 Seoul Yokocho	Upper Chapel Area	Upmarket	$27
6.9 Kiraku	Fair Haven	Upmarket	$31

Latin American *(includes Puerto Rican, Cuban, South American, Nuevo Latino)*

9.5 Roomba	Theater District	Upmarket	$52
7.9 Soul de Cuba	Theater District	Upmarket	$22
7.7 Pacifico	Theater District	Upmarket	$38
7.6 Inka	East Haven	Casual	$20
7.2 El Coquí	Fair Haven	Take-out	$7
7.2 El Caribe	Fair Haven	Casual	$25
6.9 Peroles Restaurant	Hamden	Casual	$18

Malaysian

8.5 Bentara	Ninth Square	Upmarket	$34
7.9 Warong Selera	West Haven	Counter	$11
7.0 Gunung Tahan	Westville	Casual	$23

Mexican *(includes Tex-Mex)*

8.6 Taquería Mexicana #2	West Haven	Counter	$6
7.7 El Charro	Fair Haven	Casual	$12
7.6 Guadalupe La Poblanita	Fair Haven	Casual	$10
7.5 Baja's	Orange	Casual	$23
7.4 Roomba Burrito Cart	Broadway Area	Take-out	$6
7.3 Su Casa	Branford	Casual	$22
6.9 El Charro Alegre	East Rock/Grad Ghetto	Casual	$19
6.6 Jalapeño Heaven	Branford	Casual	$23
6.5 Pancho's Cantina	Westville	Bar and grill	$22
6.4 Ixtapa Grille	Hamden	Casual	$20
6.2 Villa Del Sol	Theater District	Upmarket	$27
6.0 Fresh Taco	Financial District	Take-out	$7
5.7 Whole Enchilada	Arts District	Counter	$8
5.5 Aunt Chilada's	Hamden	Casual	$27
4.7 C.O. Jones	East Rock/Grad Ghetto	Bar and grill	$14
4.2 Bulldog Burrito	Broadway Area	Counter	$7
3.9 Chili's	Hamden	Casual	$23
1.4 El Amigo Felix	Broadway Area	Bar and grill	$23
1.2 Viva Zapata	Upper Chapel Area	Bar and grill	$18

Middle Eastern

7.3 Mediterranea	Financial District	Counter	$9
6.5 Sahara	Theater District	Counter	$9
5.6 Mamoun's	Upper Chapel Area	Casual	$9
4.8 Aladdin	Theater District	Take-out	$10
4.6 The Original Falafel	Theater District	Counter	$7

Pizza	Location	Type	Price
9.6 Sally's Apizza	Wooster Square Area	Casual	$14
9.2 Bar (Brü Room)	Theater District	Bar and grill	$15
9.1 Modern Apizza	East Rock/Grad Ghetto	Casual	$13
8.5 Frank Pepe's	Wooster Square Area	Casual	$14
8.4 Roseland Apizza	Derby	Casual	$32
8.1 Dayton St. Apizza	Westville	Take-out	$13
7.6 Stony Creek Market	Branford	Counter	$12
7.4 Gusto Italiano	Arts District	Counter	$11
7.3 Mediterranea	Financial District	Counter	$9
6.7 Alpha Delta Pizza	Broadway Area	Take-out	$7
6.5 Brick Oven Pizza	Upper Chapel Area	Counter	$9
6.4 Est Est Est	Upper Chapel Area	Counter	$8
6.1 Amato's	East Rock/Grad Ghetto	Casual	$18
5.9 Yorkside Pizza	Broadway Area	Casual	$14
5.7 Perrotti's	Wooster Square Area	Casual	$24
5.6 Pizza House	Upper Chapel Area	Take-out	$6
4.9 Naples	Financial District	Counter	$8
4.9 Xando Cosí	Broadway Area	Casual	$15
4.9 Café Java	Financial District	Counter	$8
4.8 Aladdin	Theater District	Take-out	$10
4.7 Abate Apizza	Wooster Square Area	Casual	$24
4.6 A One	Broadway Area	Counter	$6
3.8 Brazi's	Long Wharf	Casual	$22
3.6 Yalie's Pizza	Upper Chapel Area	Take-out	$6
3.2 Town Pizza	Arts District	Casual	$8

Seafood			
8.8 Stone House	Guilford	Upmarket	$38
7.7 Pacifico	Theater District	Upmarket	$38
7.3 The Place	Guilford	Casual	$19
7.1 Nikkita	Theater District	Bar and grill	$25
7.0 Scribner's	Milford	Upmarket	$32
6.6 Lenny's	Branford	Casual	$25
6.3 Chick's	West Haven	Counter	$11
6.0 Jimmies	West Haven	Casual	$22
5.3 USS Chowder Pot III	Branford	Casual	$30
5.2 Maxwell's	Orange	Upmarket	$27
4.1 Rusty Scupper	Long Wharf	Upmarket	$37

Seafood store			
Number 1 Fish Market	Hamden	Specialty grocery	-

Spanish			
9.8 Ibiza	Theater District	Upmarket	$44

Swedish			
5.1 IKEA Restaurant	Long Wharf	Counter	$6

Thai			
8.2 Som Siam	Guilford	Casual	$22
6.7 Thai Inter	East Rock/Grad Ghetto	Casual	$18
6.6 Bangkok Gardens	Upper Chapel Area	Upmarket	$20
6.5 Indochine Pavilion	Upper Chapel Area	Casual	$18
6.3 Pad Thai	Upper Chapel Area	Casual	$17
4.2 Thai Taste Food Cart	Broadway Area	Take-out	$4
3.7 Thai Taste	Upper Chapel Area	Casual	$21
2.0 Thai Pan Asian	Upper Chapel Area	Casual	$19

	Turkish	Location	Type	Price
7.3	Istanbul Café	Theater District	Upmarket	$29
	Vietnamese			
8.0	Pot-au-Pho	Arts District	Casual	$9

BY LOCATION

New Haven

Arts District

		Cuisine	Type	Price
8.7	Carmen Anthony	Steakhouse	Upmarket	$50
8.3	Koffee?	Baked goods	Café	$7
7.8	Pot-au-Pho	Vietnamese	Casual	$9
7.7	Sandra's	Southern	Casual	$21
7.7	Zoi's on Orange	Light American	Counter	$8
7.7	Anna Liffey's	Irish	Bar and grill	$21
7.7	China Great Wall	Chinese	Take-out	$5
6.6	Gusto Italiano	Italian	Counter	$11
6.3	Clark's Dairy	Short-order	Diner	$10
5.7	Judies	Baked goods	Counter	$9
5.2	Whole Enchilada	Tex-Mex	Counter	$8
4.8	Breakaway Deli	Light American	Counter	$6
3.9	Bruegger's	Light American	Fast-food chain	$6
3.7	Gourmet Heaven	Light American	Take-out	$8
3.4	Town Pizza	Pizza	Casual	$8
3.4	Sweet Relief	Light American	Counter	$7

Broadway Area

8.0	Yankee Doodle	Short-order	Diner	$6
7.7	La Piazza	Italian	Casual	$27
7.6	Roomba Burrito Cart	Tex-Mex	Take-out	$6
7.1	Royal India	Indian	Casual	$18
6.8	Mory's	Traditional Amer.	Upmarket	$28
6.7	Rudy's Restaurant	Light American	Bar and grill	$8
6.6	Ashley's Ice Cream	Sweets	Take-out	-
6.5	Koffee Too?	Light American	Café	$8
6.5	Alpha Delta Pizza	Pizza	Take-out	$7
6.0	Educated Burgher	Short-order	Counter	$7
5.9	Yorkside Pizza	Pizza	Casual	$14
5.5	Thai Taste Food Cart	Thai	Take-out	$4
5.2	Xando Cosí	Light American	Casual	$15
4.6	Main Garden	Chinese	Take-out	$9
4.1	A One	Pizza	Counter	$6
4.1	Bulldog Burrito	Tex-Mex	Counter	$7
3.8	Patricia's	Short-order	Diner	$6
3.7	Gourmet Heaven	Light American	Take-out	$8
3.0	El Amigo Felix	Tex-Mex	Bar and grill	$23
3.0	Au Bon Pain	Light American	Fast-food chain	$9
2.6	Ivy Noodle	Chinese	Casual	$8

East Rock/Grad Ghetto

8.4	Modern Apizza	Pizza	Casual	$13
8.3	Trevethan's	New American	Upmarket	$36
8.0	Christopher Martin's	Bar food	Bar and grill	$17
8.0	L'Orcio	Italian	Upmarket	$33
7.4	The Pantry	Light American	Casual	$10
7.2	Café Espresso	Light American	Café	$10
7.2	Portofino	Italian	Upmarket	$27
7.1	J.P. Dempsey's	Bar food	Bar and grill	$22
6.5	Chestnut Fine Foods	Light American	Counter	$12
6.4	Caffé Bravo	Italian	Casual	$28
6.4	Thai Inter	Thai	Casual	$18
6.3	Archie Moore's	Bar food	Bar and grill	$15
6.2	Amato's	Pizza	Casual	$18
6.2	Contois Tavern	Short-order	Bar and grill	$6

			Type	Price
6.2	Humphrey's East	Bar food	Bar and grill	$16
6.2	El Charro Alegre	Mexican	Casual	$19
5.7	C.O. Jones	Tex-Mex	Bar and grill	$14
4.2	Haya	Japanese	Casual	$22
NR	Romeo & Cesare's	Italian	Specialty grocery	-
NR	Nica's Market	Italian	Specialty grocery	-

Fair Haven

8.2	Stillwater Bistro	New American	Upmarket	$31
7.7	Geppi's	Italian	Casual	$29
7.5	Adriana's	Italian	Upmarket	$24
7.2	Kiraku	Japanese	Upmarket	$31
7.1	El Coquí	Latin American	Take-out	$7
6.7	El Caribe	Latin American	Casual	$25
6.6	El Charro	Mexican	Casual	$12
6.5	Guadalupe La Poblanita	Mexican	Casual	$10

Financial District

7.2	Jasmine Thai Cart	American	Take-out	$5
7.1	Mediterranea	Middle Eastern	Counter	$9
6.8	Moka	Light American	Café	$8
6.5	Polo Grille	Italian, Steakhouse	Upmarket	$42
6.4	Blue Pearl	New American	Upmarket	$32
6.3	Fresh Taco	Tex-Mex	Take-out	$7
6.3	Roberto's	Short-order	Diner	$9
5.8	Café Java	Light American	Counter	$8
5.7	Sidebar	Bar food	Casual	$22
5.7	Katz's 2 Go	Light American	Take-out	$9
5.3	Naples	Pizza	Counter	$8
5.3	Alpine Restaurant	Light American	Counter	$6
5.2	Joe's Hubba Hubba	Short-order	Counter	$7
4.2	Corner Deli	Light American	Counter	$6

Long Wharf

5.9	Rusty Scupper	Seafood	Upmarket	$37
5.3	IKEA Restaurant	Swedish	Counter	$6
4.8	Brazi's	Italian	Casual	$22

Medical Area/The Hill

8.3	Mother's	Jamaican	Take-out	$12
7.7	Sandra's	Southern	Casual	$21
7.4	Sage	Traditional Amer.	Upmarket	$37
7.0	Caribbean Family Pot	Jamaican	Take-out	$10
NR	Medical Area Food Carts	*various*	Take-out	$6

Ninth Square

8.7	Bentara	Malaysian	Upmarket	$34
8.3	Nini's Bistro	New American	Upmarket	$35
8.0	Central Steakhouse	Steakhouse	Upmarket	$51
7.8	Avellino's Trattoria	Italian	Upmarket	$31
7.2	Miso	Japanese	Upmarket	$25
7.1	Vito's Deli	Light American	Take-out	$6
7.0	Skappo	Italian	Upmarket	$29
6.7	Royal Palace	Chinese	Upmarket	$22
6.4	Café Nine	Bar food	Bar and grill	$9
5.8	Woodland Coffee	Light American	Café	$8

Theater District	Cuisine	Type	Price
9.3 Ibiza	Spanish	Upmarket	$44
9.2 Union League Café	French	Upmarket	$46
9.0 Roomba	Latin American	Upmarket	$52
8.5 Zinc	New American	Upmarket	$45
8.5 Bar (Brü Room)	Pizza	Bar and grill	$15
8.4 Caffé Adulis	African	Upmarket	$28
8.3 Soul de Cuba	Latin American	Upmarket	$22
8.2 Pacifico	Latin American	Upmarket	$38
7.7 Louis' Lunch	Short-order	Counter	$7
7.5 Funki Munki	Light American	Take-out	$7
7.5 Istanbul Café	Turkish	Upmarket	$29
7.4 Gastronomique	French	Take-out	$17
7.2 Temple Grill	Traditional Amer.	Bar and grill	$26
7.1 Basta!	Italian	Upmarket	$51
7.0 Scarpellino's	Italian	Take-out	$6
6.9 Café George	Light American	Counter	$8
6.7 Lalibela	African	Casual	$21
6.6 Nikkita	New American	Bar and grill	$25
6.6 Bottega Lounge	Italian	Casual	$32
6.5 Sahara	Middle Eastern	Counter	$9
6.5 Anchor	Traditional Amer.	Bar and grill	$11
6.5 Richter's	Bar food	Bar and grill	$13
6.4 Hot Tomato's	New American	Upmarket	$39
6.3 Rainbow Café	Light American	Casual	$18
6.3 Cold Stone Creamery	Sweets	Take-out	-
6.1 Oolongs Tea Bar	Light American	Café	-
6.0 Celtica	Irish	Counter	$10
6.0 Copper Kitchen	Short-order	Diner	$11
5.9 Chapel Sweet Shoppe	Sweets	Take-out	-
5.9 Villa Del Sol	Tex-Mex	Upmarket	$27
5.7 TK's American Café	Bar food	Bar and grill	$13
5.5 The Playwright	Irish	Bar and grill	$28
5.4 Quattro's	Italian	Upmarket	$33
5.3 Tasti D-Lite	Sweets	Take-out	-
5.2 John Davenport's	Traditional Amer.	Upmarket	$40
5.2 Claire's	Light American	Casual	$15
5.1 Caffé Bottega	Italian	Bar and grill	$33
4.9 Templeton's	Traditional Amer.	Upmarket	$36
4.9 Gennaro's	Italian	Upmarket	$38
4.5 Aladdin	Middle Eastern	Take-out	$10
4.4 The Original Falafel	Middle Eastern	Counter	$7
4.1 Samurai	Japanese	Upmarket	$26
2.9 China King	Chinese	Take-out	$8
2.9 Subway	Light American	Fast-food chain	$6
2.5 Dunkin' Donuts	Baked goods	Fast-food chain	$7

Upper Chapel Area			
7.6 Book Trader Café	Light American	Counter	$7
7.5 Atticus	Light American	Café	$9
7.3 Scoozzi	Italian	Upmarket	$37
7.0 Miya's	Japanese	Upmarket	$31
6.8 Seoul Yokocho	Korean	Upmarket	$27
6.7 Indochine Pavilion	Thai	Casual	$18
6.6 Zaroka	Indian	Upmarket	$24
6.5 Bangkok Gardens	Thai	Upmarket	$20
6.4 Mamoun's	Middle Eastern	Casual	$9
6.3 Tandoor	Indian	Casual	$20
6.2 Pad Thai	Thai	Casual	$17
6.2 168 York St. Café	Traditional Amer.	Casual	$13
6.1 Pizza House	Pizza	Take-out	$6
5.7 Est Est Est	Pizza	Counter	$8
5.6 Thai Taste	Thai	Casual	$21
5.2 Brick Oven Pizza	Pizza	Counter	$9

	Upper Chapel Area *continued*		Type	Price
4.9	India Palace	Indian	Casual	$18
4.7	Chap's Grille	Light American	Counter	$11
4.5	Olde Blue	Traditional Amer.	Upmarket	$26
4.4	Sullivan's	Bar food	Bar and grill	$17
4.0	Hunan Café	Chinese	Counter	$9
3.7	Yalie's Pizza	Pizza	Take-out	$6
3.4	Thai Pan Asian	Thai	Casual	$19
3.2	Viva Zapata	Tex-Mex	Bar and grill	$18
	Westville			
8.2	Lou's Big Top	Short-order	Take-out	$7
8.2	Bella Rosa Café	Light American	Casual	$17
8.0	Golden Seafood	Chinese	Casual	$22
7.4	Peppercorns	Light American	Counter	$9
7.4	Dayton St. Apizza	Pizza	Take-out	$13
7.2	Tropical Delights	Jamaican	Take-out	$8
7.1	Delaney's	Bar food	Bar and grill	$21
6.9	Pancho's Cantina	Tex-Mex	Bar and grill	$22
6.8	Gunung Tahan	Malaysian	Casual	$23
6.7	Akasaka	Japanese	Upmarket	$25
6.4	House of Chao	Chinese	Casual	$12
5.6	500 Blake St. Café	Traditional Amer.	Upmarket	$32
5.3	Athenian Diner	Short-order	Diner	$18
	Whalley			
7.9	Caribbean Connection	Jamaican	Take-out	$9
6.7	Edge of the Woods	Light American	Take-out	$13
6.6	Southern Hospitality	Southern	Take-out	$10
5.0	Stella's	Baked goods	Take-out	$9
4.3	McDonald's	Short-order	Fast-food chain	$6
3.9	Popeye's	Southern	Fast-food chain	$7
3.4	KFC	Southern	Fast-food chain	$7
2.6	Burger King	Short-order	Fast-food chain	$6
	Wooster Square Area			
8.3	Sally's Apizza	Pizza	Casual	$14
7.9	Frank Pepe's	Pizza	Casual	$14
7.7	Tre Scalini	Italian	Upmarket	$32
7.4	Consiglio's	Italian	Upmarket	$41
7.0	Tony & Lucille's	Italian	Casual	$29
5.7	Perrotti's	Italian	Casual	$24
5.3	Libby's Pastry	Baked goods	Take-out	-
4.9	Abate Apizza	Italian	Casual	$24
4.6	Cody's Diner	Short-order	Diner	$10
	Branford			
9.6	Le Petit Café	French	Upmarket	$45
8.2	Foe	New American	Upmarket	$35
8.0	Tenderloin's	Steakhouse	Upmarket	$39
8.0	Stony Creek Market	Light American	Counter	$12
7.7	Darbar India	Indian	Upmarket	$20
7.7	Su Casa	Tex-Mex	Casual	$22
7.6	Billy's Pasta Così	Italian	Upmarket	$30
7.4	Assaggio	Italian	Upmarket	$33
7.3	Jalapeño Heaven	Tex-Mex	Casual	$23
7.2	Kampai	Japanese	Upmarket	$28
7.1	Lenny's	Seafood	Casual	$25
6.4	Donovan's Reef	Bar food	Bar and grill	$25
6.1	SBC	Bar food	Bar and grill	$23
6.0	Avra Grille	Greek	Upmarket	$30
5.9	USS Chowder Pot III	Seafood	Casual	$30
5.4	Parthenon Diner	Short-order	Diner	$17

Derby

	Cuisine	Type	Price
8.2 Roseland Apizza	Pizza	Casual	$32

East Haven

	Cuisine	Type	Price
7.2 Inka	Latin American	Casual	$20
6.1 The Rib House	Southern	Casual	$21

Guilford

	Cuisine	Type	Price
8.6 Stone House	Seafood	Upmarket	$38
8.1 The Place	Seafood	Casual	$19
7.9 Martin's American Café	New American	Upmarket	$39
7.7 Som Siam	Thai	Casual	$22
7.3 Quattro's	Italian	Upmarket	$32

Hamden

	Cuisine	Type	Price
8.1 Wentworth's	Sweets	Take-out	-
7.8 Hama	Japanese	Casual	$18
7.5 Luce	Italian	Upmarket	$36
7.5 Glenwood Drive-In	Short-order	Counter	$5
7.0 Kumo	Japanese	Upmarket	$28
7.0 Peroles Restaurant	Latin American	Casual	$18
6.9 The Playwright	Irish	Bar and grill	$22
6.5 Ixtapa Grille	Tex-Mex	Casual	$20
6.1 East Buffet	Chinese	Casual	$16
6.1 Aunt Chilada's	Tex-Mex	Casual	$27
5.6 Brown Stone House	Traditional Amer.	Casual	$8
4.8 Chili's	Bar food	Casual	$23
4.5 Colonial Tymes	Traditional Amer.	Upmarket	$32
NR Number 1 Fish Market	Seafood	Specialty grocery	

Milford

	Cuisine	Type	Price
8.8 East Japanese	Japanese	Upmarket	$32
8.7 Jeffrey's	New American	Upmarket	$44
7.5 Rainbow Gardens Inn	New American	Upmarket	$24
7.3 Citrus	New American	Upmarket	$39
7.1 Scribner's	Seafood	Upmarket	$32

North Haven

	Cuisine	Type	Price
NR Liuzzi's Cheese Shop	Italian	Specialty grocery	-

Orange

	Cuisine	Type	Price
8.3 Wild Ginger	Japanese	Upmarket	$33
7.0 Uncle Willie's BBQ	Southern	Casual	$16
6.7 Baja's	Mexican	Casual	$23
6.3 China Pavilion	Chinese	Upmarket	$21
6.0 Maxwell's	Steakhouse	Upmarket	$27

West Haven

	Cuisine	Type	Price
8.1 Swagat	Indian	Casual	$7
7.9 Daiko (Jerry-San's)	Japanese	Casual	$22
7.2 Warong Selera	Malaysian	Counter	$11
7.2 Chuck's Steak House	Steakhouse	Upmarket	$22
7.1 Taquería Mexicana	Mexican	Counter	$6
6.9 Jimmies	Seafood	Casual	$22
6.5 Chick's	Seafood	Counter	$11

Woodbridge	Cuisine	Type	Price
7.3 Pazza Cucina	Italian	Upmarket	$36
6.6 Katz's Restaurant	Light American	Casual	$16

Welcome to town

Places that have opened since *The Menu's* First Edition

	Restaurant	Cuisine	Location	Type	Price
8.9	Carmen Anthony	Steakhouse	Arts District	Upmarket	$50
8.7	Wild Ginger	Japanese	Orange	Upmarket	$33
8.3	Lou's Big Top	Short-order	Westville	Take-out	$7
8.3	Trevethan's	New American	E. Rock/Grad Ghetto	Upmarket	$36
8.3	Foe	New American	Branford	Upmarket	$35
8.3	Caribbean Connection	Jamaican	Whalley	Take-out	$9
8.2	Central Steakhouse	Steakhouse	Ninth Square	Upmarket	$51
8.1	Golden Seafood	Chinese	Westville	Casual	$22
8.0	Pot-au-Pho	Vietnamese	Arts District	Casual	$9
7.9	Warong Selera	Malaysian	West Haven	Counter	$11
7.9	Soul de Cuba	Latin American	Theater District	Upmarket	$22
7.8	Avellino's Trattoria	Italian	Ninth Square	Upmarket	$31
7.7	Pacifico	Latin American	Theater District	Upmarket	$38
7.5	Nini's Bistro	New American	Ninth Square	Upmarket	$35
7.4	Gusto Italiano	Italian	Arts District	Counter	$11
7.4	Zoi's on Orange	Light American	Arts District	Counter	$8
7.4	Stillwater Bistro	New American	Fair Haven	Upmarket	$31
7.3	La Piazza	Italian	Broadway Area	Casual	$27
7.1	Nikkita	New American	Theater District	Bar and grill	$25
7.1	Temple Grill	Traditional Amer.	Theater District	Bar and grill	$26
7.1	Basta!	Italian	Theater District	Upmarket	$51
7.0	Café George by Paula	Light American	Theater District	Counter	$8
6.9	Peroles Restaurant	Latin American	Hamden	Casual	$18
6.9	Pazza Cucina	Italian	Woodbridge	Upmarket	$36
6.9	Uncle Willie's BBQ	Southern	Orange	Casual	$16
6.8	Kumo	Japanese	Hamden	Upmarket	$28
6.8	Assaggio	Italian	Branford	Upmarket	$33
6.8	Funki Munki	Light American	Theater District	Take-out	$7
6.2	Moka	Light American	Financial District	Café	$8
5.8	Avra Grille	Greek	Branford	Upmarket	$30
5.8	Sidebar	Bar food	Financial District	Casual	$22
5.5	Caffé Bottega	Italian	Theater District	Bar and grill	$33
5.4	Cold Stone Creamery	Sweets	Theater District	Take-out	-
5.3	Woodland Coffee	Light American	Ninth Square	Café	$8
5.2	Skappo	Italian	Ninth Square	Upmarket	$29
5.1	Blue Pearl	New American	Financial District	Upmarket	$32
5.1	IKEA Restaurant	Swedish	Long Wharf	Counter	$6
4.9	Oolongs Tea Bar	Light American	Theater District	Café	-
4.8	Joe's Hubba Hubba	Short-order	Financial District	Counter	$7
4.5	Tasti D-Lite	Sweets	Theater District	Take-out	-
4.3	Quattro's	Italian	Theater District	Upmarket	$33
4.2	Bulldog Burrito	Tex-Mex	Broadway Area	Counter	$7
3.8	Olde Blue	Traditional Amer.	Upper Chapel Area	Upmarket	$26
NR	Dolce Java	Baked goods	Upper Chapel Area	Café	-
NR	Nica's Market	Italian	E. Rock/Grad Ghetto	Spec. grocery	-

LISTED IN ORDER OF OVERALL RATING OUT OF 10

Good Dates

		Cuisine	Location	Type	Price
9.6	Le Petit Café	French	Branford	Upmarket	$45
9.3	Ibiza	Spanish	Theater District	Upmarket	$44
9.2	Union League Café	French	Theater District	Upmarket	$46
9.0	Roomba	Latin American	Theater District	Upmarket	$52
8.7	Carmen Anthony	Steakhouse	Arts District	Upmarket	$50
8.7	Bentara	Malaysian	Ninth Square	Upmarket	$34
8.6	Stone House	Seafood	Guilford	Upmarket	$38
8.5	Bar (Brü Room)	Pizza	Theater District	Bar and grill	$15
8.5	Zinc	New American	Theater District	Upmarket	$45
8.4	Caffé Adulis	African	Theater District	Upmarket	$28
8.3	Soul de Cuba	Latin American	Theater District	Upmarket	$22
8.3	Trevethan's	New American	E. Rock/Grad Ghetto	Upmarket	$36
8.3	Nini's Bistro	New American	Ninth Square	Upmarket	$35
8.2	Pacifico	Latin American	Theater District	Upmarket	$38
8.2	Bella Rosa Café	Light American	Westville	Casual	$17
8.2	Stillwater Bistro	New American	Fair Haven	Upmarket	$31
8.2	Foe	New American	Branford	Upmarket	$35
8.1	The Place	Seafood	Guilford	Casual	$19
8.0	L'Orcio	Italian	E. Rock/Grad Ghetto	Upmarket	$33
8.0	Central Steakhouse	Steakhouse	Ninth Square	Upmarket	$51
8.0	Tenderloin's	Steakhouse	Branford	Upmarket	$39
8.0	Stony Creek Market	Light American	Branford	Counter	$12
7.9	Martin's Amer. Café	New American	Guilford	Upmarket	$39
7.8	Avellino's Trattoria	Italian	Ninth Square	Upmarket	$31
7.7	Geppi's	Italian	Fair Haven	Casual	$29
7.7	Sandra's	Southern	Arts District, The Hill	Casual	$21
7.7	Tre Scalini	Italian	Wooster Square	Upmarket	$32
7.7	Su Casa	Tex-Mex	Branford	Casual	$22
7.7	Anna Liffey's	Irish	Arts District	Bar and grill	$21
7.6	Billy's Pasta Così	Italian	Branford	Upmarket	$30
7.5	Rainbow Gardens	New American	Milford	Upmarket	$24
7.5	Luce	Italian	Hamden	Upmarket	$36
7.4	Gastronomique	French	Theater District	Take-out	$17
7.4	Consiglio's	Italian	Wooster Square	Upmarket	$41
7.4	Sage	Traditional American	Med. Area/The Hill	Upmarket	$37
7.3	Pazza Cucina	Italian	Woodbridge	Upmarket	$36
7.3	Scoozzi	Italian	Upper Chapel Area	Upmarket	$37
7.3	Jalapeño Heaven	Tex-Mex	Branford	Casual	$23
7.1	Lenny's	Seafood	Branford	Casual	$25
7.1	Royal India	Indian	Broadway Area	Casual	$18
7.1	Basta!	Italian	Theater District	Upmarket	$51
7.0	Tony & Lucille's	Italian	Wooster Square	Casual	$29
7.0	Skappo	Italian	Ninth Square	Upmarket	$29
7.0	Miya's	Japanese	Upper Chapel Area	Upmarket	$31
6.9	The Playwright	Irish	Hamden	Bar and grill	$22
6.7	Rudy's Restaurant	Light American	Broadway Area	Bar and grill	$8
6.7	Lalibela	African	Theater District	Casual	$21
6.6	Bottega Lounge	Italian	Theater District	Casual	$32
6.5	Anchor	Traditional Amer.ican	Theater District	Bar and grill	$11
6.5	Richter's	Bar food	Theater District	Bar and grill	$13
6.5	Chick's	Seafood	West Haven	Counter	$11
6.4	Hot Tomato's	New American	Theater District	Upmarket	$39
6.4	Blue Pearl	New American	Financial District	Upmarket	$32
6.2	168 York St. Café	Traditional American	Upper Chapel Area	Casual	$13
5.7	C.O. Jones	Tex-Mex	E. Rock/Grad Ghetto	Bar and grill	$14

Outdoor Dining *listed in order of **food** rating*

9.5	Roomba	Latin American	Theater District	Upmarket	$52
8.7	Jeffrey's	New American	Milford	Upmarket	$44
8.0	Tenderloin's	Steakhouse	Branford	Upmarket	$39
7.8	Martin's Amer. Café	New American	Guilford	Upmarket	$39
7.7	Caffé Adulis	African	Theater District	Upmarket	$28
7.6	Stony Creek Market	Light American	Branford	Counter	$12
7.4	Stillwater Bistro	New American	Fair Haven	Upmarket	$31
7.4	Billy's Pasta Così	Italian	Branford	Upmarket	$30
7.3	The Place	Seafood	Guilford	Casual	$19
7.3	Citrus	New American	Milford	Upmarket	$39
7.3	Su Casa	Tex-Mex	Branford	Casual	$22
7.3	La Piazza	Italian	Broadway Area	Casual	$27
7.1	Consiglio's	Italian	Wooster Square	Upmarket	$41
7.1	Miso	Japanese	Ninth Square	Upmarket	$25
7.1	Basta!	Italian	Theater District	Upmarket	$51
7.0	Book Trader Café	Light American	Upper Chapel Area	Counter	$7
6.9	Kiraku	Japanese	Fair Haven	Upmarket	$31
6.8	Assaggio	Italian	Branford	Upmarket	$33
6.7	Sage	Traditional American	Med. Area/The Hill	Upmarket	$37
6.7	Scoozzi	Italian	Upper Chapel Area	Upmarket	$37
6.6	Lenny's	Seafood	Branford	Casual	$25
6.6	Jalapeño Heaven	Tex-Mex	Branford	Casual	$23
6.5	Caffé Bravo	Italian	E. Rock/Grad Ghetto	Casual	$28
6.4	The Playwright	Irish	Hamden	Bar and grill	$22
6.3	Chick's	Seafood	West Haven	Counter	$11
6.3	Pad Thai	Thai	Upper Chapel Area	Casual	$18
6.2	Bottega Lounge	Italian	Theater District	Casual	$32
6.1	Amato's	Pizza	E. Rock/Grad Ghetto	Casual	$18
6.0	168 York St. Café	Traditional American	Upper Chapel Area	Casual	$13
6.0	Delaney's	Bar food	Westville	Bar and grill	$21
6.0	J.P. Dempsey's	Bar food	E. Rock/Grad Ghetto	Bar and grill	$22
5.9	Yorkside Pizza	Pizza	Broadway Area	Casual	$14
5.8	Tony & Lucille's	Italian	Wooster Square	Casual	$29
5.7	TK's American Café	Bar food	Theater District	Bar and grill	$13
5.6	SBC	Bar food	Branford	Bar and grill	$23
5.5	Humphrey's East	Bar food	E. Rock/Grad Ghetto	Bar and grill	$16
5.5	Aunt Chilada's	Tex-Mex	Hamden	Casual	$27
5.3	USS Chowder Pot III	Seafood	Branford	Casual	$30
5.3	Gennaro's	Italian	Theater District	Upmarket	$38
5.1	Blue Pearl	New American	Financial District	Upmarket	$32
5.0	Chap's Grille	Light American	Upper Chapel Area	Counter	$11
4.9	Xando Cosí	Light American	Broadway Area	Casual	$15
4.7	C.O. Jones	Tex-Mex	E. Rock/Grad Ghetto	Bar and grill	$14
4.1	Rusty Scupper	Seafood	Long Wharf	Upmarket	$37
3.9	Sweet Relief	Light American	Arts District	Counter	$7
3.5	Sullivan's	Bar food	Upper Chapel Area	Bar and grill	$17
2.6	Haya	Japanese	E. Rock/Grad Ghetto	Casual	$22
2.4	Au Bon Pain	Light American	Broadway Area	Fast food	$9
2.2	Colonial Tymes	Traditional American	Hamden	Upmarket	$32
2.0	Thai Pan Asian	Thai	Upper Chapel Area	Casual	$19
NR	Lulu's	Baked goods	E. Rock/Grad Ghetto	Café	-
NR	Nica's Market	Italian	E. Rock/Grad Ghetto	Spec. grocery	-
NR	Romeo & Cesare's	Italian	E. Rock/Grad Ghetto	Spec. grocery	-
NR	Willoughby's	Baked goods	Financial District	Café	-

Free Wireless Internet *listed in order of **overall** rating*

8.3	Koffee?	Baked goods	Arts District	Café
8.0	Dolce Java	Baked goods	Upper Chapel Area	Café
6.8	Moka	Light American	Financial District	Café
6.5	Koffee Too?	Light American	Broadway Area	Café
5.8	Woodland Coffee	Light American	Ninth Square	Café
5.1	Caffé Bottega	Italian	Theater District	Bar and grill

BYO *listed in order of* **overall** *rating*

8.0	Tenderloin's	Steakhouse	Branford	Upmarket	$39
8.3	Nini's Bistro	New American	Ninth Square	Upmarket	$35
8.1	The Place	Seafood	Guilford	Casual	$19
8.0	Stony Creek Market	Light American, Pizza	Branford	Counter	$12
7.5	Istanbul Café	Turkish	Theater District	Upmarket	$29
7.0	Uncle Willie's BBQ	Southern	Orange	Casual	$16
6.4	House of Chao	Chinese	Westville	Casual	$12
6.4	Mamoun's	Middle Eastern	Upper Chapel Area	Casual	$9
6.4	Caffé Bravo	Italian	E. Rock/Grad Ghetto	Casual	$28
6.3	Rainbow Café	Light American	Theater District	Casual	$18

Water Views *listed in order of* **overall** *rating*

8.6	Stone House	Seafood	Guilford	Upmarket	$38
8.2	Stillwater Bistro	New American	Fair Haven	Upmarket	$31
8.0	Stony Creek Market	Light American, Pizza	Branford	Counter	$12
7.4	Sage	Traditional American	Med. Area/The Hill	Upmarket	$37
7.2	Kiraku	Japanese	Fair Haven	Upmarket	$31
6.9	Jimmies of Savin Rock	Seafood	West Haven	Casual	$22
6.5	Chick's	Seafood	West Haven	Counter	$11
5.9	Rusty Scupper	Seafood	Long Wharf	Upmarket	$37

Best Wine Lists *listed in order of quality (considers both breadth and value)*

1	Luce	Italian	Hamden	Upmarket	$36
2	Polo Grille	New American	Fair Haven	Upmarket	$31
3	Central Steakhouse	Steakhouse	Ninth Square	Upmarket	$51
4	Bentara	Malaysian	Ninth Square	Upmarket	$34
5	Carmen Anthony	Steakhouse	Arts District	Upmarket	$50
6	Sage	Traditional American	Med. Area/The Hill	Upmarket	$37
7	Union League Café	French	Theater District	Upmarket	$46
8	Ibiza	Spanish	Theater District	Upmarket	$44
9	Skappo	Italian	Ninth Square	Upmarket	$29
10	Zinc	New American	Theater District	Upmarket	$45

Delivery *listed in order of* **food** *rating*

8.1	Dayton St. Apizza	Pizza	Westville	Take-out	$13
8.1	Gastronomique	French	Theater District	Take-out	$17
7.8	Royal Palace	Chinese	Ninth Square	Upmarket	$22
7.4	Gusto Italiano	Italian	Arts District	Counter	$11
7.3	Mediterranea	Middle Eastern	Financial District	Counter	$9
7.2	El Caribe	Latin American	Fair Haven	Casual	$25
6.7	Alpha Delta Pizza	Pizza	Broadway Area	Take-out	$7
6.5	Royal India	Indian	Broadway Area	Casual	$18
6.5	Sahara	Middle Eastern	Theater District	Counter	$9
6.5	Brick Oven Pizza	Pizza	Upper Chapel Area	Counter	$9
6.5	Indochine Pavilion	Thai	Upper Chapel Area	Casual	$18
6.4	Est Est Est	Pizza	Upper Chapel Area	Counter	$8
6.4	Southern Hospitality	Southern	Whalley	Take-out	$10
6.3	Pad Thai	Thai	Upper Chapel Area	Casual	$17
6.1	Amato's	Pizza	E. Rock/Grad Ghetto	Casual	$18
6.0	Fresh Taco	Tex-Mex	Financial District	Take-out	$7
5.9	India Palace	Indian	Upper Chapel Area	Casual	$18
5.8	Tandoor	Indian	Upper Chapel Area	Casual	$20
5.5	Katz's 2 Go	Light American	Financial District	Take-out	$9
4.8	Aladdin	Middle Eastern	Theater District	Take-out	$10
4.7	Abate Apizza	Italian	Wooster Square Area	Casual	$24
4.1	Hunan Café	Chinese	Upper Chapel Area	Counter	$9
4.0	Corner Deli	Light American	Financial District	Counter	$6
3.9	Sweet Relief	Light American	Arts District	Counter	$7
3.6	Yalie's Pizza	Pizza	Upper Chapel Area	Take-out	$6
3.4	Main Garden	Chinese	Broadway Area	Take-out	$9
3.4	China King	Chinese	Theater District	Take-out	$8
2.0	Thai Pan Asian	Thai	Upper Chapel Area	Casual	$19

LATE-NIGHT DINING GUIDE

Each of the following lists of late-night options is comprehensive, covering all establishments that will still be open at a given hour on a given night, including take-out options. "Weekday" means Sunday to Thursday or Monday to Thursday; "weekend" means Friday and Saturday.
All lists are ordered by food rating.

Weekday food after 9pm

			Location	Type	Price
9.3	Ibiza	Spanish	Theater District	Upmarket	$44
9.2	Union League Café	French	Theater District	Upmarket	$46
9.0	Roomba	Latin American	Theater District	Upmarket	$52
8.8	East Japanese	Japanese	Milford	Upmarket	$32
8.7	Carmen Anthony	Steakhouse	Arts District	Upmarket	$50
8.7	Jeffrey's	New American	Milford	Upmarket	$44
8.7	Bentara	Malaysian	Ninth Square	Upmarket	$34
8.5	Bar (Brü Room)	Pizza	Theater District	Bar and grill	$15
8.5	Zinc	New American	Theater District	Upmarket	$45
8.4	Modern Apizza	Pizza	E. Rock/Grad Ghetto	Casual	$13
8.4	Caffé Adulis	African	Theater District	Upmarket	$28
8.3	Soul de Cuba	Latin American	Theater District	Upmarket	$22
8.3	Trevethan's	New American	E. Rock/Grad Ghetto	Upmarket	$36
8.3	Wild Ginger	Japanese	Orange	Upmarket	$33
8.3	Sally's Apizza	Pizza	Wooster Sq. Area	Casual	$14
8.3	Koffee?	Baked goods	Arts District	Café	$7
8.2	Roseland Apizza	Pizza	Derby	Casual	$32
8.2	Stillwater Bistro	New American	Fair Haven	Upmarket	$31
8.2	Foe	New American	Branford	Upmarket	$35
8.2	Pacifico	Latin American	Theater District	Upmarket	$38
8.1	Swagat	Indian	West Haven	Casual	$7
8.0	L'Orcio	Italian	E. Rock/Grad Ghetto	Upmarket	$33
8.0	Central Steakhouse	Steakhouse	Ninth Square	Upmarket	$51
8.0	Golden Seafood	Chinese	Westville	Casual	$22
8.0	Christopher Martin's	Bar food	E. Rock/Grad Ghetto	Bar and grill	$17
8.0	Tenderloin's	Steakhouse	Branford	Upmarket	$39
8.0	Dolce Java	Baked goods	Upper Chapel Area	Café	-
7.9	Daiko (Jerry-San's)	Japanese	West Haven	Casual	$22
7.9	Frank Pepe's	Pizza	Wooster Sq. Area	Casual	$14
7.8	Avellino's Trattoria	Italian	Ninth Square	Upmarket	$31
7.8	Hama	Japanese	Hamden	Casual	$18
7.7	La Piazza	Italian	Broadway Area	Casual	$27
7.7	Som Siam	Thai	Guilford	Casual	$22
7.7	Tre Scalini	Italian	Wooster Sq. Area	Upmarket	$32
7.7	Darbar India	Indian	Branford	Upmarket	$20
7.7	Su Casa	Tex-Mex	Branford	Casual	$22
7.7	Anna Liffey's	Irish	Arts District	Bar and grill	$21
7.7	China Great Wall	Chinese	Arts District	Take-out	$5
7.6	Billy's Pasta Cosi	Italian	Branford	Upmarket	$30
7.5	Atticus	Light American	Upper Chapel Area	Café	$9
7.5	Istanbul Café	Turkish	Theater District	Upmarket	$29
7.5	Glenwood Drive-In	Short-order	Hamden	Counter	$5
7.4	Sage	Traditional Amer.	Med. Area/The Hill	Upmarket	$37
7.4	Dayton St. Apizza	Pizza	Westville	Take-out	$13
7.3	Pazza Cucina	Italian	Woodbridge	Upmarket	$36
7.2	Kampai	Japanese	Branford	Upmarket	$28
7.2	Kiraku	Japanese	Fair Haven	Upmarket	$31
7.2	Warong Selera	Malaysian	West Haven	Counter	$11
7.2	Miso	Japanese	Ninth Square	Upmarket	$25
7.2	Inka	Latin American	East Haven	Casual	$20
7.2	Temple Grill	Traditional Amer.	Theater District	Bar and grill	$26
7.1	Lenny's	Seafood	Branford	Casual	$25
7.1	Royal India	Indian	Broadway Area	Casual	$18
7.1	Taquería Mexicana	Mexican	West Haven	Counter	$6

		Location	Type	Price
7.1 Delaney's	Bar food	Westville	Bar and grill	$21
7.1 J.P. Dempsey's	Bar food	E. Rock/Grad Ghetto	Bar and grill	$22
7.1 Starbucks	Baked goods	Theater District	Café	-
7.0 Kumo	Japanese	Hamden	Upmarket	$28
7.0 Tony & Lucille's	Italian	Wooster Sq. Area	Casual	$29
7.0 Skappo	Italian	Ninth Square	Upmarket	$29
7.0 Miya's	Japanese	Upper Chapel Area	Upmarket	$31
6.9 The Playwright	Irish	Hamden	Bar and grill	$22
6.9 Jimmies	Seafood	West Haven	Casual	$22
6.9 Pancho's Cantina	Tex-Mex	Westville	Bar and grill	$22
6.8 Gunung Tahan	Malaysian	Westville	Casual	$23
6.8 Seoul Yokocho	Korean	Upper Chapel Area	Upmarket	$27
6.8 Basta!	Italian	Theater District	Upmarket	$51
6.7 Akasaka	Japanese	Westville	Upmarket	$25
6.7 Baja's	Mexican	Orange	Casual	$23
6.7 Indochine Pavilion	Thai	Upper Chapel Area	Casual	$18
6.7 Royal Palace	Chinese	Ninth Square	Upmarket	$22
6.7 Rudy's Restaurant	Light American	Broadway Area	Bar and grill	$8
6.7 El Caribe	Latin American	Fair Haven	Casual	$25
6.7 Lalibela	African	Theater District	Casual	$21
6.6 Bottega Lounge	Italian	Theater District	Casual	$32
6.6 Nikkita	New American	Theater District	Bar and grill	$25
6.6 Zaroka	Indian	Upper Chapel Area	Upmarket	$24
6.6 Southern Hospitality	Southern	Whalley	Take-out	$10
6.6 Ashley's Ice Cream	Sweets	Broadway Area	Take-out	-
6.5 Anchor	Traditional Amer.	Theater District	Bar and grill	$11
6.5 Ixtapa Grille	Tex-Mex	Hamden	Casual	$20
6.5 Chick's	Seafood	West Haven	Counter	$11
6.5 Bangkok Gardens	Thai	Upper Chapel Area	Upmarket	$20
6.5 Sahara	Middle Eastern	Theater District	Counter	$9
6.5 Alpha Delta Pizza	Pizza	Broadway Area	Take-out	$7
6.4 Hot Tomato's	New American	Theater District	Upmarket	$39
6.4 House of Chao	Chinese	Westville	Casual	$12
6.4 Blue Pearl	New American	Financial District	Upmarket	$32
6.4 Donovan's Reef	Bar food	Branford	Bar and grill	$25
6.4 Mamoun's	Middle Eastern	Upper Chapel Area	Casual	$9
6.3 Fresh Taco	Tex-Mex	Financial District	Take-out	$7
6.3 Tandoor	Indian	Upper Chapel Area	Casual	$20
6.3 Clark's Dairy	Short-order	Arts District	Diner	$10
6.3 China Pavilion	Chinese	Orange	Upmarket	$21
6.3 Archie Moore's	Bar food	E. Rock/Grad Ghetto	Bar and grill	$15
6.3 Cold Stone Creamery	Sweets	Theater District	Take-out	-
6.2 El Charro Alegre	Mexican	E. Rock/Grad Ghetto	Casual	$19
6.2 Pad Thai	Thai	Upper Chapel Area	Casual	$17
6.2 168 York St. Café	Traditional Amer.	Upper Chapel Area	Casual	$13
6.2 Amato's	Pizza	E. Rock/Grad Ghetto	Casual	$18
6.2 Humphrey's East	Bar food	E. Rock/Grad Ghetto	Bar and grill	$16
6.1 The Rib House	Southern	East Haven	Casual	$21
6.1 SBC	Bar food	Branford	Bar and grill	$23
6.1 East Buffet	Chinese	Hamden	Casual	$16
6.1 Aunt Chilada's	Tex-Mex	Hamden	Casual	$27
6.1 Pizza House	Pizza	Upper Chapel Area	Take-out	$6
6.0 Avra Grille	Greek	Branford	Upmarket	$30
6.0 Maxwell's	Steakhouse	Orange	Upmarket	$27
6.0 Educated Burgher	Short-order	Broadway Area	Counter	$7
5.9 Yorkside Pizza	Pizza	Broadway Area	Casual	$14
5.9 Villa Del Sol	Tex-Mex	Theater District	Upmarket	$27
5.9 Rusty Scupper	Seafood	Long Wharf	Upmarket	$37
5.7 Est Est Est	Pizza	Upper Chapel Area	Counter	$8
5.7 Sidebar	Bar food	Financial District	Casual	$22
5.7 TK's American Café	Bar food	Theater District	Bar and grill	$13
5.7 C.O. Jones	Tex-Mex	E. Rock/Grad Ghetto	Bar and grill	$14
5.6 Thai Taste	Thai	Upper Chapel Area	Casual	$21

		Location	Type	Price
5.5	The Playwright	Irish	Theater District	Bar and grill	$28
5.4	Quattro's	Italian	Theater District	Upmarket	$33
5.4	Parthenon Diner	Short-order	Branford	Diner	$17
5.3	Libby's Pastry	Baked goods	Wooster Sq. Area	Take-out	-
5.3	Tasti D-Lite	Sweets	Theater District	Take-out	-
5.3	Athenian Diner	Short-order	Westville	Diner	$18
5.2	Xando Cosí	Light American	Broadway Area	Casual	$15
5.2	Brick Oven Pizza	Pizza	Upper Chapel Area	Counter	$9
5.2	John Davenport's	Traditional Amer.	Theater District	Upmarket	$40
5.1	Caffé Bottega	Italian	Theater District	Bar and grill	$33
4.9	India Palace	Indian U	pper Chapel Area	Casual	$18
4.9	Gennaro's	Italian	Theater District	Upmarket	$38
4.9	Templeton's	Traditional Amer.	Theater District	Upmarket	$36
4.8	Chili's	Bar food	Hamden	Casual	$23
4.8	Brazi's	Italian	Long Wharf	Casual	$22
4.7	Chap's Grille	Light American	Upper Chapel Area	Counter	$11
4.6	Cody's Diner	Short-order	Wooster Sq. Area	Diner	$10
4.6	Main Garden	Chinese	Broadway Area	Take-out	$9
4.5	Aladdin	Middle Eastern	Theater District	Take-out	$10
4.5	Olde Blue	Traditional Amer.	Upper Chapel Area	Upmarket	$26
4.5	Colonial Tymes	Traditional Amer.	Hamden	Upmarket	$32
4.4	Sullivan's	Bar food	Upper Chapel Area	Bar and grill	$17
4.3	McDonald's	Short-order	Whalley	Fast food	$6
4.2	Haya	Japanese	E. Rock/Grad Ghetto	Casual	$22
4.1	Bulldog Burrito	Tex-Mex	Broadway Area	Counter	$7
4.1	Samurai	Japanese	Theater District	Upmarket	$26
4.1	A One	Pizza	Broadway Area	Counter	$6
4.0	Hunan Café	Chinese	Upper Chapel Area	Counter	$9
3.9	Popeye's	Southern	Whalley	Fast food	$7
3.7	Yalie's Pizza	Pizza	Upper Chapel Area	Take-out	$6
3.6	Gourmet Heaven	Light American	Broadway, Arts Dist.	Take-out	$8
3.4	Town Pizza	Pizza	Arts District	Casual	$8
3.4	Thai Pan Asian	Thai	Upper Chapel Area	Casual	$19
3.4	KFC	Southern	Whalley	Fast food	$7
3.2	Viva Zapata	Tex-Mex	Upper Chapel Area	Bar and grill	$18
3.0	Au Bon Pain	Light American	Broadway Area	Fast food	$9
3.0	El Amigo Felix	Tex-Mex	Broadway Area	Bar and grill	$23
2.9	China King	Chinese	Theater District	Take-out	$8
2.9	Subway	Light American	Theater District	Fast food	$6
2.6	Burger King	Short-order	Whalley	Fast food	$6
2.6	Ivy Noodle	Chinese	Broadway Area	Casual	$8
2.5	Dunkin' Donuts	Baked goods	Theater District	Fast food	$7

Weekday food after 10pm

8.4	Modern Apizza	Pizza	E. Rock/Grad Ghetto	Casual	$13
8.4	Caffé Adulis	African	Theater District	Upmarket	$28
8.3	Sally's Apizza	Pizza	Wooster Sq. Area	Casual	$14
8.0	Christopher Martin's	Bar food	E. Rock/Grad Ghetto	Bar and grill	$17
7.7	La Piazza	Italian	Broadway Area	Casual	$27
7.7	Darbar India	Indian	Branford	Upmarket	$20
7.7	Anna Liffey's	Irish	Arts District	Bar and grill	$21
7.5	Atticus	Light American	Upper Chapel Area	Café	$9
7.2	Kampai	Japanese	Branford	Upmarket	$28
7.1	Royal India	Indian	Broadway Area	Casual	$18
7.1	Delaney's	Bar food	Westville	Bar and grill	$21
7.1	J.P. Dempsey's	Bar food	E. Rock/Grad Ghetto	Bar and grill	$22
7.1	Starbucks	Baked goods	Theater District	Café	-
7.0	Kumo	Japanese	Hamden	Upmarket	$28
7.0	Skappo	Italian	Ninth Square	Upmarket	$29
7.0	Miya's	Japanese	Upper Chapel Area	Upmarket	$31
6.9	The Playwright	Irish	Hamden	Bar and grill	$22
6.9	Pancho's Cantina	Tex-Mex	Westville	Bar and grill	$22

		Location	Type	Price
Weekday food after 10pm *continued*				
6.7	Rudy's Restaurant	Light American	Broadway Area	Bar and grill	$8
6.6	Bottega Lounge	Italian	Theater District	Casual	$32
6.6	Ashley's Ice Cream	Sweets	Broadway Area	Take-out	-
6.5	Sahara	Middle Eastern	Theater District	Counter	$9
6.5	Alpha Delta Pizza	Pizza	Broadway Area	Take-out	$7
6.4	Blue Pearl	New American	Financial District	Upmarket	$32
6.4	Mamoun's	Middle Eastern	Upper Chapel Area	Casual	$9
6.3	Fresh Taco	Tex-Mex	Financial District	Take-out	$7
6.3	Tandoor	Indian	Upper Chapel Area	Casual	$20
6.3	China Pavilion	Chinese	Orange	Upmarket	$21
6.3	Archie Moore's	Bar food	E. Rock/Grad Ghetto	Bar and grill	$15
6.3	Cold Stone Creamery	Sweets	Theater District	Take-out	-
6.2	Humphrey's East	Bar food	E. Rock/Grad Ghetto	Bar and grill	$16
6.1	Pizza House	Pizza	Upper Chapel Area	Take-out	$6
5.9	Yorkside Pizza	Pizza	Broadway Area	Casual	$14
5.9	Villa Del Sol	Tex-Mex	Theater District	Upmarket	$27
5.7	Est Est Est	Pizza	Upper Chapel Area	Counter	$8
5.7	TK's American Café	Bar food	Theater District	Bar and grill	$13
5.7	C.O. Jones	Tex-Mex	E. Rock/Grad Ghetto	Bar and grill	$14
5.4	Quattro's	Italian	Theater District	Upmarket	$33
5.4	Parthenon Diner	Short-order	Branford	Diner	$17
5.3	Athenian Diner	Short-order	Westville	Diner	$18
5.2	Xando Cosí	Light American	Broadway Area	Casual	$15
5.2	Brick Oven Pizza	Pizza	Upper Chapel Area	Counter	$9
4.9	India Palace	Indian	Upper Chapel Area	Casual	$18
4.8	Chili's	Bar food	Hamden	Casual	$23
4.7	Chap's Grille	Light American	Upper Chapel Area	Counter	$11
4.6	Cody's Diner	Short-order	Wooster Sq. Area	Diner	$10
4.6	Main Garden	Chinese	Broadway Area	Take-out	$9
4.5	Aladdin	Middle Eastern	Theater District	Take-out	$10
4.3	McDonald's	Short-order	Whalley	Fast food	$6
4.1	Bulldog Burrito	Tex-Mex	Broadway Area	Counter	$7
4.1	A One	Pizza	Broadway Area	Counter	$6
4.0	Hunan Café	Chinese	Upper Chapel Area	Counter	$9
3.9	Popeye's	Southern	Whalley	Fast food	$7
3.7	Yalie's Pizza	Pizza	Upper Chapel Area	Take-out	$6
3.6	Gourmet Heaven	Light American	Broadway, Arts Dist.	Take-out	$8
3.4	KFC	Southern	Whalley	Fast food	$7
3.2	Viva Zapata	Tex-Mex	Upper Chapel Area	Bar and grill	$18
3.0	Au Bon Pain	Light American	Broadway Area	Fast food	$9
3.0	El Amigo Felix	Tex-Mex	Broadway Area	Bar and grill	$23
2.9	China King	Chinese	Theater District	Take-out	$8
2.9	Subway	Light American	Theater District	Fast food	$6
2.6	Burger King	Short-order	Whalley	Fast food	$6
2.6	Ivy Noodle	Chinese	Broadway Area	Casual	$8
2.5	Dunkin' Donuts	Baked goods	Theater District	Fast food	$7

Weekday food after 11pm

8.0	Christopher Martin's	Bar food	E. Rock/Grad Ghetto	Bar and grill	$17
7.5	Atticus	Light American	Upper Chapel Area	Café	$9
7.1	Delaney's	Bar food	Westville	Bar and grill	$21
7.1	Starbucks	Baked goods	Theater District	Café	-
7.0	Skappo	Italian	Ninth Square	Upmarket	$29
7.0	Miya's	Japanese	Upper Chapel Area	Upmarket	$31
6.9	Pancho's Cantina	Tex-Mex	Westville	Bar and grill	$22
6.7	Rudy's Restaurant	Light American	Broadway Area	Bar and grill	$8
6.5	Alpha Delta Pizza	Pizza	Broadway Area	Take-out	$7
6.4	Mamoun's	Middle Eastern	Upper Chapel Area	Casual	$9
6.3	Archie Moore's	Bar food	E. Rock/Grad Ghetto	Bar and grill	$15
6.2	Humphrey's East	Bar food	E. Rock/Grad Ghetto	Bar and grill	$16
5.9	Yorkside Pizza	Pizza	Broadway Area	Casual	$14
5.7	TK's American Café	Bar food	Theater District	Bar and grill	$13

Weekday food after 11pm *continued*

			Location	Type	Price
5.7	Est Est Est	Pizza	Upper Chapel Area	Counter	$8
5.4	Parthenon Diner	Short-order	Branford	Diner	$17
5.3	Athenian Diner	Short-order	Westville	Diner	$18
5.2	Xando Cosí	Light American	Broadway Area	Casual	$15
5.2	Brick Oven Pizza	Pizza	Upper Chapel Area	Counter	$9
4.6	Main Garden	Chinese	Broadway Area	Take-out	$9
4.6	Cody's Diner	Short-order	Wooster Sq. Area	Diner	$10
4.5	Aladdin	Middle Eastern	Theater District	Take-out	$10
4.3	McDonald's	Short-order	Whalley	Fast food	$6
4.1	Bulldog Burrito	Tex-Mex	Broadway Area	Counter	$7
4.1	A One	Pizza	Broadway Area	Counter	$6
3.9	Popeye's	Southern	Whalley	Fast food	$7
3.7	Yalie's Pizza	Pizza	Upper Chapel Area	Take-out	$6
3.6	Gourmet Heaven	Light American	Broadway, Arts Dist.	Take-out	$8
3.4	KFC	Southern	Whalley	Fast food	$7
3.2	Viva Zapata	Tex-Mex	Upper Chapel Area	Bar and grill	$18
3.0	Au Bon Pain	Light American	Broadway Area	Fast food	$9
2.9	Subway	Light American	Theater District	Fast food	$6
2.6	Ivy Noodle	Chinese	Broadway Area	Casual	$8
2.5	Dunkin' Donuts	Baked goods	Theater District	Fast food	$7

Weekday food after midnight

6.7	Rudy's Restaurant	Light American	Broadway Area	Bar and grill	$8
6.5	Alpha Delta Pizza	Pizza	Broadway Area	Take-out	$7
6.4	Mamoun's	Middle Eastern	Upper Chapel Area	Casual	$9
5.9	Yorkside Pizza	Pizza	Broadway Area	Casual	$14
5.7	Est Est Est	Pizza	Upper Chapel Area	Counter	$8
5.4	Parthenon Diner	Short-order	Branford	Diner	$17
5.3	Athenian Diner	Short-order	Westville	Diner	$18
5.2	Brick Oven Pizza	Pizza	Upper Chapel Area	Counter	$9
4.6	Cody's Diner	Short-order	Wooster Sq. Area	Diner	$10
4.6	Main Garden	Chinese	Broadway Area	Take-out	$9
4.5	Aladdin	Middle Eastern	Theater District	Take-out	$10
4.1	Bulldog Burrito	Tex-Mex	Broadway Area	Counter	$7
4.1	A One	Pizza	Broadway Area	Counter	$6
3.7	Yalie's Pizza	Pizza	Upper Chapel Area	Take-out	$6
3.6	Gourmet Heaven	Light American	Broadway, Arts Dist.	Take-out	$8
3.4	KFC	Southern	Whalley	Fast food	$7
2.6	Ivy Noodle	Chinese	Broadway Area	Casual	$8
2.5	Dunkin' Donuts	Baked goods	Theater District	Fast food	$7

Weekday food after 1am

6.5	Alpha Delta Pizza	Pizza	Broadway Area	Take-out	$7
6.4	Mamoun's	Middle Eastern	Upper Chapel Area	Casual	$9
5.4	Parthenon Diner	Short-order	Branford	Diner	$17
5.3	Athenian Diner	Short-order	Westville	Diner	$18
5.2	Brick Oven Pizza	Pizza	Upper Chapel Area	Counter	$9
4.6	Cody's Diner	Short-order	Wooster Sq. Area	Diner	$10
4.5	Aladdin	Middle Eastern	Theater District	Take-out	$10
4.1	A One	Pizza	Broadway Area	Counter	$6
3.6	Gourmet Heaven	Light American	Broadway, Arts Dist.	Take-out	$8
3.4	KFC	Southern	Whalley	Fast food	$7
2.6	Ivy Noodle	Chinese	Broadway Area	Casual	$8
2.5	Dunkin' Donuts	Baked goods	Theater District	Fast food	$7

Weekday food after 2am

6.5	Alpha Delta Pizza	Pizza	Broadway Area	Take-out	$7
6.4	Mamoun's	Middle Eastern	Upper Chapel Area	Casual	$9
5.4	Parthenon Diner	Short-order	Branford	Diner	$17
5.3	Athenian Diner	Short-order	Westville	Diner	$18

		Location	Type	Price
5.2	Brick Oven Pizza	Pizza	Upper Chapel Area	Counter	$9
4.6	˙Cody's Diner	Short-order	Wooster Sq. Area	Diner	$10
4.1	A One	Pizza	Broadway Area	Counter	$6
3.6	Gourmet Heaven	Light American	Broadway, Arts Dist.	Take-out	$8
3.4	KFC	Southern	Whalley	Fast food	$7
2.5	Dunkin' Donuts	Baked goods	Theater District	Fast food	$7

Weekend food after 10pm

9.3	Ibiza	Spanish	Theater District	Upmarket	$44
9.0	Roomba	Latin American	Theater District	Upmarket	$52
8.8	East Japanese	Japanese	Milford	Upmarket	$32
8.7	Carmen Anthony	Steakhouse	Arts District	Upmarket	$50
8.7	Bentara	Malaysian	Ninth Square	Upmarket	$34
8.5	Zinc	New American	Theater District	Upmarket	$45
8.4	Modern Apizza	Pizza	E. Rock/Grad Ghetto	Casual	$13
8.4	Caffé Adulis	African	Theater District	Upmarket	$28
8.3	Wild Ginger	Japanese	Orange	Upmarket	$33
8.3	Sally's Apizza	Pizza	Wooster Sq. Area	Casual	$14
8.2	Foe	New American	Branford	Upmarket	$35
8.2	Pacifico	Latin American	Theater District	Upmarket	$38
8.0	L'Orcio	Italian	E. Rock/Grad Ghetto	Upmarket	$33
8.0	Central Steakhouse	Steakhouse	Ninth Square	Upmarket	$51
8.0	Christopher Martin's	Bar food	E. Rock/Grad Ghetto	Bar and grill	$17
8.0	Tenderloin's	Steakhouse	Branford	Upmarket	$39
7.9	Frank Pepe's	Pizza	Wooster Sq. Area	Casual	$14
7.9	Daiko (Jerry-San's)	Japanese	West Haven	Casual	$22
7.7	Louis' Lunch	Short-order	Theater District	Counter	$7
7.7	Darbar India	Indian	Branford	Upmarket	$20
7.7	Tre Scalini	Italian	Wooster Sq. Area	Upmarket	$32
7.7	Su Casa	Tex-Mex	Branford	Casual	$22
7.7	Anna Liffey's	Irish	Arts District	Bar and grill	$21
7.5	Atticus	Light American	Upper Chapel Area	Café	$9
7.4	Sage	Traditional Amer.	Med. Area/The Hill	Upmarket	$37
7.3	Pazza Cucina	Italian	Woodbridge	Upmarket	$36
7.3	Jalapeño Heaven	Tex-Mex	Branford	Casual	$23
7.2	Kampai	Japanese	Branford	Upmarket	$28
7.2	Miso	Japanese	Ninth Square	Upmarket	$25
7.2	Temple Grill	Traditional Amer.	Theater District	Bar and grill	$26
7.2	Portofino	Italian	E. Rock/Grad Ghetto	Upmarket	$27
7.1	Lenny's	Seafood	Branford	Casual	$25
7.1	Royal India	Indian	Broadway Area	Casual	$18
7.1	Delaney's	Bar food	Westville	Bar and grill	$21
7.1	J.P. Dempsey's	Bar food	E. Rock/Grad Ghetto	Bar and grill	$22
7.1	Starbucks	Baked goods	Theater District	Café	-
7.0	Kumo	Japanese	Hamden	Upmarket	$28
7.0	Skappo	Italian	Ninth Square	Upmarket	$29
7.0	Miya's	Japanese	Upper Chapel Area	Upmarket	$31
6.9	The Playwright	Irish	Hamden	Bar and grill	$22
6.9	Jimmies	Seafood	West Haven	Casual	$22
6.9	Pancho's Cantina	Tex-Mex	Westville	Bar and grill	$22
6.8	Gunung Tahan	Malaysian	Westville	Casual	$23
6.8	Seoul Yokocho	Korean	Upper Chapel Area	Upmarket	$27
6.8	Basta!	Italian	Theater District	Upmarket	$51
6.7	Akasaka	Japanese	Westville	Upmarket	$25
6.7	Indochine Pavilion	Thai	Upper Chapel Area	Casual	$18
6.7	Rudy's Restaurant	Light American	Broadway Area	Bar and grill	$8
6.7	Royal Palace	Chinese	Ninth Square	Upmarket	$22
6.7	Lalibela	African	Theater District	Casual	$21
6.6	Bottega Lounge	Italian	Theater District	Casual	$32
6.6	Nikkita	New American	Theater District	Bar and grill	$25
6.6	Zaroka	Indian	Upper Chapel Area	Upmarket	$24
6.6	Ashley's Ice Cream	Sweets	Broadway Area	Take-out	

	Weekend food after 10pm *continued*		Location	Type	Price
6.6	Southern Hospitality	Southern	Whalley	Take-out	$10
6.5	Ixtapa Grille	Tex-Mex	Hamden	Casual	$20
6.5	Bangkok Gardens	Thai	Upper Chapel Area	Upmarket	$20
6.5	Sahara	Middle Eastern	Theater District	Counter	$9
6.5	Alpha Delta Pizza	Pizza	Broadway Area	Take-out	$7
6.4	Blue Pearl	New American	Financial District	Upmarket	$32
6.4	Mamoun's	Middle Eastern	Upper Chapel Area	Casual	$9
6.3	Fresh Taco	Tex-Mex	Financial District	Take-out	$7
6.3	Tandoor	Indian	Upper Chapel Area	Casual	$20
6.3	China Pavilion	Chinese	Orange	Upmarket	$21
6.3	Archie Moore's	Bar food	E. Rock/Grad Ghetto	Bar and grill	$15
6.3	Cold Stone Creamery	Sweets	Theater District	Take-out	-
6.2	Pad Thai	Thai	Upper Chapel Area	Casual	$17
6.2	Amato's	Pizza	E. Rock/Grad Ghetto	Casual	$18
6.2	Humphrey's East	Bar food	E. Rock/Grad Ghetto	Bar and grill	$16
6.1	The Rib House	Southern	East Haven	Casual	$21
6.1	SBC	Bar food	Branford	Bar and grill	$23
6.1	East Buffet	Chinese	Hamden	Casual	$16
6.1	Aunt Chilada's	Tex-Mex	Hamden	Casual	$27
6.1	Pizza House	Pizza	Upper Chapel Area	Take-out	$6
6.0	Avra Grille	Greek	Branford	Upmarket	$30
6.0	Maxwell's	Steakhouse	Orange	Upmarket	$27
5.9	Yorkside Pizza	Pizza	Broadway Area	Casual	$14
5.9	Villa Del Sol	Tex-Mex	Theater District	Upmarket	$27
5.7	Est Est Est	Pizza	Upper Chapel Area	Counter	$8
5.7	TK's American Café	Bar food	Theater District	Bar and grill	$13
5.7	C.O. Jones	Tex-Mex	E. Rock/Grad Ghetto	Bar and grill	$14
5.6	Thai Taste	Thai	Upper Chapel Area	Casual	$21
5.4	Quattro's	Italian	Theater District	Upmarket	$33
5.4	Parthenon Diner	Short-order	Branford	Diner	$17
5.3	Libby's Pastry	Baked goods	Wooster Sq. Area	Take-out	-
5.3	Athenian Diner	Short-order	Westville	Diner	$18
5.2	Xando Cosí	Light American	Broadway Area	Casual	$15
5.2	Brick Oven Pizza	Pizza	Upper Chapel Area	Counter	$9
5.2	John Davenport's	Traditional Amer.	Theater District	Upmarket	$40
5.1	Caffé Bottega	Italian	Theater District	Bar and grill	$33
4.9	India Palace	Indian	Upper Chapel Area	Casual	$18
4.8	Chili's	Bar food	Hamden	Casual	$23
4.8	Brazi's	Italian	Long Wharf	Casual	$22
4.7	Chap's Grille	Light American	Upper Chapel Area	Counter	$11
4.6	Cody's Diner	Short-order	Wooster Sq. Area	Diner	$10
4.6	Main Garden	Chinese	Broadway Area	Take-out	$9
4.5	Aladdin	Middle Eastern	Theater District	Take-out	$10
4.5	Colonial Tymes	Traditional Amer.	Hamden	Upmarket	$32
4.3	McDonald's	Short-order	Whalley	Fast food	$6
4.1	Bulldog Burrito	Tex-Mex	Broadway Area	Counter	$7
4.1	Samurai	Japanese	Theater District	Upmarket	$26
4.1	A One	Pizza	Broadway Area	Counter	$6
4.0	Hunan Café	Chinese	Upper Chapel Area	Counter	$9
3.9	Popeye's	Southern	Whalley	Fast food	$7
3.7	Yalie's Pizza	Pizza	Upper Chapel Area	Take-out	$6
3.6	Gourmet Heaven	Light American	Broadway, Arts Dist.	Take-out	$8
3.4	KFC	Southern	Whalley	Fast food	$7
3.4	Thai Pan Asian	Thai	Upper Chapel Area	Casual	$19
3.2	Viva Zapata	Tex-Mex	Upper Chapel Area	Bar and grill	$18
3.0	Au Bon Pain	Light American	Broadway Area	Fast food	$9
3.0	El Amigo Felix	Tex-Mex	Broadway Area	Bar and grill	$23
2.9	China King	Chinese	Theater District	Take-out	$8
2.9	Subway	Light American	Theater District	Fast food	$6
2.6	Burger King	Short-order	Whalley	Fast food	$6
2.6	Ivy Noodle	Chinese	Broadway Area	Casual	$8
2.5	Dunkin' Donuts	Baked goods	Theater District	Fast food	$7

Weekend food after 11pm

8.4	Modern Apizza	Pizza	E. Rock/Grad Ghetto	Casual	$13
8.3	Sally's Apizza	Pizza	Wooster Sq. Area	Casual	$14
8.2	Pacifico	Latin American	Theater District	Upmarket	$38
8.0	Christopher Martin's	Bar food	E. Rock/Grad Ghetto	Bar and grill	$17
7.9	Frank Pepe's	Pizza	Wooster Sq. Area	Casual	$14
7.7	Louis' Lunch	Short-order	Theater District	Counter	$7
7.5	Atticus	Light American	Upper Chapel Area	Café	$9
7.3	Pazza Cucina	Italian	Woodbridge	Upmarket	$36
7.1	Delaney's	Bar food	Westville	Bar and grill	$21
7.1	J.P. Dempsey's	Bar food	E. Rock/Grad Ghetto	Bar and grill	$22
7.1	Starbucks	Baked goods	Theater District	Café	-
7.0	Skappo	Italian	Ninth Square	Upmarket	$29
7.0	Miya's	Japanese	Upper Chapel Area	Upmarket	$31
6.9	The Playwright	Irish	Hamden	Bar and grill	$22
6.9	Pancho's Cantina	Tex-Mex	Westville	Bar and grill	$22
6.7	Rudy's Restaurant	Light American	Broadway Area	Bar and grill	$8
6.6	Nikkita	New American	Theater District	Bar and grill	$25
6.5	Sahara	Middle Eastern	Theater District	Counter	$9
6.5	Alpha Delta Pizza	Pizza	Broadway Area	Take-out	$7
6.4	Mamoun's	Middle Eastern	Upper Chapel Area	Casual	$9
6.3	Archie Moore's	Bar food	E. Rock/Grad Ghetto	Bar and grill	$15
6.3	Cold Stone Creamery	Sweets	Theater District	Take-out	-
6.2	Humphrey's East	Bar food	E. Rock/Grad Ghetto	Bar and grill	$16
6.1	Pizza House	Pizza	Upper Chapel Area	Take-out	$6
5.9	Yorkside Pizza	Pizza	Broadway Area	Casual	$14
5.7	Est Est Est	Pizza	Upper Chapel Area	Counter	$8
5.7	TK's American Café	Bar food	Theater District	Bar and grill	$13
5.4	Parthenon Diner	Short-order	Branford	Diner	$17
5.3	Athenian Diner	Short-order	Westville	Diner	$18
5.2	Xando Cosí	Light American	Broadway Area	Casual	$15
5.2	Brick Oven Pizza	Pizza	Upper Chapel Area	Counter	$9
4.8	Chili's	Bar food	Hamden	Casual	$23
4.7	Chap's Grille	Light American	Upper Chapel Area	Counter	$11
4.6	Cody's Diner	Short-order	Wooster Sq. Area	Diner	$10
4.6	Main Garden	Chinese	Broadway Area	Take-out	$9
4.5	Aladdin	Middle Eastern	Theater District	Take-out	$10
4.3	McDonald's	Short-order	Whalley	Fast food	$6
4.1	Bulldog Burrito	Tex-Mex	Broadway Area	Counter	$7
4.1	A One	Pizza	Broadway Area	Counter	$6
3.9	Popeye's	Southern	Whalley	Fast food	$7
3.7	Yalie's Pizza	Pizza	Upper Chapel Area	Take-out	$6
3.6	Gourmet Heaven	Light American	Broadway, Arts Dist.	Take-out	$8
3.4	KFC	Southern	Whalley	Fast food	$7
3.2	Viva Zapata	Tex-Mex	Upper Chapel Area	Bar and grill	$18
3.0	Au Bon Pain	Light American	Broadway Area	Fast food	$9
3.0	El Amigo Felix	Tex-Mex	Broadway Area	Bar and grill	$23
2.9	China King	Chinese	Theater District	Take-out	$8
2.9	Subway	Light American	Theater District	Fast food	$6
2.6	Burger King	Short-order	Whalley	Fast food	$6
2.6	Ivy Noodle	Chinese	Broadway Area	Casual	$8
2.5	Dunkin' Donuts	Baked goods	Theater District	Fast food	$7

Weekend food after midnight

8.2	Pacifico	Latin American	Theater District	Upmarket	$38
7.7	Louis' Lunch	Short-order	Theater District	Counter	$7
7.1	Delaney's	Bar food	Westville	Bar and grill	$21
7.1	J.P. Dempsey's	Bar food	E. Rock/Grad Ghetto	Bar and grill	$22
6.7	Rudy's Restaurant	Light American	Broadway Area	Bar and grill	$8
6.6	Nikkita	New American	Theater District	Bar and grill	$25
6.5	Sahara	Middle Eastern	Theater District	Counter	$9
6.5	Alpha Delta Pizza	Pizza	Broadway Area	Take-out	$7
6.4	Mamoun's	Middle Eastern	Upper Chapel Area	Casual	$9

			Type	Price
6.3	Archie Moore's	Bar food	E. Rock/Grad Ghetto	Bar and grill	$15
6.1	Pizza House	Pizza	Upper Chapel Area	Take-out	$6
5.9	Yorkside Pizza	Pizza	Broadway Area	Casual	$14
5.7	Est Est Est	Pizza	Upper Chapel Area	Counter	$8
5.4	Parthenon Diner	Short-order	Branford	Diner	$17
5.3	Athenian Diner	Short-order	Westville	Diner	$18
5.2	Xando Cosí	Light American	Broadway Area	Casual	$15
5.2	Brick Oven Pizza	Pizza	Upper Chapel Area	Counter	$9
4.6	Cody's Diner	Short-order	Wooster Sq. Area	Diner	$10
4.6	Main Garden	Chinese	Broadway Area	Take-out	$9
4.5	Aladdin	Middle Eastern	Theater District	Take-out	$10
4.1	Bulldog Burrito	Tex-Mex	Broadway Area	Counter	$7
4.1	A One	Pizza	Broadway Area	Counter	$6
3.9	Popeye's	Southern	Whalley	Fast food	$7
3.7	Yalie's Pizza	Pizza	Upper Chapel Area	Take-out	$6
3.6	Gourmet Heaven	Light American	Broadway, Arts Dist.	Take-out	$8
3.4	KFC	Southern	Whalley	Fast food	$7
2.6	Ivy Noodle	Chinese	Broadway Area	Casual	$8
2.5	Dunkin' Donuts	Baked goods	Theater District	Fast food	$7

Weekend food after 1am

7.7	Louis' Lunch	Short-order	Theater District	Counter	$7
6.7	Rudy's Restaurant	Light American	Broadway Area	Bar and grill	$8
6.5	Sahara	Middle Eastern	Theater District	Counter	$9
6.5	Alpha Delta Pizza	Pizza	Broadway Area	Take-out	$7
6.4	Mamoun's	Middle Eastern	Upper Chapel Area	Casual	$9
5.9	Yorkside Pizza	Pizza	Broadway Area	Casual	$14
5.7	Est Est Est	Pizza	Upper Chapel Area	Counter	$8
5.4	Parthenon Diner	Short-order	Branford	Diner	$17
5.3	Athenian Diner	Short-order	Westville	Diner	$18
5.2	Brick Oven Pizza	Pizza	Upper Chapel Area	Counter	$9
4.6	Cody's Diner	Short-order	Wooster Sq. Area	Diner	$10
4.6	Main Garden	Chinese	Broadway Area	Take-out	$9
4.5	Aladdin	Middle Eastern	Theater District	Take-out	$10
4.1	Bulldog Burrito	Tex-Mex	Broadway Area	Counter	$7
4.1	A One	Pizza	Broadway Area	Counter	$6
3.9	Popeye's	Southern	Whalley	Fast food	$7
3.7	Yalie's Pizza	Pizza	Upper Chapel Area	Take-out	$6
3.6	Gourmet Heaven	Light American	Broadway, Arts Dist.	Take-out	$8
3.4	KFC	Southern	Whalley	Fast food	$7
2.6	Ivy Noodle	Chinese	Broadway Area	Casual	$8
2.5	Dunkin' Donuts	Baked goods	Theater District	Fast food	$7

Weekend food after 2am

6.5	Sahara	Middle Eastern	Theater District	Counter	$9
6.5	Alpha Delta Pizza	Pizza	Broadway Area	Take-out	$7
6.4	Mamoun's	Middle Eastern	Upper Chapel Area	Casual	$9
5.7	Est Est Est	Pizza	Upper Chapel Area	Counter	$8
5.4	Parthenon Diner	Short-order	Branford	Diner	$17
5.3	Athenian Diner	Short-order	Westville	Diner	$18
5.2	Brick Oven Pizza	Pizza	Upper Chapel Area	Counter	$9
4.6	Cody's Diner	Short-order	Wooster Sq. Area	Diner	$10
4.1	A One	Pizza	Broadway Area	Counter	$6
3.9	Popeye's	Southern	Whalley	Fast food	$7
3.7	Yalie's Pizza	Pizza	Upper Chapel Area	Take-out	$6
3.6	Gourmet Heaven	Light American	Broadway, Arts Dist.	Take-out	$8
3.4	KFC	Southern	Whalley	Fast food	$7
2.5	Dunkin' Donuts	Baked goods	Theater District	Fast food	$7

VEGETARIAN DINING GUIDE

LISTED IN ORDER OF OVERALL RATING OUT OF 10

All vegetarian-friendly restaurants

Rating	Name	Cuisine	Area	Type	Price
8.7	Bentara	Malaysian	Ninth Square	Upmarket	$34
8.5	Bar (Brü Room)	Pizza	Theater District	Bar and grill	$15
8.4	Modern Apizza	Pizza	E. Rock/Grad Ghetto	Casual	$13
8.4	Caffé Adulis	African	Theater District	Upmarket	$28
8.3	Willoughby's	Baked goods	Financial District	Café	-
8.3	Sally's Apizza	Pizza	Wooster Sq. Area	Casual	$14
8.3	Koffee?	Baked goods	Arts District	Café	$7
8.3	Trevethan's	New American	E. Rock/Grad Ghetto	Upmarket	$36
8.2	Roseland Apizza	Pizza	Derby	Casual	$32
8.2	Bella Rosa Café	Light American	Westville	Casual	$17
8.1	Swagat	Indian	West Haven	Casual	$7
8.1	Wentworth's	Sweets	Hamden	Take-out	-
8.0	Dolce Java	Baked goods	Upper Chapel Area	Café	-
8.0	Stony Creek Market	Light American	Branford	Counter	$12
7.9	Frank Pepe's	Pizza	Wooster Sq. Area	Casual	$14
7.8	Pot-au-Pho	Vietnamese	Arts District	Casual	$9
7.8	Hama	Japanese	Hamden	Casual	$18
7.7	Tre Scalini	Italian	Wooster Sq. Area	Upmarket	$32
7.7	Som Siam	Thai	Guilford	Casual	$22
7.7	Zoi's on Orange	Light American	Arts District	Counter	$8
7.7	Darbar India	Indian	Branford	Upmarket	$20
7.7	China Great Wall	Chinese	Arts District	Take-out	$5
7.6	Book Trader Café	Light American	Upper Chapel Area	Counter	$7
7.6	Billy's Pasta Così	Italian	Branford	Upmarket	$30
7.6	Roomba Burrito Cart	Tex-Mex	Broadway Area	Take-out	$6
7.5	Funki Munki	Light American	Theater District	Take-out	$7
7.5	Istanbul Café	Turkish	Theater District	Upmarket	$29
7.5	Atticus	Light American	Upper Chapel Area	Café	$9
7.5	Rainbow Gardens	New American	Milford	Upmarket	$24
7.4	Gastronomique	French	Theater District	Take-out	$17
7.4	Dayton St. Apizza	Pizza	Westville	Take-out	$13
7.4	The Pantry	Light American	E. Rock/Grad Ghetto	Casual	$10
7.3	Scoozzi	Italian	Upper Chapel Area	Upmarket	$37
7.2	Jasmine Thai Cart	American	Financial District	Take-out	$5
7.2	Warong Selera	Malaysian	West Haven	Counter	$11
7.2	Café Espresso	Light American	E. Rock/Grad Ghetto	Café	$10
7.1	Royal India	Indian	Broadway Area	Casual	$18
7.1	Basta!	Italian	Theater District	Upmarket	$51
7.1	Mediterranea	Middle Eastern	Financial District	Counter	$9
7.0	Tony & Lucille's	Italian	Wooster Sq. Area	Casual	$29
7.0	Miya's	Japanese	Upper Chapel Area	Upmarket	$31
6.8	Gunung Tahan	Malaysian	Westville	Casual	$23
6.8	Seoul Yokocho	Korean	Upper Chapel Area	Upmarket	$27
6.8	Moka	Light American	Financial District	Café	$8
6.7	Indochine Pavilion	Thai	Upper Chapel Area	Casual	$18
6.7	Lalibela	African	Theater District	Casual	$21
6.7	Royal Palace	Chinese	Ninth Square	Upmarket	$22
6.7	Edge of the Woods	Light American	Whalley	Take-out	$13
6.6	Bottega Lounge	Italian	Theater District	Casual	$32
6.6	Gusto Italiano	Italian	Arts District	Counter	$11
6.6	Zaroka	Indian	Upper Chapel Area	Upmarket	$24
6.6	Ashley's Ice Cream	Sweets	Broadway Area	Take-out	-
6.5	Chestnut Fine Foods	Light American	E. Rock/Grad Ghetto	Counter	$12
6.5	Koffee Too?	Light American	Broadway Area	Café	$8
6.5	Bangkok Gardens	Thai	Upper Chapel Area	Upmarket	$20

	All vegetarian-friendly *continued*		Location	Type	Price
6.5	Sahara	Middle Eastern	Theater District	Counter	$9
6.4	Caffé Bravo	Italian	E. Rock/Grad Ghetto	Casual	$28
6.4	Blue Pearl	New American	Financial District	Upmarket	$32
6.4	Mamoun's	Middle Eastern	Upper Chapel Area	Casual	$9
6.3	Fresh Taco	Tex-Mex	Financial District	Take-out	$7
6.3	Rainbow Café	Light American	Theater District	Casual	$18
6.3	Tandoor	Indian	Upper Chapel Area	Casual	$20
6.3	Cold Stone Creamery	Sweets	Theater District	Take-out	-
6.2	Pad Thai	Thai	Upper Chapel Area	Casual	$17
6.2	Amato's	Pizza	E. Rock/Grad Ghetto	Casual	$18
6.1	East Buffet	Chinese	Hamden	Casual	$16
6.1	Pizza House	Pizza	Upper Chapel Area	Take-out	$6
5.9	Chapel Sweet Shoppe	Sweets	Theater District	Take-out	-
5.9	Yorkside Pizza	Pizza	Broadway Area	Casual	$14
5.8	Woodland Coffee	Light American	Ninth Square	Café	$8
5.8	Café Java	Light American	Financial District	Counter	$8
5.7	Est Est Est	Pizza	Upper Chapel Area	Counter	$8
5.7	C.O. Jones	Tex-Mex	E. Rock/Grad Ghetto	Bar and grill	$14
5.6	Thai Taste	Thai	Upper Chapel Area	Casual	$21
5.5	Thai Taste Food Cart	Thai	Broadway Area	Take-out	$4
5.3	Tasti D-Lite	Sweets	Theater District	Take-out	-
5.3	Libby's Pastry	Baked goods	Wooster Sq. Area	Take-out	-
5.2	Brick Oven Pizza	Pizza	Upper Chapel Area	Counter	$9
5.2	Xando Cosí	Light American	Broadway Area	Casual	$15
5.2	Whole Enchilada	Tex-Mex	Arts District	Counter	$8
5.2	Claire's	Light American	Theater District	Casual	$15
5.1	Caffé Bottega	Italian	Theater District	Bar and grill	$33
5.0	Stella's	Baked goods	Whalley	Take-out	$9
4.9	India Palace	Indian	Upper Chapel Area	Casual	$18
4.9	Abate Apizza	Italian	Wooster Sq. Area	Casual	$24
4.8	Brazi's	Italian	Long Wharf	Casual	$22
4.7	Chap's Grille	Light American	Upper Chapel Area	Counter	$11
4.5	Aladdin	Middle Eastern	Theater District	Take-out	$10
4.4	The Original Falafel	Middle Eastern	Theater District	Counter	$7
4.2	Haya	Japanese	E. Rock/Grad Ghetto	Casual	$22
4.1	A One	Pizza	Broadway Area	Counter	$6
4.1	Bulldog Burrito	Tex-Mex	Broadway Area	Counter	$7
3.9	Bruegger's	Light American	Arts District	Fast food	$6
3.7	Yalie's Pizza	Pizza	Upper Chapel Area	Take-out	$6
3.6	Gourmet Heaven	Light American	Broadway, Arts Dist.	Take-out	$8
3.4	Thai Pan Asian	Thai	Upper Chapel Area	Casual	$19
3.4	Sweet Relief	Light American	Arts District	Counter	$7
3.4	Town Pizza	Pizza	Arts District	Casual	$8
3.0	Au Bon Pain	Light American	Broadway Area	Fast food	$9
2.6	Ivy Noodle	Chinese	Broadway Area	Casual	$8
2.5	Dunkin' Donuts	Baked goods	Theater District	Fast food	$7

Vegetarian-friendly top 50 food *listed in order of food rating*

9.6	Sally's Apizza	Pizza	Wooster Sq. Area	Casual	$14
9.2	Bar (Brü Room)	Pizza	Theater District	Bar and grill	$15
9.1	Modern Apizza	Pizza	E. Rock/Grad Ghetto	Casual	$13
8.5	Swagat	Indian	West Haven	Casual	$7
8.5	Bentara	Malaysian	Ninth Square	Upmarket	$34
8.5	Frank Pepe's	Pizza	Wooster Sq. Area	Casual	$14
8.4	Roseland Apizza	Pizza	Derby	Casual	$32
8.3	Bella Rosa Café	Light American	Westville	Casual	$17
8.3	Trevethan's	New American	E. Rock/Grad Ghetto	Upmarket	$36
8.2	Som Siam	Thai	Guilford	Casual	$22
8.1	Dayton St. Apizza	Pizza	Westville	Take-out	$13
8.1	Wentworth's	Sweets	Hamden	Take-out	-
8.1	Hama	Japanese	Hamden	Casual	$18
8.1	Gastronomique	French	Theater District	Take-out	$17

Vegetarian-friendly top food *continued*

			Location	Type	Price
8.0	Darbar India	Indian	Branford	Upmarket	$20
8.0	China Great Wall	Chinese	Arts District	Take-out	$5
8.0	Pot-au-Pho	Vietnamese	Arts District	Casual	$9
7.9	Warong Selera	Malaysian	West Haven	Counter	$11
7.8	Royal Palace	Chinese	Ninth Square	Upmarket	$22
7.7	Caffé Adulis	African	Theater District	Upmarket	$28
7.6	Stony Creek Market	Light American	Branford	Counter	$12
7.6	Seoul Yokocho	Korean	Upper Chapel Area	Upmarket	$27
7.5	Tre Scalini	Italian	Wooster Sq. Area	Upmarket	$32
7.5	The Pantry	Light American	E. Rock/Grad Ghetto	Casual	$10
7.4	Zoi's on Orange	Light American	Arts District	Counter	$8
7.4	Gusto Italiano	Italian	Arts District	Counter	$11
7.4	Billy's Pasta Così	Italian	Branford	Upmarket	$30
7.4	Roomba Burrito Cart	Tex-Mex	Broadway Area	Take-out	$6
7.3	Istanbul Café	Turkish	Theater District	Upmarket	$29
7.3	Mediterranea	Middle Eastern	Financial District	Counter	$9
7.0	Book Trader Café	Light American	Upper Chapel Area	Counter	$7
7.0	Gunung Tahan	Malaysian	Westville	Casual	$23
7.0	East Buffet	Chinese	Hamden	Casual	$16
6.8	Jasmine Thai Cart	American	Financial District	Take-out	$5
6.8	Funki Munki	Light American	Theater District	Take-out	$7
6.8	Rainbow Gardens Inn	New American	Milford	Upmarket	$24
6.8	Basta!	Italian	Theater District	Upmarket	$51
6.7	Scoozzi	Italian	Upper Chapel Area	Upmarket	$37
6.7	Café Espresso	Light American	E. Rock/Grad Ghetto	Café	$10
6.6	Bangkok Gardens	Thai	Upper Chapel Area	Upmarket	$20
6.5	Sahara	Middle Eastern	Theater District	Counter	$9
6.5	Indochine Pavilion	Thai	Upper Chapel Area	Casual	$18
6.5	Caffé Bravo	Italian	E. Rock/Grad Ghetto	Casual	$28
6.5	Brick Oven Pizza	Pizza	Upper Chapel Area	Counter	$9
6.5	Royal India	Indian	Broadway Area	Casual	$18
6.4	Atticus	Light American	Upper Chapel Area	Café	$9
6.4	Est Est Est	Pizza	Upper Chapel Area	Counter	$8
6.4	Ashley's Ice Cream	Sweets	Broadway Area	Take-out	-
6.3	Zaroka	Indian	Upper Chapel Area	Upmarket	$24

Vegetarian-friendly top 50 atmosphere
*listed in order of **atmosphere** rating*

9.5	Atticus	Light American	Upper Chapel Area	Café	$9
9.5	Bentara	Malaysian	Ninth Square	Upmarket	$34
9.5	Caffé Adulis	African	Theater District	Upmarket	$28
9.0	Tony & Lucille's	Italian	Wooster Sq. Area	Casual	$29
9.0	Miya's	Japanese	Upper Chapel Area	Upmarket	$31
9.0	Koffee?	Baked goods	Arts District	Café	$7
9.0	Blue Pearl	New American	Financial District	Upmarket	$32
9.0	Stony Creek Market	Light American	Branford	Counter	$12
9.0	Thai Taste	Thai	Upper Chapel Area	Casual	$21
9.0	Book Trader Café	Light American	Upper Chapel Area	Counter	$7
9.0	Scoozzi	Italian	Upper Chapel Area	Upmarket	$37
9.0	Bar (Brü Room)	Pizza	Theater District	Bar and grill	$15
9.0	Bottega Lounge	Italian	Theater District	Casual	$32
8.5	Rainbow Gardens	New American	Milford	Upmarket	$24
8.5	Bella Rosa Café	Light American	Westville	Casual	$17
8.5	C.O. Jones	Tex-Mex	E. Rock/Grad Ghetto	Bar and grill	$14
8.5	Claire's	Light American	Theater District	Casual	$15
8.0	Mamoun's	Middle Eastern	Upper Chapel Area	Casual	$9
8.0	Willoughby's	Baked goods	Financial District	Café	-
8.0	Koffee Too?	Light American	Broadway Area	Café	$8
8.0	Rainbow Café	Light American	Theater District	Casual	$18
8.0	Istanbul Café	Turkish	Theater District	Upmarket	$29
8.0	Tre Scalini	Italian	Wooster Sq. Area	Upmarket	$32
8.0	Trevethan's	New American	E. Rock/Grad Ghetto	Upmarket	$36

			Type	Price
8.0	Roseland Apizza	Pizza	Derby	Casual	$32
8.0	Royal India	Indian	Broadway Area	Casual	$18
8.0	Lalibela	African	Theater District	Casual	$21
8.0	Chestnut Fine Foods	Light American	E. Rock/Grad Ghetto	Counter	$12
8.0	Dolce Java	Baked goods	Upper Chapel Area	Café	-
8.0	Billy's Pasta Così	Italian	Branford	Upmarket	$30
8.0	Zoi's on Orange	Light American	Arts District	Counter	$8
8.0	Woodland Coffee	Light American	Ninth Square	Café	$8
8.0	The Pantry	Light American	E. Rock/Grad Ghetto	Casual	$10
8.0	Moka	Light American	Financial District	Café	$8
7.5	Hama	Japanese	Hamden	Casual	$18
7.5	Café Espresso	Light American	E. Rock/Grad Ghetto	Café	$10
7.5	Tandoor	Indian	Upper Chapel Area	Casual	$20
7.5	Café Java	Light American	Financial District	Counter	$8
7.5	Modern Apizza	Pizza	E. Rock/Grad Ghetto	Casual	$13
7.5	Frank Pepe's	Pizza	Wooster Sq. Area	Casual	$14
7.5	Starbucks	Baked goods	Theater District	Café	-
7.5	Basta!	Italian	Theater District	Upmarket	$51
7.0	Xando Cosí	Light American	Broadway Area	Casual	$15
7.0	Zaroka	Indian	Upper Chapel Area	Upmarket	$24
7.0	Pot-au-Pho	Vietnamese	Arts District	Casual	$9
7.0	Sally's Apizza	Pizza	Wooster Sq. Area	Casual	$14
7.0	Indochine Pavilion	Thai	Upper Chapel Area	Casual	$18
7.0	Haya	Japanese	E. Rock/Grad Ghetto	Casual	$22
7.0	Swagat	Indian	West Haven	Casual	$7
7.0	Darbar India	Indian	Branford	Upmarket	$20

Good dates for vegetarians *listed in order of **overall** rating*

8.7	Bentara	Malaysian	Ninth Square	Upmarket	$34
8.5	Bar (Brü Room)	Pizza	Theater District	Bar and grill	$15
8.4	Caffé Adulis	African	Theater District	Upmarket	$28
8.3	Trevethan's	New American	E. Rock/Grad Ghetto	Upmarket	$36
8.2	Bella Rosa Café	Light American	Westville	Casual	$17
8.0	Stony Creek Market	Light American	Branford	Counter	$12
7.7	Tre Scalini	Italian	Wooster Sq. Area	Upmarket	$32
7.6	Billy's Pasta Così	Italian	Branford	Upmarket	$30
7.5	Rainbow Gardens	New American	Milford	Upmarket	$24
7.4	Gastronomique	French	Theater District	Take-out	$17
7.3	Scoozzi	Italian	Upper Chapel Area	Upmarket	$37
7.1	Royal India	Indian	Broadway Area	Casual	$18
7.1	Basta!	Italian	Theater District	Upmarket	$51
7.0	Tony & Lucille's	Italian	Wooster Sq. Area	Casual	$29
7.0	Miya's	Japanese	Upper Chapel Area	Upmarket	$31
6.7	Lalibela	African	Theater District	Casual	$21
6.6	Bottega Lounge	Italian	Theater District	Casual	$32
6.4	Blue Pearl	New American	Financial District	Upmarket	$32
5.7	C.O. Jones	Tex-Mex	E. Rock/Grad Ghetto	Bar and grill	$14

Vegetarian-friendly delivery *listed in order of **food** rating*

7.4	Gastronomique	French	Theater District	Take-out	$17
7.4	Dayton St. Apizza	Pizza	Westville	Take-out	$13
7.1	Royal India	Indian	Broadway Area	Casual	$18
7.1	Mediterranea	Middle Eastern	Financial District	Counter	$9
6.7	Royal Palace	Chinese	Ninth Square	Upmarket	$22
6.7	Indochine Pavilion	Thai	Upper Chapel Area	Casual	$18
6.6	Gusto Italiano	Italian	Arts District	Counter	$11
6.5	Sahara	Middle Eastern	Theater District	Counter	$9
6.3	Fresh Taco	Tex-Mex	Financial District	Take-out	$7
6.3	Tandoor	Indian	Upper Chapel Area	Casual	$20
6.2	Pad Thai	Thai	Upper Chapel Area	Casual	$17
6.2	Amato's	Pizza	E. Rock/Grad Ghetto	Casual	$18

	Vegetarian-friendly delivery *continued*		*Location*	*Type*	*Price*
5.7	Est Est Est	Pizza	Upper Chapel Area	Counter	$8
5.2	Brick Oven Pizza	Pizza	Upper Chapel Area	Counter	$9
4.9	Abate Apizza	Italian	Wooster Sq. Area	Casual	$24
4.9	India Palace	Indian	Upper Chapel Area	Casual	$18
4.5	Aladdin	Middle Eastern	Theater District	Take-out	$10
3.7	Yalie's Pizza	Pizza	Upper Chapel Area	Take-out	$6
3.4	Sweet Relief	Light American	Arts District	Counter	$7
3.4	Thai Pan Asian	Thai	Upper Chapel Area	Casual	$19

BEST OF *THE MENU:*

67 NOTABLE DISHES

Bacon, egg, and cheese sandwich, Yankee Doodle
Bahn mi bo kho, Pot-au-Pho
Baklava, Avra Grille
Beef patty, Tropical Delights
Beef two soy, Bentara
Bloody Mary and oysters, Sage
Buffalo chicken salad, Sidebar
Buffalo wings, Christopher Martin's
Ceviche mixto, Inka
Cheese works, Louis' Lunch
Cheeseburger, Lou's Big Top
Chicken curry croissant, Stony Creek Market
Chicken mole, Guadalupe la Poblanita
Chive pocket, Peking Edo food cart
Chocolate chip cookie, Rainbow Café
Chocolate fondue, Blue Pearl
Cranberry nut bread, toasted with butter, Atticus
Creamed spinach, Chuck's Steak House
Codfish croquettes, Ibiza
Duck confit, Union League Café
Dungeness crab, Golden Restaurant
Espresso, Romeo & Cesare's
French fries with Belgian mayonnaise, Rudy's
French toast, Bella Rosa Café
Fresh tomato and garlic pizza, Sally's Apizza
Fried calamari, Adriana's
Fried calamari, Stillwater American Bistro
Gelato, Avellino's Trattoria
Gelato, Caffé Bottega
Gnocchi, Luce
Goat curry, Mother's

Half-yard, Richter's
Hot dog well done, Glenwood Drive-In
Hush puppies, Sandra's
Iceberg wedge, Carmen Anthony Steakhouse
Japaleño kampachi, East Japanese Restaurant
Key lime tart, Jeffrey's
Lithuanian coffee cake, Claire's Corner Copia
Lobster bisque, Le Petit Café
Mashed potato, bacon, and onion pizza, Bar
Meatloaf, Temple Grill
Mofongo, El Coquí
Mojito, Soul de Cuba
Oxtail, Caribbean Family Pot
Piega, Peppercorns
Pizza Basta, Basta
Pollo al horno con maní, Pacifico
Pulled-pork burrito, Roomba Burrito Cart
Roasted lobster, The Place
Roti canai, Gunung Tahan
Sausage pizza, Modern
Seafood pot pie, Stone House
Seafood succotash, Foe
Self-selected sushi combination, Hama
Shrimp Casino pizza, Roseland Apizza
Smoked duck nachos, Zinc
Steamed pork buns, China Great Wall
Stone pot bibimbap, Seoul Yokocho
Tacos de barbacoa, Taquería Mexicana #2
Tres leches, Roomba
Uni sushi, Wild Ginger
Uttapam, Swagat
Vanilla ice cream, Wentworth's
Water beef, Royal Palace
Wenzel's sub, Alpha Delta Pizza
White chocolate martini, Bottega Lounge
White clam pizza, Frank Pepe's

REVIEWS

A One Pizza Restaurant

4.1
10

Mediocre pizza, slightly better sandwiches, and
okay breakfast fare, but it's open all night long

Pizza, Short-Order American $ **6**   *Broadway Area*

4.6 /10   **3.0** /10   **4.0** /10   **5.1** /10
Food   *Atmosphere*   *Attitude*   *Value*

Counter service   21 Broadway   ***Bar*** None
Daily 24 hrs.   New Haven   ***Credit Cards*** Visa and MC
Breakfast. Vegetarian-friendly.   (203) 865-8888   ***Reservations*** Not accepted

When A One (also known as 21 Broadway) arrived, night owls all over
New Haven rejoiced: finally, a 24-hour eatery within walking distance of
downtown. The all-night schedule is certainly A One's most
distinguishing feature; otherwise, it's just a little storefront with some
tables, a place that hawks okay food and overpriced cigarettes. The
atmosphere is strangely antiseptic, like a simple neighborhood pizzeria-
sandwich shop without any of the friendliness or charm. But at 4am,
long after most other establishments have turned out the lights, our
sheer delight that New Haven finally has a downtown all-night eatery
goes a long way.

The food itself is nothing more than standard fare. There's breakfast
night and day; there are also grinders, hot and cold wraps, and edible
but uninspired pizza. Crusts are fairly thin, and ingredients seem fresh
enough, but there's some taste and tang missing here. Sandwiches,
similarly, are perfectly tolerable but not noteworthy. All in all, it's what
you'd expect. The steak-and-cheese sandwich, with lettuce, tomato,
mayonnaise, and hot peppers, is a perfectly good version, with a high
taste-to-grease ratio. Omelettes are basic and large. The Greek omelette
with feta cheese, potato, onions, and tomato, along with the souvlaki,
promotes a vaguely Hellenic theme. The French toast is sliced thick, in
the typical New York diner style.

Nothing here will impress you. But chances are, in the wee hours,
you're not in the most discriminating mood. Inexplicable is the
interminable wait between ordering and actually being served food, but
then, where are you rushing off to at this hour?

Abate Apizza & Seafood

4.9
/10

Your basic Wooster Street Italian-American gorge-fest, served up by a warm, fuzzy staff

Italian, Pizza   **$24**   *Wooster Square Area*

4.7 /10   **4.0** /10   **9.0** /10   **4.1** /10
Food   *Atmosphere*   *Attitude*   *Value*

Casual restaurant   129 Wooster St.   *Bar* Full
Mon.-Thurs. 11:30am-9pm; Fri.   New Haven   *Credit Cards* Visa, MC, AmEx
11:30am-10pm; Sat. noon-10pm;   (203) 776-4334   *Reservations* Accepted
Sun. noon-9pm. Kitchen closes 15
min. earlier. *Delivery. Vegetarian-friendly.*

Abate is known to most as a proud member of the old gang of Wooster Street Italian restaurants. What keeps it going, in addition to the stream of overflow customers from the nearby Pepe's and Sally's, is the generations of families that know the place and return year after year—they have discovered comfort in the routine of neighborhood friendliness. And the service is definitely friendly; it's a real New Haven place. You'll feel welcome, perhaps even loved, as Bill and Hillary seemed to when they frequented the joint during their days at Yale Law School.

But nowadays, we can't report that the food measures up to the feeling. Dishes like chicken marsala are too rich, overcooked, and bland. Just about everything comes with well-done pasta, which fares scarcely better. Dishes like the combo Florentine (veal, chicken, and shrimp sautéed with lemon and spinach over pasta) are over-ambitious, diluting whatever individual flavors might otherwise be in evidence. This is not to mention the daily all-you-can-eat buffet, which is just plain overwhelming.

Pizza, fried seafood, and veal are probably your best bets. The Captain's Platter has fried scallops, clams, and shrimp with fries, cole slaw, and toast—not a bad choice, but if you're after seafood, there are plenty of better choices around. We recommend avoiding all fish that's not fried, and all chicken. Portions are huge, so you might not want to order more than one main dish for every two people. Prices are not as high as some of the more upscale Wooster Street competition, but they're none too low either. The atmosphere is equally unexciting—a big, open space of mostly empty tables and an incongruous atrium area.

Adriana's

A classic gem of a Grand Avenue Italian-American
restaurant that gets just about everything right

Italian $**24**   *Fair Haven*

7.7 /10   **6.5** /10   **9.0** /10   **7.1** /10
Food   *Atmosphere*   *Attitude*   *Value*

Upmarket restaurant   771 Grand Ave.   *Bar* Full
Mon.-Fri. 11:30am-2:30pm, 5pm-   New Haven   *Credit Cards* Visa, MC, AmEx
10pm; Sat. 5pm-11pm; closed Sun. (203) 865-6474   *Reservations* Accepted
Kitchen closes Mon.-Fri. 9pm;   www.adrianasrestaurant.com
Sat. 9:30pm.

Turn back the clock: this is American-style Italian the way it's supposed
to be. Adriana's (#3 in *The Menu* for Italian) is the quintessential old-
school family restaurant, with a menu that's longer, more interesting,
and tastier than most other Italian options in town. Perhaps this is in
part because of its location: across the tracks, down Grand Avenue
toward Fair Haven. As such, the place is off the beaten path, at least if
the path is downtown. The restaurant's wonderfully friendly
management depends on word of mouth rather than proactive
marketing, so the place tends to host local families rather than tourists
or Yale parents in town for just one evening.

   Everything about Adriana's is genuine, from the décor complete
with frosted glass partitions—done in what's been aptly described as
the "wedding-cake style"—to the proprietor himself, who hails from
Caserta (near Naples). And it shows. The fried calamari, the ultimate
litmus test for Italian-American food, are superb. The savory batter is
perfectly crisp, and the squid somehow achieves a wonderful balance
between firm and tender. Even the marinara sauce is just right. Pane
cotto is just decent, but there's also a bewildering array of veal dishes
and some authentic Italian pasta selections (alla matriciana, for
example, the traditional Roman red sauce, with pancetta and onions).

   An almost impossibly friendly attitude has long been one of the
hallmarks of New Haven's great tradition of Italian-American
restaurants, and Adriana's is no exception: the welcome is warm, and
the service is professional yet genuine in a very rare way. This is
gracious hospitality incarnate. Though still little known downtown,
Adriana's is among the top Italian-American choices in the city.

Caffé Adulis

A modern, perennially popular downtown standby
that makes Eritrean fusion downright sexy

African **$28** *Theater District*

7.7/10
Food

9.5/10
Atmosphere

9.0/10
Attitude

7.9/10
Value

Upmarket restaurant
Mon.-Thurs. 5pm-12:30am; Fri.-
Sat. 5pm-2am; Sun. 5pm-10pm.
Kitchen closes Mon.-Sat. 11pm.
Date-friendly. Good wine list. Outdoor dining. Vegetarian-friendly.

228 College St.
New Haven
(203) 777-5081
www.opentable.com (reservations only)

Bar Full
Credit Cards Visa, MC, AmEx
Reservations Essential

Gideon Ghebreyesus is the consummate restaurateur. He treats you
right, he hires a beautiful waitstaff, he serves you a mangotini and
great food, and you go home happy. Caffé Adulis, his brainchild, is a
modern Eritrean joint that has emerged as one of the most dependable
restaurants in town.

Eritrean food is a lot like Ethiopian, served family-style and sopped
with sourdough injera. But Eritrean is liberally interpreted at Adulis,
with fresh, colorful ingredients and a distinct Italian spin. This restaurant
has a particular way with shrimp: the wonderfully textured Adulis
Appetizer—the best way to start—is seared shrimp sautéed with
tomato, scallions, and a lot of cabbage in a cream sauce. Mains include
shrimp Barka, another crustacean standout. Much more sweet than
salty, it integrates a creamy tomato-basil sauce, coconut, dates, basmati
rice, and parmesan.

The Mambo Gold, another notable choice, combines fettuccine with
a tomato pesto sauce, parmesan, chicken, and shrimp—sounds
jumbled, but the flavor is coherent. We also like the vegetable mains,
especially the lentils; make sure you include at least one in your order.
And the tortellini beat many of New Haven's Italian-American
restaurants on their own turf. Impressive also are the wine list and the
global selection of twenty rare beers.

With appropriately dim lighting and outdoor seating in warm
weather, Adulis is an ideal blend of hip and laid-back, and it adapts
equally well to a spontaneous bite to eat or an anniversary dinner. It's
quiet enough for conversation but bustling enough to disarm awkward
moments of first-date silence. The young servers—often
undergraduates—can be a bit slow, but they're also spectacular. It all
makes for an effortlessly pleasant evening, whatever the occasion or
the company.

Akasaka

6.7
/10

Decent sushi and Japanese food at reasonable
prices from a welcoming staff in costume

Japanese $25   *Westville*

6.9/10   **6.0**/10   **8.0**/10   **6.1**/10
Food   *Atmosphere*   *Attitude*   *Value*

Upmarket restaurant   1450 Whalley Ave.   *Bar* Full
Mon-Thurs. 11:30am-3pm, 5pm-   New Haven   *Credit Cards* Visa, MC, AmEx
10pm; Fri-Sat. 11:30am-3pm, 5pm- (203) 387-4898   *Reservations* Accepted
11pm; Sun. 3pm-10pm.

Akasaka is a Westville neighborhood favorite for reliable sushi and
cooked Japanese classics that are better than the norm. The best pieces
of nigiri sushi, at our most recent visit, were the basics, salmon and
tuna, along with fluke and red snapper. There are some faults:
yellowtail and mackerel have been more variable, and we'd get our sea
urchin elsewhere, as it has the right texture but some strong off-notes.

There are also some interesting modern Japanese concoctions,
including a miso-marinated cod misoyaki, which is well marinated,
tender, rich, and peppery, served with a side of almost raw asparagus.
We also like the interesting preparation of "green mussels," baked with
a flavorful mix including mayonnaise and tobiko. Soft-shell crab, when
in season, has soft meat and is delicately fried. Chuka hotate, a
marinated scallop salad, is chewy but with a nice soy-sauce flavor.
These are all dishes that it would be hard to find at most area Japanese
restaurants.

Prices are reasonable at Akasaka, if not particularly cheap. The place
lies well outside downtown New Haven, although it's no further by car
than Daiko or Hama, two of the other local sushi champions. We also
like the attitude; the servers, who are clad in bright red traditional
Japanese garb (it's hard to decide if the outfits are cheesy or charming),
welcome you with open arms and then dote on you.

Although we tend to prefer dim, buzzing haunts, Akasaka is located
in a supremely suburban stretch up Whalley Avenue, out a bit past
Westville, nestled jarringly amidst car dealerships and fast-food chains.
But it doesn't aspire to be anything more than a simple, friendly
Japanese restaurant that serves reasonable sushi at reasonable prices to
a local crowd. And it does so. None of which is anything at all to
complain about.

Aladdin Crown Pizza

4.5
10

Just average Middle Eastern food in an unavoidably
prime location with late, late, late hours

Middle Eastern, Pizza $**10**   *Theater District*

4.8 /10   **4.0** /10   **4.6** /10
Food   *Attitude*   *Value*

Take-out   260 Crown St.   *Bar* None
Mon.-Sat. 11am-2am; Sun. 2pm-   New Haven   *Credit Cards* Visa, MC, AmEx
1am. *Delivery. Vegetarian-friendly.*   (203) 773-3772   *Reservations* Not accepted

This late-night favorite on Crown Street does some of its best business
after the bars close at 1am or 2am, when throngs of ungratified young
people, irate at Connecticut's puritanical alcohol curfew, seek to soothe
their sorrows with pizza and falafel. Aladdin serves very average pizza
by the slice, along with an array of Middle Eastern short-order
specialties such as gyros, the standby falafel sandwich (ask for hot
sauce), and a few more unusual preparations, such as Damascus
moujadarah (steamed lentils with fried onions).

The lamb shawarma, strips of rotisserie-roasted lamb with lettuce,
tomato, parsley, and onion, topped with tahini sauce and served on
pita, is a standard version, not bad but not remarkable either. The
stuffed pizza, which might be filled with some combination of broccoli,
spinach, tomato, basil, ricotta, and mozzarella, has a following; we
concede that it's better than the regular pizza, but it's also inexplicably
expensive for late-night take-out grub. Ditto for the rest of the menu—
it's monopoly (or perhaps oligopoly) pricing, and so the tab for a
handful of small Middle Eastern dishes can really add up.

During the wee weekend hours, Aladdin's only competition on the
block is Louis' Lunch across the street. The location, speed, variety, and
hours make Aladdin Crown a great favorite among undergraduates,
and its success along those axes is well deserved. Late-night delivery is
also a welcome surprise. In terms of atmosphere, it's nothing more than
a brightly-lit take-out joint with a few token tables; unless the weather
is unforgiving, most choose the Crown Street sidewalk as the preferred
venue for frenzied consumption.

Alpha Delta Pizza

6.5
/10

A good sub and gyro purveyor that is open
spectacularly late, although the pizza is just okay

Pizza, Light American, Greek   **$ 7**   *Broadway Area*

6.7 /10
Food

6.0 /10
Attitude

7.8 /10
Value

Take-out
Mon.-Wed. 11am-3am; Thurs.-Fri.
11am-4am; Sun. 3pm-3am. *Delivery.*

371 Elm St.
New Haven
(203) 787-3333

Bar None
Credit Cards Visa, MC, AmEx
Reservations Accepted

Alpha Delta is a conveniently situated late-night take-out option for
subs, gyros, or slices, outlasting even the venerable Mamoun's on
Thursday through Saturday by staying open until 4am. Alpha Delta sits
at a crossroads of sorts, across from Rudy's, where Elm meets Howe. It's
close to Broadway, Yale, and the beginning of Whalley Avenue, and
near the university's small but loud frat scene. But Alpha Delta is also
close to the Howe Street neighborhood where a lot of New Haven's
reasonably priced apartments sit. The joint's large sign is unmistakable
as you pass that corner; it has become a New Haven landmark of sorts.

   And for good reason. Subs are the best choice here, followed by
gyros and slices, in that order. The Wenzel's sub, a buffalo chicken
sandwich with the works, including mayo and hot peppers, is a rich,
spicy, textured delight with some interesting flavor counterpoints. It's
their best work. Other subs and standard gyros are average or a bit
above.

   The pizza, however, which figures into the name of the place, is
somewhat greasy—it's far from the best in town. We wonder why so
many of the drunken post-party Yalies looking to satiate their late-night
appetites—choose the pizza. Granted, it's cheaper. But subs are still
reasonably priced, so much better, and a large one can easily be split
between two people. We highly recommend taking out rather than
eating in: you'll want to avoid sitting in the drab, bluish room adjacent
to the counter. But of course this place isn't about atmosphere. It's
about late-night grub. So enjoy.

Alpine Restaurant

5.3
10

Just an extremely basic downtown cafeteria, with a mediocre catch-all Chinese-American buffet

Light American   **$ 6**   *Financial District*

5.3/10   **5.0**/10   **6.0**/10   **6.3**/10
Food   *Atmosphere*   *Attitude*   *Value*

Counter service   100 Elm St.   *Bar* None
Mon.-Fri. 6:30am-2:30pm; closed   New Haven   *Credit Cards* Visa, MC, AmEx
Sat.-Sun. *Breakfast.*   (203) 776-6117   *Reservations* Not accepted

This is just another downtown breakfast and lunch spot, appropriately located in the ground floor of an office building. The simple, white room is furnished with institutional-style blond-wood tables and cheaply framed photos of cities and pastoral scenes, making the Alpine Restaurant feel like nothing so much as a hospital cafeteria. It's improved, though, by well-lit views of the downtown buildings through picture windows. The space is curiously divided up into two sections by a frilly, painted-glass barrier with plants. One side is table service only, and its tables have place settings and bottles of ketchup. On the other side of Alpine, bare tables await your counter-service trays. It's rather like an airplane divided into first and coach, divider and all. And as in an airplane, most people choose the simpler option (though in this case, it's just to save tip money).

The best things at Alpine are the inexpensive, eminently standard deli sandwiches and breakfast fare (omelettes and so on). A bacon, egg, and cheese sandwich, for instance, is perfectly competent, with the white American cheese well melted, the bacon fried for the right amount of time, and the egg as runny as you request it. The coffee's not bad either.

After 11am, there is also a catch-all Chinese-American buffet evocative of the New York gourmet deli concept: fried rice, assorted stir-fry plates with broccoli and the like, Chinese noodles…and then comes the fried chicken, boiled chicken breasts, vaguely Italian pasta dishes, sliced sausage, and so on. As a rule, places that try to do absolutely everything do virtually nothing well, and Alpine is no exception. The haphazard buffet is like a culinary minefield, with one item overcooked and tasteless, the next dried out from sitting in the buffet for so long. Stick to the printed menu.

Amato's

6.2
10

A solid State Street standby for subs and pizza by the slice, with unbelievably welcoming service

Pizza, Italian   **$18**   *East Rock/Grad Ghetto*

6.1/10   **5.0**/10   **10**/10   **5.9**/10
Food   *Atmosphere* *Attitude* *Value*

Casual restaurant   858 State St.   *Bar* Wine and beer only
Mon. & Wed. 11am-10pm; Thurs.- New Haven   *Credit Cards* Visa, MC, AmEx
Sat. 11am-11pm; Sun. noon-10pm; (203) 562-2760   *Reservations* Not accepted
closed Tues. *Delivery. Outdoor dining. Vegetarian-friendly.*

Amato's is a State Street neighborhood pizzeria that's an old standby for the Grad Ghetto folk. The welcoming staff here makes you feel as if you've chosen wisely by shunning the much-hyped Modern just a block away. And, although Modern makes better pies, Amato's is a good place to go if there's too long a wait down the street. It's also a solid choice—especially during the day—for take-out pizza by the slice, an option not available at Modern. And don't worry; the reliably good pizza at Amato's does justice to its New Haven appellation. Subs, including the chicken parmesan and Italian cold cut versions, are equally good—it's easily the best place on State Street for that sort of fare. There's delivery until 8pm, but only to businesses.

Sometimes a bit empty, Amato's feels like little more than your neighborhood slice shop; the atmosphere is not a revelation. There are some traditional Italian-American pasta dishes served as well, though, a few of them quite elaborate: a zuppa di pesce, for example, combines clams, mussels, scallops, calamari, shrimp, and scungilli over pasta with red or white sauce. We think there are plenty of better places in town to enjoy more ambitious Italian-American mains such as those, especially when they involve fish. But Amato's has nice homemade cannoli, and the service is dazzlingly open-armed—they'll know your name by your third or fourth visit. So don't overlook Amato's: the pizza is tasty, the price is right, and the people are outstanding.

Anchor

6.5
10

The dive bar to end all dive bars, equally beloved
by locals and students for its time-frozen charm

Traditional American $**11**   *Theater District*

5.7/10   **9.0**/10   **4.0**/10   **7.0**/10
Food   *Atmosphere*   *Attitude*   *Value*

Bar and grill
Mon.-Thurs.11am-2:30pm, 5pm-
1am; Fri.-Sat. 11am-2:30pm, 5pm-
2am; Sun. noon-1am. Kitchen
closes daily at 8:30pm. *Date-friendly.*

272 College St.
New Haven
(203) 865-1512

Bar Full
Credit Cards None
Reservations Not accepted

For a real drink at a real bar, any night you please, the Anchor is the
obvious choice—we might say the only choice. There may be no better-
preserved, no more self-consciously hip postwar watering hole in New
Haven. And no local bar is such a perennial and reliable crowd-pleaser.
In the very heart of town, this is the beloved favorite of generations of
Taft residents, law and grad students, and just about everyone else in
New Haven with a taste for kitsch, cheap beer, a wink, and a smile. The
Anchor serves passable, well-priced comfort food at lunchtime: burgers
and traditional American classics like liver, bacon, and onions (yeah!).
But the Anchor comes into its own during the post-school hours, as the
crowd slowly starts to assemble.

Fast-forward seven hours. It's packed. The last shift of Roomba and
Union League kitchen staff sidles up to the bar. Regulars have
commandeered their usual tables, and the jukebox is stacked with
classics. Grad students squirm in their plastic booths, sitting knee to
knee in observance of some irrational fire code prohibiting more
comfortable configurations. Gone, sadly, are the $1.75 bottles of
Schaefer's on Mondays; they've been replaced by cans of Rheingold,
another nostalgic American beer. "How's the Rheingold?" we asked
our server one day. "Terrible," he answered. So of course we had to
order one. Right he was—it tasted like sweetened dishwashing
detergent.

The bartenders turn into psychotic last-call drill sergeants at the
untimely hour of 12:45. (Anchor closes a little early. Always. Even the
clock on the wall is fast.) As regulars whine and guzzle while
intimidated novices file out obediently, the jukebox calmly spins its
classic tunes. Life is as it should be at the Anchor, and we only wish
that the soundtrack could follow us home.

Anna Liffey's

7.7

10

An authentic, subterranean Irish pub often
overlooked as a laid-back brunch or dinner spot

Irish, Bar food   **$21**   *Arts District*

7.1 /10   **9.0** /10   **7.0** /10   **7.5** /10
Food   *Atmosphere*   *Attitude*   *Value*

Bar and grill   17 Whitney Ave.   **Bar** Full
Sun.-Thurs. 11:30am-1am; Fri.-Sat.   New Haven   **Credit Cards** Visa, MC, AmEx
11:30am-2am. Kitchen closes daily   (203) 773-1776   **Reservations** Accepted
at 10:30pm. *Brunch. Date-friendly.*   www.annaliffeys.com

Anna Liffey's is a classic local hangout; it's also pretty authentic as Irish
pubs go. The waitstaff and bartenders, for example, hail from the
homeland. You'll have to descend a flight of stairs to enter the pub,
during which your cell phone will stop working (thank God), and you'll
find yourself in a subterranean Irish wonderland, a dark haunt with
wooden tables and benches, free-flowing Guinness and Harp, and a
gregarious town-gown mix among patrons.

   Anna Liffey's is an easy place to strike up conversations, and it's also
a great place for big groups on weeknights. Mondays feature live Irish
music, and Tuesday is trivia night, an entertaining ritual that's taken
damn seriously. There's Smithwick's, a tasty Irish bitter, on tap; a good
Irish coffee; and even hot grog, if you ask nicely. (When we were law
students, this pub was dear to our hearts as the Wednesday night
gathering place.)

   You might not think of an Irish pub as a place to eat, but Anna
Liffey's delivers on that front as well. The dinner menu, which is usually
offered until 10pm, shouldn't be overlooked. Your meal might include
starters like smoked salmon on Irish brown bread with dill cream
cheese, capers and onion, or the classic shepherd's pie (minced steak,
peas, carrots, mashed potatoes, and grated cheddar cheese). Giant
burgers are juicy, not overcooked, and served with fresh, clean cole
slaw. The huge curried chicken salad can be undersalted. A limited bar
menu is sometimes served until 11pm, and do check out the free food
(chicken fingers and buffalo wings, perhaps) for happy hour. A
deliciously artery-clogging Irish breakfast featuring Irish sausage is
among the several compelling options offered for Sunday brunch. With
that, you'll definitely need a pint, or a Bloody Mary.

Archie Moore's

6.3 / 10

An archetypal American watering hole with a local feel, notable wings, and a Coca-Cola fetish

Bar food   **$15**   *East Rock/Grad Ghetto*

5.7 /10
Food

7.5 /10
Atmosphere

6.0 /10
Attitude

6.3 /10
Value

Bar and grill
Sun.-Thurs. 11:30am-1am; Fri.-Sat.
11:30am-2am. Kitchen closes Sun.-
Thurs. midnight; Fri.-Sat. 1am.

188 Willow St.
New Haven
(203) 773-9870

Bar Full
Credit Cards Visa, MC, AmEx
Reservations Not accepted

Archie Moore's is a leading example of the classic New Haven/American bar-and-grill model that is as appealing today as it was 50 years ago. No nonsense here. As bar food goes, Archie Moore's, generally speaking, is a slight notch below Christopher Martin's, and significantly better than Sullivan's. But they're all in the same general ballpark. Archie's, unique among the pub-food mainstays, has an improbable residential East Rock location that draws in a large contingent of Grad Ghetto-resident students to complement the regulars that grew up in the neighborhood. It's one of the classic spots to meet a bunch of the guys for a burger and a beer—to watch the playoffs, perhaps, or just for a night of inane banter.

In terms of food, Archie Moore's is known first and foremost for their buffalo wings—one of America's proudest inventions. You can even get bottled buffalo sauce from Archie Moore's at the local grocery stores. And the reputation is well deserved: the wings are solidly executed, not too spicy but with appropriate tang and a judicious blue cheese dressing. Nachos aren't bad either (the more they have on them, the better). And don't forget the steak and cheese with pepper and onions, or the pitchers of pretty good beer at pretty good prices. The bacon cheeseburger, though, another staple, seems to have gone downhill of late.

In addition to the requisite televisions everywhere, the walls reveal a unique Coca-Cola fetish, with Coke paraphernalia covering virtually every inch. The signs can be amusing, but if you're frightened by the evil empire, then the inundation of signs and plaques, white script on a red field—you know the drill—might just induce seizure.

Ashley's Ice Cream

6.6
10

A popular neighborhood pit stop that rotates
through more than 150 rich, sweet flavors

Sweets   *Broadway Area*

6.4 /10   **7.0** /10
Food   *Attitude*

Take-out   280 York St.   *Bar* None
Mon.-Sat. 11am-11pm;   New Haven   *Credit Cards* None
Sun. noon-11pm.   (203) 776-7744   *Reservations* Not accepted
Vegetarian-friendly.   www.guilfordct.com/ashleys

Other branches at Hamden Plaza, Hamden, (203) 287-7566; 1016 Main St., Branford,
(203) 481-5558; and 942 Boston Post Rd., Guilford, (203) 458-3040.

Self-touted as serving "Connecticut's Best Ice Cream," Ashley's is worth
a visit in any season, whether you choose the New Haven, Hamden,
Branford, or Guilford branch. Even if the motto smacks of puffery, the
little shop serves about 20 choices of quite decent ice cream, sorbet,
and frozen yogurt, including one fat-free and sugar-free option. (In our
opinion, though, such healthful choices do not deserve to be called ice
cream.) The derivative options run the usual gamut—milkshakes,
sundaes, cups, and cones of various sizes. The ice cream is rich, sweet
(but not too sweet), and very creamy. Flavors span from traditional to
adventurous; if you are lucky with your timing, White Russian may be
among the flavors on offer—try it. The hot fudge topping is, in a word,
amazing.

The décor at the New Haven branch is a pleasant combination of
blond wood, high round bar tables, and corresponding stools. The
atmosphere is good enough for the year-round enthusiasts. Still, most
people take out, especially in good weather.

This particular York Street storefront has a checkered history of
food-service failures—honk if you remember Whimsels, the ill-fated
crêpe place. Ashley's, however, seems to be the best idea yet for the
space, perhaps because ice cream is something (unlike crêpes) that
many people are able to eat just about every day. And for variation,
Ashley's ice cream also comes shaped into cakes, which are prized for
birthdays and other celebrations (order ahead). Baked goods include
some allegedly famous and incredibly rich chocolate fudge. If you like
to get your daily allowance of sugar and fat in one sitting, this is one
way to do it. There's a stable of permanent flavors, others rotate daily
in summer months, permuting through a total of at least 150 varieties.

Assaggio

Italian food in an upmarket environment with a menu that has more style than substance

Italian $33   *Branford*

6.8 /10	8.5 /10	8.0 /10	6.5 /10
Food	*Atmosphere*	*Attitude*	*Value*

Upmarket restaurant
Mon.-Thurs. 11:30am-2:30pm,
5pm-9pm; Fri. 11:30am-2:30pm,
5pm-10pm; Sat. 5pm-10pm; Sun.
4pm-8pm. *Outdoor dining.*

168 Montowese St.
Branford
(203) 483-5426

Bar Full
Credit Cards Visa, MC, AmEx
Reservations Recommended

Assaggio is the consummate upscale Connecticut restaurant. Jazz. Little red candles. Swervy track lighting. Cool mirrors. A happy atrium with exposed windows. In good weather, there are even outdoor seats, although they're a bit close to the road for our taste. Dinner will likely begin with the habit of dipping the bread into the plate of olive oil. They don't do this in Italy, but they do it here; it's one of the many tidbits that have made Italian restaurants in America into a unique genre: not authentic, but not bad either.

Assaggio's crespelle is an uneventful appetizer of pasta stuffed with ricotta, broccoli rabe, and sausage, covered by tomato cream sauce; the ingredients are undersalted and all that's left is richness. Gnocchi with "duck Bolognese confit," a special one day, was a good idea, but ours was too salty. Perhaps the sauce was overreduced, but the salt ruined the dish. Equally disappointing has been the seared tuna, which has the opposite problem: it's undersalted, as are the vegetables it's served with, although the mashed potatoes are decent. Soft-shell crab, which we tried in season, was slightly better, well paired with angel hair pasta, but the dish was overwhelmed by too many capers, and they weren't the best, and in spite of the great caper caper, the crab still needed a bit of salt.

On the one hand, we want to salute Assaggio for its ambition. This is more than your standard Italian-American restaurant, and we love the atmosphere, but it's frustrating when such ambition and high prices are not necessarily backed up by technical proficiency, careful seasoning, and interesting flavors.

Athenian Diner

5.3
10

The Greek-Italian-American 24-hour diner so typical
it's like a caricature

Short-order American, Greek $**18**   *Westville*

5.8/10
Food

4.0/10
Atmosphere

6.0/10
Attitude

4.9/10
Value

Diner
Daily 24 hrs. *Breakfast.*

1426 Whalley Ave.
New Haven
(203) 397-1556

Bar Full
Credit Cards Visa, MC, AmEx
Reservations Accepted

You might be on Whalley Avenue in Westville, but you'll swear you're
in Queens when you get one look at this classic 24-hour (yay!) diner,
beginning with its very shape, a boxy apparition in a lonely parking lot.
All of it could hardly be any more typical: there are the tinted-glass
windows; the big, incongruous pink neon lines; the colorful assortment
of customers from every imaginable walk of life, especially late at night,
after the bars close. Then there are the brightly lit booths and the big,
glossy everything-but-the-kitchen-sink menus, which you are apparently
expected to have speed-read in the 45 seconds before the waiter or
waitress arrives, expectantly tapping pen on pad.

Or maybe they don't even expect you to order off the menu. After
all, the whole process reinforces our deep sense of bafflement at these
sorts of menus at these sorts of places: does anyone ever *really* order
the $24.95 twin lobster tail special? What about the elaborate Italian-
American veal dishes? When was the last time they sold an order of the
baked red snapper? Who in their right mind would spend that kind of
money at an all-night diner rather than at a restaurant with some
ambience? It really boggles the mind.

We prefer to stick to the diner classics, such as a well-executed
Reuben, with beefy slices of meat that stand up to the properly fried
bread, decent sauerkraut, and Russian dressing. Good also are the few
available Greek-ish dishes, which can be hard to find in the New Haven
area—a rich, creamy, and indulgently satisfying moussaka, for example,
which comes with a simple, if uninspiring, salad whose herbed dressing
has a subtle sprinkling of feta. Stick to the basic diner fare, and you
won't be disappointed.

Atticus

A bookstore-café pioneer in the genre, with artisanal breads to complement the fiction

Light American, Baked goods $ 9   *Upper Chapel Area*

6.4/10   **9.5**/10   **8.0**/10   **8.8**/10
Food   *Atmosphere*   *Attitude*   *Value*

Café   1082 Chapel St.   *Bar* None
Daily 7am-midnight.   New Haven   *Credit Cards* Visa, MC, AmEx
Breakfast. Vegetarian-friendly. (203) 776-4040   *Reservations* Not accepted

Bring together good books, good coffee, a great bakery, and a warm, open space, and you've set the stage for a legendary institution. Warm yet studious, hip yet professorial, intellectual yet flirtatious, Atticus is a college-town classic and a true American pioneer in the bookstore-café genre when it added a café section in 1986. An academic buzz permeates the place from dawn until midnight, when the doors finally close. There's scarcely an hour in the day when Atticus isn't hopping with everyone from book-signing authors to travel-guide browsers to over-caffeinated, pre-exam collegians. They come to drink coffee and taste the artisanal fruits of an oven that the Atticus folks hauled over all the way from France. The baking bread and brewing coffee together create a memorable aroma, which is welcome even if you're just browsing for books.

The Atticus menu is short and sweet. A sandwich is a simple solution: roasted turkey, ham and Swiss, or cheddar cheese on a baguette or ciabatta straight from the famous oven. The cranberry nut bread, our favorite, is best served toasted with butter, and the soup is great too; the black bean soup is particularly hearty and satisfying, though non-vegetarian (say yes to the dash of sour cream and chopped fresh onions proffered). The garden salad, meanwhile, comes with Atticus' trademark shredded carrots and a notable Dijon dressing. The bread pudding is rich, decadent, and delicious, perhaps not surprising considering the bread it begins with.

The two-floor independent bookstore is formidable in its own right, with one of New Haven's best selections of fiction and nonfiction and easily the city's best lineup of readings by well-known authors, with a particular focus on those with Yale and New England affiliations.

Au Bon Pain

3.0
10

A bright McSandwich joint peddling mediocre
baked items, sandwiches, and unimpressive coffee

Light American   **$ 9**   *Broadway Area*

2.4 /10   **4.0** /10   **4.0** /10   **3.8** /10
Food   *Atmosphere*   *Attitude*   *Value*

Fast-food chain Mon.-Sat. 7am-midnight; Sun. 8am-midnight. *Breakfast. Outdoor dining. Vegetarian-friendly.*	1 Broadway New Haven (203) 865-5554 www.aubonpain.com	*Bar* None *Credit Cards* None *Reservations* Not accepted

This McSandwich café-restaurant chain is hyper-convenient to Yale Law
School, which is part of why ABP perennially contends with the Law
School Dining Hall (along with Yorkside and Koffee Too?) in the battle
for lunchtime hegemony over lawyers-to-be. This can make for a
considerable queue at peak times.

The best place to sit here—weather permitting—is outdoors, where
a few metal tables and chairs are frequented by some of New Haven's
more legendary street characters. You probably won't even get caught
if you bring better food over from Yankee Doodle or Roomba Burrito
Cart across the street. The bright and bustling but fast-food-style room
is updated in simple shades of yellow, in line with ABP's new look, but
the vibe remains the same, with tables and booths that are as likely to
be occupied by a laptop date as by a friendly couple or gregarious
group. The service is nothing more than perfunctory, but if you position
yourself right, you can monitor the person assembling your sandwich,
making last-minute requests for more of this or none of that.

The baked goods are hit-or-miss. We don't mind the stuffed
croissants—particularly the ham and cheese, spinach and cheese, and
raspberry and cheese versions—they're satisfying, if reheated and
overpriced. Scones, bagels, and plain croissants are less impressive, and,
anyway, they've eliminated the half-price bake sale from 4pm-6pm,
which had been one of their only selling points. The sandwiches are the
other focus of the menu, and the new "café sandwiches" like BBQ
pulled pork are the best choices. Still, ingredients aren't the freshest in
town. The prices, which were once clearly too high, have remained
more or less stable while some competitors' have gone up, bringing
ABP more in line with industry norms. Soups rotate daily, and can be
okay, but the watery coffee does not impress.

Aunt Chilada's

6.1
10

A festive Tex-Mex mecca popular for the free-flowing margaritas and satisfying grub

Tex-Mex, Bar food $27 *Hamden*

5.5/10   **7.5**/10   **5.0**/10   **5.3**/10
Food   *Atmosphere*   *Attitude*   *Value*

Casual restaurant   3931 Whitney Ave.   *Bar* Full
Sun.-Thurs. 11am-10pm; Fri.-Sat.   Hamden   *Credit Cards* Visa, MC, AmEx
11am-11pm.   (203) 230-4640   *Reservations* Accepted
Outdoor dining.   www.auntchiladas.com

This enormous suburban Tex-Mex restaurant and bar is just what you'd expect: huge portions of enchiladas, burritos, and tacos overflowing with cheese, rice, and refried beans; giant appetizer platters of artery-clogging but satisfying New-England-meets-border food; easy-to-drink margaritas; and a raucous bar that caters largely to the frat crowd from nearby Quinnipiac College and other local schools. There's cavernous seating in the huge, two-floor wooden house, so even when it hops on weekends, it's not hard to get a seat. We recommend sitting in the room to the left as you enter the restaurant, because it has a fireplace and a cozier feel. The atmosphere, regardless, is festive, perhaps because so many of the patrons are sipping the sweet margaritas (the house version is fine).

Our favorite starter is the "Santa Fe egg rolls," which are rich, deep-fried pastries with Mexican fillings and a good, creamy dip. As mains go, we recommend sticking to the Mexican combinations or the fajitas rather than the "dinners." The enchiladas with ground beef and chiles rellenos, for example, are satisfying in just the way you'd expect.

Some dishes, however, disappoint. A spinach con queso dip tastes of melted American-style cheese without much of the chile tang we'd hoped for. Shrimp Anaheim, with penne pasta, a cream sauce, chorizo, and large, impressively succulent shrimp, is a solid choice, but the sauce, while peppery, doesn't have enough flavor. Boneless buffalo wings have an unusual Mexican-style bent, but we'd prefer the standard, more vinegary variety. Prices are startlingly high, but go to the web site and you can find coupons for a free appetizer or two meals for the price of one. In the end, Aunt Chilada's delivers Tex-Mex comfort food basically as expected. No more, no less.

Avellino's Trattoria

7.8
10

A relaxing new Italian-American restaurant with
great food that has refreshingly authentic touches

Italian   **$31**   *Ninth Square*

7.8/10   **7.5**/10   **9.0**/10   **6.9**/10
Food   *Atmosphere*   *Attitude*   *Value*

Upmarket restaurant   4 Orange St.   *Bar* Full
Tues.-Sun. 11am-2:30pm, 5pm-   New Haven   *Credit Cards* Visa, MC, AmEx
9:30pm; closed Mon. *Date-friendly.* (203) 777-1177   *Reservations* Accepted

Avellino's Trattoria and Wine Bar, one of the newest restaurants in this
book, is in the large Ninth Square space that was formerly occupied by
Fat Cats, across the street from Miso. As of press time, the restaurant
still feels brand new, but the layout is simple and pleasant, and ambient
lighting is appropriately dim. Avellino's is the second branch of a
popular Italian restaurant in Fairfield (it's unrelated to Avellino's Apizza
of Grand Avenue).

The menu, though technically Italian-American, has a few
interestingly authentic Italian notes, and initial impressions have been
extremely promising. A margherita (small pizza) is slightly doughy but
tasty, clearly from the fresh-tomatoes-rather-than-sauce school of
thought. An insalata caprese is made with decent mozzarella that's
created in-house and 25-year-old balsamic vinegar, but out of season its
tomatoes are not the ripest. Al ceppo amatriciana features a nicely
reduced, fully flavored version of the classic Roman sauce of tomatoes,
onions, and pancetta. Amatriciana is usually done with bucatini—
slender pasta tubes—but Avellino's chooses the similar but more
interesting pasta al ceppo (rolls of pasta that are shaped almost exactly
like cinnamon sticks). It's a unique and successful pairing—and it comes
happily al dente.

The more classic linguine with a well-bound clam sauce boasts fresh
mollusks, but it can come slightly undersalted. The pollo fantastico, a
boneless chicken breast with onions, roasted red peppers, prosciutto di
Parma, and melted fontina, is a heavy undertaking, but it's also
satisfying, with a deep, rich sauce that's both sweet and salty. Not to be
missed for dessert are several flavors of homemade gelato, including
such memorable flavors as Sicilian blood orange (squeezed in-house
and very impressive) and Nutella (creamy and wonderful). The $15 prix-
fixe two-course lunch includes most dinner mains as options, making
the deal—like this place as a whole—pretty sweet.

Avra Grille

6.0
10

A haphazardly pan-Mediterranean restaurant with
some interesting but unmemorable Greek dishes

Greek, Italian $**30**   *Branford*

5.8/10   **6.5**/10   **6.0**/10   **5.1**/10
Food   *Atmosphere*   *Attitude*   *Value*

Upmarket restaurant Sun.-Thurs. 11:30am-9pm; Fri.-Sat. 11:30am-11pm. *Brunch.*	1114 Main St. Branford (203) 488-8161 www.avragrille.com	*Bar* Full *Credit Cards* Visa, MC, AmEx *Reservations* Accepted

This downtown Branford restaurant, on the town's main drag not far
from the town green, was once the Shore Point Café. Now, it's a self-
described "eclectic Mediterranean" restaurant with a particular focus
on Greece, but bringing in elements, and dishes, from Tunisia, Italy, and
elsewhere. We were intrigued, upon our first visit, by the prospect of a
good upmarket Greek restaurant, which isn't common in these parts.
There's whole grilled fish here, for instance—a true rarity—but
unfortunately you can only get it on weekends.

Avra has its ups and downs, but we're still looking for our Greek
promised land. Among the few dishes on the menu with a real Greek
slant, we like the Mediterranean braised lamb shank. The preparation is
like a tagine, with an interesting and well seasoned chunky sauce with
oranges and sweet potatoes; we would have liked the meat much more
tender, and with more preserved lemon flavor, but the overall effect is
pleasant enough. Less successful is a Chilean sea bass (or Patagonian
toothfish, if you're PC), again seasoned well but overcooked and poorly
paired with an equally white—and equally dry—bed of mashed
potatoes. Another losing dish is the saganaki, an appetizer of
overwhelmingly salty graveira cheese marinated in brandy and fried; it's
one of those things of which one or two bites is more than enough.
Not so for the moist and delicious baklava, perhaps the best Greek
thing on Avra's menu.

The room feels refined, with elegant place settings, but the service is
that of your typical casual New Haven Italian-American joint, from the
special veal chop topped with "mootzarell" to the obligatory inquiry,
after each course (even the fried cheese appetizer), about whether you
wanna take it home. Not unpleasant, just incongruous; this
restaurant—Greek or not—lacks focus.

Baja's

A little-known choice for authentic Mexican, albeit with an empty, strip-mall atmosphere

Mexican $23   Orange

7.5 /10   **5.0** /10   **7.0** /10   **6.2** /10
Food   Atmosphere   Attitude   Value

Casual restaurant   63 Boston Post Rd.   *Bar* Full
Mon. 11:30am-9pm; Tues.-Thurs.   Orange   *Credit Cards* Visa, MC, AmEx
11:30am-9:30pm; Fri. 11:30am-   (203) 799-2252   *Reservations* Accepted
10pm; Sat. noon-10pm;
Sun. noon-9pm.

Stuck in the middle of a nondescript strip mall on that very pinnacle of New Haven suburban strip mall culture—Route 1, the old Boston Post Road—Baja's secretly serves up some of the most legitimate regional Mexican food in the area. It's real Northern Mexico/Baja California/dusty borderland grub, from the machaca, a dried beef and egg mixture that's just about the only thing real burritos are ever stuffed with anywhere in Mexico (outside of Tijuana, that is), to the illustrious lineup of Mexican beers—down-and-dirty and prestigious alike.

The menu includes all the old standbys, from tacos to chiles rellenos. In addition to such antojitos, there are a host of more ambitious mains, including carnitas, center-cut pork loin cooked for five hours in a tomato salsa and then grilled, served with rice, beans, guacamole, and tortillas. We've had a ceviche that was fairly authentic, too, with that careful balance of lime. It's all pretty good, if not transcendent. But more to the point, Baja's is a refreshing and somewhat unusual break from the Tex-Mex menu that you might be used to.

As can be the case in strip malls, Baja's atmosphere can seem a little strange and depressing, especially if you show up when no one else happens to be around. That said, there are colorful murals of Baja California—the restaurant's culinary inspiration—and an equally colorful bartender hawking gargantuan margaritas at the improbably-placed central bar. Everything is supremely casual, and there's a salsa bar with endless toppings for tortilla chips or just about anything else you order. But why not try something truly Baja—go for the machaca.

Bangkok Gardens

6.5
/10

About the best you can do around Chapel Street
for Thai, as long as you sit in the atrium

Thai $**20**   *Upper Chapel Area*

6.6 /10   **6.0** /10   **7.0** /10   **6.2** /10
Food   *Atmosphere*   *Attitude*   *Value*

Upmarket restaurant   172 York St.   *Bar* Half
Mon.-Fri. 11:30am-10pm; Sat.   New Haven   *Credit Cards* Visa, MC, AmEx
noon-11pm; Sun. noon-10pm.   (203) 789-8684   *Reservations* Accepted
Vegetarian-friendly.

The aptly-named Bangkok Gardens is something of an icon. In a city
with a lot of Thai restaurants—a lot of them, in fact, on the same
block—Bangkok Gardens is a standout, serving better Thai food at
prices only a bit higher than their competitors. The hoa mouk, which
features on the bargain-priced lunch menu, is a tender cake of chopped
chicken, cabbage, basil leaf, and Thai lemon leaf, covered with a
homemade sauce that includes coconut; it's a unique, interesting, and
tasty Thai specialty you'll almost never see elsewhere, but it has also
gone downhill in recent years, with the cake becoming drier and the
sauce more scarce.

While just about everything else on the menu—lunch or dinner—is
at least reliable, we've noticed more variability in quality lately among
favorites like drunken noodle and yum nua (beef salad infused with
citrus and cilantro). It's not in the same league as Som Siam in Guilford,
but for now, Bangkok Gardens still edges out the downtown Thai
competition.

At the same time, there's something unsatisfying about dining here.
Maybe it's the atmosphere; too much glass and the formal, black-
bowtied waitstaff make you much less comfortable than you should be.
Or maybe it's the bland décor and starchy tablecloths. A sunny atrium
in the front area of the restaurant provides warm respite from the day,
especially welcome in winter. At lunch, when the sun is out, the room
bustles with midday energy, and the price is right. It's a good way to go
if you are lucky enough to find seating in the atrium. In the evenings,
the shortcomings of décor and lighting are harder to ignore, and prices
are higher. Take-out is always an option.

Bar (Brü Room)

8.5/10

A landmark microbrewery, with great beer, thin-crust pizza to rival the best, and a bar scene too

Pizza $**15**   *Theater District*

9.2/10
Food

9.0/10
Atmosphere

3.0/10
Attitude

9.3/10
Value

Bar and grill
Mon.-Tues. 4pm-1am; Wed.-Thurs.
11:30am-2:30pm, 4pm-1am; Fri.
11:30am-2:30pm, 4pm-2am; Sat.
4pm-2am; Sun. 4pm-1am. Kitchen
closes at 10pm; slices sometimes
available later. *Vegetarian-friendly.*

254 Crown St.
New Haven
(203) 495-8924;
Pizza, (203) 495-1111
www.barnightclub.com

Bar Full
Credit Cards Visa, MC, AmEx
Reservations Not accepted

One of the elite pizzerias of New Haven, Bar proudly guards over its choice strip of Crown Street with a masterful post-hip vibe. Bar has gracefully graduated into an age when the microbrewery concept is no longer novel, an age when exposed brick and steel pipes are no longer the revelation they were in the early '90s. But Bar still wears them well, and still manages to create a crawling pick-up scene in the adjoining bar and back-room dance floor. Officially they're two separate but openly connected establishments—Bar and Brü Room—but everyone just calls it all Bar.

We love Bar (#7 in *The Menu* for food, #11 overall) for the pizza, not the town-gown debauchery. Prices are reasonable, so why not start with Bar's classic New American formula salad (greens, sliced pears, caramelized pecans, crumbled blue cheese, and a light vinaigrette—works like a charm), and get a pitcher of microbrewed Pale Ale, a hoppy American classic.

But the big, razor-thin, oval pies are spectacular—so good that they almost make you forget about the uniformly snotty and indifferent service. Back in the day, Pepe's and Sally's crusts were considered thin. Now, even your mom makes thin-crust pizza; but Bar takes it to the next level. The crust is so delicate it's almost invisible, and tomatoes are fresh. We love the combination of spinach and bacon, and the mashed-potato pizza (best with bacon and onion) has a cult following. Hot peppers are great. If there's a long wait, order a pie at the counter and take it into the bar room. Bar pizza has a very short half-life in cool air, so don't bother with the after-hours slices that are sitting there, asymptoting.

In the end, though, it's increasingly hard to avoid the hushed comparisons to Wooster Street. Better than Pepe's? Yep—we said it.

Basta!

7.1
10

From the Claire's team, a cute, fresh, and tasty but
extremely expensive new Italian restaurant

Italian, Pizza $51   *Theater District*

6.8/10   **7.5**/10   **8.0**/10   **3.3**/10
Food   *Atmosphere*   *Attitude*   *Value*

Upmarket restaurant   1006 Chapel St.   *Bar* Wine and beer only
Mon.-Wed. 11:30am-3pm, 5pm-   New Haven   *Credit Cards* Visa, MC, AmEx
9:30pm; Thurs.-Fri. 11:30am-3pm, (203) 772-1715   *Reservations* Essential
5pm-11pm; Sat. 5pm-11pm; Sun.
5pm-9:30pm. *Date-friendly. Outdoor dining. Vegetarian-friendly.*

Basta opened in January next door to, and under the same ownership
as, Claire's, New Haven's vegetarian/kosher college-town eclecticopia on
the corner of Chapel and College Streets. Here, however, meat and fish
are served, and the menu is far more ambitious, beginning with the
prices—dinner mains go as high as $34, and one pizza on the *lunch*
menu costs $18. This makes Basta as expensive as Ibiza and Union
League Café.

But for this food, it's just not worth it. One of the only things on the
menu that justifies its price is the superb, wood-fired Pizza Basta: sliced
almonds, pears, and caramelized onions carefully counterbalance each
other while setting off the saltiness of a creamy gorgonzola that's
spread onto a richly textured crust, and a subtle drizzle of honey is
inspired. Another appetizer arguably worth the money is a generous
and garlicky "zuppa di clams"—undersalted but otherwise wonderful.

The rest of the menu isn't bad, but nothing else reaches the lofty
heights of the pizza. The emphasis is on excellent primary ingredients,
such as fresh fish, wonderful greens, and artisanal ricotta cheese.
Chicken Milano is pounded, breaded, and nicely fried, with a rich,
indulgent lemon sauce. Simple pasta dishes like penne arrabbiata are
fine, if seriously overpriced; fish mains, such as salmon livornese, are
worse, and even more ridiculously expensive.

The space feels lunchy and casual, with blue skies and chubby
cherubs frolicking gleefully among cotton candy clouds. Below the
Divine Hand, a rectangular pane of glass provides a view into the
bustling little kitchen, which is barely wider than an Amtrak railway car.
Service is folksy and friendly.

As fans of organic and local produce, it pains us to complain about
Basta's prices. We know how expensive these ingredients are. But we
also know what people expect from a restaurant when they're paying
such stratospheric prices, and it's something more than this.

Bella Rosa Café

8.2
10

The best and most creative brunch in New Haven—
by a fair margin

Light American   **$17**   *Westville*

8.3 /10   **8.5** /10   **7.0** /10   **8.6** /10
Food   *Atmosphere*   *Attitude*   *Value*

Casual restaurant   896 Whalley Ave.   *Bar* None
Tues.-Fri. 7am-3pm; Sat.-Sun.   New Haven   *Credit Cards* Visa, MC, AmEx
8am-2pm; closed Mon.   (203) 387-7107   *Reservations* Not accepted
Breakfast. Brunch. Date-friendly. Vegetarian-friendly.

Okay, we'll admit it: Bella Rosa was a truly egregious omission from the last edition of *The Menu*, because this legendary Westville establishment serves the best brunch in New Haven. It all begins with the cheery neighborhood atmosphere—the small room is lovely and informal, bright and airy, cozy and intimate, as if Parisian and American at the same time. When God envisioned a casual brunch, He surely envisioned this.

Specials vary day to day, but at one recent visit, a memorable offering combined black bean soup, salsa, sour cream, avocado, cheese, and two perfectly runny but not too runny poached eggs. It was an inspired combination with good counterpoints, even better when ordered with a side of toast. Delicious, too, is the chili pepper sausage, which can be ordered on the side.

Bella Rosa Café also makes the best French toast in New Haven, hands down. There are several incarnations, and often a French toast special, such as Panettone French toast with orange crème anglaise—a concoction that might have been too rich for breakfast, but was also a soft and buttery treat that was worth every indulgent bite.

The service here tends to be friendly, but—especially at peak times—almost intolerably slow. Still, with these yellow walls, this menu, and this vibe, it barely matters. You want the experience to last. Waits at prime time on weekend mornings can be considerable, but interestingly, Bella Rosa still seems unknown to many downtowners— like so many places in Westville, it's only a ten-minute drive from the center of New Haven. In a neighborhood that conceals many gems, but Bella Rosa Café must be its crowning achievement.

Bentara

One of New Haven's most reliable experiences: consistent Malaysian food, nice wines, a good vibe

8.7 / 10

Malaysian

$34 *Ninth Square*

8.5 /10
Food

9.5 /10
Atmosphere

7.0 /10
Attitude

7.9 /10
Value

Upmarket restaurant
Mon.-Thurs. 11:30am-3pm, 5pm-10pm; Fri.-Sat. 11:30am-3pm, 5pm-11pm; Sun. 11:30am-3pm, 5pm-10pm. *Date-friendly. Good wine list. Vegetarian-friendly.*

76 Orange St.
New Haven
(203) 562-2511
www.bentara.com

Bar Full
Credit Cards Visa, MC, AmEx
Reservations Essential

Bentara is one of the most dependable spots in New Haven for an excellent meal, and it's made all the more appealing by the reasonable prices and warm, hip, beautiful space. Perhaps surprisingly, Bentara (our #6 overall restaurant) also has one of the best wine lists in New Haven. Hard-to-find Burgundies and Super-Tuscans dot Bentara's star-studded lineup, and they're fairly priced.

As for the food, it's impossible to choose badly from among the options on Bentara's expansive and exciting Malaysian menu. The rich roti murtabak is a great way to start—griddle-fried, unleavened ghee bread filled with ground beef, onions, eggs and spices, served with curry lentil sauce and sweet-and-sour red onion sauces. Both sauces are so good that it's hard to know whether to dip in one, the other, or both. We recommend ordering your mains family-style to share, as most do. Chicken two soy has a thick emulsion of sweet and salty soy sauces, along with onions and peppers. It's a bold and memorable flavor. Curries, especially those with coconut milk, are uniformly good. The popular Bentara Filet is a filet mignon drowned in one of a rotating selection of interesting sauces.

Vegetarians will also be delighted with the options. Koreng kang kong, wok-fried Asian water spinach with hot chili peppers and shrimp paste, is light and wonderful. The lunch menu is a great deal. Bentara also deserves praise for being a Ninth Square pioneer—the first smart restaurant to venture into this struggling old neighborhood with beautiful, old brick storefronts but not enough foot traffic. What a great example to set; others have since followed. In short, Bentara is not just one of the best restaurants in town, but also a landmark in New Haven's history, a gleaming beacon of a new urban renaissance.

Billy's Pasta Cosi

7.6
10

Above-average modern Italian food with a pleasant vibe and some very Connecticut touches

Italian $**30**   *Branford*

7.4/10   **8.0**/10   **8.0**/10   **6.8**/10
Food   Atmosphere   Attitude   Value

Upmarket restaurant   3 Linden Ave.   *Bar* Wine and beer only
Tues.-Sat. 5pm-10pm; Sun. 5pm-   Branford   *Credit Cards* Visa, MC
9pm, closed Mon. *Date-friendly.* (203) 483-9397   *Reservations* Accepted
Outdoor dining. Vegetarian-friendly. www.pastacosi.com

The first thing that might hit you when entering this cozy little Italian-American joint is the dramatic music. The soundtrack might well take you through the cheesiest arias of all time. The room is a really pleasant place in which to sit, with comforting yellow walls, super-glossy wooden surfaces sans tablecloths, and other such touches of modern restaurant-catalog chic.

Rock-star/chef Jacques Pepin may favor this place, but that doesn't mean it's straight outta Rome. Although, unlike Xando "Cosí," they get the accent on their name right, the menu is otherwise rife with misspelled Italian, and when your waitperson arrives, you'll likely notice the very Connecticut touches like the pronunciations ("proshoot," "mootzarell," and "antipast"), and main courses that come complete with a pasta side.

One welcome surprise at Pasta Cosí is the interesting wine list, which is well priced at the bottom end (if not as much so at the top). The bruschetta is of the hot variety, with grated parmesan cheese, and it's tasty, if largely for the pleasant sogginess of the bread. On the recommendation of the house, we have tried braciola, which was dry (as, it bears mention, it often is) but endowed with a sweetness from raisins and a crunch from chubby pine nuts. The filling in lobster ravioli is a bit granular, and that dish isn't amazing either.

We are more convinced by a dish of "Rigatoni Pasta Cosí," which features white beans, sausage, broccoli rabe, sun-dried tomatoes, and a garlicky broth. The short, carefully salted tubes of pasta glisten with oil. The pairing of beans with pasta—starch with starch—is unusual, but the plate is good, elemental, even if its coherence flutters in and out from bite to bite. Even if the atmosphere is more memorable than the food, Billy's is a nice, if not groundbreaking, addition to the area Italian-American landscape.

Blue Pearl

6.4
10

A flowing, hipper-than-thou space that's hit-or-miss for dinner but notable for chocolate fondue

New American   **$32**   *Financial District*

5.1 /10   **9.0** /10   **6.0** /10   **5.4** /10
Food   *Atmosphere*   *Attitude*   *Value*

Upmarket restaurant   130 Court St.   *Bar* Full
Tues.-Thurs. 5pm-1am; Fri.-Sat.   New Haven   *Credit Cards* Visa, MC, AmEx
5pm-2am; closed Sun.-Mon.   (203) 789-6370   *Reservations* Accepted
Kitchen closes at 11pm.   www.thebluepearlnewhaven.com
Date-friendly. Outdoor dining. Vegetarian-friendly.

Blue Pearl is New Haven's answer to New York's Asia de Cuba and Miami's Delano: a fantasy of flowing curtains in pale shades, ultra-hip lighting and art-deco furniture, a place clearly meant to attract beautiful people for strong martinis and successful dates. The backyard, in season, is a grittily romantic space, especially well suited to drinks or dessert. But this is also a fairly ambitious restaurant, bringing fondues to New Haven as well as riffs on traditional American comfort food.

The martinis are good, but the best thing we've had at Blue Pearl is the delicious chocolate fondue. It's a fun and underrepresented genre, and New Haven is the better for it. Unfortunately, we also tried a cheese fondue—parmesan and artichoke—which was lumpy, salty, and overbearing. Rumor has it that the chef (who, we also hear, has since left) didn't monitor the stirring of the fondue during its preparation, which is essential to preserve a smooth consistency. The white bread for dipping was pretty blah; better were the rye bread and nicely blanched broccoli. Still, this was nothing like what we look for in a cheese fondue.

Among the non-fondue offerings, we loved the fried oysters; they're fresh, plump, and spicy. We've also had a decent lobster roll, which comes on an appropriate soft potato roll with cole slaw that has a distinctly fruity flavor. A "vegetable stack" appetizer with goat cheese isn't bad in terms of taste, although its tomato is underseasoned and the eggplant chewy. So it's hit or miss with the savories; again, we say you're best sticking to drinks and dessert.

Book Trader Café

An airy used bookstore with a good, fresh selection of veggie-friendly sandwiches and soups

Light American   **$ 7**   *Upper Chapel Area*

7.0/10   **9.0**/10   **7.0**/10   **9.5**/10
Food   *Atmosphere*   *Attitude*   *Value*

Counter service   1140 Chapel St.   *Bar* None
Mon.-Fri. 7:30am-9pm;   New Haven   *Credit Cards* Visa, MC, AmEx
Sat.-Sun. 9am-9pm.   (203) 787-6147   *Reservations* Not accepted
Breakfast. Outdoor dining. Vegetarian-friendly.

Book Trader's expansive, sunny atrium is one of the best places in New Haven for that great American college-town tradition—the casual solo lunch with a book, or its modern cousin, a laptop. A Yale-heavy crowd of budding intellectuals and artists sidle up to the counter and place orders for good dark-roast coffee (they call it the Black Cow), a muffin, or one of an array of pun-heavy sandwiches scrawled across a chalkboard. These offerings combine fresh ingredients like fior-di-latte mozzarella, plum tomatoes, and basil pesto (that one's the Tempesto) between hunks of crusty bread (the seven-grain is top-notch).

Book Trader is, appropriately enough, a used bookstore as well, and a good one at that. Perhaps predictably, it's also a haven for vegetarians and vegans; soy chicken (which is surprisingly firm and flavorful) and oven-roasted vegetables with caramelized onions are among the sandwich fillings. There's also a daily vegan soup option. And then there are the green salads, perhaps Book Trader's crowning achievement. A fresh array of field greens is topped with a superlative balsamic vinaigrette, a syrupy delight with an emergent sweetness that works well paired with a scoop of chicken salad for a dollar and a half extra. Accompanied by a slice of fresh bread, the small salad should be enough lunch for most appetites. You might want to ask for extra dressing.

Perhaps it is the atrium's easy acoustics that lend Book Trader a certain talking-across-tables aspect among the contingent of single Yalies. You're well advised to avert your gaze if you aren't in the mood for a mid-afternoon flirtation—or for the classically awkward exchange of credentials and summer plans.

Bottega Lounge

6.6
10

An Italian restaurant and club that is all about the
outdoor tables and sidewalk scene in summer

Italian $32   *Theater District*

6.2/10   **9.0**/10   **2.0**/10   **5.6**/10
Food   *Atmosphere*   *Attitude*   *Value*

Casual restaurant   954 Chapel St.   *Bar* Full
Wed.-Thurs. 7pm-1am; Fri.-Sat.   (entrance through   *Credit Cards* Visa, MC, AmEx
7pm-2am; closed Sun.-Tues.   Temple St. courtyard)   *Reservations* Recommended
Kitchen closes at 11pm.   New Haven
Date-friendly. Good wine list. (203) 562-5566
Outdoor dining. Vegetarian-friendly. www.bottegagiuliana.net

This lively bar, grill, and hopping nightclub, affiliated with the Bottega
Giuliana clothing store and Café Bottega, occupies that limbo space in
the Taft-Liberty passageway right downtown between College and
Temple streets, and it is all about the outdoor seating in summer,
whether you prefer to sit up on the balconies or out on the sidewalk
below. Above loom the concrete twists and turns of the Taft parking
garage, but the gregarious buzz beneath, which is quite a scene on
weekends—everyone's decked out for the party—makes you stop
noticing, or caring about, the garage.

A good, if pricey, Italian wine selection—by the glass or bottle—
accompanies the standard cocktail lineup and a better-than-average
selection of Italian dishes: for instance, tasty little grilled pizzette (mini
pizzas) with tomato, mozzarella, basil, and olive oil. But the food is hit
or miss here. We've had delicious lobster ravioli with a tomato cream
sauce, and fresh crab cakes that were decent but studded with chunky
and jarring vegetables. We've had a lamb that was dry and chewy,
albeit with a beautifully reduced sauce; great pappardelle that
accompanied a not-so-great tomato-based zuppa (fish stew) without
much emergent flavor; a decent brownie-ish chocolate soufflé cake;
and the best white chocolate martini in town, among other good
drinks. The service, however, is iffy at best, and often downright
abrasive, especially when they're crowded, or when it nears 1am.

Back Room is certainly not as much fun in the winter, when you're
forced into the bowels of the bar's interior, which is a dance club with a
dizzying hodge-podge of psychedelic color and DJ paraphernalia. Of
course, sometimes that's what you want, in which case it can be even
more fun indoors. (Just beware of angry bouncers come curfew.) Back
Room is trying to be many things, but at the very least, it is a well-
mixed town-gown social scene.

Brazi's Italian Restaurant

4.8
10

A garden-variety Italian-American place popular for
the friendly service—it couldn't be the boring food

Italian, Pizza   **$22**   *Long Wharf*

3.8 /10   **6.5** /10   **6.0** /10   **4.1** /10
Food   *Atmosphere*   *Attitude*   *Value*

Casual restaurant   201 Food Terminal   *Bar* Full
Mon.-Thurs. 11:30am-9:30pm;   Plaza, New Haven   *Credit Cards* Visa, MC, AmEx
Fri.-Sat. 11:30am-10:30pm;   (203) 498-2488   *Reservations* Accepted
Sun. noon-9pm. *Vegetarian-friendly.*

Brazi's, out by the Food Terminal area that has become a chaotic
hotspot since the opening of New Haven's own IKEA, is endlessly
popular, bringing in a large cadre of regulars even for weekday lunches.
Why, we have no idea. It couldn't be for the watery pasta—a bland,
undersalted dish of penne, for example, whose red sauce is largely
dissociated from the pasta itself.

Nor is it likely that the crowds would flock in for the predictable
dinner salads, with olives and cherry tomatoes, or for the tough meats
like "veal caprese," with seemingly unsalted red sauce and basil that's
cooked so as to sap it of all flavor. A vegetable side, at our last visit,
featured peas, canned green beans, carrots, onions, and zucchini, all as
limp, watery, and underseasoned as hospital food. If you do end up at
Brazi's, stick with the pizza, which is made in a brick oven, resulting in a
decent crust. The tomatoes aren't bad, and (unlike in the veal caprese)
the basil is fresh. But the cheese falls short flavor-wise, especially by the
standards of this pizza town.

The mystery remains. Why do they come? Is it for the atmosphere?
We suppose it's possible that the cafeteria-fancy furnishings and muzak
appeal to some people, or that certain New Haveners have a particular
taste for dated ceiling fans, mirrors, and big, canopied columns that lie
somewhere in the aesthetic middle ground between Las Vegas' Caesar's
Palace and the restaurant of a Holiday Inn. At least the service is very
friendly, in a folksy kind of way. You might see the regulars in playful
banter with the staff, asking for another free refill of the hot but chewy
salami rolls. Sometimes a smile of recognition goes a long, long way.

Breakaway Deli

4.8
10

A cheap lunch stop with cafeteria-style food, below average even within its quick, short-order category

Light American   **$ 6**   *Arts District*

4.3 /10   **5.5** /10   **6.0** /10   **5.5** /10
Food   *Atmosphere*   *Attitude*   *Value*

Counter service   24 Whitney Ave.   *Bar* None
Mon.-Fri. 8am-4pm;   New Haven   *Credit Cards* None
closed Sat.-Sun.   (203) 865-5946   *Reservations* Not accepted

There is a certain kind of short-order deli and lunch counter, in a certain part of New Haven, that's geared to a certain kind of crowd. Within this group of lunch spots price ranges and menu offerings are often essentially similar, and it can be hard to distinguish one place from the next. That's where we come in. The Breakaway Deli, conveniently located next to the FedEx office on Whitney, is not our first choice among these places. There's a lot of pink and purple in the interior decorating, and there's something amusing about the sports-centered décor; as good, upstanding Red Sox and Pats fans (this is a glorious time for New England sports), we can't complain about that theme.

The prices are low, but the food misses the mark. To begin with, it's hard to prepare things that should be cooked on a skillet without such a skillet—all they have is a little electric contraption, and so the eggs in the breakfast sandwiches are pre-cooked and then microwaved. Cold cuts, too, are below average, basic and cheap; get "the works" on a sandwich and it becomes an incoherent mess with things like raw mushrooms (why?) and insufficient condiment application. Provolone is tasteless and the tomatoes, at our last visit, were unripe. Hard rolls, meanwhile, are soft, a tad chewy, not the best but not exactly bad. A chicken noodle soup is well seasoned, but the chicken within is hard to find and the noodles so mushy that they barely taste like pasta. The chocolate pudding is instant.

There's a "low-carb menu" that features things such as no-sauce pizza and "meatwiches" (vegetables wrapped inside the meat). But we don't advise trying such unusual dishes at a place that executes so poorly on the basics.

Brick Oven Pizza

5.2
10

Reliable thin-crust pizza and unexpectedly good subs—even at 2:45am

Pizza   **$ 9**   *Upper Chapel Area*

6.5/10   **3.0**/10   **4.0**/10   **5.7**/10
Food   *Atmosphere*   *Attitude*   *Value*

Counter service   122 Howe St.   *Bar* BYO
Daily 11am-3am.   New Haven   *Credit Cards* Visa and MC
                        (203) 777-4444   *Reservations* Not accepted

Brick Oven Pizza scores points with consistently good thin-crust pizza and decent chicken subs (here they're called grinders, in the small-town New England style). And it's open daily until 3am, making it one of the best late-night take-out options in the city. We make reference to take-out for a reason, though: the atmosphere inside the restaurant is fast-food style. Bright lights and an array of empty tables are backed by an incongruous wall of bricks with an oven. It's not our favorite place to sit. Even the sign outside has a distinct 1990s fast-food aesthetic that makes you want to get in and get out. And while it's not far from downtown and fairly near the late-night post-bar scene, Brick Oven Pizza is also in a neighborhood that can sometimes feel deserted in the wee hours. For take-out pies in those hours, though, Brick Oven is a welcome surprise.

The pizza itself is fairly thin, with a crust that is generally well seared. Although the sauce and cheese aren't in the league of New Haven's champions, it's a sizeable notch above the norm. Along with the usual pizza repertoire, there are some unusual combinations here, like the Sweetie Pie (with peas, tomatoes, mozzarella, ricotta, parsley, and basil) and the Black Sea (shrimp and garlic). The grilled chicken grinder with lettuce, tomato, cheese, and mayo is better than you'd expect for a mostly-take-out pizza joint: the chicken is moist, with charcoal flavor in evidence; vegetables are fresh; and the mayo adds another layer of texture. It all sits on very fresh bread. We recommend adding hot sauce. There's also a very cheap dinner special that comes with pasta and a salad. It's not the best pasta, but at 2:45am, you can't ask for much more.

Brown Stone House

5.6
10

Like a simple museum of Americana, with a menu
that seems not to have changed since the 1950s

Traditional American   **$ 8**   *Hamden*

5.1 /10   **6.5** /10   **6.0** /10   **6.3** /10
Food   *Atmosphere*   *Attitude*   *Value*

Casual restaurant   2365 Whitney Ave.   *Bar* None
Mon.-Fri. 6am-3pm; Sat 6am-2pm;   Hamden   *Credit Cards* None
Sun. 7am-1pm. *Breakfast.*   (203) 281-0446   *Reservations* Not accepted

At one of the main intersections of sleepy downtown Hamden, the
Brown Stone House is a treasure of Americana, a relic from another era.
Here you can have an open-faced turkey sandwich with gravy and a
vanilla milkshake, items which are in all likelihood identical to what you
would have gotten in 1955.

That doesn't mean that America hasn't made culinary advances
since that era, however, and a lot of the food is pretty unexciting. In
order to appreciate a meal at the Brown Stone House, you need to
have a taste for the simple, even the bland—and for nostalgia. The
soda fountain, for starters, is no replica—it's been here all along. In
addition to the menu, all the paraphernalia and appliances behind the
counter, and even the sign on the door, are unselfconsciously frozen in
a dreamlike postwar America.

And so are the customers. The years show up more dramatically on
a man's face than on a stainless-steel refrigerator. You'll notice such a
theme among the clientele, who all seem to be (not coincidentally) on a
first-name basis with the servers. For all these reasons, if you're a
youngster, it might be hard not to feel out of place here. But you also
won't feel anything less than warmly welcome—and, when you leave,
perhaps also heartsick for a kinder, simpler age that may never have
been.

Bruegger's Bagel Bakery

3.9
10

A mediocre McBagel chain where you must avoid the horrible breakfast sandwiches at all costs

Light American $ **6**   *Arts District*

4.0 /10   **3.0** /10   **6.0** /10   **5.3** /10
Food   *Atmosphere*   *Attitude*   *Value*

Fast-food chain   1 Whitney Ave.   *Bar* None
Mon.-Fri. 6am-5pm; Sat.-Sun.   New Haven   *Credit Cards* None
6am-4pm. *Breakfast.*   (203) 773-3199   *Reservations* Not accepted
Vegetarian-friendly.   www.brueggers.com

Bruegger's gets a lot of mileage from its location on Church Street only a few steps from Yale and the Green. The reliably brisk walk-in business surely bolsters their sales of mediocre-at-best bagels and sandwiches. This is not the only place to buy a bagel (some cafés even get deliveries from H&H), but if you have an especially specific bagel craving, Bruegger's does boast a greater variety of offerings than other places around town. You won't forget that it's a fast-food chain, but it's a bit brighter and airier than most; the corner location and big plate-glass windows onto Church Street brighten things up. You can eat in at one of the plastic countertops or booths. The space has a feel that's particularly conducive to breakfast.

Most people, though, order take-out. The place is fine for one or a half-dozen to go, with flavored cream cheese. The dense, pasty bagels are baked in the store, but they won't exactly transport you to New York. Smoked-salmon spread and chive cheese are both perfectly acceptable. We like the bacon-and-scallion cream cheese the best, especially with a garlic or onion bagel. The Fresh Samantha juices make us happy. Sandwiches like the Herby-Turkey (a bagel with turkey, sun-dried tomato spread, lettuce, and onions with garlic cream cheese) are edible but unexciting. We prefer the "Softwiches," which are made with bigger, breadier, softer, and more square bagels that are indeed, as Bruegger's advertises, better suited to sandwiches; among the Softwich breads, we favor the Parmesan asiago.

Most unimpressive are the breakfast options, made with prefabricated slabs of egg product that's peeled out of little plastic baggies, then paired with cold, processed bacon and cheese. For such compound breakfast items, you can do much better almost anywhere else—especially anywhere that owns a heating device other than a microwave.

Bulldog Burrito

A cheap, mediocre, student-centered overstuffed-
Cali-burrito joint—at least it's open late

Tex-Mex $ 7   *Broadway Area*

4.2 /10   **3.0** /10   **7.0** /10   **5.4** /10
Food   *Atmosphere*   *Attitude*   *Value*

Counter service   320 Elm St.   ***Bar*** Wine and beer only
Mon.-Thurs. 11am-1am; Fri.-Sat.   New Haven   ***Credit Cards*** Visa and MC
11am-2am; Sunday noon-10pm.   (203) 495-8600   ***Reservations*** Not accepted
Vegetarian-friendly.   www.bulldogburrito.com

Bulldog Burrito is only slightly different from its predecessor, the
MexiCali Grille, a quick, inexpensive California-style burrito joint on Elm
near Broadway. As you may gather from the name, the joint caters
directly to Yalies, especially undergrads stuck in the limbo times
between dining-hall meals.

It works like this: you line up at the counter and watch as a sweet,
tender, oversized flour tortilla (the highlight) is flash-steamed and then
stuffed with rice, beans, salsa, lettuce, cheese, and sour cream. We like
the creamy chipotle sauce, which adds another layer of flavor to the
mix. Curiously, this condiment is not always volunteered to customers
as an option; don't let yourself forget that it's there.

Unfortunately, our favorite filling from MexiCali—the BBQ pork—
disappeared with the conversion to Bulldog, and while grilled chicken
cubes have smoky notes of charcoal, the meat, at recent visits, has
been somewhat dry and under-flavored, with the least inspiring of all
being the chewy steak. The burritos are competent if you like the
Californian everything-but-the-kitchen-sink approach to fillings. If you're
Californian, though, you'll be disappointed with the fillings themselves.
At least the price is right; we think the regular burrito—a steal in the
five-to-six-dollar range—can actually satisfy two normal-sized appetites
(even leaving aside the handful of insipid, stale tortilla chips). By the
pound, from the taco salads to the quesadillas, the price is absolutely
righteous. Still, certain adamant aficionados would rather brave the
elements at the Roomba burrito cart two blocks away, at Elm Street.

Eating in at Bulldog—which not so many people do—means
claiming one of the functional but pleasingly harmonious wooden
tables and tackling your burrito in a bright, modern room where photo
art hangs from the walls. The late hours are refreshing. All told, it's not
terrible, especially at this price point, but suffice it to say that we don't
find ourselves returning to Bulldog very often.

Burger King

2.6
10

Burgers that are unhealthier than their
counterparts at McDonalds—and taste worse too

Short-order American   **$ 6**   *Whalley*

3.0 /10   **1.0** /10   **5.0** /10   **3.7** /10
Food   *Atmosphere*   *Attitude*   *Value*

Fast-food chain   1329 Whalley Ave.   *Bar* None
Mon.-Thurs. 6am-11pm; Fri.-Sat.   New Haven   *Credit Cards* Visa, MC, AmEx
6am-midnight; Sun. 7am-11pm.   (203) 397-8426   *Reservations* Not accepted
Breakfast.   www.burgerking.com

"Come on over, the fire's ready." That's the new motto of Burger King,
whose garish neon outlets dot the strip-mall landscape in the New
Haven area. According to BK's TV commercials, highway billboards, and
musical web site, their burgers are now "fire grilled." Previously, they
were "flame broiled." Whatever. The burgers are microwaved. And
they're not just microwaved—they're microwaved *right in front of you!*
Just how stupid do they think we are? BK's customer service line, in
response to our incredulous query, informed us that the microwave was
necessary "only to melt the cheese," and that one could specially
request a plain burger straight off the "grill."

Either way, the burgers taste as bad as ever: insipid, flimsy,
overcooked slabs of gristly meat that are much worse than the
competition—and don't get us started on the mushy, flavorless fries. Is
the food here healthier, at least? Not by a long shot. The Double
Whopper with Cheese, for example, packs in 1,060 calories and 69
grams of fat, while McDonald's Double Quarter Pounder with Cheese—
the unhealthiest item on their menu—has roughly 35% fewer calories
and 45% less fat. Step up to BK's King Size meal, and you're in for
2,050 calories and 99 grams of fat—more than most people should
consume in an entire day.

It does seem that Burger King manifests a desire—however hidden
or under-utilized—to beat McDonald's. But BK executes so poorly on its
innovations—from "French toast sticks" to the new "baguettes" to the
infamous Whaler—that McDonald's doesn't even have to keep up. Even
the atmosphere at BK is one of the least inspiring of all fast-food
chains, with an aesthetic of flashy sleaze that has all the subtlety of
Saturday morning TV. So come on over, the microwave's beeping.

C.O. Jones

5.7
10

A State Street favorite for strong and easy-to-down margaritas, though service is dodgy

Tex-Mex   **$14**   *East Rock/Grad Ghetto*

4.7 /10   **8.5**/10   **3.0** /10   **5.6**/10
Food   *Atmosphere*   *Attitude*   *Value*

Bar and grill   969 State St.   *Bar* Full
Sun.-Thurs. 5pm-1am;   New Haven   *Credit Cards* Visa, MC, AmEx
Fri.-Sat. 5pm-2am.   (203) 773-3344   *Reservations* Accepted
Kitchen closes daily at 11pm. www.cojones.com
Date-friendly. Outdoor dining. Vegetarian-friendly.

Perhaps it's because the margaritas are so potent and easy to drink that you always come away with warm (if foggy) memories of this Grad Ghetto Tex-Mex bar and grill with the double-entendre name (if you don't get it, ask a Spanish speaker). A lively mélange of grad students and a smattering of locals and suburban denizens flocks into the dimly-lit, sombrero-laden bar mostly just for drinks, although there's also a menu of burritos and border-style appetizers. Weekend nights hop with jolly carousers, as do nightly happy hours from 5-7pm—with half-price house margaritas—and Mondays, when happy hour continues until 10pm.

It bears mention that the house margarita recipe isn't the best, with a sticky-sweet, sour-mix-type flavor that seems to have gotten sour-mixier in recent years. We're more convinced by the pricier versions on the menu. During non-happy hour, you should definitely try some of the more inventive options like the prickly-pear margarita—or savor a top-shelf tequila like limey Tarantula (for budding connoisseurs, the tequila samplers are a good deal). We can't condone the service, however, which is extremely erratic, often distracted, and occasionally downright rude.

But here's the kicker: if you have good timing, C.O. Jones offers the cheapest meal in all of New Haven. That's because weeknight happy hours (5-7pm only) also feature a free, all-you-can-eat buffet of bean burritos, with lettuce, tomato, sour cream, and salsa to accompany your drinks. Wings are also half-price during happy hour. With just one small half-price 'rita as the minimum, a starving student can actually pile up the free burritos and eat a two-dollar dinner. That said, the food, burritos in particular, is less than stellar. Still, it's a fun place, a good pickup scene, and a mainstay on the New Haven bar-and-grill map.

Café Espresso

7.2
10

A quintessential neighborhood café with wonderful
service and eclectic American food

Light American $10   *East Rock/Grad Ghetto*

6.7/10   **7.5**/10   **9.0**/10   **8.2**/10
Food   *Atmosphere*   *Attitude*   *Value*

Café   981 State St.   *Bar* None
Mon.-Fri. 7:30am-3:30pm; New Haven   *Credit Cards* None
closed Sat.-Sun.   (203) 776-7477   *Reservations* Not accepted
Breakfast. Vegetarian-friendly.

This cute little café up State Street hits just the right breakfast-and-
lunch vibe. The bright, airy, casual room just feels like the perfect place
for a cup of coffee or an easy bite, whether to catch up with a friend or
on your reading. At least four varieties of coffee are on offer daily;
French roast and espresso are both above average, and they're served
to you with a big smile. Cappuccino, too, is well executed. There's good
music and a warm feeling. For some reason, this neighborhood place
attracts an inordinately female crowd.

Basic, eclectic-American food offerings, which are scrawled across a
chalkboard, change daily. They're generally tasty and many are also
effortlessly healthy. Particularly notable are the great homemade soups
(clam chowder and chili with cornbread both get high marks) and the
big salads. Sandwiches, which might include a chicken cutlet, are made
with fresh, crusty French bread and crisp vegetables. The bread might
slightly overpower the ingredients, but the flavors are satisfying. The
grilled cheese and tomato is also very good.

Muffins and scones are fine, and the creamy mint cake gets
particularly high marks—it almost reminds us of a crème-de-menthe
parfait. Prices are quite reasonable all around. At last check, there were
pizzas on Fridays and even lobster rolls.

We wish the hours were more extensive—you can't get a cup of
coffee here after 3:30pm. On weekends—our favorite time for lazy
late-morning coffee—the place is completely closed. (Not that there's
anything wrong with taking weekends off.) But we wish there were
one of these on every corner, because when it's open, Café Espresso is
a much-needed morning reminder that the world is basically all right.

Café George by Paula

6.9
10

A friendly weekday lunch spot hidden in an office building, with careful execution of simple favorites

Light American   **$ 8**   *Theater District*

7.0 /10   **6.0** /10   **9.0** /10   **8.2** /10
Food   *Atmosphere*   *Attitude*   *Value*

Counter service	300 George St.	*Bar* None
Mon.-Fri. 7am-3pm;	New Haven	*Credit Cards* Visa, MC, AmEx
closed Sat.-Sun. *Breakfast.*	(203) 777-1414	*Reservations* Not accepted

Paula recently moved from a cozy location on the corner of Orange and Grove Streets (now Zoi's on Orange) to the more spacious current location, which is a bit harder to find; it's inside an office building on George Street that is frequented more by those in the building or in the know than by walk-ins. The move to the larger space was driven by Paula's successful catering business; word has it she needed a larger kitchen in order to accommodate the increasing frequency and size of orders. Still, a reliable crowd shows up for breakfast and lunch at this weekday-only, cafeteria-style operation.

The service at Café George by Paula could hardly be any more friendly or welcoming; if you're a first-timer, you may well be acknowledged as such, helped through the menu, encouraged to come back. It's the little things, sometimes, that improve not just a customer's lunch, but his or her day; and it's the little things, often, that translate to success in the difficult food service business.

The key to Paula's success is consistently skillful execution of simple favorites. We love, most of all, the sandwiches, although prepared dishes are almost as good. A chicken cutlet sandwich with bacon, for example, benefits from supremely fresh ingredients, a crispy fried cutlet, well-paired bread, and proper seasoning. It is a blend that can be surprisingly difficult to pull off, but Paula's hand is steady. Ditto for the salads, whose vegetables are some of the freshest around. Breakfast, too, is a treat here; eggs are handled with ease. If you can find your way here at lunchtime, through the tinted glass doors and office-building lobbies, you'll be richly rewarded.

Café Java

5.8
10

A simple lunch joint, geared toward take-out, with underperforming panini but passable pizza

Light American, Pizza   **$ 8**   *Financial District*

4.9/10   **7.5**/10   **6.0**/10   **6.5**/10
Food   *Atmosphere*   *Attitude*   *Value*

Counter service   59 Elm St.   *Bar* None
Mon.-Fri. 7am-4pm; closed Sat.-   New Haven   *Credit Cards* Visa, MC, AmEx
Sun. *Breakfast. Vegetarian-friendly.* (203) 624-1275   *Reservations* Not accepted

The décor at Café Java would have you believe that you are somewhere else. The stucco walls of this downtown lunch spot are coated in a rich acrylic burgundy, and every table bears a collage of guidebook clippings from a different European country. If your dining companion stands you up, there's always a bold Union Jack or a cut-out Spanish bullfighter to keep you company.

But a glimpse at the café's menu offerings reminds you that you're still squarely on this side of the Atlantic. You can choose from a half-dozen sandwiches and a sampling of pizzas, plus a few standard pastries. After a taste of the over-ripe fruit or dry bagels, however, the three varieties of packaged Skittles candies begin to look like a viable lunch option.

Despite their promising nomenclature, the panini have little to recommend them. A soupy mess of ingredients—only some of them fresh—are layered between two slices of sourdough bread that is then embossed with defining grill marks. The sandwich tends to fall apart long before it can be consumed in full.

Yet Café Java is well-located near New Haven's business district, which provides it a steady stream of suited customers. The place is not terrible for a quick lunch or a morning coffee; just skip the brown, watery espresso, and don't expect marvels. The atmosphere is pleasant, but the café's saving grace is its pizza: although oily and not on par with this town's finest, the personal pies make a satisfying meal. The crust is appropriately crisp, and the pizzas are cooked for each customer on the spot (expect to wait about 10 minutes). It's nice to be reminded of what New Haven does best: for pizza, even this little corner of downtown beats a Parisian bistro, any day. –*Coco Krumme*

Café Nine

6.4
10

A classic dive bar with reasonable bar food and a
deep commitment to the local music scene

Bar food   **$ 9**   *Ninth Square*

5.0 /10   **9.0**/10   **7.0** /10   **7.1**/10
Food   *Atmosphere*   *Attitude*   *Value*

Bar and grill   250 State St.   *Bar* Full
Sun.-Thurs. 11am-1am; Fri.-Sat.   New Haven   *Credit Cards* Visa, MC, AmEx
11am-2am. Kitchen open Sun.-   (203) 789-8281   *Reservations* Not accepted
Thurs. noon-9pm; Fri.-Sat. noon-   www.cafenine.com
10pm. *Brunch.*

For years, Café Nine has been one of our favorite places to have a drink
and listen to live local music. Some of the music is laid back—like acid
jazz with a deep groove—and some of it is just plain loud. Either way,
as a venue, Café Nine (named for its Ninth Square location) is just right.
There seems to be some act or other any time you show up, day or
night. At either time, the crowd lies at the awkward nexus of working-
class seniors, vintage-clothed Ivy League rockers, and goth suburbanites
that can make the edges of New Haven into such a fascinating scene.

The staff is friendly and unpretentious, and the well-worn, well-
stocked bar runs along one side of the room. Even the cheap furniture
feels right at home; for atmosphere, we give it a Nine. Café Nine also
functions as an eating place of sorts, with a tiny kitchen that turns out
a standard bar menu of comfort food, which you order at the bar and
eat either right there (as many do) or at a table. There's a popular
pulled-pork sandwich, which was oversalted on a recent visit, causing
parched diners to reach for their drinks more often than usual. It's a
shame, because the sandwich was otherwise impressive—it was tender
and exceptionally flavorful, if closer to roast pork than smoky barbecue.

No fries are in sight, but the potato salad—"Jody's Famous"—is.
Except for needing salt, Jody's concoction is a good representative of
the skin-on, medium-mayo school of potato salad. Macaroni and
cheese doesn't fare as well; while the cheese sauce is at least average
and properly seasoned, the noodles are often overcooked and soggy.

But you should realize that this is all beside the point. This is a bar,
not a restaurant, and the food is there because bar patrons sometimes
get hungry. Come to Café Nine to drink, come to listen, and let
yourself relax into the rhythm of whatever band happens to be rocking
the house.

Caffé Bottega

5.1 / 10

A new downtown jack-of-all-trades—bar, café, club, and restaurant—but master only of gelato

Italian   **$33**   *Theater District*

5.5 /10   **5.0** /10   **3.0** /10   **4.1** /10
Food   *Atmosphere*   *Attitude*   *Value*

Bar and grill   910 Chapel St.   *Bar* Full
Mon. 10am-11pm; Tues.-Thurs.   New Haven   *Credit Cards* Visa, MC, AmEx
10am-1am; Fri.-Sat. 10am-2am. (203) 624-6200   *Reservations* Not accepted
Closed Sun. Kitchen closes Mon.- www.bottegagiuliana.net
Thurs. 10pm; Fri.-Sat. 11pm. Lunch,
noon-3pm only. *Breakfast. Vegetarian-friendly. Wireless Internet.*

This gleaming new establishment proclaims its ambition with bold, colorful artwork; huge windows looking across to the Green; and imposing glass doors announcing the gelato, the coffee, the Internet, the raging bar scene, the live music, the comedy, and even the monthly fashion show. Clearly, Caffé Bottega wants to be everything at once.

Most successful are the espresso and the silky, effusive gelato, made in-house with machinery imported from Italy. Fruit flavors like blackberry are sugary but dead-on. Chocolate is not too bitter, not too sweet, the best in town. The décor, like the menu, is in-your-face eclectic: industrial spotlights, tinselly beads, and kissy pink lip-seats. Chairs in transparent neon colors accent the room like Hi-Liters. It's 50% Blade Runner, 50% Vaudeville, and 100% weird.

On weekdays, a big business lunch crowd downs bland salads or thin but brittle personal pizzas, which have cheese that doesn't meld with the characterless sauce. Panini are better, with good, crisp bread and decent ingredients—the chicken cutlet is our favorite—but the sandwiches are sometimes not pressed for long enough to melt the cheese. Asian fusion dishes like spring rolls and stir-fries flail off into faux-fusion land.

Dinner is more ambitious and more deeply flawed. Best is the "creamy asparagus orzo," like the illicit love child of risotto and mac and cheese. Chicken dishes, however, are horribly dry. Lobster ravioli are undersalted. And at one visit, two of our three overcooked sea scallops were orange, and one was white. (We were told that the chef's purveyor, upon questioning, had assured him it was "just minerals.") The attractive waitpeople have absolutely no idea what they're doing, especially with respect to serving the overpriced wine, which ranges up to the $90s—yet another endeavor here whose ambition is ruined by poor execution.

Caffé Bravo

6.4
10

A decent and unpretentious but unspectacular
Italian BYO with a curious cult following

Italian   **$28**   *East Rock/Grad Ghetto*

6.5 /10   **6.5** /10   **5.0** /10   **5.6** /10
Food   *Atmosphere*   *Attitude*   *Value*

Casual restaurant   794 Orange St.   *Bar* BYO
Mon.-Fri. 11am-3:30pm, 4:30pm-   New Haven   *Credit Cards* Visa, MC, AmEx
9pm; Sat. noon-3:30pm, 4:30pm-   (203) 772-2728   *Reservations* Not accepted
9pm; closed Sun. *Outdoor dining. Vegetarian-friendly.*

This casual Italian way out toward East Rock has a small but significant
cult following in New Haven, especially among neighborhood grad
students, with some even claiming that it's the top Italian in town. That
may be hyperbole, but there's something to the theory, because even if
Caffé Bravo's is straightforward Italian-American food without much
innovation or regional authenticity, they do display a particular skill in
preparing pasta. Penne and filled pasta alike are carefully prepared and
refreshingly al dente; the effect is both satisfying and refreshing.

Pane cotto is a good way to start; the white beans have an
appropriate texture, cooked exactly the right amount, while the bread is
soft and rich; it's like a casserole. More complex dishes aren't bad
either—peppery veal marsala, for instance, is tender with a sweet and
well developed brown sauce with deliciously fresh mushrooms; at last
visit, it needed an extra touch of salt, but it was still satisfying. Gnocchi
with tomato sauce, unfortunately, are of the pre-packaged variety, and
lack the silkiness of an excellent version of that dish. The tomato sauce,
too, tends to be undersalted. Plenty of parmesan helps.

There's not much to say about the atmosphere. It has a certain
neighborhood charm, but orderly rows of nameless, faceless tables with
cafeteria-style furnishings stare up at you in bright boredom—so keep
in mind that this restaurant is a good takeout option. Summer dining is
a welcome treat, when luck and patience may grant you one of the
few outdoor tables. Sit in the evening warmth, and BYO (it's allowed,
as Caffé Bravo has no liquor license), perhaps a bottle from the Wine
Thief, not so far away on Whitney—and now we're talking. Above-
average espresso makes a good finish; so does the cognac pumpkin
cheesecake.

Caribbean Connection

One of New Haven's tiniest—and best—Jamaican take-out spots

Jamaican

$ 9 *Whalley*

8.3 /10
Food

7.0 /10
Attitude

9.5 /10
Value

Take-out
Mon.-Sat. 8am-9pm; closed Sun.
Breakfast.

364 Whalley Ave.
New Haven
(203) 777-9080

Bar None
Credit Cards None
Reservations Not accepted

It can be easy to miss if you're driving down Whalley Avenue between downtown and Westville with tunnel vision, but this stretch of road is quite a culinary melting pot, from soul food to new-age vegetarian to Chinese to Eastern European Jewish. Caribbean Connection, next door to Stella's kosher bakery, is a representative of New Haven's Jamaican community—and one of the easiest of all to miss. The storefront is barely wider than the entrance to an apartment building.

The tiny take-out window inside the door, where there's barely enough room for two or three people to stand and order at the little counter, offers some of the best Jamaican even in a town of excellent Jamaican finds. Jerk chicken, not always available, is top-notch, with a good kick and moist texture. Oxtail is soft and rich, just as it should be, even if it isn't quite up to the gold standard of Mother's. Curry goat and stew chicken benefit from well-balanced seasoning, and plenty of sauce. (Note that the curry might be gone by 7pm or so.) They even serve breakfast—ackee (the Jamaican national fruit) and salt fish with a fried dumpling, and callaloo (a leafy green) with a fried dumpling.

Plenty of sauce is something that can't be taken for granted at these sorts of Jamaican places—there's significant variation in how generously the liquid from the stew is ladled over the meat and allowed to permeate through the rice-and-peas accompaniment as well. With cooking by extraction (stewing, for instance), much of the flavor seeps from the meat into the liquid, and the sauce is where it's at. Caribbean Connection clearly understands this. Meat patties, too, are reliable, and service comes with a smile. And don't forget to consult the list of daily specials at this little treasure.

Caribbean Family Pot

7.0
/10

Characteristic Jamaican take-out that takes the concept of no frills to a whole new level

Jamaican   **$10**   *Medical Area/The Hill*

7.0 /10   **7.0** /10   **7.9** /10
Food   *Attitude*   *Value*

Take-out   560 Congress Ave.   *Bar* None
Mon.-Sat. noon-8pm; closed Sun.   New Haven   *Credit Cards* None
                           No phone   *Reservations* Not accepted

Out of all of New Haven's distinguished Caribbean take-out windows, this is surely the most window-like. In fact, you order through a panel of transparent material, a pane so scratched that it's difficult to make out the face of the person to whom you're talking. The man who's usually there, though, is an absolute hoot. Come ready to decode an extremely thick Jamaican accent, and be prepared for an in-depth discussion of current events.

The menu is a simple list of the Jamaican basics: curry goat, oxtail, jerk chicken, stew chicken, and so on. The meat patties at the Caribbean Family Pot, however, are not as good as some others we've had—they have a soggier crust and a more insipid filling—and the rice and peas (translation: rice and red kidney beans) tend to come virtually unseasoned. A deliciously syrupy, salty rendition of oxtail, with the requisite melting fat, is the best choice, while goat curry is average for the genre (that's still a compliment).

As is the case with most area Jamaican food, portions are enormous—a large order can easily feed two people dinner for less than 10 dollars. The value proposition at New Haven's Jamaican take-out joints continues to astound us, but not as much as the fact that they are still so little known amongst the Yale crowd—and none are less known than the Caribbean Family Pot. As at the other Jamaican take-out places in town, the food here is an inexpensive and welcome break from the downtown ethnic take-out norm, and it's in a neighborhood in which you might not otherwise find yourself. In short, just check it out....

Carmen Anthony Steakhouse

8.7
/10

An outstanding, high-priced steakhouse that
follows a well-tested formula—but follows it well

Steakhouse, Traditional American   **$50**   *Arts District*

8.9/10
Food

8.5/10
Atmosphere

8.0/10
Attitude

7.2/10
Value

Upmarket restaurant
Mon.-Thurs. 11:30am-4pm, 5pm-
10pm; Fri. 11:30am-4pm, 5pm-
11pm; Sat. 5pm-11pm; Sun. 4pm-
9pm. *Date-friendly. Good wine list.*

660 State St.
New Haven
(203) 773-1444
www.carmenanthony.com

Bar Full
Credit Cards Visa, MC, AmEx
Reservations Recommended

This new addition to New Haven's rather sparse steakhouse landscape is
the fifth restaurant that Carmen Anthony Vacalebre has opened in
Connecticut since 1996. In keeping with the chain restaurant theme,
the building—not far from downtown but on a lonely stretch of State
Street—is strictly office-park material.

But looks can be deceiving, especially in the restaurant business.
Inside, the design is careful and understated; globe lamps, which might
be left too bright in less able hands, are dimmed enough to turn into
friendly orbs, removing the blemishes from your date's face. Such
elaborate place settings, uncontained, might be stuffy, but here they're
protected by the gregarious, clubby buzz of the humanity that inhabits
them.

Clubby is really the point here, after all; we understand that we
really *should* be starting out with martinis (excellent), jumbo shrimp
cocktail (good), an iceberg lettuce wedge (superb, with homemade blue
cheese dressing masterfully paired with warm pieces of bacon), or
perhaps the crab cakes (exemplary, crusted with shredded potato). But
what's even more exciting is that this is one of New Haven's few
restaurants where rare orders are fully honored. The beef is not dry-
aged, but it is still flavorful, juicy, and well crusted with spices. The New
York strip and the fattier ribeye are equally good (skip the filet). Even
the tricked-out "specialty steaks," a category that we generally try to
avoid at steakhouses, was much better than expected: the "sliced New
York Florentine" is redolent of garlic and drizzled with olive oil that
seeps into every flavorful flap of the slices, like in a rustic Italian tagliata
di manzo.

That's not to say that you'll get out cheaply. Even the excellent wine
list is one of the most expensive in New Haven—but, like everything
else, worth every penny.

Celtica

6.0
10

A calming Irish tea room in the back of a store,
whose tea is preferable to microwaved hot food

Irish, Light American   **$10**   *Theater District*

5.3 /10   **6.5** /10   **9.0** /10   **6.5** /10
Food   *Atmosphere*   *Attitude*   *Value*

Counter service   260 College St.   *Bar* None
Mon.-Sat. 11:30am-4:30pm; Sun. New Haven   *Credit Cards* Visa, MC, AmEx
noon-4:30pm.   (203) 785-8034   *Reservations* Not accepted
                               www.gotirish.com

The domain name says it all: your Irish fetish will be well fed by the
downtown Celtica store and its little tea room in the back, whose
friendly service and calming vibe create a little world apart from the
bustle of College Street. The store itself, which you will walk through
along the way, peddles all manner of Irish curios—Celtica, if you will.
The tea room, too, aside its few brown tables and chairs and a counter
in back, has walls that are lined with boxes of Irish this and Irish that—
boxes of Bewley's Irish Tea, biscuits, and so on. There's even a blooming
shamrock, like an Irish chia pet.

Easily the best thing to eat at Celtica is the amazing Irish brown
bread, whose sweetness and soft mouth feel make you want to eat
more and more of it. We're told that it comes from the Emerald Bakery
in Milford, you can buy it for a few bucks per loaf at Celtica, too. The
brown bread is served with good Wisconsin butter and comes with
soups and salads. It's also used to make an open-faced tuna melt,
which is otherwise unremarkable, with standard tuna and cheese that's
melted in the microwave.

In fact, that microwave performs a lot of duties at this restaurant,
such as reheating the quiche of the day, resulting in a spongy top and
chewy crust. But we can't blame the microwave for the bland and
underseasoned potato-leek soup, made in the thick and chunky style,
which, at our last visit, featured sandy leeks. The salads, though, are
good and fresh, with mixed greens, cherry tomatoes, cucumbers, red
onion, and a properly emulsified dressing. We also like the pot of Irish
tea, which is served in a French press. Like Celtica itself, it's warm and
soothing.

Central Steakhouse

8.0
/10

A hip, modern, and pricey new Ninth Square
steakhouse with a casual vibe and good wine list

Steakhouse, Traditional American $**51**   *Ninth Square*

8.2/10   **8.0**/10   **7.0**/10   **6.5**/10
Food   *Atmosphere*   *Attitude*   *Value*

Upmarket restaurant
Mon.-Thurs. 5pm-10pm; Fri.-Sat.
5pm-11pm; closed Sun. Kitchen
closes 30 min. earlier.
Date-friendly. Good wine list.

99 Orange St.
New Haven
(203) 787-7885
www.centralsteakhouse.com

Bar Full
Credit Cards Visa, MC, AmEx
Reservations Accepted

In early 2003, six years after opening their iconic Malaysian restaurant
in then-edgy Ninth Square, the Bentara folks were at it again, inspired
by the runaway success of the "Bentara filet," and they opened a
steakhouse virtually across the street from their first venture. New
Haven is the better for it. Central ably fills what had been a gaping hole
in the local dining scene, albeit with very high prices and occasional
inconsistency.

It is immediately apparent, upon entering the room, that these two
Ninth Square restaurateurs have a few tricks up their sleeve. The first
one is the slick set of TV monitors above the open kitchen, on which
you can watch your steak being grilled. The second is a spectacular
wine cellar/private dining room beneath. It's booked for groups by
reservation only, but this ultra-romantic, candle-lit, bottle-clad
wonderland would make Poe proud. The dining room for mere mortals
is in good taste too, if less unusual, with a slick bar, dark booths, and a
casually elegant vibe that's much better when the place is full of
people.

The cuts of beef, if not earth-shattering, are generally good. Central
uses mesquite and pecan wood on the grill, and the simple, classic
steakhouse preparations are just so, with a nice crust. It's pleasing,
especially if the meat is rare. Skip the filet mignon and go for the more
flavorful top sirloin, which is USDA Prime. Among Asian-fusion-themed
apps, the rock shrimp spring rolls, perhaps a nod across the street to
Bentara, are a solid choice. Fried calamari, on the other hand, aren't the
crispiest we've had. There's room for improvement, too, with the side
dishes; creamed spinach isn't very creamy. Fortunately, we've already
seen considerable betterment in every area, from service to cooking
times, since Central's rookie year.

Chapel Sweet Shoppe

5.9
10

An old-fashioned candy shop and ice cream store in the very heart of downtown

Sweets   *Theater District*

5.4 /10
Food

7.0 /10
Attitude

Take-out
Mon.-Thurs. 10am-6:30pm;
Fri.-Sun. 10pm-9pm.
Outdoor dining. Vegetarian-friendly.

1042 Chapel St.
New Haven
(203) 624-2411

Bar None
Credit Cards Visa, MC, AmEx
Reservations Not accepted

If you consider chocolate to be its own food group, then Chapel Sweet Shoppe may become your favorite place in town. This purveyor of things sweet and sugary offers everything from novelty candy by the piece (or the handful, as the case may be) to packaged candy gift boxes and imported handmade truffles. You can also count on the Sweet Shoppe for all requisite holiday theme candy. In short, it's candy—what more can we say?

Well, we can say this: there's also an ice cream counter at Chapel Sweet Shoppe, which offers the usual flavors, including sorbet, and a few surprises; seasonal specials like pumpkin are often advertised on an easel outside the store. Then there are the usual derivative treats, most notably extra-thick milkshakes and sundaes loaded with goodies. In summer, you can take your ice cream confection and sit outside at the adjacent sidewalk tables and chairs, as many do, to watch the world go by.

After all, this is the quaintest stretch of Chapel, New Haven's most quaint street. And what would such a stretch be, in New England, without its local candy store? Whether due more to the proliferation of South Beach dieters or to the structure of the premium candy manufacturers, we can all sit and be quietly thankful that candy shops have not yet gone the way of coffee and fast food, succumbing to chains that take over all the local businesses—the industry is still a ray of light in a landscape of proliferating franchises.

Chap's Grille

4.7
10

Everything about this lunchroom is average, except its central location and extensive hours

Light American   **$11**   *Upper Chapel Area*

5.0/10   **3.0**/10   **8.0**/10   **4.7**/10
Food   *Atmosphere*   *Attitude*   *Value*

Counter service   1174 Chapel St.   *Bar* None
Sun.-Wed. 7:30am-11pm;   New Haven   *Credit Cards* Visa, MC, AmEx
Thurs.-Sat. 7:30am-midnight. (203) 562-3966   *Reservations* Not accepted
Breakfast. Outdoor dining. Vegetarian-friendly.

If food means little more than sustenance to you, then Chap's may fit the bill. Centrally located and open late, part lunchroom, part diner, the final product is a quiet, tiled dining area with cheesy picket-fence detail by the window and an uneventful short-order menu. The atmosphere, as a glance inside from the street quickly reveals, is not exactly depressing, but neither is it much to write about. There are a few simple tables and chairs, and that's just about it. In fact, almost everything about Chap's is average, although the offerings make erratic forays into unlikely territory. There's "Egyptian-style" moussaka and a version of Indian chicken tikka. Hmm. At least there are also some specifically vegan options.

For sheer nourishment, the best option here is breakfast, which seems to have a small but loyal following. For a cheap way to start your day, the breakfast special, served until 11am, offers two eggs, toast, and hash browns for $2.65. Other morning options include the Big Breakfast with all the usuals: French toast (thickly cut, thankfully), a stack of pancakes, or an omelette with hash browns and bacon. Of the breakfast standards, all are good except the hash browns, which are too soft and somewhat soggy, as though they've been heated and re-heated endlessly. For lunch and dinner, the sandwich wraps are as good a choice as any—try the chicken wrap with couscous. Or try nothing at all.

Chestnut Fine Foods

6.5
10

A cutesy, relaxing breakfast-and-lunch spot with "gourmet food" that's starting to feel dated

Light American, Baked goods   **$12**   *East Rock/Grad Ghetto*

5.6/10
Food

8.0/10
Atmosphere

7.0/10
Attitude

6.9/10
Value

Counter service	1012 State St.	***Bar*** None
Mon.-Fri. 9am-7pm; Sat. 9am-4pm;	New Haven	***Credit Cards*** Visa, MC, AmEx
closed Sun.	(203) 782-6767	***Reservations*** Not accepted
Breakfast. Vegetarian-friendly.	www.chestnutfinefoods.com	

Chestnut Fine Foods and Confections has been well known to New Haven for almost two decades. For most of that time, the popular gourmet bread, cheese, and prepared-food shop was in the Wooster Square neighborhood. Its new locale, a 19th-century building up State Street, is certainly cute. Some might say it's a bit precious, with low-hanging feathered lamps, pale pink walls, and other aunt's-house frills. But we like it; the atmosphere at Chestnut is truly refreshing, in a timeless way—like a whimsical tea room. Perhaps unsurprisingly, the clientele seems skewed toward cool, calm, and collected middle-aged women.

Given the vibe, one might expect the service here to be extraordinary. In reality, the staff seems polite but not effusive; a chatty "what do you recommend," for instance, might be met with nothing but a shrug. (That's where *The Menu* comes in.) The superb artisanal bread, which can be bought by the loaf, is easily the best thing at Chestnut; second place goes to the cheese selection. Perhaps surprisingly, sandwiches can be boring. One recent version, with goat cheese, bottled or canned artichoke hearts, and "sun-dried tomato pesto," was like a roll call of yuppie-food-magazine trends that went out of style in the 1990s. Salads, meanwhile, are pre-made and put into plastic—not our favorite practice—and at a recent visit, the salmon chowder turned out to be a clear broth that tasted of fishy water, waxy potatoes, and little else—like an insipid Eating Well recipe.

There's a catering operation, too. "Dated gourmet" might be the best way to put it all. Still, ingredients are prime, it's vegetarian-friendly, and clearly, a lot of love goes into the preparations here. Even if the food style is not really to our taste, we still love the space—and oh, that bread.

Chick's

A classic seafood shack for lobster rolls and fried clams across from the beach—or on the beach

Seafood $**11**   *West Haven*

6.3 /10   **7.0** /10   **6.0** /10   **7.1** /10
Food   *Atmosphere*   *Attitude*   *Value*

Counter service   183 Beach St.   *Bar* None
Daily 11am-9:45pm.   West Haven   *Credit Cards* None
Date-friendly. Outdoor dining.   (203) 934-4510   *Reservations* Not accepted

It just wouldn't be New England without the clams. They're certainly at home steamed, in chowder, or on a pizza (just ask Frank Pepe), but old-school New Englanders love them fried most of all. And Chick's is just the place for that preparation: it's a timeless Shoreline seafood shack with a beach right across the street.

Chick's is strictly downmarket—it looks like the sign has been there for ages, and the whole place has a sort of run-down-beach-town feel, like the place you might have gone as a little kid for fried clams after a day on the sand along Boston's South Shore.

Aside from those immortal fried clams, Chick's dishes out hot Connecticut-style lobster rolls, New England clam chowder (the creamy kind), and soft-shell crabs when in season. Although the lobster rolls are decent (the meat is a bit more shredded than we prefer), it's the fried seafood that really excels at Chick's. It might not be the best in the area—it can be greasy at times—but the preparations are eminently typical, deeply in touch with regional tradition.

The service is at the counter only; you can sit at any of the informal tables inside, or, in good weather, outside, across from the water. Although the amply outfitted parking lot (they don't call it "drive inn" for nothing) figures prominently into the view from Chick's proper, it's just as easy to take your paper boxes and bags across the street and enjoy their spoils while actually sitting on the beach. Still, some people do the truly old-school thing and eat the clams and fries in their car. A convertible, of course, is best.

Chili's

4.8
/10

Unselfconsciously mediocre suburban-chain antics—
better after a few margaritas

Bar food, Tex-Mex $23   *Hamden*

3.9/10   **6.0**/10   **7.0**/10   **4.0**/10
Food   *Atmosphere*   *Attitude*   *Value*

Casual restaurant   2100 Dixwell Ave.   *Bar* Full
Sun.-Thurs. 11am-11pm;   Hamden   *Credit Cards* Visa, MC, AmEx
Fri.-Sat. 11am-midnight.   (203) 248-2283   *Reservations* Not accepted
                             www.chilis.com

This Mexican chain is an American suburban "casual dining" mainstay
with one branch up Dixwell Avenue in Hamden and another just off
Route 95 in East Haven. Populated in equal numbers by families and
frat boys, Chili's has certainly hit on a successful formula. The main
reason it works is its Disneyesque version of Tex-Mex iconography. The
fact that Chili's is packed during peak dinner hours, especially on
weekends, adds to the atmospheric effect and makes it a fun place in
which to hang out. Margaritas might not be as stiff as you'd hoped,
but they're easy to drink and they're requisite.

   The food is actually not as bad as some people say it is—try not to
be too put off by the glossy, mass-produced menus or dishes with
intentionally cute titles. But you do have to be careful what you order.
Stick to things that are either fried or slathered in sauce or cheese. The
surfeit of flavor compensates for bland and overcooked primary
ingredients. Grilled baby back ribs with barbecue sauce, though
expensive, are a good example of this rule—they might not be subtle or
down-home authentic, but who would come to Chili's expecting
authenticity?

   Avoid the steaks and fajitas, where beef and chicken are liable to be
overcooked and dry. Burgers, including the chipotle blue cheese bacon
burger, are fine. Aside from the fajitas, chicken might actually be the
best category, particularly the boneless buffalo wings and
"southwestern egg rolls," which are flour tortillas wrapped around
smoked chicken, black beans, corn and jalapeño jack cheese with red
peppers, spinach, and an avocado-ranch dipping sauce. Avoid fish at all
costs. Appetizers are generally better than main courses, but that's
almost needless to say; at Chili's, you know what you're going to get,
and you get what you come for: typical suburban-chain fun.

China Great Wall

7.7
10

A little Chinese gem in the back of the Hong Kong Grocery, with authentic food at bargain prices

Chinese   **$ 5**   *Arts District*

8.0/10   **7.0**/10   **9.8**/10
Food   *Attitude*   *Value*

Take-out   67 Whitney Ave.   *Bar* None
Mon.-Wed. 10:30am-10pm; Thurs.   New Haven   *Credit Cards* Visa and MC
10:30am-10:30pm; Fri. 10am-10pm;   (203) 777-8886   *Reservations* Not accepted
Sat.-Sun. 10am-9:30pm. *Vegetarian-friendly.*

This tiny pearl of a Chinese joint is hidden in a back room in the deepest reaches of the Hong Kong Grocery, an overwhelmingly aromatic Asian market on Whitney Avenue. China Great Wall is different from, and we think often better than, any other Chinese food in town. There are good noodle soups, weekend roast duck, and an assortment of the expected Chinese-American classics; but the crowning achievement here is the daily lunch and dinner buffet, a steaming assortment of authentic, regional Chinese dishes that make no concessions to American tastes. Your five-dollar portion includes rice plus three or four items from the uniformly excellent spread, to be scooped, with savory juices, into a Styrofoam box that will end up so full that it has to be coaxed shut with a rubber band.

Particularly notable, when available, are squid with peppers, spicy tofu, shredded pork, glistening Chinese greens, sweet string beans, anything curried, and any one of the buttery mystery meats that often make their way into a dish. Don't try to bridge the considerable language gap; just point. Great hot-and-sour soup can be added for a few cents more. With soup, the buffet lunch or dinner is more than enough for two, and at $2.50 each, it's the best deal in New Haven, anywhere, anytime.

Aside from David Grewal, the clientele is largely Chinese, which speaks volumes for the quality and authenticity here. The atmosphere is almost a joke: Formica chairs and tables and a big mural of—what else—the Great Wall. Take-out is thus a good option. As far as buffet freshness is concerned, the earlier, the better. 5:30pm or 6pm is prime time. When available, bags of six hot steamed sticky buns to go, filled with succulent pork or red beans, are impossibly cheap.

China King

2.9
/10

Predictably bad Chinese-American take-out with a
prime location but little else to recommend it

Chinese   **$ 8**   *Theater District*

3.4 /10   **2.0** /10   **3.9** /10
Food   *Attitude*   *Value*

Take-out   942 Chapel St.   ***Bar*** None
Mon.-Thurs. 11am-11pm; Fri.-Sat.   New Haven   ***Credit Cards*** Visa and MC
11am-midnight; Sun. 11am-11pm.   (203) 776-8807   ***Reservations*** Not accepted
Delivery.

It's hard to write about little Chinese take-out spots like China King. On
the one hand, you understand the value proposition—more food than
two people could possibly eat for somewhere between four dollars (at
lunch) and six or seven dollars (at dinner). There are a couple of tables,
but most customers take out. China King is right on the Green, and it
fills you up cheaply and satisfyingly if you're starving at an off hour.

   The even more frustrating thing is that there is clearly some skill and
talent in the kitchen, and yet it goes to waste on these Szechuan-
American brown-sauce preparations. We once watched the cook, in a
virtuoso performance, carefully scramble an egg inside the bowl of his
large metal spoon before dropping it into a peppery hot and sour soup,
which turned out pretty well. But another time, when we asked for a
recommendation and were told by the cashier that General Tso's
chicken was the best choice on the menu, we had to wonder whether
he just took us for Americans without taste buds. The thick, syrupy
brown sauce, which is too sweet, also saps any crunch from the pieces
of curiously spongy deep-fried chicken. It's a heavy and cloying dish.
Fried rice is well seasoned and properly textured, if unexciting, while an
egg roll is properly crispy, but its filling, which features those little red
bits of pork similar to the ones in the fried rice, is bland and
disappointing.

   And while you'd expect friendly service at this type of place, China
King fails to deliver. For example: it's a bit annoying to charge a fee for
credit-card use on purchases under $10, but it's downright sleazy to do
so without verbally warning unsuspecting customers.

   People once craved the sort of Chinese-American glop that
proliferated at these sorts of joints throughout the 20th century. But the
American palate has turned a corner, and places like China King must
now consider that they could be so much more than what they are.

China Pavilion

6.3
10

Fairly typical suburban Chinese food, but with a devoted following and endless Peking-duck fun

Chinese   **$21** *Orange*

6.1/10   **6.5**/10   **7.0**/10   **5.8**/10
Food   *Atmosphere*   *Attitude*   *Value*

Upmarket restaurant	Hitchcock Plaza,	*Bar* Full
Mon.-Sat. 11:30am-11pm;	185 Boston Post Rd.,	*Credit Cards* Visa, MC, AmEx
Sun. 12:30pm-10pm.	Orange	*Reservations* Accepted
	(203) 795-3555	
	www.chinapavilion.net	

We're not sure why this place gets so many awards. China Pavilion is little more than a welcoming suburban restaurant with some curious quirks. The décor is pink, pink, pink, while the service is friendly but sometimes scarce, especially considering the number of people working here. But most distinctive are the signature drinks and their intriguing descriptions. These fruity, punchy concoctions are fairly guaranteed to pack a wallop. Nor are they short on drama and ingenuity; a cocktail for two arrives in a large bowl adorned with ceramic figures of topless hula dancers, with a blue flame flickering in the middle of it all. The "special straws" might transport you directly back to childhood.

The menu offers a recitation of Chinese restaurant standards. Vegetable dumplings have soft skin; they're doughy with bland filling, not much different from their equivalent at your basic corner Chinese restaurant, although the sauce with scallion and chili is a notch above the norm.

We suggest that you go for the Peking duck, which is carved tableside with a flourish. Its skin is crisp, the meat is succulent. At our last visit, however, our expert carver disappeared and we waited many minutes while the glistening meat sat just a foot away, cooling. Another complaint: the moo shu-style pancakes are bland and starchy. The menu offers a one-course and a two-course version of the Peking duck; for the second course, if requested, they stir-fry the rest of the duck with celery in a basic Szechuan preparation, which is nothing to write home about. Still, the duck meat, as in the first course, is tender, and the dish has a nice sweetness. While China Pavilion may not be worth the trip to Orange, it's not a bad stop if you happen to be in the area.

Christopher Martin's

8.0
/10

A big screen, a local vibe, and the best bar food in town, plus an upscale Italian restaurant next door

Bar food   **$17** *East Rock/Grad Ghetto*

7.6/10   **8.5**/10   **9.0**/10   **8.3**/10
Food   *Atmosphere*   *Attitude*   *Value*

Bar and grill
Bar, Sun.-Thurs. 11:30pm-1am; Fri.-Sat. 11:30am-2am. Bar food menu ends at midnight. Dining room, Mon.-Thurs. 11:30am-2pm, 5pm-10pm; Fri. 11:30am-2pm, 5pm-10:30pm; Sat. 5pm-10:30pm; Sun. 5pm-9pm.

860 State St.
New Haven
(203) 776-8835

Bar Full
Credit Cards Visa, MC, AmEx
Reservations Accepted

This is a strange wedding of the classic big-screen TV sports bar serving hot food and an adjacent upmarket Italian restaurant that has an ambitious menu whose mains go as high as $25.

The restaurant side of things attracts fewer customers. Not that there's anything wrong with it; they feature Connecticut-made "Black Ledge" blue cheese, and they do a nice job with a fusion version of BBQ short ribs (with a butternut squash risotto), but we're not sure if the atmosphere there justifies the prices.

For us, though, the bar is where it's at. Christopher Martin's vies with TK's as the best place in town to watch the Pats win the Super Bowl, or to watch the Yankees' lose even with a $200 million lineup. You'll always be joined by a lively local crowd, gregarious but rarely raucous. This is the sort of place in which a hamburger should be savored for the wonder that it is.

To our delight, the food is as good as you can get in town for bar fare, and you can get it until midnight. Burgers are tender, made with high-quality beef, filled with fresh cheese, lettuce, and tomato, and the right mix of condiments. Curly fries are crispy and tangy. Buffalo wings are just as they should be—spicy, flavor-forward, meaty, and served with plenty of blue cheese. They're some of the best wings around, surpassing the less-modestly-marketed Archie Moore's for buffalo-wing supremacy in the New Haven area. Even the grilled chicken sandwich, too often a bland choice, is a winner here. The draft beer is also just so, a tour of America's best smaller mass-market breweries: Sam Adams, Sierra Nevada, and the like. Christopher Martin's is enough to make you stop and appreciate one of the proudest culinary traditions in America: bar food done right.

Chuck's Steak House

<u>7.2</u>
10

A time-frozen 1970s chain steakhouse with bargain-priced meals and correct creamed spinach

Steakhouse, Traditional American   **$22**   *West Haven*

7.2/10
Food

7.0/10
Atmosphere

8.0/10
Attitude

6.9/10
Value

Upmarket restaurant
Sun.-Mon. and Wed.-Thurs. 5pm-
9pm; Fri.-Sat. 5pm-10pm;
closed Tues.

1003 Orange Ave.
West Haven
(203) 934-5300
www.chuckssteakhouse.com

Bar Full
Credit Cards Visa, MC, AmEx
Reservations Accepted

This blast from the past is now part of a big chain of steakhouses. However, the West Haven branch was the first on the East Coast and one of the first of all, so we feel comfortable including it in *The Menu*, if not for its meticulous time-frozen 1970s feel then for its miraculous 18-dollar prix fixe that includes an all-you-can-eat salad bar, a steak (or other main), a side dish of potatoes, a dessert, and even coffee. There's a clubby bar that's straight out of the past, and there are a few different rooms that are intermittently inhabited by local families, West Haven boys' nights out, and older boys ready to finish with a cigar.

All-you-can-eat salad bars are not our favorite thing in the world, but this one's fun: you can make your own iceberg wedge salad, with a creamy if mild blue cheese dressing, and bacon bits that are actually chopped up pieces of bacon—not those disgusting little brown things that look like grape nuts and pass for bacon bits at a less worthy salad bar. Next, to our delight and surprise, a sirloin steak ordered black and blue came exactly that way—extremely rare. The steaks taste good and beefy, with a satisfying texture.

Eva, Atticus Bookstore's legendary book buyer—and one of New Haven's great creamed-spinach aficionados—clued us in not just to Chuck's Steak House itself, but to the creamed spinach there. Creamed spinach can so often go awry, with watery leaves that don't bind to the béchamel, or clumpy stuff that tastes industrial; but Chuck's version is exactly as it should be. The wine selection is not much, with nothing above cheap California cabs. But what do you expect? This is, after all, a suburban chain steakhouse. And it's a great one.

Citrus

7.3
10

A bizarrely designed restaurant with interesting
food but little to recommend it at this price range

New American   **$39** *Milford*

7.3 /10   **7.0**/10   **8.0**/10   **6.1**/10
Food   *Atmosphere*   *Attitude*   *Value*

Upmarket restaurant   56 S. Broad St.   *Bar* Full
Sun.-Thurs. 4pm-9pm; Fri.-Sat. Milford   *Credit Cards* Visa, MC, AmEx
4pm-10pm.   (203) 877-1138   *Reservations* Accepted
Outdoor dining.   www.citrus-ct.com

This has to be one of the strangest examples of restaurant design we've
ever seen. Some of the design concepts are welcome—the variation
between rooms, the architectural twists and turns. But some are just
plain weird, like the ceiling, which looks like congealed gobs of black
goo. It makes you wonder if the otherworldly substance will drip down
onto your plate, or if Sigourney Weaver is hiding around the corner.

There's outdoor dining, too, but it's like a Home Depot garden, and
the indoor window seats look out onto little more than cars zooming
by. Even the parking lot is strange: have you ever seen a restaurant with
main courses in the $30s that sternly declares a two-hour parking limit?
What is this, Walgreens?

The food is fine, more or less what you'd expect from a New
American place with high-end pretensions. Fried calamari are tender,
but not crispy enough; they come with cucumber and Bermuda onion
(a good choice), and they're tossed with lemon vinaigrette and drizzled
with chipotle aioli. The dish is satisfying but not exciting—crowd-
pleasing fusion. Spring rolls are more inspired, well executed if not
subtle, with wasabi that cuts the fried flavor.

A sweet chili-glazed shrimp cocktail comes with a segmented
orange and cucumber salad that adds a welcome note of diversity and
makes reference, perhaps, to the restaurant's name (though there
seems to be no generalized citrus theme). In the end, Citrus
underperforms within its genre and price range; and nowhere is this
more evident than in the wine list, which reads like a catalog of
advertisements in Wine Spectator. Foreign wines like Châteauneuf-du-
Pape and Chianti are better values, but however you figure it, your tab
at the end of the night is going to be fairly steep.

We're up to date...

...r u?

Come to *The Menu*'s redesigned New Haven dining website for **free book updates**, longer-format **feature reviews**, and a **relentlessly opinionated discussion board,** where you can discuss and debate our reviews...or **write your own.**

www.
newhavenmenu.
com

Claire's Corner Copia

5.2
10

A late-1970s vegetarian restaurant that dabbles in many ethnic cuisines, but succeeds only with cake

Light American $15   *Theater District*

3.1 /10   **8.5** /10   **8.0** /10   **4.9** /10
Food   *Atmosphere*   *Attitude*   *Value*

Casual restaurant   1000 Chapel St.   *Bar* None
Sun.-Thurs. 8am-9pm;   New Haven   *Credit Cards* Visa, MC, AmEx
Fri-Sat. 8am-10pm.   (203) 562-3888   *Reservations* Not accepted
Breakfast. Vegetarian-friendly.   www.clairescornercopia.com

Wonderful vegetarian dishes are found as natural subsets of indigenous culinary traditions all over the world. But the bland fare that proliferated as a result of the 1970s and '80s development of "Vegetarian Food" as a distinct culinary category, emphasizing haphazard fusion and soy-based imitations, was a misstep in the history of American cooking and a disservice to vegetarians everywhere. Claire's, one of the first of its kind in America, is a cutting-edge vegetarian restaurant, circa 1977, dabbling in American, Italian, French, Mexican, Middle Eastern, and Eastern European food all on one menu. Many concoctions are slathered with cheese and oil, stripping away even the purported health value of vegetarian food.

The best thing here is a rich, buttery, sour-cream-based Lithuanian coffee cake that gets a lot of attention; we understand its popularity. But many other offerings range from bland to an ill-inspired pan-ethnic mess. Burritos pay little homage to any Mexican tradition, with a shocking proliferation of boring, underseasoned beans. Quiches are often flavorless, as is a Japanese stir fry, with big chunks of tough broccoli stalk and implausibly enormous, woody carrot pieces.

And yet Claire's continues to draw in a reliable quorum of customers. It is one of the only kosher places around (although it's open on Saturdays), and we do understand the attractively bustling, airy college-town vibe. But perhaps Claire's success really comes from the enviable location on one of downtown's most convenient corners, or from the consistently glowing press and restaurant reviews, even from major New England regional travel guides.

We respectfully dissent. Vegetarians no longer have to compromise by eating this kind of food. New Haven dining is now a cornucopia of tasty vegetarian options, from Book Trader to Bentara, that together make Claire's seem like even more of a dinosaur.

Clark's Dairy

6.3
10

A time-frozen treasure of a local diner, even if it's a muted version

Short-order American   **$10**   *Arts District*

5.7 /10   **7.0** /10   **8.0** /10   **6.9** /10
Food   *Atmosphere*   *Attitude*   *Value*

Diner   74 Whitney Ave.   *Bar* None
Mon.-Sat. 7am-10pm;   New Haven   *Credit Cards* None
Sun. 9am-10pm. *Breakfast.* (203) 777-2728   *Reservations* Not accepted

The diner is one of our national treasures, a dying artifact that's rarely found in city centers anymore. Clark's Dairy has been around for a long while. It's family-run, it's filled with regulars, and with its 1950s appliances, menu of old standards, and warm, fuzzy service, the place is a nod to that tradition—but it's the white-bread version, without as much character as the great diner, and chances are it will leave you still thirsting for something more nostalgic or tasty. With a central kitchen-island and lunch counter, Clark's feels half diner, half Friendly's. But sit at the counter and your experience will be largely diner; you'll also be closer to the staff, who are kind and welcoming in a "What'll it be, hon?" kind of way.

The fare is comfort food, delivered quickly. Grilled cheese is always the right thing to order (anytime, anywhere). Square-cut fries are appropriately crispy. Try the cheeseburger deluxe, relentlessly traditional, with bacon, lettuce, and tomato, served with french fries and cole slaw. The tuna melt gets high marks. Milkshakes, malted if you please, are top-notch. Not so for the chicken Caesar salad, a sad, greasy mess. Ice cream sundaes, though, are sublime, and will make even the most grown-up adult feel eight years old (yum, with a cherry on top).

Adjacent to the Dairy is Clark's Restaurant (or "Clarks' Restaurant," as the sign says), an emptier, vaguely more elaborate room under the same ownership but with its own kitchen. This Clark's serves a similar menu, but adds pizza, subs, and old-school dinners like meatloaf and mashed potatoes. We're not sure what the deal is with that place. By all means stick to the Clark's Dairy room—after all, you're here for the chrome-and-Formica diner aesthetic, right?

Cody's Diner

4.6
10

A 24/7 spot for great, edgy local atmosphere and respectable diner food

Short-order American | **$10** | *Wooster Square Area*

4.4/10
Food

5.0/10
Atmosphere

5.0/10
Attitude

4.7/10
Value

Diner
Daily 24 hrs.
Breakfast.

95 Water St.
New Haven
(203) 562-0044
www.codysdiner.com

Bar None
Credit Cards Visa, MC, AmEx
Reservations Not accepted

Given that it's one of the only 24-hour food options in the whole city, it's surprising that Cody's diner is still so little known among the downtown crowd. The main reason is its location. Buried across from a highway overpass on Water Street, Cody's is actually not far from Wooster Square, but you'll need a car to get there from most of the city. This is definitely a forgotten corner of New Haven. Maybe another reason for this diner's relative obscurity is the fact that it's a big late-night hangout for cops—what, are the Yalies afraid of being arrested for staying up too late?

We like this place. It's got a great local atmosphere and respectable, if a bit greasy, diner food. That's exactly what you want at 4am. Prices are reasonable, and the service is vintage diner. It's hard to go wrong with Cody's big breakfast, which arrives on two plates: three pancakes, two eggs, sausage, bacon, and toast. But a bacon cheeseburger with onions is also fine, as is the grilled cheese, and the obligatory milkshake is appropriately thick and sweet. And beware: the grab machine game by the entrance sits there, taunting you, until you put in your quarter. The robotic arm comes across, comes down, dips its metallic paws into a bucketful of ratty little stuffed animals that have been there for years (since no one has ever won), and comes up clutching nothing but air. It's a hallowed ritual. You must lose a quarter before you leave. Don't try to fight it.

Cold Stone Creamery

6.3
10

A popular chain ice cream shop that seems to have trademarked anything and everything

Sweets   *Theater District*

5.4 /10   **8.0** /10
Food   *Attitude*

Take-out   163 Temple St.   *Bar* None
Sun.-Thurs. 11am-11pm; New Haven   *Credit Cards* Visa, MC, AmEx
Fri.-Sat. 11am-midnight. (203) 785-1555   *Reservations* Not accepted
Vegetarian-friendly. www.coldstonecreamery.com

2004 was the year of ice cream franchise stores in downtown New Haven, and Cold Stone came in as the big daddy of the genre, scooping disturbingly large quantities of industrial-style ice cream into oversized waffle cones, along with a good dose of dramatic action from the staff. Expect ensemble singing upon certain cues, and melodious thank-yous of variable enthusiasm, depending on their mood. There's also a good deal of action behind the counter for those who decide on a custom ice cream "mix-in" made with a choice of ingredients including fruit, nuts, candy pieces and crushed cookies. Your choice of ice cream is then slathered flat on a cold, granite stone (hence the name); these ingredients are incorporated in a process that, to us, is curiously reminiscent of the signature smoosh-ins at the legendary Herrell's ice cream shops in Massachusetts. Coincidence?

Whatever the process, though, the ice cream is woefully deficient compared with Herrell's—or even compared with Ashley's a few blocks away. It's bland, it's mass-produced, it's…just plain boring. But they do seem to have good lawyers: "Apple Pie à la Cold Stone," like most "Cold Stone Originals," is studded with a Federal trademark registration notice; it's sweet cream ice cream—a sweet and otherwise benign flavor—combined with Graham cracker pie crust, cinnamon, caramel, and apple pie filling. Most of these Originals (inexplicably, another trademarked term) have at least four ingredients in them.

If you think you've come across a Cold Stone elsewhere, chances are you're right. This hyper-corporate franchise is opening stores across the country; their Pyramid of Success indicates that they intend to be the number one U.S. ice cream franchise by 2009. Judging by the constant throngs in the New Haven branch, the formula is working well so far. For them, that is—less so for us.

Colonial Tymes

4.5/10

A suburban restaurant whose careful New England décor is overshadowed by terrible, overpriced food

Traditional American　　　$**32**　　*Hamden*

2.2/10
Food

8.0/10
Atmosphere

8.0/10
Attitude

2.4/10
Value

Upmarket restaurant
Tues.-Thurs. 11:30am-3:30pm,
5pm-10pm; Fri.-Sat. 11:30am-
3:30pm, 5pm-11pm; Sun. 11:30am-
2:30pm (brunch), 4pm-9pm (dinner).
Closed Mon. *Brunch. Outdoor dining.*

2389 Dixwell Ave.
Hamden
(203) 230-2301
www.colonialtymesrestaurant.com

Bar Full
Credit Cards Visa, MC, AmEx
Reservations Accepted

Colonial Tymes is situated in a real 19th-century house that was hauled over from elsewhere and plopped down along a stretch of Hamden strip mall. We'll start with the good points: a gracious outdoor patio and a well-executed old-New England theme, with impressive 18th-century wide-boarded hardwood floors restored to high sheen. There's a pleasant mix of old lanterns, and there's even a man-sized hearth in which a real fire burns for much of the winter.

Our last meal started at the bar, where we were curious and amused by a cocktail called "Fall Foliage." We asked the bartender: "Is it good?"

"No," he said. "When you mix half-and-half and sour mix, the half-and-half curdles pretty much immediately," he explained. We thanked him for his candor.

It's one thing to serve bad drinks, but to knowingly do so? What's worse, this seems a longstanding habit here: a while back, the restaurant even displayed a self-righteous sign declaring that, in political protest, no French wine would be served at the restaurant. Talk about shooting yourself in the foot.

The famous Colonial Tymes brunch begins with soggy croissants, bready little bagels, and a "smoked salmon mirror" layered with stringy fish that reminds us of our college cafeterias on Sundays. Among mains, crab cakes are soft, homogenous, doughy lumps with little to cut the richness of bread crumbs and butter, and the seafood stuffing in baked stuffed shrimp is a mushy, buttery mess. Side dishes might include insipid cauliflower and broccoli leeched of all flavor by aggressive overcooking, as if designed exclusively for ingestion by toothless inpatients of some institution. Yet the prices for main courses at Colonial Tymes move well into the mid-$20s. It boggles the mind to think that anyone would spend that kind of money on this kind of food.

Consiglio's

A high-priced Wooster Street legend with fairly standard Italian-American food in huge portions

Italian   **$41** *Wooster Square Area*

7.1 /10   **7.5** /10   **9.0** /10   **6.1** /10
Food   *Atmosphere*   *Attitude*   *Value*

Upmarket restaurant   165 Wooster St.   *Bar* Full
Mon. 4:30pm-9pm; Tues.-Thurs. New Haven   *Credit Cards* Visa, MC, AmEx
11:30am-2:30pm, 4:30pm-9pm; Fri. (203) 865-4489   *Reservations* Essential
11:30am-2:30pm, 4:30pm-10pm;   www.consiglios.com
Sat. 4:30pm-10pm; Sun. 2pm-9pm.
Date-friendly. Good wine list. Outdoor dining.

The legendary Consiglio's has long vied for supremacy with its Wooster Street rival, Tre Scalini, in the league of high-end New Haven Italian-American restaurants. A perennial favorite, Consiglio's gets consistently rave reviews from the local and regional press and other polls. It's a New Haven restaurant with a history going back to 1938. And it's a food destination that has pleased local families for generations. Fond memories of celebrations have made space for Consiglio's in many hearts. This is an enduring icon, a footnote in the history of American restaurants.

Irreproachability and popular belief aside, though, we humbly submit that New Haven is not a great town for Italian food other than pizza. While the legendary pizzerias have endured, the downward momentum at elegant Italian restaurants is palpable. Here, you get well-executed versions of suburban Italian-American food that do their best to mix in expensive-sounding ingredients. For example, veal might be sautéed with shiitake mushrooms, shrimp, and broccoli in a lobster champagne sauce. An unimpressive braciola, meanwhile, is tough and chewy.

While we cannot deny the sentimental appeal, the dining experience at Consiglio's is at best uninspiring, and at worst disappointing—especially when you're paying $27 for a main course. For this much money elsewhere, you could get true culinary excellence. Granted, the portions are enormous—enough to take home the leftovers and feed yourself for the next day—but the problem is, not everyone wants to do that.

And the atmosphere at Consiglio's is just as predictable as the menu, with overdressed tables, although the considerable crowd adds ambience. The place enjoys neither the old-school Italian kitsch value of a Tony & Lucille's nor the regional menu of a L'Orcio. Here's hoping for more creative or authentic regional Italian food in New Haven.

Contois Tavern

6.2
10

A simple old bar that serves up burgers, dogs, and
pepperoni soup to an extremely local crowd

Short-order American $ 6   East Rock/Grad Ghetto

5.9 /10   **7.0** /10   **6.0** /10   **7.6** /10
Food   *Atmosphere*   *Attitude*   *Value*

Bar and grill	Corner of Nicoll St.	*Bar* Full
Food daily 11am-2pm,	and Eagle St.,	*Credit Cards* None
sometimes until 3pm or 3:30pm.	New Haven	*Reservations* Not accepted
Bar open later.	No phone	

This is a practically unknown, no-frills bar with a lunch counter that
happens to serve some of the best burgers in town. Just off State
Street, Contois is an unapologetic local. It should be; it's been in New
Haven since 1934. But this old pub is not about hype. In a squat,
square, brick building on a residential block, Contois hides beneath
almost imperceptible dark wood signage over the door. It's
quintessentially an old-man bar, and that's what the staff is used to.

Don't look here for a swinging scene, late-night hours, or witty
post-modernisms. Don't look, in fact, for anyone that's not a 40-to-70-
year-old male slugging a bottle of Bud Light or Michelob—or an
Advocate editor. But for a quiet beer and conversation; for some great,
basic, and inexpensive lunchtime dining; or to observe a true slice of
old New Haven life, this is the spot.

Knowing that anyone who sits for long enough on a bar stool will
eventually become hungry, Contois has the good sense to serve food.
The schedule is as erratic as the menu; generally, food is available at
lunchtime until 2pm, but occasionally they're still serving at 3:30,
depending on the traffic. Hot dogs are always available, but roast beef
sandwiches usually appear later in the week. Pepperoni soup has a
particular following. Burgers on paper plates, as classic as the bar itself,
are available daily as long as the grill is on. On request, they come with
blackened onions and tomato. They're big and tasty, if browned a bit
much. The cheese is particularly good, with a memorable texture.

This is not nouvelle cuisine, nor should it be. Just stop by, pull up a
stool, and enjoy a taste of living history.

Copper Kitchen

6.0
/10

A storybook greasy-spoon diner, right downtown

Short-order American $**11**   *Theater District*

5.6 /10   **6.5** /10   **7.0** /10   **6.4** /10
Food   *Atmosphere*   *Attitude*   *Value*

Diner   1008 Chapel St.   *Bar* None
Mon.-Sat. 6am-6pm;   New Haven   *Credit Cards* None
Sun. 8am-4pm. *Breakfast.* (203) 777-8010   *Reservations* Not accepted

One of New Haven's only true downtown diners, Copper Kitchen, with its mid-century appliances, milkshake blenders, soda fountains, and coffee pitchers, is almost too typical, reducing visiting foreigners to giddy giggles. They can now die happy, having just seen a carbon copy of the diner set from whichever American TV show was dubbed into their language growing up. The evidence is in the postcards from loyal customers around the world tacked up by the register.

It's not bad food, either. They serve straightforward omelettes, with friendly service and a bottomless cup of coffee, and they're not particularly trying to pull anything off. Breakfast is definitely the way to go—and unlike certain places up State Street, you won't have to wait in line or deal with opening-hours hijinks. The weekday breakfast is an especially good deal for those up and about before 11am. Just don't ask for anything elaborate—all the tea here is Lipton's, and it's all caffeinated.

Copper Kitchen is not great for groups, since most tables seat four at most. But anyway, counter service is the most fun for your buck. Order eggs, order fried, order traditional. Order the bacon, egg, and cheese sandwich, one of America's greatest culinary achievements. Watch it be prepared, and revel in it. When you are telling your grandkids about the way things used to be, Copper Kitchen may just be what comes to mind.

Corner Deli

4.2
/10

Below-average Chinese, about-average short-order grill food, and a strange grocery-store vibe

Light American, Chinese   **$ 6**   *Financial District*

4.0 /10   **4.0** /10   **6.0** /10   **4.7** /10
Food   *Atmosphere*   *Attitude*   *Value*

Counter service
Mon.-Fri. 7am-8:30pm;
Sat. 7:30am-5:30pm; closed Sun.
Breakfast. Delivery.

181 Orange St.
New Haven
(203) 772-1611

Bar None
Credit Cards Visa, MC, AmEx
Reservations Not accepted

Corner Deli probably has the least attractive signage among all the Financial District lunch spots in downtown New Haven—and also, arguably, the least attractive interior. The place feels like a glorified grocery store, filled with soft-drink fridges, some fairly grungy tables and chairs, a few assorted retail items for sale, and a big central Chinese buffet with piles of Styrofoam and plastic containers in which to scoop its contents (sold by the pound).

It's certainly a jarring juxtaposition—not just the Chinese buffet, but also a full Chinese-American menu, along with the standard short-order grill fare (the egg sandwiches, the burgers, the deli offerings, and so on). It's not so often, after all, that eggplant parmigiana, beef curry, strawberry pancakes, a liverwurst sandwich, a bagel with cream cheese, and General Tso's chicken all share the space on one little folded paper menu. Welcome to America.

The problem is, the Chinese food at Corner Deli is awful. It's all lukewarm, the fried items are soggy and limp, the sweet sauce on the tough spare ribs tastes like cherry cough syrup, and so on. The only tasty thing we've tried from the buffet was a sort of Chinese meatloaf drowned in gummy gravy. Still, you're much better off ordering something more American, like a well-executed steak-and-cheese sandwich, whose hard roll is good, pliable, and fresh, and whose tender steak is shredded into small pieces that absorb melted cheese into their many nooks and crannies.

Maybe the lack of focus is the whole point here. For instance, if you need a cosmetic break between your first course of steamed dumplings and your second course of a tuna melt, then Corner Deli will even sell you a hairbrush. Now that's full service.

Daiko (Jerry-San's)

7.9
10

Some of the freshest sushi around in a cute little spot out near the Yale Bowl

Japanese $ **22**   *West Haven*

8.0 /10   **7.5** /10   **8.0** /10   **7.7** /10
Food   *Atmosphere*   *Attitude*   *Value*

Casual restaurant   400 Derby Ave. (Rt. 34)   *Bar* Full
Mon.-Thurs. 11:30am-3pm,   West Haven   *Credit Cards* Visa, MC, AmEx
5pm-10pm; Fri.-Sat. 11:30am-3pm, (203) 392-3626   *Reservations* Accepted
5pm-11pm; Sun. 4pm-10pm.

Improbably stuck on a strip-mall street near the Yale Bowl, Daiko is known among sushi lovers near and far as one of the best places in the area for fresh fish, regardless of atmosphere, remoteness, or randomness. You'll know it by the theatrical façade, incongruous among car dealerships and green plastic storefronts.

Albacore (white tuna) sashimi is exceptional; there's a great rotating selection of lesser-known fish scrawled on a blackboard; and almost everything, including the unusually wide assortment of reasonably priced nigiri sushi, is reliable. There's also a broad variety of specialty maki, including creations with soft-shell crab and a crunchy spicy tuna roll. Combinations are good, but the à la carte selection is so interesting and cheap that you might be best off ordering your choice of pieces until you're full.

Don't expect too much in the way of atmosphere, and you won't be disappointed. The small, curtained room with tables spanning its edges, surrounding a central sushi bar, can seem cozy on a good night (when you have dining companions), or uncomfortably weird on a bad one. Still, Daiko's small size keeps it from feeling too empty and suburban. Prices are reasonable, the fish is fresh, and the service is really friendly. It's definitely one of the best choices in the area for sushi.

Oh, and if it's your birthday, or if you say it is, they bang on a drum with a cat symbol on it; then they take a photo of everyone at the table. The photos, of which there are hundreds, go on the wall, where they stay for years. Happy birthday.

Darbar India

7.7
10

The best Indian food in the area is in Branford—
and great prices too

Indian $20   *Branford*

8.0/10   **7.0**/10   **8.0**/10   **7.6**/10
Food   *Atmosphere*   *Attitude*   *Value*

Upmarket restaurant   1070 Main St.   *Bar* Full
Sun.-Wed. 11:30am-3pm, 5pm-   Branford   *Credit Cards* Visa, MC, AmEx
10:30pm; Thurs.-Sat. 11:30am- (203) 481-8994   *Reservations* Accepted
3pm, 5pm-11pm.   www.darbarindia.com
Vegetarian-friendly.

Is it worth the trip out to Darbar on the Branford town green for the best Indian food in the area? Well, if you live in Branford, it's a no-brainer. But we think the effort is worth your while even if you're an Elm City denizen with a vehicle at your disposal. Perhaps unsurprisingly, Darbar is owned by the same folks as Royal India, one of downtown New Haven's best Indian choices. But the longer journey to Darbar is justified by even better food—plus a break from the city. What's more, if you're a Yalie on the run, you're far less likely to bump into that teaching assistant who thinks you're deathly ill or the ex who thinks you're questioning your sexuality.

The location is pleasant, right on the town green. The feeling is very classic suburban Indian restaurant, with bright lighting, deferential service, and zealous attention to the level of your water glass. The menu is also very standard for the genre—don't come here expecting to sample any unusual new regional dishes. But the food, which comes in little silver metal soup bowls with lids instead of the standard open platter, is simply impeccable. Indian standards are uniformly satisfying, including the shrimp tandoori masala and the mixed grill. Classics like chicken tikka masala are reliably excellent examples, and there is a great selection of vegetarian-dishes-after-saag-paneer; try the baigan bhartha, eggplant cooked with green peas, onions, and tomatoes with ginger and spices. The mango lassi is superb.

Portions are not particularly large for an Indian restaurant, which we actually find refreshing. Prices are quite reasonable from top to bottom, but the best value are the lunch specials, which hover in the six-dollar range, and a great all-you-can-eat buffet on Fridays, Saturdays, and Sundays.

Dayton Street Apizza

A little Westville gem of a pizzeria, with well-executed, sweetly thin-crusted pies, best taken out

Pizza $ **13**   *Westville*

8.1 /10
Food

6.0 /10
Attitude

8.0 /10
Value

Take-out
Sat.-Thurs. 11:30am-10pm,
Fri. 11:30am-11pm.
Delivery. Vegetarian-friendly.

60 Dayton St.
New Haven
(203) 389-2454

Bar None
Credit Cards Visa and MC
Reservations Not accepted

This is little more than a take-out spot, but one that makes extraordinarily good pizza. In fact, it's been compared to the giants of Wooster Street in the literature. We wouldn't go nearly that far, but the pizza is quite nice, while fuss and waits are completely nonexistent. The hallmark at Dayton is the thin crust, which is well textured with a gentle sweetness, although we'd prefer a couple more minutes of cooking. The sauce, too, is excellent, but unremarkable grated cheese on the basic mozzarella pie is too abundant. The overall effect is still great; it reminds us of the very best style of New York pizza, such as that served at the late and great Joe's on Carmine Street, only more liberally seasoned.

But here's the thing: even better—both in terms of texture and taste—is the more basic marinara pie that is simply sprinkled with parmesan cheese. It allows that wonderful crust to shine without all that mozzarella moisture. As for the rest of the menu, there are subs, which are well executed and quite worthwhile. There's also a range of pasta dishes, from gnocchi to spaghetti with clam sauce to lobster ravioli—the folks at Dayton Street bottle and sell their pasta sauce, in fact, which they dub "Bobo's"—but in our mind, the pasta dishes (and appetizers—fried mozzarella, calamari, and so on) are far less notable than the delicious pizza.

You won't want to spent too much time hanging out in the little room, which is lined with fake bricks and has a couple of soda machines for a centerpiece. Unfortunately, the pies here (as with most good pizza) have a short half-life; if you're traveling a fair distance with the box, keep it closed, and hurry!

Delaney's Grille

7.1
10

A Westville institution, with good feelings and
great drinks, even if the food is just okay

Bar food, Traditional American $**21**   *Westville*

6.0/10   **8.5**/10   **9.0**/10   **6.8**/10
Food   *Atmosphere*   *Attitude*   *Value*

Bar and grill	882 Whalley Ave.	*Bar* Full
Sun.-Thurs. 11:30am-12:30am;	New Haven	*Credit Cards* Visa, MC, AmEx
Fri.-Sat. 11:30am-1:30am.	(203) 397-5494	*Reservations* Accepted
Kitchen closes Sun.-Thurs. midnight;		
Fri.-Sat. 1am. *Outdoor dining.*		

Delaney's is a Westville neighborhood legend, pure and simple. No
fewer than three are the sections of Delaney's: the Pub Dining Room,
with a restored art-deco bar that pays homage to the 1939 World's
Fair; the Tap Room, which is more of a bar, with a limited late-night
menu; and the Main Dining Room, which is brighter and, in our view,
less atmospheric than the other two. Great also is the expansive
outdoor patio, which sits right on Westville's main drag.

First and foremost, the bar's the thing, from the dark wood paneling
to the darts to the clientele to the spectacular service, which really
couldn't be nicer. Delaney's list of libations is expansive beyond belief,
beginning with more than 20 single malts and no fewer than 35
vodkas, continuing with a spectacular beer list that takes you around
Europe with 51 options on tap, and finishing with cordials from
Gammal Dansk Bitters to cachaça (can you imagine drinking it
straight?!) to Baronjager Honey Liqueur. That's not to mention the
Ports, the Cognacs, and a list of 12 Bourbons, including one that's 124
proof. So many ways to get sauced!

As for food, Delaney's tends to execute competently on the basics,
beginning with the buffalo wings, which have a good balance of sauce.
Blue cheese dressing is chunky and flavorful. Onion rings are thickly
battered and pleasantly crispy, and french fries are of a specific bar-food
type—that is, fried with some seasoning beyond just the plentiful salt—
and sufficiently crispy.

A steak sandwich isn't bad—you'll want to keep eating it—but it's
also problematic: our view is that every bite that's presented between
two pieces of bread should be edible. Here, on the other hand, there
are periodic bites of gristle, interfering with the sandwich-eating
process. Still, the gorgonzola adds a welcome kick. As for the even
more ambitious main courses—seafood and the like—keep in mind that
this is just a bar.

Dolce Java

8.0
10

The newest and most relaxing of the downtown coffeeshops, with Internet access and an easy vibe

Baked goods   *Upper Chapel Area*

8.0/10
Atmosphere

8.0/10
Attitude

Café
Mon.-Sat. 7am-10pm;
Sun. 8am-8pm.
Breakfast. Vegetarian-friendly. Wireless Internet.

166 York St.
New Haven
(203) 772-4559

Bar None
Credit Cards Visa, MC, AmEx
Reservations Not accepted

Dolce Java is a new and welcome addition to the New Haven caffeine scene. This airy coffeeshop, which opened not long before we went to press, is right above Yalie's on York Street. Whether for its location slightly off the more heavily trafficked Chapel Street, or simply for its relative newness, the place is usually extremely low-key, without too much chaos or too many customers jockeying for space. It's more of a nook than a scene.

It's easy to find a seat at Dolce Java, and easy to crack open your laptop in peace. The walls are decked out with amusing coffee and tea paraphernalia. The resulting vibe is generally a lot more relaxing as a place to study than, say, the frenzied laptop-outlet wars of Starbucks.

As for the music, smooth jazz and soft pop can often feel saccharine, but here it seems somehow okay. The food at Dolce Java is nothing much—it's your basic assortment of garden-variety baked goods. However, there is delicious gelato imported from Italy in flavors like mixed berry, dulce de leche, and gianduia (chocolate-hazelnut). There's also a good selection of smoothies (many with ice cream) and a wide variety of flavor shots for the coffee.

Still, the food selection generally remains one of Dolce Java's relative weaknesses as compared to Atticus and Book Trader, the coffeeshop competition. Dolce Java answers back, however, with the advantage of wireless Internet access—a real boon these days.

Donovan's Reef

6.4
/10

A big, open American bar and grill, pure and simple

Bar food, Traditional American   **$25**   *Branford*

6.1/10
Food

7.0/10
Atmosphere

6.0/10
Attitude

5.7/10
Value

Bar and grill
Sun.-Thurs. 11:30am-1am;
Fri.-Sat. 11:30am-2am.
Kitchen closes at 10pm. *Brunch.*

1212 Main St.
Branford
(203) 488-5573
www.donovansreef.com

Bar Full
Credit Cards Visa, MC, AmEx
Reservations Accepted

Don't be deceived; this isn't a seafood specialist, it's a reference to *Donovan's Reef,* a 1963 John Wayne film, in which a bunch of ex-sailors are settled on a South Pacific island, one hot chick shows up, and all hell breaks loose. Ironically enough, on our last visit, the entire second and third floor ("the loft") of the airily terraced indoor space was filled only with women (it was a baby shower). The big, open room—the building once belonged to the Yale Lock company—has a soaring roof; it reminds us of a base lodge bar and grille at a ski resort. Live bands come and go, and the place is also quite a Branford bar scene at peak hours, when it feels more like your local watering hole than a restaurant.

Donovan's is a self-described "American grill," which should clue you in to what's on the menu: buffalo wings, steak, shrimp, ribs, chili, and so on. They're also known for the Sunday brunch, which is pretty standard but not bad. Generally, preparations are competent; scallops, for instance, are browned with a deep, dark crust, and served over an extremely lemony but good sauce. Crab cakes, too, are above average; it's not lump crabmeat, but it's decent shredded crab, not too bready but still well crisped on the outside, although the sweet salad beneath the cakes comes over-dressed.

The more unusual "surf and turf burger" is less successful: the delicate taste and texture of lobster meat, which is placed between burger and bun, is completely drowned out by stronger tastes and textures: the good but underseasoned meat, the enormous bun, the lettuce and tomato, the remoulade. In retrospect, we should have known better than to wander away from the American basics at such a deeply American place.

Dunkin' Donuts

You know the drill—thousands of locations, okay donuts, worse savory food

Baked goods, Light American   **$ 7**   *Theater District*

2.8/10   **1.0**/10   **5.0**/10   **3.5**/10
Food   *Atmosphere*   *Attitude*   *Value*

Fast-food chain   16 branches in   *Bar* None
Hours vary by location;   New Haven   *Credit Cards* None
81 Church St. branch open 24 hrs. (203) 497-9250   *Reservations* Not accepted
Breakfast. Vegetarian-friendly. *(770 Chapel St. branch)*
                                 www.dunkindonuts.com

Business still chugs along for the chain that's seen its entire livelihood threatened in the past few years by the explosion of the Krispy Kreme empire. Dunkin' Donuts' main marketing response to its chief competitor seems to have been to focus on the freshness of its coffee rather than to attempt to challenge the sublime taste and texture of a Krispy Kreme doughnut taken hot out of the oven. We think the coffee at Dunkin' Donuts is okay, better than some, worse than others. It does seem to be brewed frequently.

Before ordering food, ask yourself one question: is it a doughnut? The doughnuts themselves are fine, just what you'd expect, although we think they're baked in too-large batches, and not often enough, hurting their freshness. We favor the basic jelly-filled and glazed varieties. Crullers and crumb doughnuts have a less exciting texture, a bit too dry and cakey, and we find the cream-filled options too rich. Apart from doughnuts, pickings are slim indeed. The breakfast sandwiches, of the frozen-and-reheated-egg-from-the-plastic-wrapper variety, are boring and chewy. (At least they're better than the ones at Bruegger's.) Bagels and muffins are not much better.

But at least for now, New Haven is still Dunkin' Donuts country. Believe it or not, there are actually 16 branches in New Haven proper. It's the closest thing to a fast-food empire in town—this is truly staggering coverage, folks. There are *two* in Union Station. For better or for worse, sooner or later, you'll probably find yourself at one of these outlets, if only for a bottle of the excellent, rich Nestlé Quik chocolate milk. But unless you're desperate, get your food elsewhere.

East Buffet

6.1
10

An enormous all-you-can-eat Chinese buffet that
wows crowds with unusual dim-sum components

Chinese $16 Hamden

7.0 /10   **4.0** /10   **7.0** /10   **6.0** /10
Food   *Atmosphere*   *Attitude*   *Value*

Casual restaurant   2100 Dixwell Ave.   *Bar* Full
Mon.-Thurs. 11:30am-3pm,   Hamden   *Credit Cards* Visa, MC, AmEx
4:30pm-9:30pm; Fri.-Sun.   (203) 288-8898   *Reservations* Accepted
11:30am-3pm, 4:30pm-10:30pm.   www.eastbuffet.com
Brunch. Vegetarian-friendly.

One of New Haven's well-kept suburban secrets, East Buffet is situated
in the middle of a strip mall, wedged in between haircutting chains and
discount shoe stores. It's easy to miss, and upon walking in, you'll
probably assume it's another cavernous suburban Chinese joint, with
families wolfing down oversized plates of spare ribs, fried shrimp, and
beef with broccoli at 5:30pm.

That's only partly true. Those families and that food are there (kids
under four and a half feet eat free), but so is the local Chinese
population at this Cantonese diamond in the rough. The all-you-can-eat
buffet must be the largest in the entire region, which one wouldn't
necessarily assume to be a good thing. But it's also full of rare delights
that please both Lilliputians and Brobdingnagians. There's a wide
assortment of real Hong Kong dumpling fare, from doughy shrimp balls
to rice-noodle dumplings to delicious pork versions. It's like above-
average Chinatown dim sum, served buffet-style.

The secret to your East Buffet experience is selection, restraint, and
navigation around the incongruous and toward the authentic. Pick out
what looks interesting—unfamiliar versions of dumplings, strange
meats, scallion pancakes, Peking duck, steamed Chinese greens, and
shredded pork with black beans. There's even lobster in the buffet on
weekends.

You see, East is caught having to engage with the classic suburban
quantity-quality fallacy. Along those lines, there are also some strange
and disturbing sights, like all-you-can-eat sushi (the rice is suspiciously
moist and the fish isn't particularly fresh), or mac-and-cheese and
barbecued chicken that beckon from a steaming servery. All this can
distract patrons from the restaurant's true talents. Just keep your wits
about you; you know better than to dig on Southern comfort food at a
dim sum restaurant. Be wise and the rewards will be many.

East Japanese Restaurant

8.8
10

Easily the best sushi in the area—and some of the most exciting Japanese fusion too

Japanese   **$32**   *Milford*

9.4 /10
Food

7.5 /10
Atmosphere

9.0 /10
Attitude

8.1 /10
Value

Upmarket restaurant
Mon.-Thurs. 11am-3pm, 5pm-
10pm; Fri. 11am-3pm, 5pm-11pm;
Sat. 5pm-11pm; Sun. 5pm-9:30pm.

17 Turnpike Square
Milford
(203) 877-7686

Bar Full
Credit Cards Visa, MC, AmEx
Reservations Accepted

"Sometimes, customers like being told what to do." So says Jason Tay, the head chef at East, a serious but unpretentious Japanese fusion restaurant in a light, airy, and friendly dining room that is housed along an unlikely stretch of Milford strip mall. The chef will even manage the chronology of your meal: the mild hiramasa (Australian golden amberjack) sushi, for instance, must be eaten before the rich hamachi (yellowtail), which is pure, buttery pleasure, easily the best version we've had in Connecticut.

East endows even the sushi lunch combo with an unusual elegance, but there are also elaborate, fusion-heavy omakase (chef's tasting menu) meals for $55 a head and up, which might include a superb jalapeño kampachi. The amberjack is like a dream: imagine an ideal piece of yellowtail, then add a slightly starchy firmness that gives it an unexpected depth. Throw in a well-balanced soy-citrus sauce, jalapeños, some cilantro, and a tiny pile of Osetra caviar, and you approach the very essence of modern Japanese fusion.

Toro tartare in a salty, flavorful soy-wasabi sauce, at one visit, was accompanied by a syrupy bayberry, a rarely-encountered fruit. The combination simultaneously activated receptors sweet and salty, taste and touch; the crunch of the shallots amplified the ethereal softness of the toro. And almost flawless are the crispy, comforting duck spring rolls with citrus, oil, and soy sauce, like a brilliantly executed Peking duck—but with an edge.

But fusion pyrotechnics cannot succeed without good primary ingredients. When it comes to raw fish, freshness is king. The rumble of a purveyor's truck pulling up in front of a sushi restaurant, day after day, is a happy sound indeed. That is why East (#1 for Japanese, #5 overall) isn't just the best place in the New Haven area for omakase—it's also the best place for sushi.

Edge of the Woods

6.7

10

Vegetarian, kosher, healthy, and not bad at all

Light American $**13** *Whalley*

6.0 /10
Food

8.0 /10
Attitude

7.0 /10
Value

Take-out
Mon.-Fri. 8:30am-7:30pm; Sat.
8:30am-6:30pm; Sun. 9am-6pm.
Vegetarian-friendly

379 Whalley Ave.
New Haven
(203) 787-1055

Bar None
Credit Cards Visa and MC
Reservations Not accepted

For those seeking health-conscious take-out food, Edge of the Woods is definitely on the short list. Like Claire's downtown, the place is also kosher. Attached to an excellent whole-foods store of the same name, Edge of the Woods is a café, storefront, and caterer that offers vegetable pastries, vegan soups, whole-grain breads, pies, pastas and dessert. There are, however, a few tables to sit at, and they get nice light in the atrium-style enclosure. Some items on the buffet spread have perhaps been sitting there a bit too long, and thus tend toward the limp and crusty. There are some standard dishes, like eggplant parmesan, a garden-variety version here, battered and fried eggplant in a red sauce with melted parmesan and mozzarella on top. There are also interesting soups.

But Edge of the Woods also tends to freestyle. Vegan shepherd's pie features soy "un-sausage," corn, carrots, and celery in gravy topped with vegan mashed potatoes. Hmm. We prefer naturally vegetarian or vegan dishes to the sort of ill-advised attempts to simulate meat dishes that proliferated as "vegetarian cuisine" during the 1980s; along those lines, we'd prefer the tofu vegetable lasagne if it didn't have the tofu, even if it is a good source of protein.

Look carefully at the dishes before selecting, and if you fear bland fare, seek out well-spiced options. For liquid nutrition, there's a serious juice bar for wheatgrass shots, beet juice, and so on. Alternatively, you can skip directly to dessert, the equal-opportunity option, but avoid the vegan chocolate cake unless you've long since forgotten what the real thing tastes like.

The Educated Burgher

6.0/10

As the name implies, a simple American grill that does the basics well and caters to the Yale crowd

Short-order American   **$ 7**   *Broadway Area*

5.6/10   **7.0**/10   **5.0**/10   **7.1**/10
Food   *Atmosphere*   *Attitude*   *Value*

Counter service   53 Broadway   *Bar* Beer only
Mon.-Sat. 7am-10pm;   New Haven   *Credit Cards* None
Sun. 9am-10pm.   (203) 777-9198   *Reservations* Not accepted
Breakfast. Vegetarian-friendly.

If not for the looming presence of Yankee Doodle across the street, the Educated Burgher would rule its league: the short-order breakfast and lunch counter on Broadway, steps away from Yale. But the Burgher's fare isn't quite as melt-in-your-mouth good as the Doodle's (in part due to the more judicious, artery-sparing use of butter here).

The Burgher does have other advantages. Seating is plentiful, relaxed, and good for a conversation, and the menu is varied. The Burgher serves salads, for example, including a large bowl of Greek salad (although it's better at Yorkside around the corner). In addition to the standard selection of burgers, grilled cheese sandwiches, and their progeny, there are hot deli sandwiches (including a good pastrami special on rye toast with Swiss cheese, bacon, mushroom, and grilled onion), Greek-style gyros, and the like. The basics are best, though; leave the complex salads and ethnic food for elsewhere.

The room is simple and classic, if a bit dingy, with assorted Yale memorabilia and books (which no one ever has read, or ever will read) lording over a bright array of basic booths. There's very little natural light—a problem for a breakfast and lunch place—and perhaps too many mirrors. Ordering and food delivery both happen at the counter. During busy weekday lunches, this arrangement can sometimes lead to the tragic choice between a tedious standing wait and a seated wait at your table in a limbo state (neurotically glancing over your shoulder toward the kitchen every few seconds in anticipation of your order).

The Burgher might be best for breakfast, when lines are not an issue, standards like eggs over-easy with home fries, toast, and bacon are prepared reliably well, and the playful academic setting sets a light tone for the day ahead.

El Amigo Felix

Bad Tex-Mex food in a strange, dark atmosphere
that can sometimes turn into a fratty scene

Tex-Mex   **$23**   *Broadway Area*

1.4 /10   **5.0** /10   **7.0** /10   **2.2** /10
Food   *Atmosphere*   *Attitude*   *Value*

Bar and grill Tues.-Thurs. 3:30pm-12:30am; Fri.-Sat. noon-1:30am; Sun. noon- midnight; closed Mon. Kitchen closes Sun. and Tues.-Thurs. 10:30pm; Fri.-Sat. 11:30pm.	8 Whalley Ave. New Haven (203) 785-8200	*Bar* Full *Credit Cards* Visa, MC, AmEx *Reservations* Accepted

This was one of the lowest-scoring restaurants in our first edition.
Unhappy with the results, the folks at El Amigo Felix emailed us, telling
us that we knew little about Mexican food—but also asking us to try
the food again and give them another chance.

Of course, every restaurant gets another chance with every new
edition, and El Amigo Felix is no exception. But the amazing thing is
that, when we returned, the Tex-Mex food wasn't as bad as it was last
time around—it was worse. We tasted tortilla chips that were leathery,
almost unable to be chewed, served with an off-tasting salsa that
wasn't even up to the level of cheap supermarket stuff. We tasted
enchiladas whose sauce had the texture of paint cracking off the
tortilla. The beef within was implausibly tasteless, with a texture that
seemed generated by a hair dryer. Perhaps worst of all was a horrific
appetizer of chili con queso whose surface developed with a thick,
plasticky skin, with a cheese taste worse than that of any microwaved
version we've ever tried.

The décor is in the Tijuana-frat-bar vein, which is perfectly fine if
you come, as most do, to consume lots of generic alcohol. The point is,
El Amigo Felix isn't really about the food. It's a party for the college
students who come here to drink, to flirt, and to drink more. We really
do approve of so many people having such a good time. And insofar as
they are able to provide that service, we salute El Amigo Felix. But
we're also food critics, and we must review the food. Our duty is to our
readers, not the restaurants, and fulfilling that duty is not always as
much fun as it might sound.

El Caribe

6.7 /10

A big, kitschy Miami-ish restaurant with authentic Puerto Rican food including excellent mofongo

Latin American   **$25**   *Fair Haven*

7.2 /10   **5.5** /10   **7.0** /10   **6.1** /10
Food   *Atmosphere*   *Attitude*   *Value*

Casual restaurant   136 Chapel St.   *Bar* Full
Mon. 10am-2pm;   New Haven   *Credit Cards* Visa, MC, AmEx
Tues.-Sun. 10am-10pm. *Delivery.*   (203) 562-1330   *Reservations* Accepted

This Puerto Rican restaurant on a quiet, lesser-known stretch of Chapel Street sports the tropical kitsch of a Cuban diner in Miami, complete with little palm trees and even a goldfish pond in the middle of the enormous space. The brightly lit restaurant is curiously empty on most nights, however, making it feel antiseptic and not well tailored to a romantic night out. It's a shame, because this is some of the most authentic Hispanic food in the area. (They are sometimes busier for the more inexpensive midday meals, and they also deliver.)

It might all begin at El Caribe with one of the popular cocktails—a well-executed piña colada is served with a certain levity: clinging to the straw is a little paper monkey whose hindquarters are suspended just millimeters above the whipped cream. The food, though, is serious, starting with the good sausage soup that has a spicy, salty, fully developed meat flavor set off by a hint of lime. Fried appetizers are generally excellent, including the best relleno de papa in town, battered with an indulgently flaky fried dough covering a rich, knish-like potato mixture that, in turn, conceals ground beef deep within.

Prices are a bit steep for the seafood-cocktail starters and the seafood salad mains, but the excellent mofongo (mashed green plantain rolled into a ball and deep fried) with top-notch shrimp is worth every penny. The starch absorbs all the garlicky goodness of the shrimp's sauce; this dish is like a showpiece for garlic. Good also is a moist and well seasoned grilled pork chop with garlic butter; as far as sides go, stick with the maduros (sweet plantains) rather than the drier tostones (the salty ones). In the end, El Caribe is worth every minute of the short drive from downtown.

El Charro

6.6
10

A true slice of Mexico in the middle of Fair Haven

Mexican   **$12**   *Fair Haven*

7.7 /10   **5.0** /10   **5.0** /10   **7.1** /10
Food   *Atmosphere* *Attitude*   *Value*

Casual restaurant   262 Grand Ave.   *Bar* Wine and beer only
Mon. and Wed.-Sat. 10am-8pm;   New Haven   *Credit Cards* None
Sun. 10am-9pm; closed Tues.   (203) 498-7354   *Reservations* Not accepted

Those with wheels who are willing to make the trek into what to some may be unfamiliar territory—the middle of Fair Haven, up Grand Avenue, which ultimately amounts to little more than five minutes from the Green—will be well rewarded with some of the best, most authentic Mexican food around. One of the glorious, little-known Mexican champions that hide out in nooks and crannies of the New Haven area (Guadalupe La Poblanita and Taquería Mexicana #2 also come to mind), El Charro is the closest to downtown New Haven but also easy to miss amidst pawn shops, bodegas, and stereo-equipment resellers.

El Charro is a funny, bright little place, and it really feels like a slice of Mexico—all is conducted in Spanish (though English is spoken), and you're even wont to find the most traditional Mexican scene of all: the cadre of down-and-out middle-aged men in the corner, good-naturedly teasing the waitress, drowning their sorrows in jukebox tunes and 40s of Tecate. The low prices feel like Mexico too (order individual antojitos rather than the plates that come with rice and beans—they're much cheaper).

Chorizo tacos and enchiladas are good choices. There are some more sophisticated combinations, like a seafood stew that integrates lobster, clams, mussels, fish, octopus, shrimp, in a broth of shrimp stock and dry red pepper sauce, served with tostadas on the side. Everything is good, even the Mexican beer selection, although this might not quite be your spot for boozing. For some reason, only taquitos are sold after 5pm on Sundays. In all, El Charro is very much worth the trip, wherever you're coming from.

El Charro Alegre

6.2
10

Pricier, more piñata-happy, and less authentic than
its Fair Haven brother, but still good

Mexican $19   *East Rock/Grad Ghetto*

6.9 /10   **5.0**/10   **6.0** /10   **5.9**/10
Food   *Atmosphere*   *Attitude*   *Value*

Casual restaurant   14 Mechanic St.   *Bar* Full
Tues.-Sat. 11pm-10pm;   New Haven   *Credit Cards* Visa, MC, AmEx
Sun. 11am-8pm; closed Mon. (203) 752-9130   *Reservations* Accepted

You want to believe it's just an identical twin, a Grad Ghetto version of
El Charro, a duplicate branch opened in a more accessible area, à la
Sandra's on Whitney Avenue. Unfortunately, this restaurant bears only a
fleeting resemblance to the wonderfully authentic mothership on Grand
Avenue in Fair Haven—especially when it comes to atmosphere. Here,
up State Street, the hanging-sombreros-and-piñatas décor tries a lot
harder, and ends up feeling ridiculous, especially when paired with the
noticeable lack of customers. It looks like someone threw a big fiesta
for the third-graders and no one showed up.

But more importantly, prices are much higher here—almost double,
in fact (though portions are also bigger)—and the food's a lot more Tex
and a lot less Mex. We're happy to report that it's still good, though—
well above the New Haven standard, and still worth a visit. Refried
beans are rich and tasty, the melted cheese is the right kind, and
ingredients seem fresh. Fajitas are sizzling and good, although we
prefer the enchiladas and, even more, the carnitas (roasted pork with
rice, beans, guacamole, sour cream, and flour tortillas).

Even if the food is competent, though, El Charro Alegre fails to
achieve either the you-could-be-in-Mexico quality of its sister restaurant
or the merry suburban Tex-Mex appeal of a Su Casa or a Jalapeño
Heaven. As a result, it winds up as a respectable but overdressed
restaurant without a compelling draw.

El Coquí

7.1
/10

A Fair Haven take-out find with authentic Puerto Rican preparations and the best mofongo in town

Latin American

$ 7 Fair Haven

7.2 /10
Food

7.0 /10
Attitude

8.8 /10
Value

Take-out
Daily 11am-8:30pm.

286 Grand Ave.
New Haven
(203) 562-1757

Bar Wine and beer only
Credit Cards None
Reservations Not accepted

The sign outside this shabby-looking Fair Haven joint, which is basically a take-out place, advertises "Spanish food," but really, the cuisine is Latin American, with a clear focus on Puerto Rican specialties. The menu changes regularly; there is always an assortment of fried foods, various stews, chicken, and above all, pork dishes (from fried pork rinds to roast pig), most displayed behind the counter. Unless you're familiar with the dishes, even if you're a Spanish speaker, you might just want to point, rather than trying to figure out the names and ingredients of the different dishes. Ordering at El Coquí can be humbling and disorienting—but very worthwhile.

For us, the truly superlative dish at El Coquí is the mofongo; this one you can request by name. It's a famous Cuban and Caribbean dish of mashed plantain with garlic that is formed into a ball, seasoned, fried, and then covered with another topping. There are higher-priced versions of mofongo in town—at El Caribe, for instance, or at the upscale Pacifico—but with all due respect, we believe that El Coquí's is the best in town. It's like a showcase for garlic, with that flavor deeply infused into the moist but not wimpy starch, and a broth that's generously spooned on (you choose which kind; we love the beef broth) adds another dimension. It's a unique experience in the New Haven area.

Plantains are also good in their other fried forms. We've been less impressed by the empanadas, which sometimes sit around for a while and will be in your bag yet longer, cooling off, if you order take-out. Better are the moister stews, roast meats, and such. There's even beer for sale. The incredibly low prices are yet another reason to make it to this easy-to-miss food counter.

Est Est Est

5.7
/10

A well-liked New York-style pizza joint that draws throngs in the wee hours for decent pies and subs

Pizza, Italian   **$ 8**   *Upper Chapel Area*

6.4 /10   **4.0** /10   **7.0** /10   **6.5** /10
Food   *Atmosphere*   *Attitude*   *Value*

Counter service   1176 Chapel St.   *Bar* None
Mon.-Thurs. 10am-1am; Fri.-Sat.   New Haven   *Credit Cards* Visa, MC, AmEx
10am-3am; Sun. 11am-midnight.   (203) 777-2059   *Reservations* Accepted
Delivery. Vegetarian-friendly.

This is a decent New York-style pizza place that does most of its business with starving grad students (especially art and architecture students, whose headquarters are right nearby). They come especially for the low prices and late hours. On Friday and Saturday nights, Est Est Est is open until 3am, and other weeknights it closes at 1am, so it's a viable late-night option right on Chapel Street. As for the slices, the plain cheese variety is better than average. The crust is crispy in a balanced way; sauce is just tangy enough; and it's not overwhelmed with cheese (although unfortunately, the cheese itself is mediocre).

All in all, it's what you'd expect at a solid New York joint, which is nothing to be ashamed of. There are also some daring combinations that are not for the faint of heart. For instance, the chicken paisano pizza is topped with mozzarella, grilled chicken, mushrooms, tomatoes, artichoke hearts, and capers, the pizza equivalent of one-pot cooking. There's certainly enough going on there to command your attention, though pizza purists may shudder at the thought. To each his own.

Est Est Est is a take-out spot, really, although there is an array of eat-in tables that always suffers from a comical lack of attendance; even if there's a line going out the door for the $1.50 slices, you'll still not find a soul seated at one of the tables. In fact, we have yet to meet anyone who has either sat down or ever seen anyone sitting down in this dining room. Est Est Est also serves up garden-variety Italian subs. In the wee hours, the place is as good an option as any in town. Cheers to that.

500 Blake St. Café

5.6
/10

A Westville institution with a famous all-you-can-eat brunch of epic proportions, but little taste

Traditional American   **$32**   *Westville*

5.0/10   **6.0**/10   **8.0**/10   **4.6**/10
Food   *Atmosphere* *Attitude*   *Value*

Upmarket restaurant	500 Blake St.	***Bar*** Full
Sun. 11am-3:30pm; closed Mon.-	New Haven	***Credit Cards*** Visa, MC, AmEx
Sat. until re-opening of full kitchen.	(203) 387-0500	***Reservations*** Essential
Brunch.	www.500blakestreetcafe.com	

500 Blake is the 800-pound gorilla on the local brunch scene, offering a pricey, all-you-can-eat brunch of mammoth proportions. At press time, brunch was the only meal they were serving, as the kitchen was being redone. We'll limit our comments, thus, to the brunch.

The good: everyone always seems to be having a fabulous time cavorting between carvery, omelette stations, and banquet tables which groan under so many platters of food. The bad: too much of something is not always a good thing. This is a place steeped in the curious American brunch tradition of aiming to eat as much as one possibly can in a single sitting.

We do like the prosciutto, which is above average, well paired with cantaloupe if in season. The caprese salad features fresh, if unsalted, mozzarella with a lovely texture. The Italian winning streak stops short, however, with watery rigatoni. Other offerings fare scarcely better, from a seafood salad ruined by excessively chewy conch to the boring, overcooked carvery. Dessert is amply provided for those who can heave themselves to the extensive spread of assorted cakes, apple crisp, fresh waffles and the like; all are plentiful, none superlative.

It just doesn't add up. 500 Blake is consistently lauded in the local press far and near, from *Connecticut* magazine to the "Best Of" reader's survey in the *Advocate*. Why do people pay a lot for mediocre food—and keep coming back? Perhaps 500 Blake's popularity owes much to the genius of unlimited dessert, which ensures that everyone leaves with a nice, guilt-free sugar high. After all, dessert that you don't have to own up to ordering is good, clean fun for the whole family.

Foe

A relaxing but elegant vibe and careful upscale creations that are creative, not derivative

New American $35 Branford

8.3/10   **8.0**/10   **8.0**/10   **7.3**/10
Food   Atmosphere   Attitude   Value

Upmarket restaurant   576 Main St.   **Bar** Full
Tues.-Thurs. 11:30am-2:30pm,   Branford   **Credit Cards** Visa, MC, AmEx
5pm-9:30pm; Fri.-Sat. 11:30am- (203) 483-5896   **Reservations** Accepted
2:30pm, 5pm-10:30pm;
Sun. 5pm-9pm. *Date-friendly.*

You're probably wondering—here's the answer: "Foe" is the nickname of the chef of this cozy restaurant, who came over from Esteva (which is now called Martin's American Café). He's done quite a service to us all, because this is one of the more exciting restaurants to come along in a while. Foe is unpretentious, with a cute, cozy space and good, chilled-out music in the background, but it's also unselfconscious. However, dinner is meant to be taken seriously here, beginning with the opening round of honey butter, so substantive it's like an amuse-bouche, and so sweet it's like a dessert.

Fried calamari are good and crispy, served with an aioli redolent of basil, although we would have liked more hot peppers. Lamb chop "lollipops" really are that shape and size, and they're an interesting exercise in the interplay between sweet and savory. There are notes of mint, an extremely sweet sauce full of honey, and a deliciously reduced demi-glace of sorts. You'll want to dip the lamb in everything at once.

Even better is the "seafood succotash," an extremely creamy creation with bacon, scallops, and shrimp and, of course, corn. It's like the best creamed corn you've ever tasted, and it comes with grilled bread that tastes like—we kid you not—smoked toast. On our last visit, we tried a West Coast sable, which came with a superb sauce of cilantro and dill. Clearly, Foe has a way with sauces. The sable was something like black cod, soft and rich, and cooked just the right amount, although the rice was crunchily undercooked.

Foe's service is nice, the vibe just right, and the menu extremely creative. It makes us so happy to see a New American restaurant that's breaking new ground instead of replaying the greatest hits of California construction cuisine.

Fresh Taco

6.3
/10

An Asian-run lunch stop with fast, no-frills Tex-Mex food that's built upon homemade tortillas

Tex-Mex   **$ 7**   *Financial District*

6.0/10   **7.0**/10   **7.6**/10
Food   *Attitude*   *Value*

Take-out   39 Elm St.   *Bar* None
Mon.-Sat. 10:30am-11pm;   New Haven   *Credit Cards* Visa, MC, AmEx
Sun. noon-10pm.   (203) 777-3068   *Reservations* Not accepted
Delivery. Vegetarian-friendly.

Change can be a really good thing. This was one of the lowest-scoring restaurants in the first edition of *The Menu,* but since early 2004, Fresh Taco has been under new ownership. The joint has shortened its name (previously it was called the "Original Fresh Taco"), revamped its menu, and vastly improved.

Visually, Fresh Taco is still an experience in cultural dissonance. The little place screams Chinese take-out, from the Chinese and Malaysian staff to the narrow storefront and photo-board menu overhead to the alpha-numeric listings on the fold-out menu (complete with a "no MSG" assurance). But if you look more closely, things take an unexpected turn: this little shop packs up not Chinese but rather Mexican food—burritos, tacos, refried beans, guacamole, and so on. The shop caters to a lunch-break crowd, with equal parts take-outers and solo sit-down diners. Prices are low; the $10 delivery minimum means feeding at least two people.

Perhaps because of the cultural heritage of the staff and perhaps not, things taste a little bit different here than at your standard Tex-Mex quick stop. That is not necessarily a bad thing. The flour tortillas are homemade in a press, not taken out of a package, which is a most welcome touch. Their texture is somewhat unusual, more doughy than most, and almost evocative of...well...roti. Nowhere is the roti resemblance quality stronger than in the extra-puffy tortillas used for the quesadillas sincronizadas (pressed with meat and jack cheese).

Among fillings, chicken is fully flavored but crunchy around the edges, and cumin-forward "Tex-Mex chili" is okay if unusually soft. Lettuce and tomato are fresh, but the little plastic tub of salsa that's served with almost everything is subpar. And we're not sure what to make of the french fries and buffalo wings. To each his own.

Funki Munki

7.5
/10

A food cart on Chapel Street with a whimsical
approach, but a serious commitment to quality

Light American

$ 7   *Theater District*

6.8 /10
Food

9.0 /10
Attitude

9.4 /10
Value

Take-out
Mon.-Sat. 11am-4pm; closed Sun.
Vegetarian-friendly.

Chapel St.
near College St.
New Haven
(203) 988-1380

Bar None
Credit Cards None
Reservations Not accepted

Beginning with the name, this little jack-of-all-trades food cart that sits
on Chapel Street (near the Sweet Shoppe) is a fun, goofy place. It's a
refreshing gourmet riff on New Haven's more standard ethnic food carts
that dot the landscape everywhere from Elm and York to the Medical
School area. Funki Munki has a much more whimsical feel, from the
menu to the meringue music. But that's not to take anything away
from the seriousness of the food-service endeavor here: Maurice Juarez,
the owner of the cart, used to work at Union League. Now he parks
outside.

Although the friendly attitude and chummy antics are clearly a
priority, it's also evident that there's a deep concern for the quality of
the ingredients and the creativity of the preparations—and we don't
just mean the good gourmet hot dogs. Vegetables and bread are fresh,
and happily, they don't attempt anything that can't be pulled off
satisfactorily at a food cart, focusing on things like soups and sandwich
fillings that do well sitting in tubs, as is required by the medium. One
nice touch is a cooler of ice-cold water infused with the herb or fruit of
the day—free for all passers-by.

Pulled pork is a particular specialty, and we really like Funki Munki's
satisfying version; it's more sweet than spicy. They do a few different
sandwiches featuring the pulled pork and other fillings, such as a nice
tropical-tasting slaw, but the accommodating folks at the cart are more
than happy to let you create your own sandwich as well. In season,
we've tried a chunky but refreshing gazpacho. But try anything—most
of it is really reliable. What a welcome addition to the liveliest stretch of
Chapel Street.

Gastronomique

7.4
__
10

Serious French cooking from a take-out counter
that's barely bigger than a closet

French   **$17**   *Theater District*

8.1 /10   **6.0** /10   **7.6** /10
Food   *Attitude*   *Value*

Take-out   25 High St.   *Bar* None
Mon.-Sat. 10am-9pm; closed Sun. New Haven   *Credit Cards* Visa, MC, AmEx
Breakfast. Brunch. Date-friendly. (203) 776-7007   *Reservations* Not accepted
Delivery. Vegetarian-friendly. www.thegastro.com

This pint-sized take-out and catering outfit proves the adage that good
things come in small packages. Gastronomique is mostly kitchen space,
with a narrow counter separating customers from where the action is.
A chalkboard outside announces the steaming, glistening seasonal daily
specials, which might include roasted chestnuts, butternut squash soup,
or braised short ribs.

The flavor is French, and the tone is bistro, ranging from a rich,
velvety, cheesy French onion soup in the traditional style to a rich and
delicious lobster bisque. The Provençal rack of lamb, at one visit, was a
triumph, tender, sweetly crusted with forest spices and olive tapenade,
and served with a creamy potato tart, dried tomato, and shredded
fennel. A risotto with saffron, spinach, parmesan, and roasted red
pepper has been one of the only disappointing items—the flavor was
something less than the sum of its parts. There's a chubby burger that's
cooked in veal stock, though often for too long, rendering the meat
grey and burning the cheddar cheese. We were also disappointed by an
oily, chunky, almost ketchupy gazpacho; that said, it had a good kick to
it. We love the creamy chicken paté sandwich, though, accompanied by
fresh greens with a subtle vinaigrette; fruit smoothies, composed of
wondrously fresh fruit and vegetable combinations; and French toast
that makes for a decadent mid-morning breakfast.

Gastronomique is perhaps best for dinner-party augmentation or a
candlelight dinner for two, at home, no prep required. The wry chef,
who comes to High Street by way of the Culinary Institute of America
and a bevy of prestigious New York and Connecticut kitchens, also
somewhat amusingly thumbs his nose at Yale Dining Services by
offering a "student meal plan" of 30 meals per month at discounted
prices.

Gennaro's Amalfi Grille

4.9
/10

One of the most overpriced, boring, and ugly
Italian restaurants in town

Italian **$38** *Theater District*

5.3 /10
Food

4.0 /10
Atmosphere

5.0 /10
Attitude

2.7 /10
Value

Upmarket restaurant
Mon. 5pm-8:30pm; Tues.-Fri.
11:30am-2pm, 5pm-10pm;
Sat. 5pm-10pm; closed Sun. *Outdoor dining.*

196 Crown St.
New Haven
(203) 777-4745

Bar Full
Credit Cards Visa, MC, AmEx
Reservations Accepted

In a city of Italian-American restaurants, this is just another one of
many. Much of the menu is just a recitation of the most standard pasta
dishes in various combinations (with the usual overrepresentation of
cream-based sauces). There's plenty of veal, of course. Gennaro's
commits the classic New Haven Italian-American blunder—too many
rich ingredients, not enough subtle and interesting flavor—over and
over again. And the prices are steep.

It might all begin with soft, disappointing fried calamari. Next come
incoherent dishes like the inexplicably named veal "caprese," whose
overcooked cutlet is topped with asparagus, canned or bottled
artichoke hearts, unpeeled tomatoes whose skins are distracting, tough
little pieces of prosciutto, and—yup—a cream sauce, complemented by
underseasoned green beans. The gnocchi are satisfactory, which is a
minor triumph. Not so for lobster ravioli, whose salty filling tastes more
like mixed seafood with off notes. The pink sauce isn't bad, though,
and at least this pasta's not usually overcooked.

When value is not the driving force, something else should step into
the breach. Sadly, neither atmosphere nor service is up to the
assignment. The décor makes us wince (think white tulle curtains with
cheesy red velvet accents and chandeliers with touches of green), the
lighting lacks warmth, and muzak comes from a cable box. Service,
meanwhile, is well intentioned but unpolished. The location, too, lacks
something. Diners look out onto the concrete abomination of a parking
lot across from the old Chapel Square mall, or the vehicles circling in
search of a metered spot on this highly-trafficked downtown block.
Meanwhile, within a city block or two—no more—is the highest
concentration of dining options in town, on College, Crown and
Chapel. It is completely beyond us why anyone ever chooses to eat
here.

Geppi's

A classic neighborhood Italian-American spot that
matches tasty comfort food with good feelings

Italian $**29**   *Fair Haven*

7.2 /10   **8.0** /10   **10** /10   **7.0** /10
Food   *Atmosphere*   *Attitude*   *Value*

Casual restaurant   113 Grand Ave.   *Bar* Full
Tues.-Thurs. Noon-3pm, 5:30pm-   New Haven   *Credit Cards* Visa, MC, AmEx
9pm; Fri. noon-3pm, 5:30pm-10pm;   (203) 776-0100   *Reservations* Accepted
Sat. 5:30pm-10pm, Sun. 4pm-9pm;
closed Mon. *Date-friendly.*

Anyone who has been in New Haven for five minutes knows about
Wooster Square, but true acolytes of the city's Italian-American fare will
go the extra mile down Grand Avenue to visit Geppi's, which has been
feeding New Haven natives for more than two decades. Like most
restaurants of this ilk and tenure, this is a place that has seen many a
festive family meal.

The service feels like family too—equal parts brusque and attentive.
If you don't clean your plate, which is a challenge for the heartiest
appetite, you may have to answer to your server, who might well seem
personally invested in having you totally, utterly, impossibly full. The
décor is of the classic Italian-American restaurant style, but in its very
best incarnation, with a piano that's played on Friday evenings.

It all adds up to a warm, fuzzy feeling that harmonizes well with the
comfort food, which is well above average and consistently satisfying (if
not transcendental). Of the complimentary antipasto of cheese and
pickled vegetables, we like the red peppers best. Fried calamari, a
benchmark dish, is delightfully fresh. The batter is not quite crispy
enough, but the piquant cherry pepper sauce served alongside it is
really something special. An appetizer of grilled shrimp and artichokes is
competently prepared, even if the shrimp aren't the most succulent
around. Pork osso buco, too, has good flavor; the meat is tender,
though not of the falling-off-the-bone variety, and the saffron risotto is
the real, creamy deal—nothing like the rice medley that some
restaurants try to pass off as such. Among pasta dishes, we love the
lobster ravioli, which boasts generous morsels of meat with a pleasant
texture, although the sauce is slightly under-reduced.

Good food, good feelings, good times.

Glenwood Drive-In

7.5
10

A time-frozen road stop known for spectacular hot dogs, soft-shell crabs, and even vintage car shows

Short-order American   **$ 5**   *Hamden*

7.5/10   **7.5**/10   **7.0**/10   **9.7**/10
Food   *Atmosphere*   *Attitude*   *Value*

Counter service   2538 Whitney Ave.   *Bar* None
Winter, 11am-9pm daily;   Hamden   *Credit Cards* None
summer, 11am-10pm daily.   (203) 281-0604   *Reservations* Not accepted

This roadside stop famous for its hot dogs seems time-frozen in the year that it opened—1955. The postwar diner feel has been perfectly preserved, and to this day there are vintage auto shows at 6pm every Wednesday night in summer—bring your classic and join in the fun.

It's really all about the hot dogs, though, which can be grilled in three ways: normal, well done, or "burnt." The more cooking of the hot dog, of course, the more browning and crisping of the skin. This may be the first and last time within these pages that we recommend ordering any meat "well done," but here it adds a welcome new dimension. Listen as your order is efficiently turned into kitchen-speak: "One dog, two burnt, two French."

We recommend the hot dog with American cheese (it's placed between the hot dog and the bun, where it melts somewhat beneath the heat). Skip the merely average chili topping, but don't miss the condiment station off to the side, where you'll pile on sauerkraut, chopped onions, and a nice hot pepper sauce along with the other usual suspects. The bun is wonderfully browned, and the overall effect is memorable. The best hot dog in America? Who knows. The best hot dog we've had in recent memory? Easily. A steal at less than three dollars? Absolutely.

The rest of the menu—which includes seafood preparations like the classic Connecticut hot lobster roll, clam strips, and so on—might not be as superlative as the hot dogs, but the fries are crispy and well prepared and the burgers get good marks. Soft-shell crabs are another specialty when in season. Finish with the superb vanilla ice cream from the adjacent Kelly's Kone Konnection.

Golden Seafood

8.0
10

Authentic Hong Kong Cantonese cooking in
Westville, with fish so fresh it's flopping

Chinese $22 *Westville*

8.1 /10   **7.5**/10   **9.0** /10   **7.8**/10
Food   *Atmosphere*   *Attitude*   *Value*

Casual restaurant   1307 Whalley Ave.   *Bar* Wine and beer only
Daily 11am-10pm.   New Haven   *Credit Cards* Visa, MC, AmEx
                           (203) 389-6889   *Reservations* Accepted

The staff of Hong Kong natives at Golden Restaurant, an excellent and authentic Cantonese restaurant newly resident in Westville, describe it as "Chinatown-style." That is to say that although the requisite Szechuan brown-sauce dishes are on the menu, they are not the focus. It's the regional and seafood specialties—some of which are printed on the menu, some scrawled on the walls—that lie at the heart of the restaurant's wonderful offerings. The staff's willingness to translate the more obscure dishes into English reveals their welcoming attitude toward people who want to learn more about Cantonese food rather than ordering something they already know well.

Go straight for the Cantonese stuff that you rarely encounter. Steamed Chinese greens are fresh and bouncy. XO shrimp, with salt and pepper, are meant to be eaten with the heads still on—that's where the shrimpiest flavor lurks. Better yet is the succulent and deliciously garlicky Dungeness crab, steamed whole, one of the best crab dishes in Connecticut.

The *pièce de resistance*, though, is in the back of the restaurant, in the form of a large fish tank. When you order a whole fish special— such as the steamed sea bass—a man goes to the tank with a net, and then emerges demonstratively, walking toward the kitchen with a big smile on his face, his catch flopping around in front of the whole dining room.

Golden Restaurant's two rooms have the bright lighting and a few big round tables that, again, evoke Chinatown—not to mention the largely Chinese clientele, which is the best sign of all. Although it's not exactly romantic, the warm buzz of cross-generational eating creates some ambience. It's all certainly pleasant enough not to distract you from the wonderful seafood at this hidden gem of a restaurant.

Gourmet Heaven

A 24/7 deli with two downtown branches, but they're only to be used in emergencies

Light American, Chinese $ 8   Broadway Area, Arts District

3.6 /10
Food

4.0 /10
Attitude

4.5 /10
Value

Take-out
Daily 24 hrs. Deli buffet ends
at 2am. *Vegetarian-friendly.*

15 Broadway
New Haven
(203) 787-4533

Bar None
Credit Cards Visa and MC
Reservations Not accepted

Whitney Ave. branch:
Daily 24 hrs. Deli buffet ends
at 2am.

44 Whitney Ave.
New Haven
(203) 776-0400

•

We have good news and bad news. The good news is that the "revitalization" of Broadway has brought to New Haven the exact brand of omnibus, large-scale, 24-hour gourmet convenience store that New Yorkers take for granted; it comes complete with the obligatory station of salad, fruit, and a hot food buffet-by-the-pound under heat lamps. Timing is everything. The bad news is that, as is also so often the case in the New York gourmet delis, the food itself is overpriced, uninspiring, and has often been sitting around for a while. The expansive food station holds a plethora of prepared dishes, from barbecued chicken to macaroni and cheese, plantains, and even steak fries. Unlike fine wine, most of the offerings under the heat lamp do not improve with age.

But a secondary problem is that, we suspect, a few things probably weren't particularly tasty to begin with: stir fried beef tends to be tough, and pasta with cream sauce is overly creamy, bland, and undersalted. But the salads are palatable, diverse, and a slightly better value; the fresh fruit, though expensive (a handful of grapes is heavier than one might imagine), is also okay. There are also deli sandwiches, and some basic eat-in seating offered upstairs.

If you're looking for packaged food, Gourmet Heaven delivers, albeit at a premium, from cheeses, dried fruits and nuts, and upmarket sauces to the requisite instant ramen. This is also the place for various and sundry items that you won't find elsewhere at 3am, from fresh-cut flowers to prophylactics. Gourmet Heaven's second branch is at 44 Whitney Avenue, next to Sandra's. It's more of the same. Unless you're in a dire late-night situation, try to avoid these places.

Guadalupe La Poblanita

6.5
10

An unassuming highwayside Mexican restaurant
that is shockingly good, authentic, and friendly

Mexican   **$10**   *Fair Haven*

7.6/10   **4.0**/10   **7.0**/10   **7.3**/10
Food   *Atmosphere*   *Attitude*   *Value*

Casual restaurant   500 Foxon Blvd.   **Bar** Beer only
Wed.-Mon. 11am-8pm;   New Haven   **Credit Cards** None
closed Tues.   (203) 467-7732   **Reservations** Not accepted

In a town of culinary gems hidden behind the most unassuming
façades, Guadalupe La Poblanita boasts perhaps the most inverse
relationship of food to atmosphere in all of New Haven. In terms of
taste, this is the best place in town for Mexican. Everything on the
menu is good. Where some downtown haunts tend to evoke
packaged, processed Old El Paso, Guadalupe serves up truly authentic
dishes to those in the know. Don't make the mistake of coming here
for a romantic night out, though; depressing, white lights and tinny
music bear down on bright plastic abominations that pass for booths.

But Guadalupe is all about the food. The cheese is the real thing—
Mexican queso fresco, not Cracker Barrel shredded Monterey jack. The
chicken with chocolate-tinged mole, which might be the best dish on
the menu, is an excellent balance of sweet and savory, and it comes
with rice, beans, and homemade tortillas. Never take tortillas for
granted. Tostadas are fantastic; chiles rellenos, chili peppers stuffed with
beef or cheese, are just okay (the texture was difficult to tackle on a
recent visit). Simpler but well executed are the roast pork and anything
with chorizo, and there's also an impressive selection of Mexican-beer-
after-Corona, including the delicious Bohemia and even—if you're
lucky—Sol.

Portions are large, so order less rather than more; even the smaller
antojitos will satisfy most appetites. Some English is spoken, though
better would be Spanish. You'll need a car to reach this out-of-the-way
shack (take exit 8 off I-91), and even then, it's easy to miss. But keep in
mind that Guadalupe is on the way the next time your car is towed to
the suburbs for street sweeping.

Gunung Tahan

Surprise! A good, if inconsistent, Malaysian
restaurant along a suburban highway

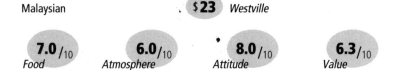

Malaysian $23   *Westville*

7.0/10   **6.0**/10   **8.0**/10   **6.3**/10
Food   *Atmosphere*   *Attitude*   *Value*

Casual restaurant	1451 Whalley Ave.	*Bar* Full
Sun.-Thurs. 11:45am-10pm;	New Haven	*Credit Cards* Visa, MC, AmEx
Fri.-Sat. 11:45am-11pm.	(203) 389-1280	*Reservations* Accepted
Vegetarian-friendly.		

Gunung Tahan is a well-kept secret. And no wonder: it's Malaysian food
in suburbia, up Whalley Avenue past Westville (near Akasaka). It's easily
worth the trip just for the spectacular roti canai (rich, flaky, unfilled
fried bread served with a bowl of curry sauce with beef and potato).
With apologies to Bentara, it's easily the best roti in the area.

There are flashes of brilliance, too, among mains; try to comb the
menu for dishes with exotic names and tastes. One star is the kari asam
udang, an entertaining mix of jumbo shrimp, tomato, okra, and
tamarind in sour curry sauce. Sting ray cooked in banana leaf with a
deep, thick red sauce is another winner. But ayam percik, a grilled
chicken leg, arrives bone-dry, and the sambal tofu is tasteless, except
for its gummy, overpowering peanut sauce. And everything comes with
a boring house salad of iceberg lettuce with ginger dressing or a
gummy, bland chicken and broccoli soup, diluting the overall
experience. Given the potential, you're left with some tantalizing what-
ifs: what if the cooking were to focus exclusively on authentic
Malaysian, rather than throwing in uninspired pan-Asian concessions to
suburban convention?

And what if the atmosphere were romantic instead of suburban?
The room is too brightly lit, as is all too common, with Malaysian
tourism posters hanging from the walls. The Unklung—large Indo-
Malay musical instruments played with a mallet—are interesting but
disappointingly silent. It seems Unklung players are hard to come by in
these parts. If the talent in the kitchen were transplanted wholesale
from this location to a cool downtown spot, and the menu pared down
to the authentic, we think this place would have unlimited potential. In
the meantime, though, why not check it out? It's still cheap, good, and
really interesting.

Gusto Italiano

6.6
/10

A downtown luncherie with welcoming service and
supremely authentic Italian panini and tramezzini

Italian, Pizza   **$11**   *Arts District*

7.4/10   **5.0**/10   **7.0**/10   **7.2**/10
Food   *Atmosphere*   *Attitude*   *Value*

Counter service   45 Grove St.   **Bar** Wine and beer only
Mon.-Fri.7:30am-8pm;   New Haven   **Credit Cards** Visa, MC, AmEx
Sat. 9am-5pm; closed Sun. (203) 777-3234   **Reservations** Not accepted
Breakfast. Delivery. Vegetarian-friendly.

Who knew that one of the most authentic Italian eateries in town
would be a counter-service cafeteria-style joint, where Avanti once sat,
near the corner of Grove and Orange? Equally convenient to the
downtown lunch crowd, to Yale University, and even to the southern
end of the Grad Ghetto neighborhood, Gusto Italiano peddles an
eminently worthwhile lunch menu to a cross-section of New Haveners
(and word is still spreading) at a crossroads of city foot traffic.

We've tried the big, fresh salads with genuinely Italian ingredients,
and panini that blow away much of the competition in terms of
ingredient quality, inspired combinations, and proper, sufficient pressing
(which is key). Tramezzini (satisfying, classic Italian white-bread
sandwiches with the crusts cut off, filled with mayonnaise and an
assortment of other ingredients) are rarely found in New Haven, and we
love them here. There are also decent, if unspectacular, pizzas; it would
be hard to scale the lofty heights of New Haven pizza without a more
elaborate brick-oven setup. You might expect an espresso to be top-
notch at such a real, live Italian place, but unfortunately, it tends not to
be very short, not up to the gold standard of Romeo & Cesare's and
Caffé Bottega. But that is one of our only complaints.

We love the counter service here, which is quite accommodating.
Your presence as a customer is clearly appreciated, not taken for
granted. The rather dark room is not quite the revelation that the menu
is; there's an assortment of basic tables and chairs that are certainly
more at home for lunch than for dinner. But we offer Gusto Italiano a
hearty welcome to town, and we hope that more such salad-and-
sandwich places will take this place as a model of authenticity.

Hama

7.8
/10

Some of the best sushi around, at the best prices—
we fully agree with the domain name

Japanese   **$18** *Hamden*

8.1 /10   **7.5** /10   **7.0** /10   **8.0** /10
Food   *Atmosphere*   *Attitude*   *Value*

Casual restaurant   1206 Dixwell Ave.   *Bar* Full
Mon.-Thurs. 11:30am-2:30pm,   Hamden   *Credit Cards* Visa, MC, AmEx
5pm-9:30pm; Fri. 11:30am-2:30pm, (203) 281-4542   *Reservations* Accepted
4:45pm-10pm; Sat. 4:45pm-10pm;   www.ilovehama.com
Sun. 5pm-9:30pm. *Vegetarian-friendly.*

You might not think that some of the best sushi in New Haven County
would be found in strip-mall suburbia, but Hama is just that—and on
value for the dollar, it's particularly hard to beat. As a result, the place is
routinely packed. The atmosphere is pretty blah; the room is too sterile
and bright. But with this sushi at these prices, who cares?

The reasonably priced menu is extensive, with a focus on dozens of
unique house rolls. Keep in mind that Math 251b (Stochastic Processes)
is a necessary prerequisite for deducing the complex formula governing
the selection of choices in the excellent-value combination lunches and
dinners. But the epitome of the appeal for the price-conscious is one
unique and unbeatable offer, usually available on weekdays (lunch or
dinner, eat-in only): an inexpensive sushi combination of seven pieces
and two rolls, all of your own choosing. This offer includes its own
ordering ritual, which begins with closing the proffered menu and
letting your server know you'd like the golf pencil and little piece of
paper used to mark your nigiri and maki choices (legend has it that the
offer is also listed on the menu, but we challenge you to find it there).

This brilliant arrangement gets past the standard sushi-combination
problem of surrendering choice to the house in order to save money,
and it requires nothing more than a basic familiarity with elementary
linear algebra and vector spaces. All the classics and more are on offer
in the combination, even uni (sea urchin), which is available at most
restaurants only at a premium. If applicable, ask for the tuna with spicy
mayo, rather than just spicy tuna. This is the best way to get your sushi
fix for under $15 and the ultimate local satisfaction for your sushi
craving.

Haya

A cute Japanese restaurant serving significantly
worse food than the nearby Japanese competition

Japanese $22   *East Rock/Grad Ghetto*

2.6 /10   **7.0** /10   **5.0** /10   **3.4** /10
Food   *Atmosphere*   *Attitude*   *Value*

Casual restaurant   93 Whitney Ave.   **Bar** Full
Mon.-Thurs. 11:30am-2:30pm,   New Haven   **Credit Cards** Visa and MC
5pm-9:30pm; Fri. 11:30am-2:30pm, (203) 562-3022   **Reservations** Accepted
5pm-10pm; Sat. 3pm-10pm;
Sun. 3pm-9:30pm. *Outdoor dining. Vegetarian-friendly.*

This little Japanese restaurant is on the downtown end of the Grad
Ghetto, scoring it some Yalie walk-by business. It's a good thing for
them, because precious few would go out of their way to come here
for the sushi. The fish is chewy, the vinegared rice is soggy, it's all
inexplicably adulterated by lemon and, more than sometimes, the
flavors lack the fresh, reassuring sweetness of the sea. While Haya is
not inordinately expensive, the combination sushi lunch special is only a
dollar cheaper than the dinner version, making it a particularly poor
choice for lunch as compared to the Big Four—Miso, Hama, Daiko, and
East.

So we advise you to forget the sushi. Your best bet might be lunch
specials like Japanese curry, which are inexpensive and not bad. Your
student ID will get you 10% off dinner, and on Wednesday and Sunday,
sake is half price. Some people like the noodle and tempura dishes (the
udon noodle soup is a soy-based broth with thick white noodles and
shrimp and vegetable tempura), but we're not big fans. Every one of
these things is better, and not much more expensive, at other Japanese
spots in town. Service is slow and strange.

Haya's atmosphere is cute, though. You enter through a beaded
curtain, and you can choose between three cozy rooms, one of them
downstairs. Warm weather brings quaint outdoor tables with sweeping
views of the Trumbull Street parking lot. But unless you're seized by an
unmanageable hunger for Japanese food while on foot between Yale
and the Grad Ghetto, you'll do better almost anywhere else.

Hot Tomato's

6.4
10

A chic, soaring space beneath the Taft where the cocktails overshadow the work of the restaurant

New American, Italian $**39**   *Theater District*

6.3/10   **8.5**/10   **1.0**/10   **5.2**/10
Food   *Atmosphere*   *Attitude*   *Value*

Upmarket restaurant   261 College St.   *Bar* Full
Mon.-Thurs. 11:30am-1am; Fri.   New Haven   *Credit Cards* Visa, MC, AmEx
11:30am-2am; Sat. 4pm-2am; Sun.   (203) 624-6331   *Reservations* Recommended
4pm-1am. Kitchen closes at 10pm.   www.hottomatos.net
Date-friendly. Good wine list.

Set in the grand old ballroom of what was once the Taft Hotel in the very heart of downtown, with exceedingly high ceilings and brass railings, Hot Tomato's effortlessly occupies a cavernous space that conveys exactly the sense of New York chic that the place is going for. The space is divided into a pricey Italian-influenced New American restaurant—most of which spreads out over second-floor balconies—and a ground-floor bar.

The popular bar is the crowning achievement. It may be too yuppie for some tastes, but it takes an elegant approach to late-night or before-dinner drinks, with a soaring space that feels like a well-executed bar in the lobby of a hip big-city hotel—except for the screw-you service from New Haven's most obnoxious bartenders. There are smart martinis and a good Scotch list. The popular double chocolate martini has Finlandia vodka and Godiva liqueur lost in a sea of Bailey's Irish Cream. The espresso martini, made with Stoli Vanil, is better balanced. The bar menu features little gems like chorizo and carnival-style fried dough at remarkably low prices.

The restaurant itself is a mish-mash of good conception and ambivalent execution, tempting but disappointing. To dine along the balconies, perched on a ledge high above the bar, is an experience that matches the verticality of what's on the plates themselves. The service at the restaurant is better than at the bar, but prices are high for the unremarkable dishes with more attitude than taste. A skirt steak is chewy and boring. Orecchiette tossed with sautéed chicken and broccoli are underflavored and incoherent (why do restaurants continue to serve pasta with chicken?). Tiramisu has little rum. And so on. Stick to the bar, and you can soak in the atmosphere without spending so much on dinner.

House of Chao

6.4
/10

A good, cheap, and basic Chinese standby that's long been quite popular with Westville locals

Chinese   **$12**   *Westville*

6.2/10   **6.5**/10   **7.0**/10   **6.8**/10
Food   *Atmosphere* *Attitude*   *Value*

Casual restaurant   898 Whalley Ave.   ***Bar*** BYO
Tues.-Sun. noon-10pm;   New Haven   ***Credit Cards*** Visa, MC, AmEx
closed Mon.   (203) 389-6624   ***Reservations*** Accepted

This inexpensive Chinese-American restaurant in downtown Westville has built up a devoted following over more than 20 years. The very local patrons (and we don't mean Chinese people) tend to arrive knowing exactly what they want. The stained, lacquered wooden surfaces, the wainscoting, the white walls, the Chinese art, and the pop piano classics are exactly what you'd expect, although lighting is refreshingly dim. The service is polite but nothing more unless you're a regular.

Most of the menu is as predictable as the décor: classics like General Tso's, lo mein, and so on. Hot and sour soup is a good version, with pleasing bits of bamboo, egg, and tofu coexisting in happy harmony; pepper is the dominant flavor there. Fried rice, another standby, is unusually dull, however, without much fried character or evidence of egg.

The dumplings are homemade and well above average, as are the other standard brown-sauce preparations, but we prefer the "house specialties," which include good, crispy fish and lamb dishes. The New Tse Chicken is a plate of large chunks of chicken that are deep fried for an effect something like chicken fingers, but not greasy and puffy like deep fried Chinese-American fare can be. It's real breast meat (not that spongy stuff), crispy enough to stand up to the sweet but largely uninteresting red sauce. Fresh vegetables, which might include broccoli, bamboo shoots, baby corn, celery, onions, and snap peas, are cooked al dente for an unexpected crunch. Decent, in short, but unmemorable.

Lunch specials are all under five dollars, in line with low market rates for lunch, and remarkably, not one dish on the menu—not even the crispy fish—costs more than $8.95. And don't forget about the value proposition of BYO. In the end, it might be the value proposition that really keeps people hooked.

Humphrey's East

6.2
10

A neighborhood bar with old-school American grub, outdoor seating, and a significant following

Bar food $16 *East Rock/Grad Ghetto*

5.5/10
Food

7.5/10
Atmosphere

6.0/10
Attitude

6.1/10
Value

Bar and grill
Sun.-Thurs. 11:30am-1am; Fri.-Sat. 11:30am-2am. Kitchen closes at midnight. *Outdoor dining.*

175 Humphrey St.
New Haven
(203) 782-1506
humphreyseastpub.com

Bar Full
Credit Cards Visa, MC, AmEx
Reservations Accepted

This classic bar and grill, with first-rate fries and burgers and free-flowing beer, enjoys a jovial escape-from-it-all atmosphere that might derive partly from its location a couple of short blocks off the beaten Grad Ghetto track. It's far enough away not to be overrun by angst-ridden academics with higher degrees, trying to decide whether or not to sell their souls to the endlessly churning econo-engine of corporate America.

The local happy hour crowd is particularly fun, especially in warm weather when the crowd flows into the sunny back room, aptly named Bogart's. On a good day the drink deal is sweetened by a raft of free bar food, of which the chicken wings are by far our favorite. On certain nights, Bogart's is also graced by live music and dancing.

The best aspect of Humphrey's East, though, is the outdoor tables in good weather. As for the food, standbys include buffalo wings, fried calamari, and well-dressed burgers. For those craving liberal servings of meat, there are barbecued ribs (which can be on the tough side, with a sweet and uninteresting BBQ sauce) and steaks sized medium to XXL. There is also a brief nod to vegetarians, and a great-value kids' menu for people under age 12. At our last visit, we were somewhat unimpressed by the burgers, though. There's also pizza, which is actually not bad.

It's mostly old-school American food as it was meant to be, and it's emblematic of one of New Haven's strengths: unpretentious grub that tastes as good to a Little Leaguer as it does to a Comp Lit professor.

Hunan Café

Typical corner Chinese-American take-out only a
slight notch above the mediocre competition

Chinese $ 9   *Upper Chapel Area*

4.1 /10   **3.0**/10   **6.0** /10   **5.0**/10
Food   *Atmosphere*   *Attitude*   *Value*

Counter service   142 York St.   ***Bar*** Wine and beer only
Mon.-Sat. 10:30am-10:30pm; New Haven   ***Credit Cards*** Visa, MC, AmEx
Sun. 11:30pm-10:30pm. *Delivery.* (203) 776-8688 ***Reservations*** Accepted

Hunan Café, on the corner of York and Crown, is the Chinese take-out
vendor of choice for this part of town, especially at lunchtime, when
the special is a value that's hard to beat: $4.50 yields a generous
portion of wok fare with rice, plus soup (egg drop, wonton, or hot and
sour) or an egg roll. In a subterranean location decorated with artificial
flowers, Hunan has little in the way of charming ambiance—this place
is all about a compelling taste-to-value ratio.

The menu touts its offerings as "exotic Chinese," but it seems that
the most exotic things here are whimsical titles for otherwise familiar
dishes, and a mysterious predilection toward pairing chicken and
shrimp (Dragon and Phoenix is just one of five such options); perhaps
this is a strategy to bulk up the servings of what is actually rather good
shrimp. Veggie options include steamed broccoli with tofu and
mushroom with brown rice and ginger sauce.

Most dishes are wok-sautéed combinations of protein and
vegetables, executed with characteristic speed. Hunan is no haute
cuisine, whatever its aspirations, but in the corner Chinese-American,
Szechuan brown-sauce model, it is a slight notch above Main Garden,
China King, and so on. Vegetables are fresh and crisp, and the
establishment guarantees that all dishes are MSG-free. The bulk of
business at Hunan is in take-out, and the free delivery for orders over
$10 is a boon to the New Haven scene, where there is still a dearth of
delivery options.

Ibiza

9.3
10

New Haven's Spanish superstar, exploring profound
and modern flavors with each new menu

Spanish   **$44**   *Theater District*

9.8/10   **8.5**/10   **9.0**/10   **8.1**/10
Food   *Atmosphere*   *Attitude*   *Value*

Upmarket restaurant   39 High St.   *Bar* Full
Tues. 5pm-10pm; Wed.-Thurs.   New Haven   *Credit Cards* Visa, MC, AmEx
11:30am-2:30pm, 5pm-10pm; Fri. (203) 865-1933   *Reservations* Essential
11:30am-2:30pm, 5pm-11pm; Sat. www.ibizanewhaven.com
noon-3pm, 5pm-11pm; Sun. 6pm-
9pm; closed Mon. *Date-friendly. Good wine list.*

Ten years ago, New Haven's top restaurants were hopelessly outdated—
fancy, perhaps, but not modern. How far we have come. Today, it is
Ibiza that is blazing the trail ahead. More than one hundred years after
Louis Lassen purportedly invented the hamburger, thus becoming the
first New Haven chef to achieve national renown, Luis Bollo—a Spanish
chef whose flights of fancy include shellfish foams, mango terrines,
tomato-caper quenelles, soy sauce-citrus juice vinaigrettes, and crispy
Manchengo cheese cookies—has become the next. To walk the few
paces from Louis' to Luis' is to traverse a century's arc of a city's, and a
nation's, culinary and cultural development.

Luis' pleasures are as complex as Louis' are simple. The menu
changes often; a recent meal began with rich but delicate codfish
croquettes, and progressed to blue point oysters marinated in mint
leaves and lime juice, with a "Bloody Mary foam" and avocado ice
cream—like an intense encounter of masculinity and femininity, with
rock salt and spicy tomato flavors overlapping with the overtly sexual
texture of ethereal foam upon creamy oyster. Other recent favorites
have included a preparation of fatty, indulgent, deeply flavored pork
belly that was set off by notes of Cabrales blue cheese, pineapple, and
garlic.

Service is serious and attentive, and the lighting and ambience have
improved in recent years. Furnishings are quite modern, and the bar,
although largely concealed from view, exudes happy feelings. Ibiza is
not a timid restaurant, and Mr. Bollo not a timid chef. His flavors are
bold, experimental, and profound. When he speaks, there is authority,
and when he cooks, there is authority. And yet he leads New Haven's
best restaurant quietly and not loudly. What a great example to follow
from a chef, and a city, that we should be proud of.

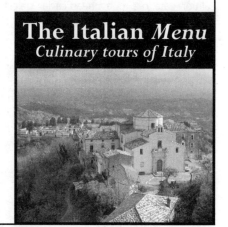

IKEA Restaurant

5.3
/10

The 99-cent breakfast might seem like a bargain—
but how much did you spend at IKEA that day?

Swedish   **$ 6**   *Long Wharf*

5.1/10   **5.5**/10   **6.0**/10   **6.3**/10
Food   *Atmosphere*   *Attitude*   *Value*

Counter service   450 Sargent Dr.   ***Bar*** None
Mon.-Fri. 9:30am-8pm; Sat. New Haven   ***Credit Cards*** Visa, MC, AmEx
9:30am-8pm; Sun. 9:30am-7pm. (203) 865-4532   ***Reservations*** Not accepted
Breakfast.   www.ikea.com

Since the opening of New Haven's IKEA, people have flocked into town
from Massachusetts, from eastern Connecticut, and even from the
northern New York City suburbs just to partake in the classic all-day
scavenger hunt for cheap Scandinavian furniture. It's a pastime so
popular that it has made Swedish founder Ingvar Kamprad one of the
world's richest men.

But Ingvar would have to sell quite a few of the 99-cent egg, bacon,
and potato breakfasts—this has to be the highest calorie-to-cent ratio
in New Haven—to add much to his $50 billion fortune. Although
breakfast represents the best value, we prefer to stick to the decent
Swedish meatballs, which taste good for frozen, processed meat.
They're well seasoned and served with mild gravy and a lingonberry
preserve that adds a pleasant tartness. But avoid at all costs the "pesto-
marinated" vegetables with soggy pasta and crayfish tails that come
with a metallic-tasting lime sauce, a multicolored mess.

Downstairs, hot dogs please the crowds, warm cinnamon buns
exude that irresistible fresh-baked smell, and frozen yogurt rings in at
under $1. The store also sells reasonably priced Swedish goods like
salmon paté in a tube, cheap caviar, delectable cloudberry jam, and
those same frozen meatballs in big bags, along with the lingonberry
sauce (Clare admits that they have, on occasion, made her quite happy
at the undiscriminating hour of 3am).

Above all, the IKEA restaurant is brilliant retail science, because it
prevents customers from leaving the store just because they're hungry.
Whether or not the store is profiting from the food, your little break
gives you that extra moment to convince yourself that you really do
need that minimalist bookcase-room divider (it's still right over there).
Like most self-made billionaires, Ingvar always knows the way to your
wallet better than you do.

India Palace

An average Indian restaurant with a lunch buffet
but not much going for it—especially décor-wise

Indian $**18**   *Upper Chapel Area*

5.9 /10   **2.0** /10   **8.0** /10   **5.5** /10
Food   *Atmosphere*   *Attitude*   *Value*

Casual restaurant   65 Howe St.   *Bar* Wine and beer only
Daily 10:30am-10:30pm.   New Haven   *Credit Cards* Visa, MC, AmEx
Delivery. Vegetarian-friendly. (203) 776-9010   *Reservations* Accepted

What India Palace loses in atmosphere, it gains back in bang for the
buck at the lunchtime buffet, but then loses again with food that's
extremely unexciting. Let's begin, though, with the décor: we've
scarcely seen anything worse. It's as if you tried to fashion an Indian
restaurant out of a deserted high school classroom, and then stopped
halfway through. The emptiness of the room (no one ever actually
seems to be eating at India Palace) makes the blank white walls seem
all the blanker. When you peer in through the front windows—even
during the lunchtime buffet, at India Palace's busiest time of day—the
atmosphere seems to have a tangible effect on the emotional states of
the customers. Otherwise gregarious groups seem somehow
disconnected, and even couples in love seem lonely.

The food is fine—unless you over-gorge to the point of physical
discomfort at the all-you-can-eat lunchtime buffet, it's a good deal at
$7.95, considering that you can conceivably reap an entire day's caloric
nourishment from the spread. India Palace serves standard versions of
all the Indian dishes you've come to expect—saag paneer, chicken tikka
masala, rogan josh, and the like. But do consider that you've got a
similar, better buffet at Royal India not so far away, and another one at
Tandoor, even closer. Not to mention Lalibela's much more interesting
Ethiopian buffet, for a dollar less; the raft of Southeast Asian options
on Chapel Street; or other quick, cheap delights such as Louis' Lunch,
China Great Wall, and so on.

Granted, India Palace isn't exactly bad, but there are better choices.
It's for no-bull advice like this that you bought our book, right?

Indochine Pavilion

6.7
10

An above-average standby for cheap pan-Southeast-Asian food

Thai $**18**   *Upper Chapel Area*

6.5/10   **7.0**/10   **7.0**/10   **6.5**/10
Food   *Atmosphere* *Attitude*   *Value*

Casual restaurant   1180 Chapel St.   ***Bar*** Full
Sun.-Thurs. 11:30am-10pm;   New Haven   ***Credit Cards*** Visa, MC, AmEx
Fri.-Sat. 11:30am-11pm.   (203) 865-5033   ***Reservations*** Accepted
Delivery. Vegetarian-friendly.

This pan-Southeast-Asian mainstay stands guard at the very western end of New Haven's miniature Thai Town on Chapel Street. It's above average for the strip, a cozy little room decorated in shades of brown that create a more careful atmosphere than some of the Chapel Street competition. We've always been a bit befuddled by the sign boldly advertising that the place got "three stars from the New York Times." We have absolutely no idea what they are talking about, but you have to respect, on some twisted level, that a bargain-basement pan-Asian joint on a New Haven street corner would be brazen enough to claim that they were on par with Le Cirque.

That said, the prices are quite reasonable, especially for the popular and incredibly cheap all-you-can-eat lunch buffet, offered daily for rock-bottom prices. The menu might be a bit too far-reaching, with Vietnamese, Cambodian and Thai all elbowing their way into print (though it's nothing compared with Thai Pan Asian half a block away). Thai hot and sour soup is pretty decent, as are the green and yellow curries of various sorts. However, we are particular fans of the larb gai (a cold, marinated, minced chicken salad with onions and a wonderful limey tang), which might be the best choice of all. The vegetarian selection is also admirable.

Service is attentive and friendly, they do a healthy take-out business, and they even deliver. In short, Indochine is a good standby if you feel like eating something flavored with some coconut, some spice, and maybe some lemongrass, without spending a lot. You'll be sharing space with a Yale-heavy crowd that's clued in on that same spice-for-the-dollar proposition that you are. Just don't expect fireworks.

Inka

7.2
10

The only Peruvian restaurant in the area, with
memorable ceviche served in an unassuming space

Latin American   **$20**   *East Haven*

7.6 /10   **6.0** /10   **8.0** /10   **7.0** /10
Food   *Atmosphere*   *Attitude*   *Value*

Casual restaurant   142 Foxon Rd. (Rt. 80)   *Bar* Wine and beer only
Thurs.-Sun. 12:30pm-10pm; closed   East Haven   *Credit Cards* Visa, MC, AmEx
Mon.-Wed. Hours vary; call first.   (203) 469-0028   *Reservations* Accepted

Peruvian food in East Haven? Yeah, baby. We're talking about Inka, a
restaurant on a lonely stretch of Foxon Road that serves what might
well be the best ceviche in the entire New Haven area—even amidst
fierce competition. Inka closed briefly for remodeling in 2005, but has
now re-opened in full force; apparently, there are now plans to beef up
the more authentic Peruvian criollo section of the menu with weekend
specials.

The staff at Inka is friendly, but the service can be slow, and the
restaurant's décor is stark, to say the least. For the time being, the small
house contains little more than white walls with a rambling collection
of paintings depicting scenes of ancient Peru, and a bunch of very basic
tables and chairs.

Regardless, you can't go wrong with the delicious (and amply
portioned) ceviche, whether it's the shrimp, fish, or mixed shellfish
version. The well balanced marinade, which has an authentic orange
hue and a healthy lime kick, does wonders for the succulent shrimp
and meltingly tender fish. Even the squid shines here, with virtually no
hint of chewiness, and big kernels of maize set off the fish nicely. Our
hearts were stolen by the anticucho, skewers of grilled veal hearts with
a deeply spiced, wonderfully savory marinade. The meat, which might
remind you of sweetbreads, has a slight bounce to it characteristic of
innards, but the hearts are cooked just enough to be tender without
stripping them of their wonderful flavor. The only disappointment at
Inka has come from the criollo main courses—specifically the arroz
chaufa de pollo, an enormous serving of fried rice and bits of chicken
and egg with a taste that is strongly reminiscent of cheap Chinese take-
out. Skip it.

Istanbul Café

7.5
10

Good Turkish food in an elaborately decorated, central location

Turkish $**29**   *Theater District*

7.3 /10   **8.0** /10   **7.0** /10   **6.8** /10
Food   *Atmosphere*   *Attitude*   *Value*

Upmarket restaurant   245 Crown St.   *Bar* BYO
Daily noon-10pm. No lunch menu   New Haven   *Credit Cards* Visa, MC, AmEx
Sundays. *Vegetarian-friendly.*   (203) 787-3881   *Reservations* Recommended

Istanbul Café is an interesting experiment: a smart Turkish restaurant in the heart of downtown New Haven. The location couldn't be more choice, around the corner from the Shubert and the Taft. And yet, judging from the empty tables, it seems that Istanbul Café has won precious few devotees in town.

We think that's a shame, because the food at Istanbul Café is great. The nohut ezme, Turkish hummus, is excellent, as is the patlican salata, a creamy purée of grilled eggplant, lemon juice, puréed garlic, vinegar, and olive oil that is reminiscent of baba ganoush, but with a bit more subtlety. Ispanak ezme, a spicy spinach purée with yogurt, is an interesting and welcome flavor combination. Stay away from the more standard Middle Eastern options; meat skewers, for instance, can lack seasoning and also be too dry. The restaurant definitely has a way with eggplant, though, and nowhere is that more evident than in the spectacular smoked eggplant purée that comes with hunkar begendi ("Sultan's Delight"), our favorite dish on the menu. Pieces of tomato-marinated cooked lamb are served atop the purée, which is wondrously rich, creamy, and flavorful, yet not overwhelming.

The room's décor is a tad too elaborate, and the empty tables don't help the ambience, but it's pleasant enough, and the service is quiet but efficacious. There is a semi-secret back room (a bit drafty in winter) that's positively romantic, with golden curtains, velvety couches, and a low table. There are even belly dancers on Friday nights, if that's your thing. Istanbul Café is expensive for New Haven—but it's in the same range as its upmarket neighbors around Crown and College. Yet Istanbul Café has yet to win a loyal following. We wish it would, because we'd like the restaurant to stick around.

Ivy Noodle

2.6
10

Not even late hours and a great location can redeem the awful Chinese food at this little joint

Chinese   **$ 8**   *Broadway Area*

1.8 /10   **3.0** /10   **6.0** /10   **4.4** /10
Food   *Atmosphere*   *Attitude*   *Value*

Casual restaurant   316 Elm St.   *Bar* None
Mon.-Sat. 11am-2am; Sun.   New Haven   *Credit Cards* Visa and MC
noon-11pm. *Vegetarian-friendly.* (203) 562-8800   *Reservations* Not accepted

When Ivy Noodle opened as the first Asian noodle shop in town, it also joined the exceedingly sparse late-night food scene in New Haven. The late hours and the low prices (a complete meal is easy to do for under $5, although the lightning-quick, nominal table service nudges you into tipping) remain its chief virtues. We're also charmed by the staff behind the counter; they work with mild gusto and a friendly eye. There's no effort whatsoever at décor or atmosphere (other than the open-air kitchen itself), but would you expect anything more, given the business model?

Unfortunately, although the extraordinarily extensive menu of rice and noodle dishes, most of them Cantonese, looks promising, all hope is destroyed in the execution. Preparations could hardly be any more bland—it seems as if virtually no seasoning at all is used in preparation, whether the sautéing of greens or simmering of soups. Compare this to China Great Wall, where the exact same soups are fully flavored. Here, adding lots of hot sauce or sliced hot peppers helps things, so don't forget to ask for some (and plenty of salt) when ordering take-out. But nothing could have possibly fixed the last noodle soup we tried, which was just disgusting. It had all the taste of warm dishwater with a distinct sheen of grease sitting on top.

If you must eat here, curry soups have more taste than the rest, and they're probably the best choice. Consider the curry chicken noodle, which is white meat chicken, noodles, and fried tofu in chicken broth with coconut milk and Asian curry spices. Always ask for extra greens, because often there aren't enough of them. But, frankly, even in the wee hours, we'd rather not eat at all than eat food that's this bad.

Ixtapa Grille

6.5
10

A basic, homey restaurant that's nothing more, or less, than slightly-above-average Tex-Mex

Tex-Mex $**20**   *Hamden*

6.4 /10   **6.5** /10   **7.0** /10   **6.6** /10
Food   *Atmosphere*   *Attitude*   *Value*

Casual restaurant   2547 Whitney Ave.   *Bar* Full
Sun.-Thurs. 11am-10pm;   Hamden   *Credit Cards* Visa, MC, AmEx
Fri.-Sat. 11am-11pm.   (203) 230-2586   *Reservations* Accepted

Ixtapa Grille is a homey restaurant decorated in bright festive colors. The menu is more Tex-Mex than traditional Mexican, with the usual tacos, quesadillas, burritos and enchiladas. There are fajitas and saucier meat, chicken, and garlicky shrimp dishes served with rice, tortillas, and a side of beans. Ixtapa also offers a fairly inexpensive club steak, for those times when you crave a piece of meat. Things here don't stray far beyond these staples. It's a shame, to us, considering that the owner, chef, and staff are all Mexican. The chef hails from Guadalajara, and we would give a lot to dip a spoon into a cooking pot from his home town rather than having yet another chimichanga. Still, these are worthwhile versions of Tex-Mex, and there's nothing wrong with Tex-Mex.

This phenomenon is quite typical for local Mexican restaurants. It is why Californians tend to pine away for the more authentic offerings available on the left coast. At first, we hypothesized that New England restaurants were often not run by Mexicans. But we have since determined that the crux of the matter lies elsewhere. Is it that our produce is disheartening to Mexican restaurateurs? A difficulty in sourcing authentic seasonings, perhaps? Or do they simply assume that the Connecticut dining public isn't interested in more regional fare?

The straight-ahead, moderately priced food menu is augmented by a prodigious drink list which includes approximately twenty margaritas and more than a dozen kinds of Mexican beer. The breadth of the margarita list reflects not just fruity flavors, but also some highly respectable tequilas. These liquid assets, combined with some charming booth seating and friendly service, make Ixtapa a good place to catch up with friends for a few drinks and conversation when it happens to be mealtime.

J.P. Dempsey's

7.1
10

A reasonable sports bar and grill with a peculiar peanut obsession

Bar food $22   *East Rock/Grad Ghetto*

6.0 /10   **7.0** /10   **6.0** /10   **5.1** /10
Food   *Atmosphere*   *Attitude*   *Value*

Bar and grill   974 State St.   *Bar* Full
Mon.-Thurs. 11:30am-1am;   New Haven   *Credit Cards* Visa, MC, AmEx
Fri. 11:30am-2am; Sat. noon-2am; (203) 624-5991   *Reservations* Accepted
Sun. noon-midnight. Kitchen closes
Sun.-Thurs. 11pm; Fri.-Sat. 12:30am.
Outdoor dining.

J.P. Dempsey's is your average American sports bar/pub/grill with slightly-above-average burger-and-bar food, an average beer selection, and an average crowd—a mix of locals and a few grad students. It's a standby when C.O. Jones is too crowded for drinks, or Modern is too crowded for pizza. The burgers and wings, as at most such solid, local spots in New Haven, are the real thing, and deserve serious respect. Perhaps the bar's best feature is a few outdoor tables on the State Street sidewalk during summer.

The menu includes fried calamari tossed with hot cherry peppers and marinara; good boneless buffalo chicken tenders; and a starter called gusto bread, which is a half loaf of Italian bread topped with diced tomatoes, onions, prosciutto, and mozzarella, baked and served with the "famous" herb plum tomato sauce, and a fantastic example of that American classic, chocolate cake. Although the menu is quite expansive, including such single-eyebrow-raisers as a sole and cheese sandwich and 17-dollar steaks, we recommend sticking to the basics.

Be forewarned: you don't want to come in here barefoot, because J.P. Dempsey's has a peculiar obsession with peanuts. A basket of peanuts is peremptorily deposited onto your table within moments of your arrival, and the bar's floor is entirely carpeted with a layer of peanut shells so thick that it's hard to tell the color underneath—in-your-face evidence that you, and thousands before and after you, will have to do the shelling yourself. If you're like us, peanuts are the sort of high-calorie, low-satisfaction food that you inadvertently eat in abundance if they're sitting there unattended for any appreciable length of time. Nonetheless, the novelty value may override any dietary fears. After all, how often do you get to experience the satisfying crunch of peanut shells underfoot?

Jalapeño Heaven

One of the most charming places in the area for
Tex-Mex fare: a little house on the side of the road

Tex-Mex   **$23**   *Branford*

6.6/10   **8.5**/10   **8.0**/10   **6.9**/10
Food   *Atmosphere*   *Attitude*   *Value*

Casual restaurant   40 North Main St.   ***Bar*** Full
Mon.-Tues. 11:30am-9pm; Wed-   Branford   ***Credit Cards*** Visa, MC, AmEx
Thurs. 11:30am-9:30pm; Fri.-Sat.   (203) 481-6759   ***Reservations*** Not accepted
11:30am-10:30pm; Sun. noon-9pm.
Date-friendly. Outdoor dining.

In the wonderful world of suburban Tex-Mex, Jalapeño Heaven is the
ultimate crowd-pleaser. These folks know what people want, and they
know how to give it to them. The restaurant is in a cute little white
house—it would certainly seem like your average two-family if not for
the kitschy sign hung on the front porch.

Inside, the kitsch continues. You might be ushered up to a charming
second floor, which is like your aunt's living room fitted with all the
standard Tex-Mex accoutrements. There's something about dining on
this particular sort of Tex-Mex food in the upstairs of a little house that
is completely unique, and uniquely wonderful. The porch, meanwhile,
houses some tables in good weather as well—after all, there's nothing
better than sipping margaritas outdoors on a sunny afternoon.

Service is smiley and endearing. Surprisingly, prices are somewhat
high given the place's random suburban location along Route 1. But
they're not through the roof. Here, as ever, jack cheese is one of the
secrets to satisfying Tex-Mex: the grilled quesadilla is filled with green
chili peppers and…plenty of cheese. We like the white enchilada, which
is filled with chicken and topped with a spicy cheese sauce rather than
the standard red sauce. Accompanying beans and rice are flavorful, and
desserts are good. But Jalapeño Heaven is really about the experience,
and it's worth it. You've got to be in that particular mood, and a
margarita or two might do the trick.

Jasmine Thai Cart

7.2/10

A friendly, reliable Thai newcomer to the New
Haven food-cart scene, in a location bereft of carts

American **$ 5** *Financial District*

6.8/10
Food

8.0/10
Attitude

9.6/10
Value

Take-out
Mon.-Fri. 11am-3pm; closed Sat.-
Sun. *Vegetarian-friendly.*

Church St. between
Grove St. and Elm St.
No phone

Bar None
Credit Cards None
Reservations Not accepted

You're never far from a food cart in New Haven, but this simple
weekday-only Thai cart, which is relatively new to the scene, sits in an
area far from most of the others. It's more easily accessible from the
downtown financial and government area, as well as the southern end
of the Grad Ghetto neighborhood, and it delivers on its promise of
cheap, competently prepared Thai basics.

The menu rotates, but you can always choose two, three, or four
items in combination. Perhaps in deference to the Atkins crowd, rice is
an option, not a baseline. Our favorite things here are the tender "Thai
BBQ chicken," which is curried and grilled right in front of your eyes—
it's improved by hot sauce—and the good Panang curry, with chicken
and green beans that still have some snap to them. Pad Thai has sweet
noodles and perhaps an under-dose of egg and peanut, but it's not
bad. Its noodles, like the pineapple fried rice (another option), quickly
begin to absorb the flavors of the other dishes that you select, adding
more flavor. It's all spooned into your Styrofoam box in prodigious
portions. After a couple of dishes, the box is bursting with food; a five-
dollar three-item combo (never mind the four-item version for less than
a dollar more) easily feeds two. We find it hard to fathom, in fact, that
any one person could complete the task of eating it all.

The service is polite, too, so it's not hard to see—given the value
proposition and slightly monopolistic location—why this place has a
loyal lunchtime following during the week.

Jeffrey's

A famous, elegant New American restaurant that's
now reinventing itself as an informal bistro

New American $44   *Milford*

8.8 /10   **8.0** /10   **10** /10   **7.4** /10
Food   *Atmosphere*   *Attitude*   *Value*

Upmarket restaurant   501 New Haven Ave.   *Bar* Full
Mon.-Sat. 11:30am-10pm;   Milford   *Credit Cards* Visa, MC, AmEx
closed Sun. *Good wine list.* (203) 878-1910   *Reservations* Accepted
Outdoor dining.

For more than a decade, Jeffrey's of Milford has been a venerable
Connecticut restaurant that has focused its attention on excellent local
ingredients and traditional preparations—albeit with a distinctly modern
New American angle and more than a handful of fusion touches. A
white house on a nondescript stretch of Milford strip mall, the
restaurant has always been traditional to the core: an elegant space
with a nice view of marshland, luxuriant place settings that happily
hover just on this side of stuffy, and a gracious outdoor patio.

So imagine our surprise at hearing that, at press time, Jeffrey's had
shut down and was reinventing itself as a much more informal place,
focused more on lunches and such. We have high hopes: this was a
place that would always impress us with the careful seasoning of the
sauces (clearly tasted in the kitchen), with a chef that unstintingly
demanded high performance from his purveyors. This showed in such
dishes as the sesame-seed-encrusted Ahi tuna with a great sesame-
ginger vinaigrette. Although this was a decade-plus-old Californian dish
that had already become the very symbol of New American fusion
cuisine before Jeffrey's started serving it, the execution here was
impeccable. The tuna had a crisp but delicate sear concealing
sensuously rare flesh within, and a "citrus wasabi aioli" added yet
another layer of flavor.

Anyway, we're excited to see what Jeffrey's is up to now that we
will (presumably) never again have to deal with such pricey mains as a
$36 filet mignon (in its defense, it was topped with truffle). In any case,
we hope that they won't stop making their spectacular key lime tart,
one of the happiest desserts in all of greater New Haven.

Jimmies of Savin Rock

6.9
10

A grand, classic seafooder sprawled right on the West Haven waterfront

Seafood, Traditional American $**22**   *West Haven*

6.0 /10
Food

8.0 /10
Atmosphere

9.0 /10
Attitude

6.5 /10
Value

Casual restaurant	5 Rock St.	*Bar* Full
Sun.-Thurs. 11am-9:30pm;	West Haven	*Credit Cards* Visa and MC
Fri.-Sat. 11am-11pm.	(203) 934-3212	*Reservations* Not accepted

From the parking lot, the outside of Jimmies of Savin Rock looks like a bunkered 1960s presidential retreat, with a vague Frank Lloyd Wright lodge aesthetic. But cast your eyes seaward and you'll see expanses of beach, boardwalk, park, gazebo. Indoors, the cacophony of seaside themes comes together in Jacquard-style prints that feature in the window dressings and carry over to the dividing wall, where they meet the wood paneling. There are painted glass portholes with multicolored, cartoonish fish, and large picture windows that look out over expanses of the real sea (okay, the Sound). There is even a lighthouse in view. Whether you're coming from downtown New Haven or nearby in West Haven, Jimmies really is a trip.

The open-armed, what-can-I-get-you-sweetie style service has real appeal. We think it's particularly appreciated by the older clientele (some of which seem to have been customers since Jimmies first opened in 1925). Start with a fresh, spicy Bloody Mary before moving on to the long and involved menu, which lists a variety of surf-and-turf variations, elaborate fish dishes, and so on. Jimmies is best known, though, for classics like hot dogs, fried clams, fried shrimp, and lobster rolls.

Some claim that the place has gone downhill, food-wise, in recent years. Perhaps, but the lobster roll is still a valuable relic. One can forget how important the "roll" part is in a lobster roll, but not here: the bun is wonderfully toasted and luxuriously buttery. The meat within, though, is unfortunately not pure lobster; it's mixed with langoustines, which gives it a texture more like shrimp. Full platters feature french fries of the cafeteria-style ruffled variety, along with absolutely enormous quantities of (usually) fried seafood. It's hard to imagine how one person, however large, could possibly take on the whole thing.

Joe's Hubba Hubba

5.2
/10

A very, very American lunch spot in the business district, with average food and not much else

Short-order American $ **7**   *Financial District*

4.8 /10   **5.5** /10   **7.0** /10   **5.9** /10
Food   *Atmosphere*   *Attitude*   *Value*

Counter service   135 Orange St.   ***Bar*** None
Mon.-Tues. 7am-4pm; Wed.-Fri. New Haven   ***Credit Cards*** None
7am-6pm; Sat. 11am-6pm;   (203) 773-1000   ***Reservations*** Not accepted
closed Sun. *Breakfast.*   www.joeshubbahubba.com

This is a new short-order spot in the business district that advertises breakfast, lunch, and dinner, although we doubt many people come for the last. The menu is American to the core, focusing on "wedges" (really just sandwiches on long rolls, cut in half), hot dogs, burgers, and wraps, along with a few other standard items like chicken tenders and fried clams. There's also a standard breakfast lineup.

The counter service is friendly and functional; there's a token attempt at retro atmosphere, but the reproductions of Americana (mostly old advertisements for food and drinks) are far too orderly and new-looking to create any nostalgia. The checkered linoleum floors and seven cafeteria-style fake wood tables are purely functional, and the blaring radio drowns out conversation; the overall effect is merely that of another lunch spot that does a healthy take-out business, although a fair number of customers stay and eat in.

Joe's logo touts the "Famous Chili," and Joe's menu touts "Hubba's Famous Wedges," so we thought the natural way to proceed would be to try something that combined all of the famous things in one—the Steak Texas wedge, with steak, onions, and chili. We added cheese for good measure. The chili is, at the least, unusual. It is extremely finely shredded beef with a kick to it, dominated more by the flavor of hot pepper than of cumin or anything else—almost like a spicy Bolognese sauce. It goes well with the whiz-type cheese; that cheese also pairs perfectly with steak, a strong argument in favor of the Philadelphia school of steak and cheese. The wedge boasts excellent fresh bread, but the steak itself, in spite of being cut into appropriately small and thin pieces, is rather tough and certainly undersalted.

Definitely not any better than anything else in this neighborhood. A bit worse, perhaps.

John Davenport's

The Omni Hotel's offensively poor excuse for a restaurant with a view

Traditional American $40   *Theater District*

4.1 /10   **7.0** /10   **6.0** /10   **2.9** /10
Food   *Atmosphere*   *Attitude*   *Value*

Upmarket restaurant
Mon.-Thurs. 6am-11am, 11:30am-2pm, 5:30pm-10pm; Fri.-Sat. 6am-11am, 11:30am-2pm, 5:30pm-11pm; Sun. 6am-2pm, 5:30pm-10pm. *Breakfast. Brunch.*

155 Temple St.
New Haven
(203) 974-6737
www.omnihotels.com

Bar Full
Credit Cards Visa, MC, AmEx
Reservations Accepted

"So," we once asked a hotel staff member, "what do people really call the restaurant, informally? Davenport's? John's? Top of the Park? JD's, perhaps?" He shrugged: "Most people just call it the restaurant at the Omni." We couldn't have said it any better, because of all the beautiful things that a place with the best view in town could be, this is just a mediocre hotel-chain restaurant whose only interest seems to be in gouging its captive expense-account guests.

It's a shame, because the view from high above the Green is spectacular. As evening sets in—if you're lucky enough not to be seated next to fussy, view-obscuring institutional drapery—you can gaze upon twinkling lights of the many restaurants in town where you can get a good meal at a fair price.

The Omni's descriptions of their New England dishes, whose prices reach past the mid-$20s, range from the nostalgic ("Rhode Island Stuffies") to the trendy ("blueberry wine demi-glace") to the just plain bizarre ("Yale greens"). A cheesy Vermont cheddar and apple bisque isn't bad, but the "sautéed wild mushrooms" on the "corn Johnnycakes" taste like microwave dinner fare. At one visit, a sirloin steak ordered rare came not just well done, but cooked to a virtually inedible deep, dark grey, and a blueberry dessert arrived still frozen in the middle.

And instead of allowing locals who don't feel like spending $65 a head for a horrible dinner to simply order a cocktail and enjoy the view, the Omni reserves window seats for full meals only; the adjoining bar is just a windowless den that might as well be in a basement. It's as if they wrote it in big letters across the penthouse of their gleaming downtown building: "Screw you, New Haven. Yours sincerely, the Omni Hotel."

Judies European Bakery

5.7
10

A local bakery that's great for fresh breads and not bad for lunch—if only they were friendlier

Baked goods, Light American   **$ 9**   *Arts District*

6.5 /10   **5.0**/10   **3.0** /10   **6.3**/10
Food   *Atmosphere*   *Attitude*   *Value*

Counter service   63 Grove St.   *Bar* None
Mon.-Fri. 7am-5:30pm;   New Haven   *Credit Cards* Visa, MC, AmEx
Sat. 7:30am-3pm; closed Sun. (203) 777-6300   *Reservations* Not accepted
Breakfast.   www.judies.net

When it comes to local bakeries, Judies may well be top dog. The bakery is located on the premises, and its bounty is lovingly displayed in and behind an L-shaped counter. There are little patisserie-style cakes and confections, as well as croissants and other breakfast pastries, but the centerpiece here is bread baked daily with artisanal attention to detail and prices to match. The standards come in all shapes and sizes, from herb baguettes (asiago and shallot, red onion and garlic, rosemary and olive) to butter rolls and sandwiches. Other breads are available on particular days; Fridays are our favorite, with, at last check, orange ricotta, Moravian sugar, brioche, and challah.

Beyond bread sold by the loaf, Judies serves mediocre breakfast sandwiches in the morning, and then serves much better lunch fare until 3pm (why stop so early?). The main drawback is the irritating service—one day unreasonably rigid, the next day unreasonably curt—which seems to us deeply antithetical to the concept of a neighborhood bakery. At one point we were actually charged 15 cents for butter for our bread. The atmosphere has little charm; it's just a bunch of cafeteria-style tables. Most people opt for take-out.

Food-wise, most options are good, but the warm, pressed panini are standouts. Good examples include a first-rate, well-seasoned sandwich of duck prosciutto, pickled cherry peppers, and mozzarella; or the grilled vegetable with taleggio cheese. Even the grilled lemon chicken escapes the blandness typical of most chicken breast sandwiches. Among the soups, the borlotti bean offering (prepared with chicken stock) is luscious. Keep your eye on the daily specials as well.

Kampai

7.2
10

The old-school, sentimental favorite for theatrical teppanyaki, with very respectable sushi too

Japanese $28   *Branford*

7.2/10   **7.0**/10   **8.0**/10   **6.5**/10
Food   *Atmosphere*   *Attitude*   *Value*

Upmarket restaurant   869 W. Main St.   *Bar* Full
Mon.-Sat. 5pm-10:30pm;   Branford   *Credit Cards* Visa, MC, AmEx
Sun. 4pm-9pm.   (203) 481-4536   *Reservations* Accepted

Kampai is the old guard of Benihana-style dining. This 20-year-old Branford restaurant has played benevolent host to innumerable birthdays, dates, and family celebrations, and it's showing its age. The service is kindly but unenergetic, and the hibachi room exudes dim, unflattering light, with a tired carpet that is actually unraveling in one corner. After two decades, the bloom is off the rose. But, like an opera diva a little past her prime, when the curtain goes up, one thinks of nothing but the performance. The knife-flipping teppanyaki theatrics (everything is cooked on the grill in front of you, with great pomp and flair) at Kampai are as good as any, eliciting oohs and aahs aplenty—especially from the kids—and the chicken here is more succulent and tender than at the young upstart, Kumo.

Kampai also bests Kumo when it comes to sushi—especially the excellent yellowtail. Unlike "hibachi" restaurants where sushi is an afterthought, Kampai is actually two restaurants, with two separate rooms; when Kampai first opened, you couldn't get your sushi at Stop and Shop, and a serious, stand-alone sushi restaurant might not yet have survived in American suburbia.

Downstairs, teppanyaki takes center stage, but upstairs, past a kitschily charming koi pond, is a very well appointed dining room complete with tatami seating, where the sushi bar takes pride of place. Although there is little to say about the standard teppanyaki menu (soup, salad, fried rice, and a choice of meat)—it's Benihana all the way—we have one uncharacteristic suggestion: get the chicken. The swordfish is dry, the steak tends toward chewy, and this is not ideal format for lobster. So go ahead and order the cheapest dinner option, then sit back and let yourself enjoy the show.

Katz's 2 Go New York Deli

5.7
10

A lunch-only take-out counter downtown that
hawks New York deli fare, with variable success

Light American   **$ 9**   *Financial District*

5.5/10   **6.0**/10   **6.2**/10
Food   *Attitude*   *Value*

Take-out	167 Orange St.	*Bar* None
Mon.-Fri. 11am-3pm;	New Haven	*Credit Cards* Visa, MC, AmEx
closed Sat.-Sun. *Delivery*.	(203) 787-5289	*Reservations* Not accepted

This is the only downtown New Haven spot that serves anything
approaching New York deli fare. It's basically nothing more than a take-
out place, but even then, there's some charm to the joint, and a cheery
menu and a cheery counter staff to go with it. It's the downtown lunch
crowd that's drawn to this place more than anyone else, and the short
hours—weekdays only, lunchtime only—quickly reveal how specific the
audience is.

The menu, at least, will be a nostalgic thing for anyone who longs
for the corner deli in Manhattan. There are blintzes here; corned beef
and pastrami sandwiches on rye (yes, with mustard); the requisite cole
slaw sides; and pickles with everything. There's a sit-down restaurant
called Katz's in Woodbridge that is loosely affiliated with this
downtown place, but they are run separately.

Pastrami and corned beef sandwiches are perfectly respectable, and
basics like cole slaw are fine. The knishes from Katz's 2 Go are
disappointing, to say the least. They're dry, crackly, and underseasoned
within. Bagels, cream cheese, and lox are a bit better, without any such
glaring flaws. Still, the fare is unremarkable. Few things here will quite
transport you to Katz's Delicatessen on Houston Street, perhaps the
most famous New York deli of them all (suffice it to say that they're
unaffiliated). Still, in a town so close to New York, it's nice to have
something like this downtown.

Katz's Restaurant

6.6
/10

A friendly, fairly successful emulation of a sit-down
New York deli, with great whitefish salad

Light American $16   *Woodbridge*

6.3 /10   **7.0** /10   **7.0** /10   **6.6** /10
Food   *Atmosphere*   *Attitude*   *Value*

Casual restaurant   1658 Litchfield Tpk.   *Bar* None
Daily 11am-8pm.   Woodbridge   *Credit Cards* Visa, MC, AmEx
Brunch.   (203) 389-5301   *Reservations* Accepted

Katz's is one of the only places in greater New Haven that fully realizes
the concept of a New York City deli, from top to bottom. The
emulation begins with the décor: a black-and-white checkerboard
theme, ringed by bright red booths. Perhaps in a nod to the racing flag
motif, service is friendly and almost impossibly swift.

To begin with, two bowls are delivered quickly to every table, one
bearing good cole slaw and the other with two delicious versions of
pickles: sour and half-sour. The chocolate egg cream is well-balanced,
with the proper level of light brown froth to top the sweet blend of
milk, soda water, and chocolate syrup. Certain foods inspire cravings,
and Katz's seems to have the master list of Jewish deli favorites,
beginning with the bagel and lox. Salmon is soft, but just average;
however, the bagels are fresh and judiciously toasted, the cream cheese
is excellent, and the overall effect quite pleasing. Even better is the
exemplary whitefish salad, with big and well textured chunks of smoky
fish mixed into a wonderfully executed cream sauce, and studded with
unusually large chunks of diced celery.

Woodbridge is home to a significant Jewish community, but this is
hardly a kosher deli (to wit: a bacon, egg, and cheese sandwich on the
menu). The traditional Jewish meats—the pastrami, the corned beef,
and so on—do take center stage; the sandwiches, in the New York
style, are many inches thick (though the meat is not up to the hot, rich,
fatty New York standard).

Speaking of enormous sandwiches, there is no official relation
between this Katz's and the Lower East Side landmark on Houston
Street, but this place is affiliated with Katz's 2 Go, a take-out-and-
delivery outpost in downtown New Haven.

KFC

3.4
10

A standard fast-food place that's open late but
loses the fast-food fried-chicken battle to Popeye's

Southern   **$ 7**   *Whalley*

4.0 /10   **2.0** /10   **4.0** /10   **4.6** /10
Food   *Atmosphere*   *Attitude*   *Value*

Fast-food chain   311 Whalley Ave.   *Bar* None
Sun.-Thurs. 10:30am-2am;   New Haven   *Credit Cards* None
Fri.-Sat. 10:30am-4am.   (203) 777-5414   *Reservations* Not accepted
                           www.kfc.com

One of the most global of all fast-food chains, Kentucky Fried
Chicken—whose self-conscious adoption of the "KFC" nickname was a
shameless (if early) concession to the acronym frenzy of the 1990s (BK,
IHOP, T2, and MIB were other notable commercial offenders)—serves
chicken, mostly fried, with standard sides like mashed potatoes and
gravy. For KFC, the abbreviation was apparently an effort to de-
emphasize the "fried," but, make no mistake, that sensibility did not
extend to the menu. The chicken, fried, comes in original or extra
crispy; we prefer the former, as it's more moist and subtle—if we can
call immersing battered chicken in a vat of fat subtle. In fact, rather
than the standard chicken, we even prefer the hot wings, the honey
barbecue and spicy crispy strips, and the fried chicken sandwiches and
their progeny.

The colonel doesn't lie, but perhaps he misleads: while the fried
chicken is famously dubbed "finger-lickin' good," we think that part of
the finger-lickin' quality is due to the equally well-known greasiness of
the batter. Keep in mind that Popeye's is better in the fried chicken fast-
food category, and it's closer to downtown. However, as fast food goes,
fried chicken is one of the better food categories; at least here you're
not subject to thin grey slabs of meat or processed chicken patties. It's
real chicken. The other thing that KFC has going for it is the
wonderfully late hours on weekends.

Kiraku

The idyllic river location puts this competent
Japanese and Korean restaurant over the top

Japanese, Korean $**31**   *Fair Haven*

6.9 /10   **7.5** /10   **8.0** /10   **6.3** /10
Food   *Atmosphere*   *Attitude*   *Value*

Upmarket restaurant	5 Clifton St.	*Bar* Full
Mon.-Fri. 11am-3pm, 5pm-10pm;	New Haven	*Credit Cards* Visa and MC
Sat.-Sun. 5pm-10pm.	(203) 469-7917	*Reservations* Accepted
Outdoor dining.		

Purple glitter walls, purple satin curtains, and purple beads hanging in
the doorway boldly announce the arrival of Kiraku, a Korean-run
restaurant that sits memorably (complete with outdoor tables) on the
Quinnipiac River, next to the even newer Stillwater Bistro.

Japanese and Korean dishes politely share space on Kiraku's menu.
A long sushi bar dispenses fish that, in our experience, has been quite
fresh and good, with a bevy of interesting roll combinations. Some of
the main course combinations are quite expensive, though. Lunch is a
better deal. There are also some more intriguing appetizers, like fried
mussels that come still in their shells. The non-sushi options can be hit-
or-miss, but more often it's hit—for instance, man-doo, handmade pork
dumplings. We're less fond of the fried dishes like kira ebi (fried
shrimp), and we don't particularly recommend the Japanese-American
standards like teriyaki (although the kids might like them).

Still, in the end, it's all about the aesthetic. Sake is artfully served in
artisanal pottery, and there's a large selection of prettily presented
tropical mixed drinks too. But it's ultimately the setting that makes
Kiraku a go-to destination. Precious few of New Haven's restaurants
take advantage of its ample contact with water, and Kiraku's Quinnipiac
riverbank location is a rare treat, delightfully relaxing, and even better in
warmer months, when you can enjoy sushi out on the torch-lit porch. If
you were any closer to the river, you'd be swimming.

Koffee Too?

6.5
/10

An immensely popular coffeeshop serving decent panini and salads to a primarily academic crowd

Light American, Baked goods $ **8**   *Broadway Area*

5.9 /10
Food

8.0 /10
Atmosphere

6.0 /10
Attitude

7.6 /10
Value

Café
Mon.-Fri. 7am-midnight; Sat.
8:30am-midnight; Sun. 9am-
midnight. Lunch menu (sandwiches,
salads, etc.) served 11am-3pm only.
Breakfast. Vegetarian-friendly. Wireless Internet.

276 York St.
New Haven
(203) 787-9929

Bar None
Credit Cards Visa and MC
Reservations Not accepted

Koffee Too?, on York Street, has blossomed into something of a mitochondrion. Just steps away from the law school, this joint is now under separate ownership from Koffee? on Audubon. Clearly, they're doing something right; there's practically not a minute of the day when you won't have to wait in line for a cup of joe, and there are many times when you have little chance of grabbing a seat. It's not hard to see why it's so popular, given the proximity to the Hall of Graduate Studies and Yale Law School, the congenial, mixed student-faculty vibe, and the very good tea selection (teas are also available by the pound).

This coffeeshop also does a brisk business with the lunchtime crowd, making its neighbor, the ubiquitous Au Bon Pain, look embarrassingly bad. Most notable are the panini, pressed grilled sandwiches on good bread, filled with any number of standard filling combinations listed on the board above the counter, as well as a daily special. The #2, a mainstay, has mozzarella and prosciutto with tomato, basil, olive oil, and balsamic vinegar on rustic Italian bread. Don't bother with the tough, chewy steak and cheese, or anything, for that matter, that prominently features meat. By way of explanation, we were once told by the staff that "almost everyone who works here is a vegetarian." That should tell you something about what to order. Much better—delicious, at its best—is a portobello mushroom and goat cheese salad with wonderful seasoning.

The staff is fun and alternative, there's always a newspaper lying around. Whether you're reading cases, skipping class, or on that awkward post-coital coffee date (because dinner would be too uncomfortable), you'll definitely feel like you're fulfilling your role as part of the Yale community.

Koffee? on Audubon

A cool coffee shop where grad students work on their dissertations or their dating prospects

Baked goods, Light American $ 7   Arts District

9.0/10   6.0/10
Atmosphere   *Attitude*

Café
Mon.-Fri. 7am-10pm; Sat 8am-
10pm; Sun. 9am-8pm.
*Breakfast. Vegetarian-friendly.
Wireless Internet.*

104 Audubon St.
New Haven
(203) 562-5454
www.koffeekoffee.com

Bar None
Credit Cards None
Reservations Not accepted

In the dog-eat-dog world of New Haven coffee, Koffee? is a force to be reckoned with. Now completely dissociated in ownership from Koffee Too? (but affiliated with the new Moka), this original, less crowded, infinitely cooler Koffee branch is in a nook on tiny Audubon Street, cleverly nestled right on the way from the Grad Ghetto to Yale. Predictably, it's absolutely dominated by grad students, but it's everything you want in a coffee shop. It may be the best place in town to chill for hours over a laptop and latte. Couches in the front room give way to chairs and tables in a sunny atrium with bright red brick. Behind that, there's a pleasant backyard. Its grass and trees make the whole setting seem almost pastoral. The music is good, especially if you like Nirvana and its progeny.

The coffee itself is also good, plenty dark. There's food, but it's pretty unspectacular. Offerings like a tomato and onion quiche, cappuccino muffins, and cheesecake brownies are generally average, but better than the bland, microwaved pasta dishes, which aren't even that cheap. But few people come here to eat. Koffee? is a particularly good place to go alone—with a book, with a computer, with a little pad of paper. In fact, most customers are solo, and WiFi wireless Internet connections even allow them to surf for Internet porn while getting their caffeine fix. The only downside to this place: picture yourself trying to sift through pages of Hegel or write the great American novel while simultaneously listening to the insufferable English Ph.D. candidate try, repeatedly and unsuccessfully, to hit on the cool Forestry girl. You're guaranteed to witness pickup attempts—so just try to tune it out (or, if you prefer, throw your hat into the ring).

Kumo

Classic suburban-style teppanyaki eatertainment, with brand-spanking-new grills

Japanese $28   Hamden

6.8/10   **7.0**/10   **8.0**/10   **6.3**/10
Food   *Atmosphere*   *Attitude*   *Value*

Upmarket restaurant
Mon.-Thurs. 11am-3pm, 4:30pm-
10:30pm; Fri.-Sat. 11am-3pm,
4:30pm-11pm; Sun. noon-10pm.

218 Skiff St.
Hamden
(203) 281-3166

Bar Full
Credit Cards Visa, MC, AmEx
Reservations Accepted

Teppanyaki cooking—with its fire and flash, with its communal tables and swashbuckling chefs—has been a crowd pleaser ever since the first Benihana restaurant opened forty years ago. But you don't necessarily want to be at a restaurant that recently held its quarterly earnings Webcast, and we're glad that the latest local purveyor of this formulaic "eatertainment" is not part of that empire. At Kumo, what's old is new. The new restaurant features glowing hardwood floors and four gleaming grills, two of which accommodate up to 20 people. There is also tatami seating, but we favor seats by the grill. If you're not here for the show, you're missing the point entirely. Likewise if you order sushi.

Kumo does very average teppanyaki: soup that is watery and hardly worth the trouble; salad, whose ginger dressing is flavorful and abundant; and a schedule of protein combinations, along with the ubiquitous teppanyaki fried rice, complete with egg impressively juggled, flipped and cracked on the edge of a spatula as it succumbs to gravity. The fiery onion volcano, another favorite, is executed with similar flair and prowess.

This cooking style tends to render all things equal, treated to the same soy-sauce-and-butter basting. By virtue of texture, steak and shrimp are the best choices. Fish is a disappointment; it gives us that not-so-fresh feeling. Chicken is bland, and frozen lobster tails barbecued at high heat while doused in soy sauce are hardly worth the premium.

Ultimately, these restaurants are about fun, not fine dining. There is something inherently festive about the genre, which makes it great for big groups and small children—or just your inner child. We defy you to go the entire evening without at least one involuntary gasp. If you can, check your pulse, because you are probably dead.

La Piazza

7.7
/10

A new Italian-American spot catering to students, with late hours, reasonable prices, and open air

Italian   **$27**   *Broadway Area*

7.3 /10   **8.5** /10   **8.0** /10   **7.1** /10
Food   *Atmosphere*   *Attitude*   *Value*

Casual restaurant
Mon.-Wed. noon-10:30pm; Thurs.-
Sat. noon-midnight; Sun. noon-
9pm. Kitchen closes at 10:30pm.
Outdoor dining.

65 Broadway
New Haven
(203) 946-0753
www.opentable.com (reservations only)

Bar Full
Credit Cards Visa, MC, AmEx
Reservations Accepted

Nestled just beyond the Barnes & Noble Yale Bookstore, and open until midnight seven days a week during the school year, La Piazza, from the Caffé Adulis folks, has brought new vitality to a walkway between Broadway and York that used to see little but collegiate traffic. The menu is squarely Italian, and the outdoor summer seating is decidedly Continental.

The menu at La Piazza is a blessedly straightforward, and affordable, thing. Expect pasta, pizza, chicken, and veal, with a selection of appetizers, salads, and sides to round things out. Pasta dishes are a mix-and-match affair, and they ring in at under $10, unless you order gnocchi. Chicken and veal are treated to traditional Italian-American preparations like Milanese and parmigiana. They're nothing groundbreaking, but we've had a delightfully crispy and well-structured version of the veal. And no recitation of Italian-American hits would be complete without calamari and shrimp scampi. Considering these value propositions, the desserts seem disproportionately priced; a chocolate caramel pyramid resembles a David Glass creation—high drama, at prices to match.

For those who prefer a liquid lunch, the martini list includes a charming La Piazza Sparkler, and the mangotini that has been lighting up the cocktail menu at Adulis for as long as we can remember. La Piazza is still quite young, and yet the place is already starting to feel like it's always been there. The space has a benignly modern feel; our favorite architectural features are high, matte-black ceilings with industrial piping, and exposed brick. Comfy banquet seating runs along the dining room perimeter. But when the weather is nice, the best seats in the house are outside, where the restaurant spills out onto the arcade, evoking a truly idyllic outdoor lifestyle. We could all use more of that.

Lalibela

The only strictly Ethiopian restaurant in town is
friendly and affordable, but the food's hit-or-miss

African $**21**   *Theater District*

5.6 /10   **8.0** /10   **9.0** /10   **6.3** /10
Food   *Atmosphere*   *Attitude*   *Value*

Casual restaurant   176 Temple St.   ***Bar*** Full
Mon-Thurs. 11:30am-2pm, 5pm-   New Haven   ***Credit Cards*** Visa, MC, AmEx
10pm; Fri. 11:30am-2pm, 5pm-   (203) 789-1232   ***Reservations*** Accepted
11pm; Sat. 5pm-11pm; Sun. 5pm-   www.lalibelarestaurant.com
10pm. *Date-friendly. Vegetarian-friendly.*

Lalibela is the only restaurant in New Haven that actually calls itself
Ethiopian. Everything comes with injera, the light and spongy
sourdough flatbread distinctive of the region, and you can even eat at
one of the traditional tables in back that looks more like a big bongo
drum than the familiar four-legged article. The room has an
unremarkable, squareish, predictable layout, but friendly faces and
genuineness on the part of the staff go a long way in creating a good
feeling.

The food is tasty and different, a great break from the Indian and
Thai places that proliferate in the area. It's not exactly haute cuisine;
don't expect African with the sort of flair and subtlety you'll find at
Adulis. Here, sauces are simpler, heavier, and darker. Flavors are bold
and deep. Texture is sometimes the driving force, as in the
recommended shuro, made with a rich chickpea puree. The rather
amusingly titled yater fitfit appetizer is dried peas cooked with garlic
and ginger root, mixed with injera and garnished with hot peppers,
served chilled. (We know, it's only funny to English speakers. But try
saying it aloud.) It's an unusual and rewarding taste. We also like dishes
with awaze, the hot-pepper paste.

Unfortunately, some dishes lack sufficient salt—like spicy lentils—
while others are too greasy or buttery, like a garlicky shrimp dish and
spicy chicken. Offerings are generally vegetarian-friendly, though, and
especially at lunch, when there's an all-you-can-eat buffet, the price is
right. In fact, although Lalibela focuses on the same part of the world
as Adulis, the two shouldn't properly be compared; Lalibela is really
competing with Chapel Street Thai, Howe Street Indian, and the like—
whether for the cheap lunch buffet or a casual, not-too-expensive grad-
student dinner. In that company, Lalibela is a worthy competitor.

Le Petit Café

9.6
/10

An outstanding, well-priced, unpretentious prix-fixe
in a cozy haunt on the Left Bank of Branford

French   **$45**   *Branford*

9.4 /10   **10** /10   **10** /10   **8.4** /10
Food   *Atmosphere*   *Attitude*   *Value*

Upmarket restaurant   225 Montowese St.   *Bar* Full
Wed.-Sat., 2 seatings at 6pm and   Branford   *Credit Cards* Visa, MC, AmEx
8:30pm; Sun., seatings at 5pm and (203) 483-9791   *Reservations* Essential
7:30pm; closed Mon.-Tues.   www.lepetitcafe.net
Date-friendly. Good wine list.

Number one overall for the second straight edition of *The Menu,* this
warmly lit, inviting little room right on the Branford town green is easily
worth the trip from anywhere in Connecticut for chef Roy Ip's
impeccable French country food and wine. Le Petit Café's artfully
crafted bistro décor wouldn't be at all out of place along a back street
on the Left Bank of the Seine in Paris—except for the reasonable prices
and the completely unassuming, open-armed attitude of Roy and his
entire staff. Reserve well in advance for one of the two nightly seatings
(only ten per week in total).

As the top end goes, Le Petit Café is not even that expensive,
considering how good the food is. Everyone is required to order the
hearty five-course prix-fixe meal for just under $40; you choose from
several starters and mains on the chalkboard, which change daily. You
can't go wrong with anything here, even if you're a foodie; meat, fish,
and fowl plates are equally spectacular. Duck cassoulet, when available,
is a guaranteed winner. It's a stew with roasted duck, armagnac duck
sausage, applewood smoked bacon, and beans; this is bistro cooking at
its best. Seared duck breast, too, has been consistently outstanding, as
has steak, which really comes rare upon request, and a tender rack of
lamb. French fries are top-notch, and a profound lobster bisque, when
available, is one of the best versions we've ever tasted.

God is also in the details, and here we are reminded of the simple
things that the French do so effortlessly well: a crusty peasant bread,
baked in-house each day; a pot of rich, earthy homemade truffle
butter; or a sauce that is reduced to nappant, as it should be—no
more, no less. Pair it all with a bottle of reasonably priced Burgundy.

Every take-out dinner with a laptop in an office is a step closer to
death. To die is human, but to savor life's pleasures in good company is
something greater. At the real dinner table, we engage with the spirit.
To dine well is to live as we should. To dine like this is to stop time.

Lenny's Indian Head Inn

7.1
/10

Oysters and beers on the back porch overlooking
the marsh: it's all that's good about New England

Seafood, Traditional American   **$25**   *Branford*

6.6/10
Food

9.5/10
Atmosphere

3.0/10
Attitude

6.5/10
Value

Casual restaurant
Sun.-Thurs. 11:30am-9:30pm;
Fri.-Sat. 11:30am-10:30pm.
Date-friendly. Outdoor dining.

205 S. Montowese St.
Branford
(203) 488-1500

Bar Full
Credit Cards None
Reservations Not accepted

Lenny's is everything that's wonderful about this part of the world. A
log cabin on a salt marsh. Summer beers on the back porch with briny
oysters on the half shell. Good, spicy Bloodies. Fresh steamed lobsters
on precarious trays overflowing with melted butter, corn on the cob,
cole slaw, and lobster bibs without even an ounce of intentional kitsch.
Rhode Island-style clam chowder as it should be: sweet, silky, and
savory, with salty oyster crackers in little clear plastic packets. A loud
suburban buzz, with an equal mix of young families, wrinkled old
couples, local college kids, and the occasional Yalie.

Seafood is king here, and portions are generally huge. Order oysters
raw, clams and lobster steamed, and everything else fried. Baked or
broiled white fish has never been New England's forte, so stay away
from it here. French fries can also tend to underperform. Truly, though,
their best work is the outstandingly tender and delicious fried soft-shell-
crab sandwich, not to be missed when it's in season. Keep in mind that
true vegetarians will have little to bite on.

We do have a couple of gripes. First, the service is murderously slow
and inattentive. Don't ever make the mistake of presuming that
anyone's aware of your table, your order, or your existence. Second, the
beautiful outdoor back porch, is inexplicably closed on many a
beautiful, sunny evening; and it's flat-out closed until so late in the
spring that most students leave for vacation before they even get a
chance to slurp oysters on the marsh. There are even some bizarre
menu restrictions on outdoor eating. But whatever you do, you need to
make your way out here anyway. Anyone without a place for Lenny's in
her heart should move back to the West Coast.

Libby's Italian Pastry Shop

5.3
10

A famous Wooster Street purveyor of Italian
desserts that are not as good as their reputation

Baked goods, Sweets

Wooster Square Area

4.5 /10
Food

7.0 /10
Attitude

Take-out
Mon. 11:30am-10pm; closed Tues.;
Wed.-Thurs. 11:30am-10pm;
Fri.-Sat. 11:30am-11pm;
Sun. 11:30am-9pm. *Vegetarian-friendly.*

139 Wooster St.
New Haven
(203) 772-0380

Bar None
Credit Cards None
Reservations Not accepted

This little post-pizza standby on Wooster Street is all about
atmosphere—and fame. Situated among a slew of pizza-only places, it
satisfies your sweet tooth. It's populated by a genuine Italian-American
crowd (along with a smattering of locals and tourists fresh from a
Pepe's or Sally's pilgrimage). The crowd is lively and festive, and the
attitude strikes a perfect balance between brusque and welcoming.

There are some idiosyncrasies here, like an espresso bar that's open
only during certain hours—in fact, truth be told, we've never actually
found it open. And as a purveyor of Italian baked goods, Libby's Pastry
Shop is overrated. But maybe the actual quality of the pastry isn't really
the point. With all of this ambience, and such a location, you'll go
home with a smile even if you could have gotten more delicate cakes
and cookies elsewhere.

Still, wouldn't it be great if the Italian pastry actually measured up?
Instead, everything is too sugary. The cannoli don't have that wonderful
ricotta that should ideally tend toward the savory rather than the
sweet. We think a good tiramisu should be moist and rummy (after all,
the word roughly translates as "throw me on my arse," a nod to the
grogginess of this classic dessert); here, though, it is sadly lacking in
libation.

Libby's fills a particular niche, and we have no doubt that it will
continue to do well. It's a neighborhood classic. But what can we say?
We're food reviewers, and nostalgia gets us only so far. If you are a
cannoli connoisseur, we hope you'll appreciate our candor.

Liuzzi's Cheese Shop

The best cheese selection around

Italian

North Haven

9.0/10
Attitude

Specialty grocery
Mon.-Sat. 8:30am-6pm; closed Sun.
Vegetarian-friendly.

322 State St.
North Haven
(203) 248-4356
www.liuzzicheese.com

Credit Cards Visa, MC, AmEx

It's not just cheese at Liuzzi's, but if you love cheese, you may never leave this store. On an average day, there are over 350 varieties, including the homemade cacciocavallo, a gourd-shaped cheese that is rarely seen in these parts. In the event of a Hollywood epic-style natural disaster, we hope to be caught here, where every inch of shelf space bears closely-stacked Italian specialties, including delightful jewel-toned soda bottles. The deli section is crammed with enormous plates of antipasti, and the butcher's counter displays perfectly marbled Angus beef alongside outsized coils of sausage. In addition to the meat counter, deli, and specialty dry goods, at lunchtime the store offers sandwiches and classic Italian entrees. Come Christmas, and there's an authentic array of panettone.

The Liuzzi's story could make for classic cinema. The family hails from Puglia, at the heel of the boot of Italy, where the original Domenico Liuzzi had a dairy farm. Domenico had a son, Pasquale, who worked beside his father, learning the art of making ricotta, among other local cheeses. Pasquale begat another Domenico, and that Domenico had his own Pasquale, who dreamt of coming to America. And so he did, in 1960, bringing with him generations of artisanal expertise. After nineteen years of managing someone else's cheese factory, he decided to go into business with his brother.

Although the store also sells a wide range of imports, to this day Liuzzi's makes cheese in-house, including sublime ricotta and "basket cheese," a deliciously fresh farmer's cheese that one could eat for breakfast or dessert. This is also the place to get fresh mozzarella, along with some stern advice about how it should be treated. ("Cut it into thin slices. Very thin. Do you have a mandoline?")

L'Orcio

8.0
/10

One of the best, most authentic Italian restaurants in town, in a gracious old State Street house

Italian   **$33**   *East Rock/Grad Ghetto*

7.8/10   **8.5**/10   **8.0**/10   **7.1**/10
Food   *Atmosphere*   *Attitude*   *Value*

Upmarket restaurant   806 State St.   *Bar* Full
Tues.-Fri. 5:30pm-9:30pm; Sat.   New Haven   *Credit Cards* Visa, MC, AmEx
5:30pm-10:30pm; Sun. 5pm-9pm;   (203) 777-6670   *Reservations* Accepted
closed Mon. *Date-friendly. Good wine list.*

This ambitious two-floored Italian restaurant occupies a gracious old house on State Street that has been lovingly restored by its new owners. It was opened by a former Italian parquet floormaker and his American wife; the couple moved to New Haven from Italy to open L'Orcio. The focus here is on Tuscan and Northern Italian cuisine. The pasta here is perhaps the firmest in town, which brings a huge smile to our faces. The Italian spellings are all correct (a rarity in the Elm City), and creations are generally about as authentic as can be found anywhere in the area. While the cooking is not quite breathtaking, the fact that L'Orcio (#2 for Italian) is so much more than your standard Italian-American goes a long way in this city.

Pastas take center stage here. Bucatini all'amatriciana is a classic Roman red-sauce dish of long, tubular pasta with onions, red pepper, and pancetta; here, the bucatini are just about as al dente as we've seen outside of Italy, adding immensely to their texture. While the sauce is not so smoothly reduced, the flavor is still a savory delight. More regional delights include a canellini bean soup with croutons and truffle oil, the sort of dish rarely seen in the Elm City. Meat courses are much more expensive but follow in the trend of creative authenticity; herb-rubbed lamb chops, for instance, are served with polenta drizzled with lamb stock reduction, a dish with true Northern sensibilities.

The room is pleasant and well lit, and the house is beautifully restored. The room upstairs is more subdued. Service is pleasant. Especially given how many eminently standard Italian-American restaurants are continuing to open downtown, we wish that more restaurateurs would follow L'Orcio's lead of offering ambitious, authentic Italian fare instead of more of the same.

Louis' Lunch

7.7
10

A New Haven institution ever since Louis Lassen invented the hamburger more than 100 years ago

Short-order American   **$ 7**   *Theater District*

7.7/10   **9.0**/10   **4.0**/10   **9.7**/10
Food   *Atmosphere*   *Attitude*   *Value*

Counter service   263 Crown St.   *Bar* None
Tues.-Wed. 11am-4pm; Thurs.-Sat.   New Haven   *Credit Cards* None
noon-2am; closed Sun.-Mon.   (203) 562-5507   *Reservations* Not accepted
                               www.louislunch.com

Whether or not Louis Lassen—the great-grandfather of the current owner of Louis' Lunch—actually invented the hamburger more than a century ago is a question that we can't claim the authority to answer. What we do know, however, is that Louis' is an absolute gem. It's New Haven—and small-town America—in all its blustery glory.

The menu and opening hours are exercises in guesswork. Do they have egg creams? Do they serve a sliced steak sandwich? Who knows. Maybe they do if they like you. What they do always have is good (if often too well done) hamburgers, made with high-quality beef that's ground in-house daily. The patties are grilled vertically on ancient cast-iron machines and served on toasted white bread, perhaps slathered with some Cheez Whiz, and accompanied by a wedge of tomato and a slice of onion. Absolutely top-notch potato salad (even better with a dash of salt) and homemade pies bolster the formidable supporting cast.

If you're a rookie, you'll need a primer: First, wait in line. When it's your turn, unhesitatingly yell out your order, indicating the number of hamburgers, followed by "cheese" for cheeseburgers, and then "works" if you want tomato and onion. "Plain" means just the meat and bread. "Rare" is something that we strongly recommend. For example, "two cheese works rare." And don't try to ask for ketchup, unless you want to get thrown out. (Really.) The order will be scrawled on a piece of paper and will be ready in anywhere from two minutes to half an hour (and please don't ask). You can take it all to go, or—if you're lucky—plop down at one of the few age-old brown wooden tables with chairs that look more like church pews. Either way, it's an unforgettable New Haven experience.

Lou's Big Top

Some of the best burgers and pulled pork in New Haven at a nostalgic and unassuming roadside stop

Short-order American $ 7   *Westville*

8.3 /10   **8.0** /10   **10** /10
Food   *Attitude*   *Value*

Take-out   1514 Whalley Ave.   *Bar* None
Mon.-Thurs. 11am-8pm; Fri.-Sat.   New Haven   *Credit Cards* Visa and MC
11am-9pm; Sun. 11am-7pm.   (203) 397-2970   *Reservations* Not accepted
Longer hours in summer.

When Doug Fantarella went to Amity High School—class of 1977—he and his classmates were addicted to the burgers and ribs at the Big Top, on the border of New Haven and Woodbridge. They would come late at night, after the bars had closed. Big Top closed in 1990; in the space, a procession of short-order restaurants came and went until late 2004, when Mr. Fantarella bought and re-opened the Big Top, naming it after Lou, his late father.

We're all lucky for the man's nostalgia, because he's now serving some of the best burgers and pulled-pork in this part of Connecticut. Lou's is a small and simple place with a long counter. There's a friendly cashier and the sounds and smells of fire-cooking from the back. There are a few stools where you can eat against the wall along the window, but the vast majority of people take out; there's even an option (we have to wonder how many exercise it) to call ahead and have your order brought out to your car.

The menu is as basic and inexpensive as the décor: you've got your burgers, fries, BBQ ribs, and a few fried-seafood options. We are happy to report that the cheeseburger is superb. It is a carefully cooked patty of fresh Angus beef, and an absolutely judicious melt of cheese, served on an interestingly sweet and doughy bun (fried onions are available off the menu). Excellent, too, is the pulled-pork sandwich, with extremely tender meat, a well-balanced barbecue sauce, and another wonderfully textured bun; add a side of cole slaw. Specials on the wall, including— at last check—an enormous steak-and-cheese sandwich. They are, like Lou's and most of its clientele, all American, and all very, very good.

Luce

7.5
10

Competent Italian food and the best wine list in the county in a warm, redesigned space

Italian $36   *Hamden*

7.1 /10
Food

8.0 /10
Atmosphere

8.0 /10
Attitude

6.4 /10
Value

Upmarket restaurant
Mon.-Fri. 11:30am-2:30pm, 5pm-9pm; Sat. 5pm-10pm; Sun. 2pm-8pm. *Date-friendly. Good wine list.*

2987 Whitney Ave.
Hamden
(203) 230-0228
www.raffaellos.net

Bar Full
Credit Cards Visa, MC, AmEx
Reservations Recommended

Wine, wine, wine. Wine! This is the biggest and best cellar in *The Menu*, with 17,000 bottles, including such Italian wonders as a vertical collection of Sassicaia with every vintage from 1990 to 2000, and a Mastroberardino Taurasi Riserva from the legendary vintage of 1968. What's more, these bottles come at extremely reasonable prices, many of them not different from what you would pay at auction—or at the wonderful Mount Carmel wine store next door.

Luce was once called Raffaello's. It's still under the same ownership, but the new name is an homage to the famed Super-Tuscan wine (a joint venture between Marchesi de' Frescobaldi and Robert Mondavi). Even the restaurant's new font and color scheme are mighty similar to the Luce wine label, although we're told there's no official affiliation.

Luce's menu is almost the same as it was when it was called Raffaello's, but the newly redesigned space is worlds better. There's a warmer, dimmer vibe, with a reddish glow. The space is divided into cozy nooks such that it feels an appropriate place to drink a 100-dollar 1990 Barolo. The food's not bad either; one memorable special has been gnocchi with duck confit in a tomato sauce. The soft, slightly sweet homemade gnocchi are Luce's best work. "Uccelletti Ticinesi," veal rolled with spinach, sun-dried tomatoes, pine nuts, and gorgonzola, is also a longtime favorite. The cognac sauce has enormous wild mushroom pieces, and a taste typical of area Italian-American. The veal is tender, and the flavors are there, though the dish needs a lot more salt. The "Orecchiette Siciliana" (pasta "ears") are delightfully firm, and they're tossed with a fairly standard sauce of crumbles of sausage (good) and bright red peppers (less well integrated).

And oh, that wine.

Lulu's

A friendly neighborhood coffeeshop that's not Starbucks—let's celebrate

Baked goods   *East Rock/Grad Ghetto*

8.0/10   **7.0**/10
Atmosphere   *Attitude*

Café   49 Cottage St.   *Bar* None
Mon. 7:30am-1pm; Tues.-Fri.   New Haven   *Credit Cards* None
7:30am-3pm; Sat.-Sun. 8:30am- (203) 785-9218   *Reservations* Not accepted
3pm. *Breakfast.*

Despite the pretensions of its title, this café serves coffee much like any other; if you actually want your espresso short in the Italian style, we suggest that you say so. Nestled on Orange Street, Lulu's is more local than foreign, a neighborhood pit stop for your daily cup of joe rather than a showcase for barista hijinks. It is a serviceable source of coffee or tea, and it serves pastries and bagels as well as drinks. The service is friendly, in a gratifying, genuine sort of way, and you can have the pleasure of supporting An Establishment Other Than Starbucks.

If it's one of those sunny New Haven mornings, the friendly banter and relaxed coffee-drinking at the tables out on the sidewalk might be just what you're looking for. At those moments, you might just feel a spiritual connection to the rest of the grad ghetto community—and after all, what's more spiritual in America than the lazy weekend-morning coffee ritual?

When weather doesn't allow for outdoor coffee, the room is small, with few indoor tables, and thus perhaps most appropriate for coffee-in-a-paper-cup on the way to somewhere else (before your Saturday morning shopping at Nica's?). This is largely because of the limited offerings and few indoor tables. We're also deeply confounded by the schedule. The place tends to close when it should be open (weekend afternoons, for example) and open just as you get used to the idea that it's so often closed. Still, in the age of Starbucks, we're rooting for Lulu's. Join us, fight the good fight, and buy local.

Main Garden

4.6
10

Mediocre, large-portioned Chinese take-out
peddled primarily to budget-conscious students

Chinese   **$ 9**   *Broadway Area*

3.4 /10   **7.0** /10   **4.7** /10
Food   *Attitude*   *Value*

Take-out   376 Elm St.   *Bar* None
Mon.-Thurs. noon-1am; Fri. noon-   New Haven   *Credit Cards* Visa and MC
1:45am; Sat. 12:30pm-1:45am;   (203) 777-3747   *Reservations* Not accepted
Sun. 12:30pm-12:30am. *Delivery.* http://maingarden.com

You can count on a basic take-out Chinese place to adhere to a
particular format, whether it's downtown, up Dixwell Avenue, in a
nearby suburb, or even in another city. Main Garden, though, has a
particular undergrad following amidst a sea of choices, which must be
in large part due to location, given that its standard take-out Chinese
fare is not particularly different from competitors'—that is to say, not
very good. At least prices are quite low, and service is known for being
good, friendly, and accommodating, especially to students.

Food-wise, you probably know what to expect. Dishes have names
like Happy Family (jumbo shrimp, sliced pork, beef, chicken, lobster
meat, and Chinese vegetables), and their content consists largely of the
standard permutations of Chinese take-out-joint ingredients. Steamed
broccoli with garlic sauce and white rice is one of the vegetarian
offerings. There are also a few quirkier combinations. Fong wan gai, for
example, is a chicken breast stuffed with roast pork, dipped in egg
batter, fried, and topped with broccoli, snow peas, baby corn, and
bamboo shoots. The place is open late (until 1am on weeknights, 2am
on Friday and Saturday), making it one of the best late-night Chinese
options in town (it easily beats the terrible Ivy Noodle, just off
Broadway).

But during the day, in the bare-bones category, we prefer China
Great Wall (albeit in a different neighborhood) for authenticity and
taste. Cheap Chinese joints like Main Garden need to learn that their
antiquated menus are fast losing their appeal as the American public is
introduced to real Chinese food, and we hope that this restaurant and
its contemporaries will someday adjust to the times and start preparing
dishes with more interesting flavors and less brown-sauce goo.

Mamoun's

A cozy, dimly lit, and legendary falafel place that
stays open until 3am every day of the year

Middle Eastern $ 9   *Upper Chapel Area*

5.6 /10   **8.0** /10   **6.0** /10   **7.2** /10
Food   *Atmosphere*   *Attitude*   *Value*

Casual restaurant	85 Howe St.	*Bar* BYO
Daily 11am-3am.	New Haven	*Credit Cards* None
Vegetarian-friendly.	(203) 562-8444	*Reservations* Accepted
	www.mamounsfalafel.com	

A true New Haven institution, Mamoun's is the sleepless student's
dream come true, serving inexpensive falafel sandwiches and other
Middle Eastern snacks in a cool, dark room that's open until 3am, 365
days a year. Go for a break; go to study (though lighting is dark, which
adds to the atmosphere but takes away from the visibility); go if you've
got the late-night munchies. Go for any reason at all.

Mamoun's is part of an elite New Haven club: places that are open
for food after 2am. And within this select group, it holds up very well.
Mamoun's opened in New Haven in 1977, making it the second in a
small chain of such falafel places. The mothership opened on McDougal
Street in Manhattan, near NYU, in 1971—and it's no small feat to do as
well there as they have.

The falafel itself is fine, if perhaps a bit overrated. But it represents
good value, and with a wonderful little cup of hot mint tea, it's a
reliable remedy for the late-night munchies. We also like the grape-leaf
sandwich. Quantity-wise, sandwiches are a much better deal than
platters, whether falafel, grape leaves, or other dishes. Baklava is well
executed. Tamarind tea is a unique sweet-tart emulsion with the
astringent tannins of tea but the relentless fruitiness of tamarind itself—
it's exotic and refreshing. Eat in; once exposed to the cold night, the
half-life of a Mamoun's sandwich, even inside a foil wrapper, is
extremely short.

The old black-and-white photo of Mamoun himself, on the wall,
inspires an inexplicable sense of hushed awe. Mamoun has achieved
cult status. He's open for business and there for us all, tonight and
forever.

Martin's American Café

7.9
10

A new incarnation of Esteva on the picturesque
Guilford Green—now sporting a breakfast menu

New American $**39** *Guilford*

7.8/10   **8.0**/10   **8.0**/10   **6.8**/10
Food   *Atmosphere*   *Attitude*   *Value*

Upmarket restaurant   25 Whitfield St. (Rt. 77) *Bar* Full
Mon. 8pm-9pm; Tues.-Thurs.   Guilford   *Credit Cards* Visa, MC, AmEx
8am-2:30pm, 5:30pm-9pm;   (203) 458-1300   *Reservations* Recommended
Fri.-Sat. 8am-2:30pm, 5:30pm-
9:30pm; Sun. 8am-3pm (brunch),
5:30pm-9pm. Breakfast menu
Mon.-Sat. 8am-noon. *Breakfast. Brunch. Date-friendly. Good wine list. Outdoor dining.*

Martin's is a new name for a classic New American spot. The
picturesque Guilford green is the quintessential New England town
scene. Old church, meeting hall, expansive lawns and majestic trees,
and quaint shopping streets with little boutiques and bookstores—
they're all in rare form here.

New ownership has changed the name of this restaurant from
Esteva to Martin's and added breakfast, but the place remains an
equally quintessential symbol of modernity with its New American
cuisine and avant-garde interior design that nonetheless fits in
harmoniously. The atmosphere inside is just so, cheery and elegant, and
the staff is extraordinarily friendly, certainly more so than in the previous
incarnation.

The kitchen is populated by a mix of the old staff at Esteva and
some new folks that are up from Fairfield, but the level of the cooking
has remained high. We'll begin with what's new: an elaborate breakfast
menu that must be the longest in the area, with enormous combination
egg dishes priced as high as fifteen dollars and a cringe-worthy list of
12 Starbucks coffee drinks (come on, guys). The lunch and dinner
menus are more similar to Esteva, but there seems to have been a slight
retreat from fusion, though that is still where our favorites here lie, as
with the duck confit and dried fruit chutney; the pappardelle with
smoked chicken and shiitake mushrooms; or grilled ginger shrimp with
chili oil.

Even if you don't feel like springing for a blowout dinner here, come
just for breakfast; it's also one of the nicest spaces anywhere in which
to sit and drink a martini, worth the trip out to Guilford just for a bit of
relaxation in such a pleasant environment away from the city.

Maxwell's Oyster Bar

6.0
10

A hit-or-miss steak-and-seafood restaurant whose attempts at elegance are strip-mall swank

Steakhouse, Seafood   **$27** *Orange*

5.2/10   **7.5**/10   **6.0**/10   **5.2**/10
Food   *Atmosphere*   *Attitude*   *Value*

Upmarket restaurant
Mon.-Thurs. 11:30am-10pm; Fri.-
Sat. 11:30am-11pm; Sun. 4pm-
9pm. Kitchen closes 1 hr. earlier.

175 Boston Post Rd.
Orange
(203) 795-8555
www.maxwellsoysterbar.com

Bar Full
Credit Cards Visa, MC, AmEx
Reservations Accepted

This suburban steakhouse and seafooder has a look that might be best described as pre-strip-club swank—it's not surprising that they're affiliated with Nikkita in downtown New Haven. The attitude, too, is almost as rude as it is at Nikkita—they actually hung up on us ("we're too busy for this <click>") when we called to fact-check for the restaurant guide.

Round mini-banquettes look out onto a rushing waterfall. Such touches can be charming, but here, in shades of red and black, they feel sleazy. And perhaps in the most cheesy-chic touch of all, a glass of sweet Asti Spumante—the cheapest of bubblies—shows up at the table before all else, along with a harmless eggplant caponata. Most people seem to order from the excellent-value prix-fixe menu (Sunday through Wednesday), which amounts to less than half of the cost of ordering à la carte.

To start, oysters and clams on the half shell are perfectly adequate, and the blue cheese dressing on an iceberg wedge is nice. The house salad dressing is decent, too, foregoing the usual sugary, gummy vinaigrette for a better-balanced lemon and oil dressing.

The plot thickens, though, with the subpar main courses. A steak ordered rare, at our last visit, came medium-plus, sapping it of any taste and texture. Route 1 is rife with overcooked steaks, and Maxwell's follows suit. But the West Haven location is no excuse for this practice. It gets even worse, though, as you move into the pasta dishes, like a horrible linguine with clam sauce. The pasta is overcooked, undersalted, with no emulsion of flavor, and no binding of sauce to noodles, while the clams are tasteless and chewy. It might end with a good chocolate cake, but it's too little, too late after such disappointing mains.

McDonald's

4.3
_10_

It may be the evil empire, but the food actually
tastes good—and nobody's willing to admit it

Short-order American   **$ 6**   _Whalley_

5.0/10   **3.0**/10   **4.0**/10   **4.9**/10
Food   _Atmosphere_   _Attitude_   _Value_

Fast-food chain   250 Whalley Ave.   _Bar_ None
Daily 6am-midnight.   New Haven   _Credit Cards_ Visa, MC, AmEx
Breakfast. Outdoor dining.   (203) 865-9195   _Reservations_ Not accepted
                            www.mcdonalds.com

We were as disturbed as others by the revelations in _Fast Food Nation_
and the hilarious _Super Size Me_, but we're food critics, not doctors or
urban planners. And while fast food is almost never particularly good
for you, McDonald's actually offers more reasonably sized sandwiches
than most chains, and the introduction of the salads and elimination of
the Super Size (whether or not it was in response to the movie) were
steps in the right direction. Even the most caloric offerings on the
McDonald's menu tend to have significantly fewer calories than their
equivalents at other chains.

The french fries might not be what they once were when they were
cooked in beef fat, but they are still by consensus some of the best
around, well crisped and well sized. Consider also the cheeseburger,
perhaps this chain's true crowning achievement, still elegant after fifty
years: The beef patty has real (if processed) flavor, the American cheese
is usually melted just as it should be, and the ketchup-rehydrated onion
taste somehow just works. Close your eyes, open your mind, and eat
(sparingly). And the Big Mac is timelessly tempting. You probably
already know better than to order the Filet o' Fish, sandwiches
featuring that chewy bacon, or any of the rotating market-test
experiments, which are usually euthanized within a few months—
remember the McRib?

Angry readers will complain, as they always do, about McDonald's
being rated higher in the food category than this or that local place.
They always do. What can we say? We know it's not pretty. But what
keeps customers coming back to McDonald's every day is not just the
excellent value proposition but also the fact that the food actually
tastes good. And nobody's willing to admit it.

Medical Area Food Carts
Special section

At least 19 lunch carts, with culinary roots spanning the globe, from West Haven to Saigon—New Haven's answer to a Singaporean hawker center

$ 6   *Medical Area/The Hill*

Take-out
Generally Mon.-Fri. 11am-3pm;
varies by cart.

Near the corner of Cedar St. and
York St., New Haven
No phone

The doctors know about it. (The doctors always know.)

The medical students know about it. (After all, they're studying to be doctors.)

Even the occasional recuperating patient can be seen wandering around the corner of Cedar and York Streets in hospital-issue pajamas, sampling epicurean delights encased in handy Styrofoam.

But what's amazing to us is how few people tend to walk the few short blocks from downtown—even if it means traversing the unsightly Air Rights Garage and the terminus of the ill-fated Route 34 extension—to sample from the eclectic collection of up to 19 food carts that cluster around the Yale-New Haven Hospital and Yale Medical School.

It's a shame, because they represent the best lunchtime value in New Haven. There are similar clusters downtown and near the School of Management, but the number of carts in those locations just doesn't compare. So many, and so diverse, are these take-out carts that they conjure up images of the hawker centers in Singapore, street-food bazaars where low overhead and fierce competition translates into spectacular eats at bargain prices. Sadly, that genre is now threatened, even in Asia, by the global fast-food chains.

While New Haven's version of the hawker center may not quite be up to Singaporean culinary standards, it is particularly heartening to see this kind of good capitalism alive even in America. It is all too rare to stumble upon a micro-economy that's driven not by manipulative marketing, but rather by simple, honest supply-and-demand forces.

To wit: virtually every dish costs between four and five dollars, and the cooks often know their customers (a lot of whom, you'll quickly notice, are clad in scrubs). On a given day, you might see a nerdy surgeon chatting in Spanish with a Mexican cook; a beefy West Haven Italian-American carefully discussing salad dressing ingredients with a nurse while assembling three sausage-and-pepper sandwiches simultaneously; or a med student asking a hospital maintenance worker about whether to go for noodles or sushi.

Medical Area food carts special section, continued

Happily, there's also a ready-made place to sit down and eat your lunch: the Medical School cafeteria just inside Harkness Hall and the large array of outdoor tables and chairs in the courtyard. It is, in fact, rather amusing to see the actual cafeteria's business stagnate. And no wonder—why choose institutional grub when such interesting options lie just outside?

To help you sift through the many options, we've compiled a list. We've made up names for the several unlabeled carts, which are marked with asterisks. (We had a bit of fun with the names.) The numbers below correspond to the numbers on the map to the right, although the carts' positions can sometimes vary from day to day.

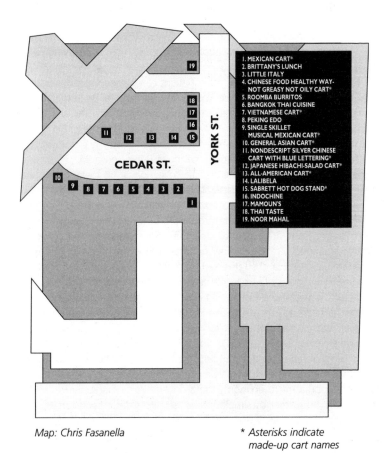

1. MEXICAN CART*
2. BRITTANY'S LUNCH
3. LITTLE ITALY
4. CHINESE FOOD HEALTHY WAY-NOT GREASY NOT OILY CART*
5. ROOMBA BURRITOS
6. BANGKOK THAI CUISINE
7. VIETNAMESE CART*
8. PEKING EDO
9. SINGLE SKILLET MUSICAL MEXICAN CART*
10. GENERAL ASIAN CART*
11. NONDESCRIPT SILVER CHINESE CART WITH BLUE LETTERING*
12. JAPANESE HIBACHI-SALAD CART*
13. ALL-AMERICAN CART*
14. LALIBELA
15. SABRETT HOT DOG STAND*
16. INDOCHINE
17. MAMOUN'S
18. THAI TASTE
19. NOOR MAHAL

CEDAR ST.

YORK ST.

Map: Chris Fasanella

Asterisks indicate made-up cart names

Medical Area food carts

Medical Area food carts special section, continued

We have sampled food from every single one of these 19 carts. All have certain things in common: enormous portion sizes, a friendly attitude, a cooler full of standard soft drinks, and minimal frills. But warm fuzzies aside, on to the judgment.

The eight best carts, food-wise, are, in the following order: the Vietnamese Cart (#7); the Mexican Cart (#1); the Roomba Burrito Cart (#5); Brittany's Lunch (#2); Peking Edo (#8); the General Asian Cart (#10); the Single-Skillet Musical Mexican Cart (#9); and the All-American Cart (#13). At the other end of the spectrum, here are five carts to avoid, in no particular order: both Chinese carts (#4 and #11); Lalibela (#14); Mamoun's (#17); and Noor Mahal, the Indian cart (#19). The rest of the carts fall somewhere in between.

The **Vietnamese Cart** (#7) was, until the recent opening of Pot-au-Pho, the only place in New Haven to get Vietnamese food. But more importantly, the food is extremely fresh: raw pieces of pork or shrimp, for instance, are laid across a real grill, painted with a savory baste, and carefully cooked to a well-balanced juiciness, easily blowing away the tough, pre-cooked meat at the Chinese carts.

Have it the typical Vietnamese way, with thin, room-temperature rice noodles, along with a peanut sauce (here it's unusually dark) or fish sauce; you can ask for both. We also like the finely sliced pickled carrots and radishes, which add a welcome vinegary note.

The **Mexican Cart** (#1) is the first one you'll encounter if you're walking from downtown on York Street, and it's also a good stop. It's strictly Tex-Mex comfort food—no cabeza or pozole here—but ingredients are fresh and well balanced. The friendly Puebla-born cook will fill all the classic antojitos with shredded or grilled chicken, steak, or cheese. Of these, we favor the cheese enchiladas, topped with a mild red sauce, briefly baked in the oven, and topped with guacamole, a chunky tomato salsa with notes of cilantro, a peppy chipotle sauce, and sour cream. Everything comes with well-executed refried beans and yellow rice. It reminds us of West Coast Mexican.

The popular **Roomba Burrito Cart** (#5), which also has a sister operation on York and Elm, is well known around town for its superbly fresh ingredients, high-quality meats, warm tortillas as big as your head, and an inventive slaw of crunchy cabbage and sweet corn. We're happy to report that the pulled-pork special is now a permanent fixture here.

Brittany's Lunch (#2), which rivals the Chinese Food Healthy-Way Not Greasy Not Oily Cart and Roomba for longest queues, is the best choice among the sandwich- and salad-makers. Their immensely popular Caesar salad is made with very fresh greens. One day, we even found some heirloom tomatoes in the mix. The extensive menu can overextend; even yaki soba and hibachi dishes make appearances. Interestingly, though, the onions and meat in our excellent steak-and-cheese tasted vaguely hibachi-style—residual soy sauce, perhaps. Whatever the intention, these Japanese notes actually improved the sandwich.

At **Peking Edo** (#8), dishes are alternately Japanese, Taiwanese, Malaysian, and Singaporean. This is the closest you'll come in New Haven to real hawker center food. Mee goreng, for example, is made of noodles with shrimp, egg, onion, tomato, curry, and—we're told—a bit of ketchup. It's interesting, although we wish it were warmer. Better is the Taiwanese stewed hard-boiled egg, which swims in a dark, salty sauce of ground pork and tofu—not subtle, but fun to eat, like a re-imagined sloppy joe. Best of all is the chive pocket, a crispy, deep-fried indulgence that's like a Chinese scallion pancake unexpectedly stuffed with rice noodles, chives, and fried egg. And try the homemade hot sauce.

We named the **General Asian Cart** (#10) for a dish on their menu that is rather hilariously called "General Chicken"—and also for the fact that when we asked the Vietnamese cook which nationality his cuisine belonged to, he simply shrugged. Regardless, he makes a pleasantly spicy, fresh-tasting dish called "spicy shrimp" (also available with chicken) in Japanese hibachi style. It's well-seasoned with soy sauce and various hot sauces, and the shrimp (which could be better deveined) and bean sprouts are, refreshingly, cooked from the raw state.

The **Single-Skillet Musical Mexican Cart** (#9), which is distinguished by an umbrella, dresses its tomato-tortilla quesadillas with a surprising fusion twist—a chunky mango salsa—as well as an exciting dose of chipotle pepper sauce; the cheese congeals quickly, though. The single pan in use at the Single-Skillet Musical Mexican Cart means slow throughput, but your wait is made into a fiesta by the Mexican music that always emanates from deep within.

The last among our top eight is the **All-American Cart** (#13), which serves the American classics: burgers, fries, grilled chicken sandwiches, and so on. There are no frills here, but the fries are freshly made to order, and the cheeseburger, which is of the thin variety, is correctly cooked on a gas grill and well balanced, with a good mix of cheese, fresh tomato, lettuce, onion, and so on. It's a simple pleasure, and at $2.25, it blows away the fast-food competition.

There are also a few big disappointments. Virtually everything we've tried at **Noor Mahal**, the Indian cart (#19), has been tragically underseasoned. Chicken in the Tikka Masala is tough, spinach has almost no flavor at all, channa (chickpeas) are spicy but otherwise bland and too soft; and haleem (made, we're told, with mashed chicken and five kinds of beans) is unnervingly mealy.

At **Mamoun's** (#17), meanwhile, the falafel is good and crispy, but we've had a kefta that was seriously undercooked. We're all for rare lamb chops, but in a ground-lamb patty at a food cart, you don't want to see so much pink in the middle. We learned our lesson there the hard way: stay away from anything other than falafel.

Medical Area food carts special section, continued

Lalibela (#14) serves Ethiopian food, but its exotic promise falls flat. Spicy chicken is indeed spicy, but it's also bland and unbelievably greasy—red oil oozes everywhere. Undersalted spicy lentils have heat but little else. Soft green beans, well flavored by tomato and onion, cross the "okay" threshold, but not so for bright yellow shrimp that drown in an over-rich sea of butter.

But perhaps the biggest failure of all is the immensely popular Chinese category. Usually the local crowds are right, but sometimes they're wrong. Here, we think they've fallen for a cheap marketing ploy. The clear market leader, which almost always boasts a long line of customers, boldly proclaims in large letters: "**Chinese Food Healthy-Way Not Greasy Not Oily**" (#4). Unfortunately, it's not tasty either. An enormous container of soup is so bland that it's hard to eat more than a spoonful—it tastes like hot water with some soggy noodles and pasty shrimp stripped of flavor. String beans with ground pork are only a little better—a thick, gummy brown sauce is poured on top, rather than being integrated into the dish, and the meat has unexpected and unpleasant flavors.

As for the **Nondescript Silver Chinese Cart with Blue Lettering** (#11), they use fresher, less overcooked ingredients and subtler sauces than the Chinese Good Healthy-Way Not Greasy Not Oily Cart, but it's still just cookie-cutter suburban Chinese-American grub. There are so many better ways to cart.

The Menu makes a tasteful gift.

Make somebody else—or yourself—happy, and order more copies of ***The Menu: New Haven*** or *The Menu: Northampton, Amherst, and the Five-College Area,* online, direct from the publisher at **www.newhavenmenu.com**. You can also order through amazon.com on our site.

Overnight shipping is available.

To order more than 10 copies at a special discount, or for information about using *The Menu* as a corporate gift, please call Off The Map Press at 203.286.1775.

Mediterranea

7.1
10

A simple purveyor of unusual Middle Eastern fare,
with excellent, little-known vegetarian specialties

Middle Eastern, Pizza   **$ 9**   *Financial District*

7.3 /10   **6.5** /10   **8.0** /10   **8.3** /10
Food   *Atmosphere*   *Attitude*   *Value*

Counter service   140 Orange St.   *Bar* None
Mon.-Sat. 9am-9pm; closed Sun.   New Haven   *Credit Cards* None
Delivery. Vegetarian-friendly.   (203) 624-0589   *Reservations* Not accepted

This simple business-district restaurant, a great choice for vegetarians,
peddles quick, cheap fare that's a lot more interesting than your
standard Middle Eastern. Chairs and tables seat quite a few people in
two rooms—the more secluded back room must be one of the only
dining rooms in New Haven with exposed brick walls on three sides.
Still, the short-order open kitchen with slice-ready pizzas on the counter
gives off a very lunchtime-take-out vibe.

The falafel, though soft, is quite nice, but we'd like to direct your
attention to some of the more unusual offerings. Don't be put off by
the name: "foul mudammas" is a vegetarian treat with a harmonious
focus on primary ingredients, beginning with the irresistible rustic
appeal of fava beans, one of the most under-utilized starches in the
universe. In a simple and elegant treatment, the cooked beans are
bathed in a well-balanced sea of olive oil, garlic, and plenty of lemon.

Moujaddarah, another vegetarian option, is a plate of lentils and
cracked wheat, with darkly browned onions that add a deep
caramelized taste—another interesting choice, though not up to the
level of the foul mudammas. The menu also includes ouzi (rice with
green peas and almonds in phyllo dough) and moussaka (eggplant,
tomatoes, ground meat, and cheese), a Greek dish that reveals the
kitchen's pan-Mediterranean aspirations. You can finish off with a
pleasant cup of the hot Syrian tea.

The pizza makes concessions to New Haven traditions ("clams
casino," for example, with clams, roasted peppers, onions, bacon, and
mozzarella), and it does have high quality cheese and a well-cooked
crust with the occasional blackened bubble, but the crust is a bit too
thick to be called true thin-crust New Haven style. Better to stick with
the little-known Middle Eastern delights.

Miso

7.2
10

The best Japanese downtown, with fresh sushi and
good cooked food in a sleek, airy setting

Japanese   **$25**   *Ninth Square*

7.1 /10   **7.0** /10   **8.0** /10   **6.7** /10
Food   *Atmosphere*   *Attitude*   *Value*

Upmarket restaurant   15 Orange St.   *Bar* Full
Mon.-Thurs. 11:30am-3pm, 5pm-   New Haven   *Credit Cards* Visa and MC
10pm; Fri.-Sat. 11:30am-3pm,   (203) 848-6472   *Reservations* Accepted
5pm-11pm; Sun. 3:30pm-10pm.   www.misorestaurant.com
Outdoor dining.

Miso was more than welcome when it moved into Ninth Square a few
years ago, and it immediately emerged as the best sushi place
downtown. It's an austere home to fresh fish and Japanese elegance.
Every aspect of Miso's design, from the spectacular light bamboo tables
and beautifully angled sushi bar to the careful layout of nigiri on
wooden tablet, stresses clean lines and airy openness. There's also a
pleasant backyard garden in summer, always a welcome addition, with
a notable modernist wave roof. Even the font spelling out "Miso" on
the restaurant's front door is an exercise in cutting-edge simplicity.

The location is equally cutting-edge; we heartily applaud Miso's
decision to follow in Bentara's footsteps and open in this revitalizing
warehouse district, although a parking lot would have been a plus.
(Don't park in that lot next door. You'll get towed. We know this from
experience.)

The service is genuine and friendly, the fish usually fresh and
tender—though not invariably so; ask the chef what's best that day. We
sometimes wish it weren't served so cold. Generally notable are the
salmon and albacore (white tuna). Substitutions within the set-meal
sushi combinations are (refreshingly) handled with grace, even for the
inexpensive nigiri lunch combination, which comes with miso soup—
easily the best sushi deal downtown. The sushi-sashimi dinner
combination is a much better selection than average, with tuna,
albacore, yellowtail, salmon, fluke, red snapper, eel, orange clam, and
even best-in-downtown uni (sea urchin), along with a tuna roll or a
spicy dragon roll.

There are also plenty of well-executed non-sushi choices on the
menu, including a nice version of katsu. Whatever you do, beware of
the low-sodium soy sauce, which can be easily confused with the
regular; ask your wonderfully friendly waitperson for emergency
assistance.

Miya's

7.0
10

A small, hip Japanese restaurant and sushi bar with an unusual menu and a young vibe

Japanese
$31
Upper Chapel Area

6.0/10
Food

9.0/10
Atmosphere

7.0/10
Attitude

6.1/10
Value

Upmarket restaurant
Sun.-Thurs. 5pm-1am; Fri.-Sat.
5pm-2am. Kitchen closes at
11:30pm. *Date-friendly. Vegetarian-friendly.*

68 Howe St.
New Haven
(203) 777-9760

Bar Full
Credit Cards Visa, MC, AmEx
Reservations Accepted

For two decades, Miya's has brought a touch of urban sophistication to the New Haven Japanese restaurant scene. Everything from the logo painted outside to the hip, wooden interior and clever menu screams out "New New Haven"—and the location couldn't be more emblematic of the transformation of the Howe Street neighborhood that Miya's inhabits.

Miya's does more than we've ever seen done with a beer-and-wine-only license, serving up sake, beer, and wonderful saketinis with fresh fruit (like watermelon) in the adjacent lounge area. There's even a sake Bloody Mary, which hits the spot. The cool, dim bar, illuminated by tea lights, draws in young droves for the cheap cans of Schaeffer's (the one beer to have when you're having more than one), and Miya's lights up evenings with a raging young bar scene.

There are also some higher-end food pretentions, including a bevy of rolls composed of substances you probably never imagined could wind up wrapped in nori and vinegared rice. Vegetarian sushi lovers, in particular, will be delighted to know that Miya's has devised ways to form maki out of almost any non-animal substance. If you want gorgonzola in your maki, this is the place to be. (Do you?)

Public opinion on the service here is bimodally distributed. The mellow, super-cool all-purpose waiter-bartender-sushi chef staff has a cult following and charms a lot of people, including many undergraduates. However, some of the more mature patrons tend to complain about slow and indifferent table service.

There's also a $29.75 sushi-plus tasting menu special on Wednesdays—not bad for the amount of food you get—and even a $67.95-and-up kaiseki option, which we haven't yet had the privilege of trying. But ultimately, we think it's the enchanting vibe, most of all, that keeps Miya's hopping.

Modern Apizza

An unpretentious, dark-horse contender for best pizza in New Haven

Pizza   **$13**   *East Rock/Grad Ghetto*

9.1/10   **7.5**/10   **7.0**/10   **9.5**/10
Food   *Atmosphere*   *Attitude*   *Value*

Casual restaurant
Tues.-Thurs. 11am-11pm; Fri.-Sat.
11am-midnight; Sun. 3pm-10pm;
closed Mon. *Vegetarian-friendly.*

874 State St.
New Haven
(203) 776-5306
www.modernapizza.com

Bar Wine and beer only
Credit Cards Visa and MC
Reservations Not accepted

This excellent, truly local pizzeria is in the heart of the Grad Ghetto, which partly explains its perennial popularity. The other part is the reliably great pies. The crust isn't quite as thin as its rivals' on Wooster Street, but some might prefer it this way: it's more like American-style brick-oven pizza at its best. The sauce is perfectly balanced, the crust is not too doughy, and oil is applied with careful restraint. Toppings, too, are more classically American here than at New Haven's other top contenders: sausage and pepperoni are among the most popular, and they're great here. Outlandish combinations of multiple ingredients are encouraged: the veggie bomb, for example, has spinach, broccoli, olives, mushrooms, red and green peppers, onion, and garlic. Our favorite combination, though, is bacon and spinach.

In fact, in the greatest American pizza town, many a diehard Modernist declares this joint the best of all—better than Sally's. While we don't think Modern quite reaches that level on a day-to-day basis, we have no complaints (it's #8 in *The Menu* for food), and we do empathize with those—like Joe Castiglione, voice of the World Champion Red Sox—who fall deeply in love with Modern's accessibility and its low-key environment.

The atmosphere at Modern is hardly romantic, but it's a pizzeria, after all—pitchers of Coke and beer, loud laughter, Formica tables, and frenzied but friendly service. There are also subs, but people come for the pizza (a large pie feeds three, a medium two). Even here, waits can be considerable at prime time on weekend nights, but they rarely reach Wooster Street proportions. Modern also runs a brisk take-out business, and if you live nearby, you may prefer the ambiance of your own apartment. In an age of the celebrity restaurant, we salute Modern, a great, laid-back, and deservedly successful New Haven institution.

Moka

A light, airy new jack-of-all-trades café and lunch
spot specializing in chocolate and crêpes

Light American, Sweets $ 8 *Financial District*

6.2 /10   **8.0** /10   **7.0** /10   **8.0** /10
Food   *Atmosphere*   *Attitude*   *Value*

Café	141 Orange St.	*Bar* None
Mon.-Fri. 7am-6pm; Sat. 8am-6pm;	New Haven	*Credit Cards* Visa, MC, AmEx
Sun. 10am-4pm. Lunch menu	(203) 752-0052	*Reservations* Not accepted

10am-2pm only. *Breakfast. Wireless Internet. Vegetarian-friendly.*

Moka bills itself as a "chocolate café"—and it's got the café part right,
at least. Those expecting a Montezuman lair (the Aztec ruler was said
to consume, daily, several dozen servings of chocolate out of golden
goblets), or, for that matter, a specialty shop, will have to look
elsewhere. Though the concept is thin and the chocolate a bit watery,
Moka has stationed itself as a reliable and even tasty spot for a
weekday lunch or an afternoon espresso.

The café marks the expansion into downtown of the consonant-
swapping "Koffee?" empire, which also includes a branch in Fair Haven
("Koffee Too?" is now under separate ownership). The mini-chain
offers atmosphere, a panorama of drink options, and airy rooms with a
big, light-filled atrium perfect for chatting or studying. Moka has added
crêpes, panini, chocolate gifts, and chocolate drinks.

The menu features an assortment of filled crêpe selections, many of
them vegetarian. A big crêpe with fresh mozzarella, sun-dried
tomatoes, and zucchini has tasty batter—a pleasant surprise, given its
whole-wheat composition and hue—but is also a bit spongy and dry,
and the veggies in the filling, though fresh, tend to slip around each
other rather than adhering to the crêpe. Chocolate drinks occupy a
disappointingly meager share of the menu, with six options ranging
from the spicy Azteka to the Exquisite Orange to a cup of Hot White.
The flavors are interesting, but for a place that claims chocolate as its
specialty, the chocolate could stand to be a little richer and more
intense. The Spanish cocoa is frothy and aromatic, though not as thick
as its billing on the menu—"melted milk chocolate with milk"—might
suggest. Even if it's not all as exotic as it sounds, with its downtown
location, Moka makes sense as a healthy lunch option. –*Coco Krumme*

Mory's

6.8
/10

The classic Yale eating club, more a monument to tradition than a serious restaurant

Traditional American   **$28**   *Broadway Area*

6.0/10
Food

9.0/10
Atmosphere

5.0/10
Attitude

6.0/10
Value

Upmarket restaurant
Mon.-Sat.11:30am-2pm,
5:30pm-10pm; closed Sun.
Kitchen closes at 8:30pm.

306 York St.
New Haven
(203) 562-3157

Bar Full
Credit Cards Visa and MC
Reservations Essential

Mory's, across from the Law School in an old house on York Street, is a funny place. Funny in all the meanings of the word: funny ha-ha, funny weird, and even funny as in "you're looking at me funny." Mory's fancies itself a "private club," but it's hardly private—nor really a club, for that matter. Back in the day, you had to charge the meal to your personal account. Nowadays, even credit cards are accepted. To join the restaurant you need forty bucks, an existing member, and some association with Yale, however tenuous. Elitist? Yes. Selective? No.

Mory's is best known for their "cups," silver bowls full of neon-colored concoctions of unnamed liquors and fruit juices (who really wants to know?). They're famously imbibed upstairs (in a sacred, ritualistic fashion), but can certainly be ordered anywhere in the more traditional worn-dark-wood-tabled, ridiculously Yale-themed, restaurant area downstairs as well. The Whiffenpoofs, Yale's best-known a cappella group, treat Mory's patrons to song every Monday. Mory's claims that you need reservations three weeks in advance for Monday dinner. What is this, Per Se?

The food is uninspired old-school men's-club fare. Some of the better choices include the grilled calf's liver, and the lunch-only Welsh rarebit (a murderously rich concoction of bread, leeks, melted cheddar cheese, beer, poached egg, and bacon, which has been on the menu for about a century). The creamy, curried "baker's soup," no doubt inspired by some 19th-century Yalie's sojourn to India, is inexplicably delicious. Lunch is not a bad deal—it's hard to spend more than ten bucks. Obviously, Mory's is not going to do particularly well in our food-rating system. But mark our words: whether for a cup or a rarebit, you've got to see this place before you skip town.

Mother's

A true Jamaican gem, best for take-out, hiding in
the side streets west of downtown New Haven

Jamaican $12   *Medical Area/The Hill*

8.4 /10
Food

8.0 /10
Attitude

9.4 /10
Value

Take-out   16 Norton St.   *Bar* None
Mon.-Sat. 7am-9pm;   New Haven   *Credit Cards* Visa and MC
Sun. 9am-5pm. *Breakfast.* (203) 562-3701   *Reservations* Accepted

This is an out-of-the-way find in a part of New Haven most Yalies
probably don't even know exists—it's somewhat west of downtown, off
Derby Ave. With a half-broken TV and ripped plastic upholstery, the
atmosphere is so drab it's almost a joke; but the place is so genuine in
its lack of intentional aesthetic that it comes off as purely endearing.
And take-out orders are the best choice anyway. Huge family-style
portions make it a great option for a dinner party or Sunday brunch.

Mother is a real, live, person, a friendly Jamaican woman who surely
knows her way around a kitchen. The Jamaican accents at the counter
are the genuine article. The tastes are vintage West Indies too: for
example, deep-fried meat pie pockets are gloriously soft and flavorful.
Red beans and rice have a texture and sweetness rarely seen in a dish
that can so often be boring in less capable hands. Ten dollars gets you
an outrageously large portion of outstanding goat curry, with
impossibly tender meat and a sauce that bursts with exotic flavors and
spicy goodness. Cabbage and collard greens are a sweet counterpoint,
melting in your mouth. You just want to eat it all—immediately. Large
portions easily serve two, bringing the actual price per person down
quite a bit.

And there's so much more. There's jerk chicken and kingfish in
gravy. There's Jamaican breakfast in the morning. There are vegetables
you've probably never heard of, like callaloo, and other unexpected
treats like mackerel, oxtail, and ackee—in New Haven! Wash it down
with a real ginger beer. We're not exaggerating when we say that
Mother's serves some of the best food in the city. You won't be
disappointed by this trek to a neighborhood unfamiliar to many
downtowners.

Naples

5.3
/10

A pizza joint that's one of the many sad casualties of America's idiotic drinking age

Pizza, Light American $ **8**   *Financial District*

4.9 /10   **6.0** /10   **6.0** /10   **5.9** /10
Food   *Atmosphere*   *Attitude*   *Value*

Counter service   90 Wall St.   *Bar* None
Mon.-Fri. 7am-9pm; Sat. 11am-   New Haven   *Credit Cards* Visa, MC, AmEx
9pm; closed Sun. *Breakfast.*   (203) 776-9021   *Reservations* Not accepted

Like a dragon without its fiery roar, Naples without its liquor license is a sad sight indeed. Back in its heyday, this place played host to generations of undergraduates who would gleefully down pitchers of beer and greasy pizza. It was, and still is, a historic college-town joint, a glorious relic from another era. Naples' dark wood tables are embedded with the tipsy inscriptions and memories of students past.

But this is America, home of the free, where adults can raise children, fly planes, and drop bombs—but can't drink beer legally. Almost every other country in the world, instead, entrusts its own citizens with learning to drink responsibly; they grow up drinking wine in moderation with their parents, building up their tolerance over time, and learning that alcohol is a complement to food and festivities, not an end in itself.

In this Puritan heartland, instead, we taunt our children with tales of sound and fury, dangling alcohol out of their reach like forbidden fruit. And so our children learn to drink by sneaking into cabinets or binge-guzzling at frat parties. How can we possibly be surprised, then, when they don't know when to stop? When the night ends in a pool of vomit or a dangerous ride home? It is *because* America has the highest drinking age in the world, not in spite of it, that we have the world's biggest drunk driving problem.

And one gray night it happened: Naples was hit with the last of many police stings, the liquor license bid Naples adieu. And now, like Jackie Paper, the undergraduates come no more. It's a shadow of its former self, simply serving Italian-style subs (steak and cheese isn't bad), thick and cheesy pizzas, iceberg-lettuce-style salads, and some basic Italian-American mains—but without that trademark buzz.

Nica's Market

A one-stop shop for quality fresh ingredients
(butcher included) and prepared food

Italian   *East Rock/Grad Ghetto*

8.0 /10
Attitude

Specialty grocery   603 Orange St.
Mon.-Sat. 7am-7pm; Sun. 7am-   New Haven   *Credit Cards* Visa, MC, AmEx
2pm. *Breakfast. Outdoor dining.* (203) 787-5919

Nica's Market is a family affair. After an un-amicable split, co-owner Joe Sabino, formerly of competing gourmet grocery Romeo and Joe's (now Romeo and Cesare's), moved a few blocks down the sam street to Nica's to join his son Tony and Tony's brother-in-law Pino in this venture, which is named after Tony's daughter (Joe's granddaughter) Veronica.

This Orange Street storefront has been turned from Prime Market, an undistinguished grocery, into a spectacular oasis of edibles with a decidedly Italian accent. Spilling out of woven baskets are artisanal breads and a bounty of fresh fruits and vegetables, including exotic seasonal produce (persimmons, anyone?) and a startling array of fresh mushrooms. A fresh meat counter is the best (and priciest) in the area, including organic chicken and a rotating selection of specialty items like duck breast, game, veal shanks destined for *osso buco*, and even kobe beef. If you have a particular cut in mind, ask for it; they'll butcher for you on the spot. Call two to four days ahead for special meat orders.

For lazybones and lunchers, Nica's offers a variety of prepared food, from foccaccia sandwiches, pizza and panini, to soups and marinated vegetables, stuffed roasted chicken, sausages (made in-house) with peppers, and hearty slabs of lasagna. They sell their pizza dough to go, too, and in a reminder that we can all do so much better than Bruegger's, they import H&H bagels from New York City.

Save room for dessert; tiramisu is a decadent, creamy, delight, and the chocolate mousse cups are memorable. We also have a weakness for the selection of gourmet ice cream and sorbets, especially Ciao Bella's unctuous fruit flavors. And the freezer holds yet more promise of home-cooked goodness, with an array of fresh pasta made locally. There's no better place in New Haven to shop for dinner.

Nikkita

6.6
/10

An almost absurdly modern bar that serves eclectic food late into the evening

New American, Seafood $**25**   *Theater District*

7.1 /10   **7.5** /10   **1.0** /10   **6.0** /10
Food   *Atmosphere*   *Attitude*   *Value*

Bar and grill
Sun.-Tues. 4pm-1am; Wed.-Thurs.
11am-1am; Fri. 11am-2am; Sat.
4pm-2am. Kitchen closes Sun.-
Tues. 10pm; Wed.-Thurs. 11pm;
Fri.-Sat. 12:30am.

200 Crown St.
New Haven
(203) 787-0227

Bar Full
Credit Cards Visa, MC, AmEx
Reservations Accepted

We must salute Nikkita, first and foremost, for serving fairly serious food later than almost anyone else in New Haven, especially on weeknights. From trendy fonts to skeletal metal to halogen spot lighting to the eclectic, vaguely Italian menu, this place is modern, modern, modern. Nikkita turns into quite a bar scene on weekend nights, with people gravitating away from the restaurant-style booths and toward the long bar and its three prominent LCD flat-screen televisions (at least one is tuned to sports, and perhaps one to Fox "News").

Drinks are solid—we like the illusion martini, which is like Campari for beginners (the tartness cut with cranberry juice). As for food, there's an extensive raw bar (oysters, clams, and so on) and a good selection of smallish plates at smallish prices. Presentations have a flair for drama. One appetizer boasts frighteningly gigantic coconut shrimp dangling almost in mid-air, while a dish of rare seared tuna crusted with sesame seeds also has virtuoso plating; still, both dishes are underseasoned and fairly bland. Osso buco is better and saltier, with a nice, cheesy risotto. The shank isn't the most tender, but the sauce is well reduced, and again, the price is right.

There are consistent, serious attitude problems here, however, even when it's quiet. On one visit, we ordered wine three times over the course of a half hour, with no luck. Halfway through our steak, we gave up and got two glasses of wine at the bar. When our passive-aggressive waitress finally reappeared at our table and saw what we had done, she stormed off, returning with two more glasses that we didn't want, and charging us for all four. It is remarkable when service is so bad that it ruins not just your meal, but your entire evening.

Nini's Bistro

8.3
10

Downtown New Haven's only BYO prix-fixe, boasting an interesting, ever-changing menu

New American $35   *Ninth Square*

7.5/10 *Food*   **9.5**/10 *Atmosphere*   **9.0**/10 *Attitude*   **7.4**/10 *Value*

Upmarket restaurant Wed.-Sat., 2 seatings at 6pm and 8:15pm. *Date-friendly.*	40 Orange St. New Haven (203) 562-6464 www.ninisbistro.com	*Bar* BYO *Credit Cards* Visa, MC, AmEx *Reservations* Essential

Nini's is a wonderfully welcome addition to Ninth Square. Although the name and font make the place look, from the outside, like just another cookie-cutter Italian-American restaurant, Nini's Bistro is neither Italian-American nor just another restaurant; it is, rather, an unbelievably well-priced BYO prix-fixe concept that is completely unique in town, with an atmosphere that's dim, cozy, and romantic.

Keep in mind that the menu at Nini's changes every two weeks, so what we've sampled may have no correlation with what you'll get. That's a good thing; we love the concept so much that we're willing to overlook the weak points—our starter of boquerones rebozados (anchovies), for instance, was heavy and a bit greasy, without the lightness that we'd hope for from a Mediterranean fried fish (although the "spicy caper aioli" was fine). The second course usually involves soup or salad; we don't like to harp on misspellings, but we couldn't help but be amused by the description of a salad whose first ingredient was simply "mescaline."

Unfortunately, the overcooking of the grilled "culotte steak" was not a hallucination. We did like the fantastically interesting chipotle nut salsa with which the steak was served; it had a dry heat that complemented the slightly charred surface of the meat well. Asian fusion preparations are generally more exciting than simple American options, which do, however, utilize very fresh ingredients. A bourbon bread pudding with banana cream sauce was rich and superb, perhaps the best thing we've tried at Nini's.

Keep in mind that the hours are quite limited. It's easy to forget that the place is closed Sunday, Monday, and Tuesday. But do make it here, especially if you have a good bottle of wine waiting in the wings. It's a worthwhile, if not quite psychedelic, experience.

Number One Fish Market

The name says it all

Seafood   *Hamden*

9.0 /10
Attitude

Specialty grocery   2239 State St.
Mon.-Sat. 9am-6pm; closed Sun.   Hamden   *Credit Cards* Visa, MC, AmEx
                                     (203) 624-6171
                                     www.numberonefish.com

For a city on the Sound, New Haven has a frustrating paucity of excellent seafood. Number One Fish Market, although just a store, is the exception to this rule. Nestled in a gentle bend on State Street just beyond the New Haven-Hamden city line, this first-rate fishmonger is a boon to seafood aficionados all over the county, and a particular favorite of Yale faculty and Japanese transplants—the latter is perhaps the highest praise possible for a purveyor of fish.

Robert McNeil is passionate about fish. He fell in love with handling fish while in a job driving a delivery truck full of it. He soon realized that New Haven County desperately needed his expertise, and opened Number One a quarter century ago. To this day, Bobby regularly makes the pre-dawn trip to Fulton Fish Market, inspecting the global catch (being half Sicilian, Bobby knows how to look a swordfish in the eye), and speeding his selections back to Hamden. He also sources directly from Stonington to Nova Scotia; when shad roe season arrives in early spring, Bobby offers Connecticut River shad to first takers, some of whom (us, for example) consume copious amounts of roe before the season ends a few short weeks after it begins. Number One Fish is also the place for soft-shell crabs, lobsters, and all variety of delicious mollusks.

Our only quarrel with Number One is over the patrician hours. The store shutters its windows at 6pm, which is difficult for the after-work crowd, precipitating many a mad dash down two-lane State Street. (Another red light!) For those who arrive after closing time, or who simply don't care to cook at home, another option is to follow the Number One truck around town; the store operates a thriving wholesale operation serving local restaurants.

Olde Blue Publick House

4.5
10

The Colony Hotel's attempt at a Yankee throwback, but it's really just an average hotel restaurant

Traditional American $**26**   *Upper Chapel Area*

3.8 /10   **5.5** /10   **6.0** /10   **3.6** /10
Food   *Atmosphere*   *Attitude*   *Value*

Upmarket restaurant
Sun.-Thurs. 6:30am-midnight; Fri.-
Sat. 6:30am-1am. Kitchen closes at
10pm. *Breakfast. Brunch.*

1157 Chapel St.
New Haven
(203) 562-2221
www.colonyatyale.com

Bar Full
Credit Cards Visa, MC, AmEx
Reservations Accepted

This is the restaurant of the Colony Hotel at Yale; the space formerly housed TJ Tucker's, which was a popular place for raucous karaoke but not much else. Olde Blue is a different concept, more of a family restaurant somewhere between a steakhouse and a bar and grill. The interior decoration was reinvented and redesigned, with—you guessed it—blue as the dominant color. Clearly, the goal here is to appeal to the Yale crowd, particularly visiting parents. The "Publick House" designation, we must admit, is pretty amusing, and at the least they do pour a decent glass of ale—their own, for instance, dubbed "Olde Blue Pale Ale." It's a hoppy, New England-style brew, not bad at all.

The portion sizes are big, with none bigger than the enormous "Cowboy" New York strip. But this isn't necessarily a good thing, because some of this is the sort of food you want to eat less of, not more. Buffalo chicken spring rolls, for instance, are bland and greasy, referred to as "spicy" yet without much heat or spice—or any taste resembling that of buffalo sauce. Even the blue cheese is bad.

As for a personal pizza, it comes complete with grill marks, but its bubbly mozzarella is thick, viscous, almost too chewy to eat. The flavor is vanishingly sparse, and the crust, at our last visit, somehow arrived partly soggy and partly burnt, while the flavor was cooked out of the basil.

The music is depressing, and while we appreciate that the booths and tables try to execute a sort of antique-New-England feel in accordance with the name of the place, they instead feel cafeteria-like. Why is it that nothing named "Olde" ever has even a hint of authenticity—or age?

168 York Street Café

6.2 /10

A well-kept secret for brunch—especially given the big, cheap pitchers of Bloodies

Traditional American   **$13**   *Upper Chapel Area*

6.0/10   **6.0**/10   **8.0**/10   **6.4**/10
Food   *Atmosphere*   *Attitude*   *Value*

Casual restaurant Mon.-Sat. 5:30pm-9:30pm; Sun. 11am-3pm. Bar is open until 1am, until 2am on Fri.-Sat. *Brunch. Date-friendly. Outdoor dining.*	168 York St. New Haven (203) 789-1915	*Bar* Full *Credit Cards* Visa and MC *Reservations* Accepted

When you are hung over and cash-strapped on Sunday morning, you can't beat the jumbo-sized Bloody Mary pitchers at 168 York, otherwise known as York Street Café. Bloody Marys are mixed from scratch, and, at only a few bucks for a 60-ounce pitcher, this concoction (though lacking in horseradish) is perhaps New Haven's best alcoholic bargain. Your brunch options won't blow you away, but they're not half bad either. For well under ten dollars, you can choose from a comforting array of late-morning classics: thick-cut French toast, saucy eggs benedict, and pancakes speckled with the fruit-of-the-day. We recommend two eggs over easy, which achieves a good balance of runniness, with a tender and salty country sausage patty and a hearty mound of soft, well-seasoned home fries. Bacon is some of the thickest we've encountered. Blintzes are less impressive.

Although brunch is tasty and cheap, you might want to satisfy your nocturnal urges elsewhere. Dinners at York Street verge on the surreal; somewhat misplaced epicurean aspirations result in some ill-inspired concepts. This is not to say that there's not the occasional success; the meatloaf is reliably good, and for the low price, it's hard to go wrong. There's a prime rib, but we'd rather go with a burger (also on the brunch menu), which they do quite well here. In short, stick to the comfort food. There is no regular menu, just daily specials, so dinner can be a gamble, albeit an affordable one.

After hours, the York Street Café is transformed into one of the city's two week-round gay bars. But check the calendar before you go. Each night has a different theme; on some nights the bar is jumping, but on other nights it can be rather barren.

Oolongs Tea Bar

6.1
10

Rest, relaxation, and 70 teas in Sherman's Alley

Light American   *Theater District*

4.9/10   **7.5**/10   **9.0**/10
Food   *Atmosphere*   *Attitude*

Café
Mon.-Thurs. 9am-9pm; Fri.-Sat.
9am-10pm; Sun. 10am-6pm.
Breakfast.

1044 Chapel St.,
Sherman's Alley
New Haven
(203) 752-0718
www.oolongsteabar.com

Bar None
Credit Cards Visa and MC
Reservations Not accepted

Downtown New Haven now has its very own temple to tea, brought to you in part by the people who brew your coffee—one of the owners founded Koffee? and now co-owns Koffee Too?. Oolongs Tea Bar is a serene 14-seat space on Sherman Alley, a bricked walkway off Chapel Street that runs alongside Union League Cafe, whose building was once home to General Sherman. Sherman Alley is an ideal spot for Oolongs, a few steps away from the hustle and bustle of Chapel Street. This place offers the yin to coffeeshop yang, enveloping visitors in a quiet calm, complete with leafy green bamboo and gurgling water sculpture.

But Oolongs is also serious about tea, with over 70 varieties on offer, from nutty green teas, to refined white-tipped varieties, fruit tisanes, and flowering teas that miraculously unfold into floating lotuses when steeped in hot water. We haven't tried every single one, but for herbal tea drinkers, the African Outback blend is a standout. To find your own favorite, take some time to peruse the printed menu, a heavy, solid tome that offers a catalog of teas by style, along with tasting notes. If you prefer to follow your nose, head for the row of apothecary jars which line the wall opposite the tea bar; inside each is a sample that you can smell and touch, if that strikes your fancy.

Although purists will have plenty to consider, those interested in the pop culture of tea are also taken care of here, with bubble teas, tea lattes (they have a new-fangled espresso-like machine for these), tea soda, and of course, iced tea. Oolongs also peddles basic but mediocre food (sandwiches and such); for our money, the best stuff here is in your cup.

The Original Falafel

A no-frills joint serving bland falafel that's not even particularly cheap

Middle Eastern   **$ 7**   *Theater District*

4.6/10   **4.0**/10   **4.0**/10   **4.8**/10
Food   *Atmosphere*   *Attitude*   *Value*

Counter service   240 College St.   *Bar* None
Daily 11am-9pm.   New Haven   *Credit Cards* Visa, MC, AmEx
Vegetarian-friendly.   (203) 777-8884   *Reservations* Not accepted

Part of a 21st-century explosion of falafel places in town, the Original Falafel, which opened in 2002, offers all the usual sandwich fillings plus a few more unusual fillings, including fried cauliflower. The look is haphazard and unusual: a bizarre array of giant signs, red on white, advertises the low prices a bit too forwardly, tipping you off right from the start that the focus here might not be on the quality. These huge banner-style ads, with their bulbous 1980s-style font (reminiscent of the infamous Cooper Black), might as well be selling refurbished electronic equipment at discount rates on 42nd Street.

Unfortunately, though, they're selling food. In classic 42nd Street style, the prices here are reasonable, but actually no lower than they are anywhere else; five bucks for a falafel sandwich with hummus and tabbouleh (it's called the Super Falafel) is not exactly a steal, although there are some cheaper lunchtime discounts. The falafel balls themselves aren't bad—they're soft within, crispy without, and they're scooped and fried to order, four to a sandwich. Other ingredients are weak, from the tasteless tomato to the bland hummus (which, on one particular visit a few years ago, actually tasted carbonated). The tabbouleh has even less flavor, and everything, including the falafel, comes undersalted. The pita bread, meanwhile, tastes and feels like the flimsy out-of-the-bag variety, a poor specimen that's barely warmed on the griddle.

Service at the counter is merely perfunctory, and in terms of atmosphere, aside from the signage, Original Falafel feels like nothing more than a take-out place, but there's plenty of seating inside, and many people do seem to eat in. Either way, you can do so much better, both for falafel quality and environment, at other falafel places downtown.

Pacifico

A vibrant and exciting Nuevo Latino hotspot that
hops with activity late into the evening

Latin American, Seafood $**38**   *Theater District*

7.7 /10   **9.5** /10   **7.0** /10   **7.1** /10
Food   *Atmosphere*   *Attitude*   *Value*

Upmarket restaurant
Mon.-Thurs. 5pm-10pm; Fri.-Sat.
5pm-11pm. Kitchen closes 30 min.
earlier, but Menu de Media Noche
(abridged menu) available Thurs.-
Sun. 10:30pm-1am. *Date-friendly*.

220 College St.
New Haven
(203) 772-4002

Bar Full
Credit Cards Visa, MC, AmEx
Reservations Recommended

Primary colors: that's the first thing that hits you when you walk into
Pacifico, Colombian restaurateur and cookbook author Rafael
Palomino's new seafood-focused Nuevo Latino restaurant, which
inhabits the space once occupied by Tibwin. The primary colors are
everywhere: the walls, the tiles, the little fish that swim through the
upholstery of the restaurant's wonderfully varied configurations of
banquettes. The warm human buzz in the two-floor space plays off the
colors and the open kitchen to emulsify an atmosphere that is more
than the sum of its parts.

It's still in the early stages, but so far, among appetizers, the most
impressive thing has been the trio de langosta, a pricey but interesting
plate of succulent lobster meat in three preparations (a quinoa and
lobster hash brown, for instance). Also great are the ostras con
mofongo, meltingly tender fried oysters with a chunky sweet plantain
puree. Less impressive are vegetable empanadas, which have an
inspired goat-cheese filling but are a tad greasy.

The best main so far has been pollo al horno con maní y pure de
papa con azafrán—superbly crusted, juicy chicken with a well-
developed flavor and wonderful peanut sauce. A gently roasted corvina
(a species sometimes called "Mediterranean bass") is cooked whole, its
flesh sweet and delicate, but its sides are boring. We've had steak a la
parilla requested rare come out medium-plus, which was disheartening,
although the meat was nicely marinated. The vegetable paella was a
bland disappointment.

Pacifico has also developed quite a bar scene (try the delicious
pineapple mojito) and refreshingly late kitchen hours. And Mr.
Palomino, going in his own direction, plans to offer cooking classes
every other Wednesday. It's all quite impressive for a restaurant still so
early in a lifespan that we hope will be long and happy.

Pad Thai

10

A simple, unexciting restaurant that is nonetheless
one of the better options on Thai restaurant row

Thai $**17**   *Upper Chapel Area*

6.3 /10   **5.5**/10   **8.0**/10   **6.0**/10
Food   *Atmosphere*   *Attitude*   *Value*

Casual restaurant   1170 Chapel St.   *Bar* Wine and beer only
Sun.-Thurs. 11:30am-3:30pm, 5pm-   New Haven   *Credit Cards* Visa, MC, AmEx
10pm; Fri. 11:30am-3:30pm, 5pm-   (203) 562-0322   *Reservations* Accepted
10:30pm; Sat. 11:30am-10:30pm.   culinarymenus.com/padthai.htm
Vegetarian-friendly. Outdoor dining.

As the name suggests, this is fairly standard Thai fare, but it's actually
above average amidst this bland stretch of Chapel Street ethnic
restaurants. The room isn't bad—they seem to have redecorated and
dimmed the lights in recent years—although the décor is still
uninspiring. There are, however, a few outdoor tables in the summer—
a definite plus. While preparations are competent here, some of the
flavors have been toned down from their traditional levels in what we
suspect is a misguided concession to the American palate; as elsewhere
in downtown New Haven, they lack the spice-and-texture zing of Thai
food at its best. Slightly more interesting "chef's specials" have
attendant prices that are a bit dear.

If you do find yourself here, we suggest that you order anything but
the eponymous Pad Thai, an already bland dish that gains nothing from
this lackluster treatment. Well-priced noodle options abound, and the
standard meat-and-vegetable stir-fry dishes are all in attendance—the
usual low-priced options for those on a grad-student stipend, with free
delivery for minimum orders of at least $15 (which can be a bit hard to
achieve at lunch). Chef's specials yield some more interesting options,
like dishes of soft-shell crab and "Long Island Fish," a fried whole fish
with onion, bell pepper, coriander, and sweet and sour sauce (takes you
right back to Long Island, doesn't it)? There's even a wild boar curry
with basil.

Perhaps because of the rather sterile atmosphere, the place rarely
seems crowded; they seem to do much of their business on a take-out
basis. There is one advantage to Pad Thai, though: with the big glass
front window on upper Chapel, you can spot your arch-nemesis dining
inside from clear across the street, in plenty of time to turn tail and go
elsewhere.

Pancho's Cantina

A crowd-pleasing Tex-Mex hotspot in downtown Westville

Tex-Mex, Bar food $22   *Westville*

6.5/10   **7.5**/10   **7.0**/10   **6.5**/10
Food   *Atmosphere* *Attitude*   *Value*

Bar and grill
Sun.-Thurs. 11am-1am; Fri.-Sat. 11am-2am. Kitchen closes at midnight.

883 Whalley Ave.
New Haven
(203) 397-3300

Bar Full
Credit Cards Visa, MC, AmEx
Reservations Accepted

It is not so surprising that this well-known downtown Westville haunt attracts so many Southern students, night after night: the Tex-Mex fare is simple but tasty; the well-executed, free-flowing margaritas come in cactus glasses; and, of course, the location is prime.

The space is divided into two areas: one that feels more like a restaurant, and another with throbbing music that feels more like a frat bar, complete with all the neon beer signs, chili peppers, pinball machine, "I got floored at Pancho's" T-shirts for sale, and so on. There are often hip-hop dance classics piped through the formidable sound system, and on a weekend night, the place rages. DJ dance parties are not out of the ordinary—if you're here for dinner, don't worry, you're not required to join the line winding out the door. The bar area is not just for getting wasted, though; you can also eat there, and on the quieter nights, it's the only area with much restaurant activity.

A meal will surely begin with chips and salsa, as it should; the salsa is chunky and garlicky, not hot but still good. After that, we recommend sticking with the Tex-Mex classics—that is, the ones replete with red sauce and melted cheese: chiles rellenos, enchiladas, and so on. Such dishes are just about on par with the area's best Tex-Mex; they're moist, not dried out, and they're freshly prepared with good tortillas. The dirty rice and beans are particularly satisfying.

Some of the other menu options are less Tex-Mex, like "spicy shrimp," which are redolent of Tabasco rather than Mexican spices. And then some are just bar food (wings, for instance). These tend to fare less well, relatively speaking, but they're still competent. Desserts include plátanos de Oaxaca, a concoction of bananas with coconut syrup and whipped cream that arrives in flames. It's yet another crowd-pleaser.

The Pantry

7.4
10

A great, casual breakfast and brunch spot—with
endless queues to prove it

Light American   **$10**   *East Rock/Grad Ghetto*

7.5/10   **8.0**/10   **5.0**/10   **8.5**/10
Food   *Atmosphere*   *Attitude*   *Value*

Casual restaurant	2 Mechanic St.	*Bar* None
Tues.-Sat. 7am-2pm;	New Haven	*Credit Cards* None
Sun. 8am-3pm; closed Mon.	(203) 787-0392	*Reservations* Not accepted
Breakfast. Brunch. Vegetarian-friendly.		

Much vaunted as the place for brunch in New Haven, the Pantry has a
loyal following. The result is a daunting queue of the hungry and
hopeful; it may be Sunday morning, but you'll feel like you're still
outside the club the night before. Once you get in—if you get in—the
atmosphere feels distinctly late-1970s Portland, Oregon. The soothing
sounds of jazz and the coziness of the two small rooms contribute to
the hipsterish allure.

The breakfast classics are all here—French toast, eggs over easy,
bacon (refreshingly not overdone—speak up if you like it crispy), and
home fries, all well executed. But breakfast here is also intended to be
something more than mainstream; dishes come garnished with fresh
fruit and herbs, feta and spinach work their way into the omelette mix,
and there are nouvelle brunches like lox benedict. The hollandaise here
is great; so are pancakes and French toast. Salads, too, have fresh
ingredients, but they're less interesting.

The Pantry's true strength is not so much inspirational dining as
atmosphere and Grad Ghetto location. But perhaps its greatest asset of
all is the lack of competition. Brunch, a weekend tradition to so many,
can still be a challenge to find in New Haven, and it's the imbalance of
supply and demand that really leads to the infamous Pantry queues. So
the Pantry operates like a monopolist, advertising "Breakfast All Day"
and then shutting their doors whenever they feel like it—which, in spite
of posted hours, can be as early as 1:30pm. It can add up to a level of
stress and frustration that feels fundamentally antithetical to the brunch
aesthetic. On the other hand, the longer you have to wait, the better it
will all taste when you finally get in.

Parthenon Diner

5.4
/10

A standard 24-hour diner with below-average
Greek-American food—and almost everything else

Short-order American, Greek   **$17**   *Branford*

5.0 /10   **5.5** /10   **7.0** /10   **5.0** /10
Food   *Atmosphere*   *Attitude*   *Value*

Diner   374 E. Main St.   **Bar** Full
Daily 24 hrs.   Branford   **Credit Cards** Visa, MC, AmEx
Breakfast.   (203) 481-0333   **Reservations** Not accepted
                     www.parthenondiner.com

This is one of the only 24-hour restaurants in the New Haven area. As
at the Athenian Diners in Westville and Milford, the Parthenon Diner is
much like your typical all-night diner in Queens or on Long Island,
sporting a colorful and encyclopedic menu that traverses Greece, Italy,
and most of America. There is wine from the Aegean Islands, cocktails
including Ouzo and Metaxa, and a platter of sea scallops with artichoke
hearts in white wine sauce. There are Belgian waffles and pizza bagels,
spanikopita and T-bone steaks, and tapioca pudding. On the one hand,
the idea that one restaurant would try to do this many things at once
offends our food sensibilities (especially when some of the things are so
questionable in and of themselves). On the other hand, if there are only
two or three places open at 4am, it's nice to be able to find absolutely
anything you crave at Parthenon.

Hamburgers and such might be the best choice, although there's a
short list of Greek choices that include grape leaves, moussaka,
souvlaki, and so on. The best thing about the gyro at Parthenon might
be the pita—it's the good kind, with some nice girth to it. The meat on
top is salty (very salty) but satisfying, and the tsatsiki is refreshing, but
copious lettuce, chopped onion, and under-ripe tomatoes flood the
plate, adding little but logistical difficulty. French fries are also subpar,
with a mealy, tasteless interior. Coffee is weak, but that's closer to par
for the diner course.

Suffice it to say that we can see little reason for frequenting
Parthenon during the regular business hours of regular restaurants. But
at those other times, beggars can't be choosers, and it is then that we
salute Parthenon for their commitment not to sleep.

Patricia's Restaurant

3.8
10

A gritty diner that's been around for 50 years—it's more about nostalgia than food

Short-order American   **$ 6**   *Broadway Area*

3.3/10   **4.0**/10   **6.0**/10   **5.1**/10
Food   *Atmosphere*   *Attitude*   *Value*

Diner   18 Whalley Ave.   *Bar* None
Tues.-Sun. 7:30am-2:30pm;   New Haven   *Credit Cards* None
closed Mon. *Breakfast.*   (203) 787-4500   *Reservations* Not accepted

After a half century's tenure as a diner, Patricia's Restaurant may feel that it has nothing to prove. The décor is haphazard and unassuming, the menu brief, and the rules explicit: No Substitutions. This old dame of the downtown coterie of cheap diners offers the kinds of things you would expect from a diner. It can be hard to find a solid American breakfast in New Haven, and Patricia's delivers at true thrift-shop prices; two eggs with home fries and toast can be had for pocket change.

The dining room offers a collection of mismatched chairs and tables and uninspired lighting. Those lucky enough to get a booth are confronted with a bizarre reflection of themselves in a round mirror, tinged faintly blue, for that hung-over look any time of day or night. The one advantage of the proliferation of mirrors is that they make the space look larger and more exciting; a big gilt mirror on the back wall faithfully reflects the comings and goings on the street beyond the glass facade. Everything is steeped in the history of a space that has been serving (albeit under different managements) for over half a century, so many a New Havener has a place in her heart for Patricia's.

But when it comes to food, there's not much to write about. The French toast, made with squares of Wonder-style bread, is a pale shadow of what it could be. Omelettes, served up without flounce or frills, are downright boring. And a note of caution to those patrons who may indeed be hung over: take special care when looking for the loo. The egress provided is a precipitous descent to the facilities (and said facilities are bare-bones at best). Please, watch your step.

Pazza Cucina

7.3
/10

Finally, an ambitious and atmospheric restaurant in
Woodbridge, a bit more than your standard Italian

Italian   **$36**   *Woodbridge*

6.9 /10   **8.0** /10   **8.0** /10   **6.2** /10
Food   *Atmosphere*   *Attitude*   *Value*

Upmarket restaurant   208 Amity Rd.   *Bar* Full
Sun.-Thurs. 5pm-9:30pm;   Woodbridge   *Credit Cards* Visa, MC, AmEx
Fri.-Sat. 5pm-midnight. Kitchen (203) 397-8882   *Reservations* Recommended
closes Sun.-Thurs. 9:30pm; Fri.-Sat. 10pm. *Date-friendly.*

Woodbridge needed Pazza Cucina, and Pazza Cucina needed
Woodbridge. An upscale suburb without a single distinguished Italian
restaurant—especially in an area known for Italian restaurants—is a
market primed for success, and judging from Pazza Cucina's attendance
even on weeknights, it's working. The carefully lit room hits that
upmarket-casual-chic feel that seems to have equal appeal for young
professionals and affluent families.

The food here toes the line between Italian-American and Italian. On
the former front, fried calamari make an excellent starter, some of the
tops in town. The batter has a wonderfully crispy texture, the squid is
tender, and the sauce is one of the most interesting tomato sauces that
we've had with fried calamari—oven-dried tomatoes make for darker,
fuller taste. There are perhaps too many olives in the mix, but hot
peppers are a welcome addition.

Chicken Milanese comes well breaded and crusted, but the cutlets
should be pounded thinner than they are—pounded and pounded—
before dredging and frying, for the crispier overall effect that is the
hallmark of a good Milanese (or its distinguished cousin, the Wiener
schnitzel). We appreciate the fennel and shaved parmesan on the
accompanying salad, though. As for pasta, a dish of penne
all'amatriciana comes properly al dente, with a sauce that has an
essential smokiness, but it's improperly reduced, with a texture too
chunky and watery, so the sauce doesn't bind well to the pasta.

Pazza Cucina's new wine list is very respectable, although its
predecessor (a smaller list) had a larger selection of inexpensive wines.
Still, the value proposition is as good as ever, and many of the higher-
end Italian wines are serious, rarely found, well-priced bottles—surely
another first in Woodbridge.

Frank Pepe's

7.9
10

Still a legendary pizzeria with long queues to show
for it, even if they've lost a step in recent years

Pizza   **$14** *Wooster Square Area*

8.5 /10   **7.5** /10   **5.0** /10   **8.6** /10
Food   *Atmosphere*   *Attitude*   *Value*

Casual restaurant   157 Wooster St.   *Bar* Wine and beer only
Mon. 4pm-10pm; Wed.-Thurs.   New Haven   *Credit Cards* None
4pm-10pm; Fri.-Sat. 11:30am- (203) 865-5762   *Reservations* Not accepted
11:30pm; Sun. 2:30pm-10pm;
closed Tues. *Vegetarian-friendly.*

The Spot: Tues.-Thurs. 4pm-10pm;   163 Wooster St.
Fri.-Sat. 4pm-11pm;   New Haven
Sun. 3pm-10pm; closed Mon.   (203) 865-7602

Frank Pepe's, one of the two most famous restaurants in New Haven
and among the best-known in all New England, is the oft-disputed
champion of New Haven's venerable tradition of pizza. An icon of the
old Wooster Street Neapolitan community, this inimitable pizzeria has
long held its ground. You'll have quite a while to ponder its illustrious
history during your epic wait for seating (it's worst 6pm-8pm
Wednesday through Saturday).

Although it's still a worthwhile trip if the wait is not too long, we're
sad to report that Frank Pepe's has slipped a bit in recent years. Rumors
abound about family feuds, but all we know is that the flaky, bubbly
crust that is gently seared by the soot of decades-old brick has gotten
less flaky, less bubbly, and—we dare say—thicker and brittler. The
famed white clam and bacon pie—still our favorite—has come too salty
and not oily enough a couple of times recently; we still love it, though.
And a basic margherita with tomato and mozzarella still boasts that
delicious sauce, even if it also sports too much cheese and has less of
that ethereality.

If Pepe's is not what it once was, it's still a great pizza place. Few
details of the pizza-making process have changed since 1936. The turn-
of-the-century brick oven is still tended with long wooden spatulas. The
room is too bright, and your order is taken with a direct, tongue-in-
cheek briskness. Some traditionalist aspects are just plain annoying,
such as Pepe's refusal to take credit cards, or above all, to take
reservations. Pepe's The Spot, next door, helps with this problem by
offering similar pizza, with shorter lines, in a room that's more drab and
less historic. The Spot is also open on Tuesdays, when the mothership is
closed.

Peppercorns

7.4
10

One taste of the piega, and you'll see that this is more than just a Westville sandwich shop

Light American $ **9**   *Westville*

7.5 /10   **6.5** /10   **9.0** /10   **8.7** /10
Food   *Atmosphere*   *Attitude*   *Value*

Counter service   1302 Whalley Ave.   *Bar* None
Mon.-Fri. 7am-6pm; Sat. 7am-3pm;   New Haven   *Credit Cards* None
closed Sun. *Breakfast.*   (203) 397-0782   *Reservations* Not accepted

Whether coming from nearby Westville center or all the way from New Haven, many a foodie has been charmed enough to make the drive to the unlikely location of Peppercorns, a gourmand's sandwich shop with excellent, affable service. Although many carry out, the food can also be eaten at a handful of tables.

The signature sandwich bread at Peppercorns is the piega, baked fresh on the premises; it's a delightful flatbread of which the folks here are justly proud. There are also standard bread options, but who cares? The piega is the perfect vehicle for a variety of fillings, which are ordered by number. We love the #6, for example: crispy chicken, caramelized onion, and ancho chili mayonnaise. Yum. There are other offerings aside from sandwiches, but we feel the same way about them as we do about all that other bread. French fries are not the specialty here; they can be soggy, as though the temperature on the deep fryer needs a good nudge upwards. Likewise, we find the Caesar salad lackluster; it features unremarkable dressing and unimpressive cold sliced chicken breast.

After the piega, Peppercorn's greatest asset is its people—smiling, friendly souls who clearly feel good about what they do. On a recent visit, we and the other late lunch eat-in customers were all spontaneously offered complimentary cookies. A free cookie is a good cookie, and so these were, though of the dense and doughy variety. But if you are actually on a mission for something sweet to end your meal, head straight for the spectacular apple spice cake, a heated delight of moist butter cake, pieces of seasoned apple, and golden raisins, topped with a generous mound of whipped cream. It's one of the most memorable cakes around.

Peroles Restaurant

The best—and only—Colombian food in town, in stark and simple Dixwell digs

Latin American $18   *Hamden*

6.9/10   **6.5**/10   **9.0**/10   **6.9**/10
Food   *Atmosphere*   *Attitude*   *Value*

Casual restaurant   1832 Dixwell Ave.   *Bar* Full
Tues.-Thurs. 11am-9pm; Fri.-Sat.   Hamden   *Credit Cards* Visa, MC, AmEx
11am-10pm; Sun. 11am-9pm;   (203) 287-9646   *Reservations* Accepted
closed Mon. *Brunch.*

This, the only Colombian restaurant in the New Haven area, is an unusual treat. It lies in a little house along Dixwell Avenue, and still seems little known, in spite of the pleasant executions of Latin American dishes that are hard to find in the area. The room is simple, sparse, and a bit dark, with a few tables that are spottily illuminated, but friendly service makes up for the uninspired décor. Anyway, this is more or less what you'd expect from a simple South American restaurant, so it's hard to fault the authenticity.

To begin with, arepas, soft white corn cakes, are somewhat bland, but empanadas are better, with a pleasant crispness surrounding the soft fillings. And the moist and immensely flavorful morcilla (blood sausage—which Robin is still trying to get Clare to like as much as he does) is the best around, stuffed with rice and the trademark notes of cinnamon and sweet spice.

At Peroles, you'll get hearty food and hearty portions, too. At lunchtime, seven bucks or so buys you an enormous serving, enough for two people. Fried plantains are good and sweet, and arroz con pollo is a tour de force, with moist chicken and well-textured yellow rice. It's a filling dish, full of energy (we prefer to add hot sauce and salt). A plate called "Bandejita Paisa Peroles" features a combination of some of the traditional Colombian specialties, including a great fried pork belly and soft, soothing beans. The combo has some weak points— fried beef is underseasoned and avocado just okay—but it's a good introduction to South American cuisine.

And there's more. A full bar. Tropical fruit shakes. Even if not every item on the menu is up to the lofty standards of the morcilla, empanadas, and arroz con pollo, we really love this place.

Perrotti's

5.7
/10

Just another cookie-cutter Wooster Street Italian-
American restaurant—no more, no less

Italian, Pizza $24   *Wooster Square Area*

5.7 /10   **6.0** /10   **5.0** /10   **5.0** /10
Food   *Atmosphere*   *Attitude*   *Value*

Casual restaurant   127 Wooster St.   **Bar** Wine and beer only
Mon.-Thurs. 11:30am-9pm; Fri.   New Haven   **Credit Cards** Visa, MC, AmEx
11:30am-10pm; Sat. noon-10pm;   (203) 624-4407   **Reservations** Accepted
Sun. 1pm-9pm.

Some restaurants are such perfect archetypes of a genre that they almost seem to be caricatures of themselves. Perrotti's, the classic New Haven Italian-American restaurant on the classic strip of Wooster Street, almost precisely meets our modest expectations for such a place—without exceeding them a bit.

In sharp contrast with Tony & Lucille's (the kitschy Wooster Street competition), Perrotti's dining room is far too brightly lit, taking away whatever enjoyable ambience might have otherwise existed. Not that there would have been much; the tables and place settings are downmarket, the walls are decorated with misplaced murals of the Amalfi Coast, and the service is merely perfunctory. To be fair, though, it's a place aimed at families, probably not intended for romantic dates or furtive tête-à-têtes.

The food, too, is just as expected, including the above-average fried calamari, which are thickly crispy with a batter that's very light-colored—almost white—and served with a decent red sauce. Perrotti's also has a way with eggplant, and the eggplant parmigiana (in the soft and tender school of eggplant) is another highlight. While we were once directed by the staff toward the lasagna, we found it unexciting and under-flavored. Even worse are the stuffed shells and manicotti—both feature watery, overcooked pasta filled with disappointingly grainy and tasteless cheese. And while chicken Diane, with a white wine sauce and mushrooms, isn't particularly bad—the chicken is fairly tender—it's entirely predictable. Do people really love the enormous plate of pan-fried white meat (chicken breast or veal cutlet) with the sweetish wine-and-stock sauce *so much* that it deserves to be replicated exactly in more than a hundred greater New Haven eateries?

Are Perrotti's and its lookalikes still what customers want, or are these restaurants just increasingly out of touch with reality?

Pizza House

6.1
10

A simple, utilitarian slice joint that's open late

Pizza

$ 6   *Upper Chapel Area*

5.6/10
Food

7.0/10
Attitude

7.4/10
Value

Take-out
Sun.-Thurs. 11am-11pm; Fri.-Sat.
11am-1am; closed Mon.
Vegetarian-friendly.

89 Howe St.
New Haven
(203) 865-3345

Bar None
Credit Cards None
Reservations Not accepted

The first glimpse you get of Pizza House is an inauspicious one: every inch of free space behind the small counter is piled high with cardboard pizza boxes, and most of the dozen or so wooden tables are empty. This utilitarianism permeates the establishment to the last square foot: there's absolutely nothing fancy or superfluous here; even the name of the place offers the necessary information, and no more. The only frill in Pizza House seems to be the mandatory straw dispensed with each can of soda you order, a charming touch offered by an equally charming but often taciturn staff.

With these prices—$1.50 for a slice of cheese, a quarter more for pepperoni or sausage—it's hard to find cause for complaint. The pizza is not too thick, but also not thin, and while the slices are far from extraordinary, they're definitely not a greasy mess, either. Although the pies would benefit from a little more sauce, the cheese is good and stringy, the crust the right medley of crisp and soft, and the toppings are fresh and copious. Pizza House is a paper-plate type of place (no utensils are offered; if forks exist they are without a doubt plastic ones), but within its category, this restaurant is above-average.

Most customers prefer take-out. Pizza House is open until 1am on Fridays and Saturdays, making it an okay option for a late night slice. But if you're in this neighborhood—especially if you feel like actually sitting down—you might as well walk a block and shell out a couple more quarters for Brick Oven Pizza, which makes a better pie and offers some of the frills that Pizza House can't muster. *–Coco Krumme*

The Place

8.1
10

A magical summer spot to enjoy great grilled seafood while sitting on tree stumps in open air

Seafood   **$19**   *Guilford*

7.3 /10   **10** /10   **7.0** /10   **8.2** /10
Food   *Atmosphere*   *Attitude*   *Value*

Casual restaurant	901 Boston Post Rd.	*Bar* BYO
Summer only (generally May	Guilford	*Credit Cards* None
through October), lunch and dinner.	(203) 453-9276	*Reservations* Not accepted
Hours are unpredictable; call		
ahead for details. *Date-friendly. Outdoor dining.*		

Don't wear your Sunday best to this friendly outdoor picnic-style cookout in Guilford, which is open only in good weather. Every dish on the menu is messy, beginning with the inexplicably alluring roasted clams with a barbecue sauce that everyone in the whole place seems to be enjoying. Actually, even the menu itself is messy, carved in block letters on slabs of wood towering above a smoking barbecue pit. You eat at rustic picnic tables, sitting on tree stumps, under lights that are strung up overhead. It's an absolute dream—but remember to bring along some bug spray to ward off the mosquitoes that are as entranced by you as you are by the barbecue.

Most seafood here is excellent, but nothing is better than the succulent lobsters and fresh crabs. The price is right, and the Place has some of the best lobsters in New Haven County. They're not overcooked, and they're served with plenty of melted butter. Other butter-worthy options are the excellent grilled corn on the cob and the great baked potatoes.

Be forewarned that straight fish dishes (bluefish and so on) can tend to dry out on the grill. There's nothing in the way of sides; if you desire salad, bread, booze, or dessert, just bring your own. They'll provide corkscrew and plastic-cup services. Bring anything. Bring a keg.

Although it's a bit of a trek from New Haven, when the weather is warm (keep in mind that the Place is closed when it's cold or rainy), this experience is worth every necessary mile of highway driving. Some things make you proud to be a New Englander. The Place is just such a gem.

The Playwright

6.9
/10

The older and better of the Playwrights: a country Irish feel, outdoor seats, and good burgers

Irish, Bar food $22   *Hamden*

6.4/10   **8.0**/10   **7.0**/10   **6.5**/10
Food   *Atmosphere*   *Attitude*   *Value*

Bar and grill   1232 Whitney Ave.   *Bar* Full
Mon.-Thurs 11:30am-1am; Fri.-Sat.   Hamden   *Credit Cards* Visa, MC, AmEx
11:30am-2am; Sun. 10am-1am.   (203) 287-2401   *Reservations* Accepted
Kitchen closes Sun.-Thurs. 10:30pm;   www.niteimage.com/clubs/Playwright_Hamden
Fri.-Sat. 11:30pm. *Brunch. Date-friendly. Outdoor dining.*

The difference between this, the original neighborhood Playwright pub in Hamden, and the gargantuan branch on Temple Street in downtown New Haven, could hardly be any greater. This one is a local legend, and it feels so much more like a local, from the photos of Irish heroes on the walls to the harmonious and elegant bar to the authentic furniture and stained glass, imported directly from Ireland, that still feels somehow restrained. The dining room, meanwhile, is more like a charming rural Irish cottage, from the antiques and knick-knacks that sit here and there, to the delightful stone fireplaces, to the exposed wood beams that are actually Irish railroad ties.

Apps might include nice Irish smoked salmon, crispy beer-battered mushrooms, and good, meaty buffalo wings. Guinness stew, which comes with a swirl of mashed potatoes, is tender with well-developed flavor, while the shepherd's pie, at last visit, was much better seasoned at this joint than at the younger, bigger brother in the 'Have. In the end, though, we favor the burgers here, which are well executed, with fresh, crisp french fries. An Irish whiskey BBQ burger, for instance, with "house whiskey BBQ sauce" and melted cheddar, strikes just the right pub note.

The Irish pub, when done right, is able to play a specific, comforting role in restaurant culture and even the collective consciousness of a community, and the Hamden branch of Playwright fits that bill. It's the sort of standby that is there for you, night after night. Whether it's for a Black and Tan at the bar, or for something more substantial by the fireplace, you just know that you'll be back.

The Playwright

5.5
10

A brash and cavernous sibling to the Hamden standby, with a raging crowd and so-so Irish meals

Irish, Bar food   **$28**   *Theater District*

5.1 /10   **7.0**/10   **3.0** /10   **4.6**/10
Food   *Atmosphere*   *Attitude*   *Value*

Bar and grill   144 Temple St.   *Bar* Full
Mon.-Thurs. 11:30am-1am; Fri.-   New Haven   *Credit Cards* Visa, MC, AmEx
Sat. 11:30am-2am; Sun. noon-1am. (203) 752-0450   *Reservations* Accepted
Kitchen closes at 10pm. *Brunch.*   www.niteimage.com/clubs/Playwright_NewHaven

This Temple Street Irish pub is so big that it defies proportions. Any one of its cascade of rooms and floors might by itself look like the biggest bar in New Haven…until you enter the next room, which is even bigger. And on weekends, the Playwright somehow seems to fill them all. It's a young, loud, and boisterous crowd. The beer flows, the TVs blare, the lights flash, the overworked waitstaff scurries around, and the Playwright rakes in the cash.

As for the Irish dinners here, you do best with simple dishes like a fine Guinness lamb stew, made with carrots, peas, and potatoes, or a shepherd's pie, which is well browned and decently flavored. As for the pub fare, the burgers are perfectly decent, but fries are tasteless and mealy. The menu is a minefield: we've had an appetizer of tuna with panko bread crumbs that was curiously served cold (panko bread crumbs don't like the cold), a strange salad in a taco shell, and a horribly overcooked steak. A French onion soup has cheese that's not browned and little evidence of Port or Madeira, and potato skins with corned beef and cheese have too high a ratio of bland, dry potato to other ingredients. The wine list, reasonably long yet devoid of even one interesting selection, is like a parody; it is a roll call of almost every California mass-marketed supermarket selection you can possibly imagine.

We prefer the place at non-peak hours, when the ambience is a lot more mellow and you can actually stop and appreciate the exquisitely Disneyesque, imitation-Irish detail of this cavernous pub. A lot of thought went into every etch of glass, every angle of wood. You can decide for yourself whether they've gone too far in the Irish theming— or just meditate on the mind-boggling square footage.

Polo Grille & Wine Bar

6.5 /10

Wonderful wines and an elaborate menu, but fancy
ingredients don't always mean good food

Italian, Steakhouse   **$42**   *Financial District*

6.6 /10   **6.0** /10   **7.0** /10   **5.2** /10
Food   *Atmosphere*   *Attitude*   *Value*

Upmarket restaurant
Mon.-Thurs. 11:30am-3pm, 5pm-
9pm, Fri.-Sat. 11:30am-3pm, 5pm-
10pm; closed Sun. *Good wine list.*

5 Elm St.
New Haven
(203) 787-9000
www.pologrille.com

Bar Full
Credit Cards Visa, MC, AmEx
Reservations Recommended

Sometimes it seems that each of New Haven's many misguided
attempts at expensive Italian food misses in a slightly different way. Polo
is the Jason Giambi of the lot: pumped up with steroids, it takes a
massive home-run swing but still strikes out. We understand that
there's now a new chef, who came over from Tre Scalini, but things
don't seem to have changed much.

As it always has, Polo presents an ambitious, high-priced menu of
Italian-American specialties such as grilled filet mignon topped with
grilled portobello mushrooms and lobster meat, served in a cognac
gorgonzola cream sauce. This misguided dish seems conceived with the
fallacy that good food results simply from throwing together expensive
ingredients (and could there be any more on one plate?). The result is
neither Italian, nor particularly American—nor particularly good. In this
case, individual flavors are obscured, not heightened. At one recent
visit, there was a filet mignon special whose cream sauce featured
berries and champagne. Need we say more?

There are some simpler steaks too, but they're undistinguished, and
they're often cooked more than requested. Pasta dishes can actually be
better than the meat options, particularly the specials. But they, too,
often suffer under the weight of heavy cream sauces. Polo's décor is
ridiculous in a similar way to the food: too much, too much, too much.
One room has a ceiling painted with blue sky and white clouds.
Another tries, and fails, to feel clubby, like a New York City steakhouse.
One high note, however, is the Italian wine list, which is not only
fantastic, but wonderfully well priced. Even southern Italy is well
represented, with even more excellent values. We'll toast to that.

Popeye's

3.9
10

They serve much better chicken than KFC, and they stay open late—still, fast food is fast food

Southern   **$ 7**   *Whalley*

5.3 /10   **1.0** /10   **4.0** /10   **5.3** /10
Food   *Atmosphere*   *Attitude*   *Value*

Fast-food chain   35 Whalley Ave.   *Bar* None
Sun.-Wed. 11am-midnight; Thurs.   New Haven   *Credit Cards* None
11am-1am; Fri.-Sat. 11am-3am.   (203) 562-7674   *Reservations* Not accepted
                                  www.popeyes.com

Popeye's is one of the most redeeming of American fast-food chains, both for its reliably decent fried chicken and for its classic logo. The theme is officially Louisiana (po-boys, crawfish, and jambalaya may be found on the menu), but the place is really all about the chicken and the sides. The fried chicken is correct. It's crispy, properly seasoned and salted, and just plain good. Dark meat is better than light, and also marginally cheaper. Spicy chicken strips are also a fine choice; the chicken sandwich is solid. Well-textured red beans and rice are a great accompaniment. The mashed potatoes with "Cajun gravy" are of the whipped variety (ergo, very likely reconstituted), but we like them. The fries are well spiced and crispy, tasty but greasy, and of dubious residual nutritional value; there is very little evidence of the original potato.

There's nothing in the way of atmosphere, unless you have a thing for fast-food decor. Take-out is certainly the way to go. The Popeye's in New Haven is right across from the Holiday Inn at the beginning of Whalley Avenue, making it an easy stop on the way to Staples, the supermarket, or the futon store. It's one of the few places where Yalies tend to mix with residents of the Dixwell neighborhood. Popeye's also has a walk-up window which is open until 3am on the weekends—bless their hearts.

Portofino

7.2
10

Friendly, mid-priced, red-sauce Italian—what else is new—but with fair prices and good execution

Italian   **$27**   *East Rock/Grad Ghetto*

7.1 /10   **7.0** /10   **8.0** /10   **6.5** /10
Food   *Atmosphere*   *Attitude*   *Value*

Upmarket restaurant   937 State St.   *Bar* Full
Mon.-Fri. 11:45am-2:30pm and   New Haven   *Credit Cards* Visa, MC, AmEx
5pm-9pm; Sat. 5pm-10:30pm;   (203) 562-1414   *Reservations* Accepted
Sun. 4pm-8:30pm.

From the outside, in a town of Italian restaurants, Portofino has precious little to distinguish it from the incumbents. You walk in anticipating another boring Italian-American restaurant. However, that all changes once you walk past the lively bar into the main dining room. Every aspect of the decorating is more tasteful than expected. Subdued lighting emanates from a network of pretty chandeliers with miniature lampshades. Tables are tastefully outfitted. Service is pleasant and unobtrusive.

Although Portofino's menu is an almost comically typical list of Italian-American basics, the restaurant exercises unusual restraint. Simple preparations focus on fresh ingredients and elemental flavors, instead of the jumbled mess of expensive ingredients that we sometimes encounter at New Haven Italian-American spots. It's not perfect, but there are some pleasant surprises, such as the fettuccine alla Bolognese, a superb example of this Northern Italian standard—a dish that is so often misunderstood and misconstrued. At Portofino, it's a simple sauce of wonderfully textured ground beef with a tomato base that sparkles with the savory flavors of emulsified vegetables. Still, it needs salt. Other highlights are an ideally prepared veal parmigiana and excellent homemade meatballs. Veal Francese is a bit too soft and not delicate, though, and braciola is dry.

But, mamma mia, what portions! Mains come with (albeit undistinguished) appetizer salads, eliminating the need to order other appetizers (which include good, crispy fried calamari with a nice marinara). This further boosts the value proposition here: while the main courses are not dirt cheap, they're not expensive either, and one might be all you'll need for two people. The wine list is reasonable too. The moral of the story: Portofino is one of the better deals in town for upscale Italian-American, and it deserves more attention than you might think.

Pot-au-Pho

7.8

10

A welcome new Vietnamese place that's delicious, airy, relaxing, and so, so cheap

Vietnamese
$ 9
Arts District

8.0 /10
Food

7.0 /10
Atmosphere

9.0 /10
Attitude

9.3 /10
Value

Casual restaurant
Mon.-Sat. 11am-8pm; closed Sun.
Vegetarian-friendly.

77 Whitney Ave.
New Haven
(203) 776-2248

Bar None
Credit Cards Visa, MC, AmEx
Reservations Not accepted

It's refreshing to finally have a Vietnamese place in New Haven. But it's positively exciting to have one that is this good. The menu here is short and easy to process, with prices that are almost stunningly student-friendly.

Truly impressive is the French-dippish bahn mi bo kho. It's dubbed a "sandwich," but it's really a bowl of a delicious braised beef stew with carrots, served with a few big pieces of crusty French bread for dipping. The beef is wondrously tender, and the liquid has a flavor that's deep and well-developed (though it's a tiny bit oily). Wait for the broth to cool before jumping in with the spoon or dipping in the bread, which is an uncanny match with the broth; the flavor somehow takes on more complexity as it absorbs into soft, bready goodness. Sprigs of cilantro and slices of onion, meanwhile, play with other parts of your palate. For a portion that would feed two normal appetites, this has to be the best six dollars you can spend in New Haven.

The braised beef also makes up part of another delicious dish—an egg noodle soup. The five-spice braised duck and shiitake mushroom noodle soup is also superb. Even the lighter, simpler broths such as the hu tieu (rice noodle with roast pork, shrimp, fried shallots, and cilantro) and the basic pho are well executed, with proper background seasoning. Shrimp are juicy, not overcooked, and the roast pork respectable; some soups benefit from adding hot sauce. The bubble teas and Vietnamese coffees, too, are welcome treats unavailable elsewhere.

The space is simple, with a few counter spaces and a few tables; it's particularly well suited to solo diners. The service is friendly and welcoming—a winning attitude—and, we are certain, a recipe for success.

Quattro's

A deservedly well-known Guilford Italian-American
mainstay with rich food in a calming environment

Italian   **$32** *Guilford*

7.2/10	**7.5**/10	**7.0**/10	**6.4**/10
Food	*Atmosphere*	*Attitude*	*Value*

Upmarket restaurant	1300 Boston Post Rd.	*Bar* Full
Mon.-Thurs. 11:30am-2:30pm,	Guilford	*Credit Cards* Visa, MC, AmEx
5pm-9pm; Fri.-Sat. 11:30am-	(203) 453-6575	*Reservations* Recommended
2:30pm, 5pm-9:30pm;		
Sun. 11am-9pm. *Brunch.*		

Little known within the borders of New Haven until the opening of a
sister branch downtown, Quattro's is one of the better Italian
restaurants in the entire metropolitan area. At the Guilford branch,
which is about 15 minutes from the Elm City, dishes are prepared with
panache. Fried calamari are delicate and not too chewy. Veal is a
specialty, tender and satisfying in any of its many incarnations.
Generally speaking, portions are huge, and recipes are rich compilations
rather than showcases for individual ingredients. Sea scallops, for
example, are wrapped with bacon and topped with lobster sauce;
they're too rich and absolutely delicious. Jumbo shrimp are stuffed with
asparagus and mozzarella and wrapped in prosciutto, grilled with
scallops and served in a pesto cream sauce. Perhaps overzealous, but
surely satisfying. Better are the preparations of fresh salmon, which, on
request, can be cooked rare—a refreshing change.

    Strangely, the recently opened downtown New Haven branch of
Quattro's is not up to the standard of the Guilford mothership. Much
seems to have been lost in the translation. Our only complaint with the
Guilford Quattro's, though, relates not to what it does do, but only to
what it doesn't do: either true regional Italian recipes or anything
resembling Northern Italian or New Italian. But Quattro's is what it is.
It's suburban Italian-American, but it's a superlative example of the
designation—surprising considering that the place is in the middle of a
strip mall. The décor might be considered bland by some, but we like it.
It's just a simple room, quiet, calm, refined, no bar, no fuss. The lighting
is muted. And the service is courteous and accommodating. Quattro's
might not survive in New York, serving this food at these prices, but
we're quite happy that this one is in Guilford.

Quattro's

5.4
/10

A new downtown Italian-American spot that, like most sequels, isn't nearly as good the first

Italian   **$33**   *Theater District*

4.3 /10   **7.0** /10   **7.0** /10   **3.3** /10
Food   *Atmosphere*   *Attitude*   *Value*

Upmarket restaurant   172 Temple St.   *Bar* Full
Mon.-Thurs. 11am-3pm, , 5pm-   New Haven   *Credit Cards* Visa, MC, AmEx
10pm; Fri.-Sat. 11am-3pm,5pm- (203) 787-6705   *Reservations* Accepted
10:30pm; Sun. noon-9pm. *Outdoor dining. Vegetarian-friendly.*

This space has gone through many incarnations, most recently as Del Monaco's, an Italian restaurant with an old Wooster Street history that moved downtown and never quite made it. Especially because the folks behind Quattro's are so successful—their Guilford branch, which has been open almost ten years, is popular and well regarded around the state—you would think that, before jumping in, they would have looked at the old Del Monaco's and contemplated the reasons behind its failure (a staggering number of virtually identical Italian-American restaurants all over New Haven).

You'd be wrong. Instead, they changed little about the space; a redecoration didn't alter the substantive feel, nor does the menu—a standard Italian-American roll call—differ so much from the one at Del Monaco's. What's truly mind-boggling, though, is that not only is the downtown Quattro's not distinguished from the competition, it's also significantly worse than the first Quattro's. Although prices aren't through the roof—there are many options under $20—it's not a bargain, given what you're getting.

A strip steak, for instance, comes with an overbearing vinaigrette reduction that features mushrooms, and the steak is chewy, chewy, chewy—but not as chewy as the clams in an incoherent linguine with clam sauce, that sports little in the way of sauce. It's one of the worst versions we've tried. Other pasta, too, comes overcooked and sauced without coherence, while fish dishes tend toward dry, bland, or both.

We won't bore you with any more of the details; perhaps in restaurants, as in the movies, the sequel is never as good as the original. But given the prime real estate, we're especially disappointed that this space couldn't have been used for something even a little bit new or different.

Rainbow Café

Unfocused, overpriced pseudo-vegetarian and
pseudo-hippie food with pseudo-service

Light American　　　　　$18　　Theater District

5.7 /10
Food

8.0 /10
Atmosphere

5.0 /10
Attitude

6.0 /10
Value

Casual restaurant
Mon.-Fri. 11am-8pm; Sat. 10am-
9pm; Sun. 10am-8pm.
Brunch. Vegetarian-friendly.

1022 Chapel St.
New Haven
(203) 777-2390

Bar BYO
Credit Cards Visa, MC, AmEx
Reservations Not accepted

This subterranean Chapel Street joint is a lunch spot with its own
particular form of pseudo-service: First, you place your order at the
counter; then, when your food is ready, someone will bring it to you on
a tray. After that, the process is strictly self-help. The room is light and
cheery, as is the crowd. The portions are big and the vegetables are
fresh.

But unfortunately, Rainbow Café doesn't stop there. Some of the
menu seems vaguely Mexican, while other parts of it reveal a misguided
Californian sensibility. The raspberry chicken explosion is a good
example of this—mixed greens with slices of chicken, apples, grapes,
raspberries and blue cheese, with a raspberry vinaigrette dressing and a
croissant. Grilled cheese and avocado is a less ambitious but equally
representative option. Neither is particularly good.

Vegetarians will be delighted by the plethora of meatless offerings,
until they taste them. A salad has raw white mushrooms with a jarring
texture, and mediocre dressing that comes in a little plastic container. A
crab cake in a sandwich is soggy instead of crispy. A gorgonzola onion
burger is some of their best work, though, and the high point, by all
accounts, is the giant saucer-like chocolate-chip cookie. People (more
women than men) come from miles around…okay, blocks.

Let's cut to the chase, though: the place is just plain ill-conceived.
Even with the 10% Yale Student ID discount, it's terribly overpriced. It
lacks a clear focus. It's trying, and failing, to be hippie. It's not even
vegetarian. First you serve yourself, and then you have to deal with
your own dirty dishes. However many hot hippie wannabes you may
meet along the way, there's no pot of gold—or any pot at all, for that
matter—at the end of this Rainbow.

Rainbow Gardens Inn

7.5
/10

An almost-too-cute, haphazardly eclectic New England inn with an immensely popular lunch

New American   **$24**   *Milford*

6.8 /10   **8.5** /10   **9.0** /10   **7.1** /10
Food   *Atmosphere*   *Attitude*   *Value*

Upmarket restaurant
Tues.-Thurs. 11am-3pm, 5pm-9pm;
Fri.-Sat. 11am-3pm, 5pm-9:30pm;
Sun. 4pm-8pm.
Brunch. Date-friendly. Vegetarian-friendly.

117 North Broad St.
Milford
(203) 878-2500
www.rainbowgardens.org

Bar Full
Credit Cards Visa, MC, AmEx
Reservations Essential

The immeasurable quaintness of the Rainbow Gardens Inn explains why it is so popular that you need to make reservations well in advance, even (or perhaps especially) for lunch. So finely realized is the cute New England aesthetic that walking up to the porch and into the space is like stepping into a vacation in a Vermont resort town (the Inn also rents rooms). Place settings are just so, and many windows look out onto the street and Milford's elongated town green. The restaurant is divided into smaller spaces, making every seat in the old house feel cozy.

It might come as no surprise, thus, that this establishment is generally frequented by an older crowd. They come not just for the escapist charm but also for the menu of American cuisine, which is eclectic almost to a fault—Asian here, Italian there. Cutesy, too, is the menu, with descriptions that range from the funny ("racey garlic butter") to the drugged-out ("mystic mountain") to the just plain weird (a "trinity of love apples").

The "Mount Gorgonzola" is a sandwich whose name we actually find to be borderline disturbing. Like many preparations here, it's competent but not extraordinary. It's essentially a chicken club, with a fresh chicken breast that's not overcooked, along with lettuce, tomato, bacon, and of course the gorgonzola, which works pretty well. Strangest of all, on a recent visit, was a special of sweet, loud coconut shrimp atop an overdressed Caesar salad that practically swam in a thick, strong dressing, intermingled with a mango concoction even sweeter than the shrimp. But even if it's more the atmosphere than the food that keeps Rainbow Gardens Inn so popular, the place is nonetheless an absolute hoot.

Rib House, The

6.1
10

A typically suburban family restaurant that makes some of the best barbecue in the area

Southern   **$21** *East Haven*

6.4/10 **6.0**/10 **5.0**/10 **5.6**/10
Food   *Atmosphere* *Attitude*   *Value*

Casual restaurant
Mon.-Thurs. 4pm-10pm; Fri. 4pm-
11pm; Sat. 3pm-11pm; Sun. 1pm-
9pm in winter, 4pm-10pm in summer.

16 Main St.
East Haven
(203) 468-6695

Bar Full
Credit Cards Visa, MC, AmEx
Reservations Accepted

The Rib House is exactly what it sounds like. Just up Main Street in East Haven, this purveyor of barbecued ribs and chicken is a reliable source of hearty fare. The main dining room is a series of lodge-like wooden tables, chairs, and booths, with an impressive spit roast occupying the large hearth that dominates one wall. The décor is one hundred percent suburban, as befits the location; a great place for a group of hungry people, or for families, The Rib House has its clearly defined place in the landscape of local eateries.

The ribs are pretty good, and they're easily your best choice here. A large order is a generous rack and a half, plenty for two hungry people, and perhaps even enough for three. The ribs are slow-cooked in a trademark barbecue sauce, more sweet than spicy, but quite tasty. You'll have a choice between baby back ribs and St. Louis-style side ribs (there are no beef ribs). It all comes with decent french fries and mediocre cole slaw. If you insist on something other than ribs, there are a few other listed options, from barbecued shrimp served over rice to steak by the ounce, but this isn't really the place for steak. Chicken, although well flavored with a spice rub, tends to be less succulent than one would want it to be, as is often the fate of barbecued chicken.

Skip the seafood offerings entirely (you did not come here to eat scrod), and exercise restraint when ordering appetizers; portions are huge. There's a kids' menu, and, with its down-home barbecue feel, the Rib House should generally make young people happy. In short, this is about as well as you can do in the area for barbecue.

Richter's

6.5
/10

An atmospheric former speakeasy known for its
half-yards, good burgers, and old-Yale theme

Bar food   **$13**   *Theater District*

6.0/10   **8.0**/10   **5.0**/10   **6.8**/10
Food   *Atmosphere*   *Attitude*   *Value*

Bar and grill Mon.-Thurs. 11:30am-1am; Fri.- Sat. 11:30am-2am; Sun. 11am- 1am. Kitchen closes at 9pm. *Date-friendly*.	990 Chapel St. New Haven (203) 777-0400	*Bar* Full *Credit Cards* Visa, MC, AmEx *Reservations* Not accepted

Once a speakeasy (for the Taft, back when it was a hotel)—which gets
it automatic points—Richter's is a pretty relaxing place for half-yards
and burgers amidst a healthy mix of undergrads and grads engaged in
the age-old human activity of getting drunk. A half-yard, for the
uninitiated, is an artistically shaped glass of draft beer (there's a good
selection—Sierra Nevada, the British Isles standbys, and an oddball or
two) that is in fact somewhere near one-and-a-half feet tall, and more
or less the liquid equivalent of two-and-a-half pints. But since it all
comes at once, and in such a beguiling format, you'll find it goes down
easier—that is, quicker—than your average two-and-a-half beers.
Perhaps this is why they're not served after about 12am.

Richter's is a great neighborhood standby. The front room has a TV
with NCAA basketball and classic patron-bartender banter, and is pretty
much your typical American bar scene. The atmospheric back room is
decorated with old Yaleiana, and has a fireplace and more intimate sit-
down tables, where you can order off the short food menu, which
includes quite good burgers, fries, and the like, and set about carving
your name into a table. The juicy and tender ribs also have a devoted
following.

It's in the back room that the half-yard phenomenon comes into its
own. Group psychology plays in when you've got a table of six—how
can you not order a half-yard. It is thus that even the prudent are
intimidated into inebriation. And that's what a speakeasy is all about.

Roberto's Restaurant

A friendly diner where you know exactly what you're going to get

Short-order American   **$ 9**   *Financial District*

6.4 /10   **5.5** /10   **8.0** /10   **7.1** /10
Food   *Atmosphere*   *Attitude*   *Value*

Diner   418 State St.   *Bar* None
Mon.-Fri. 6am-4pm; Sat. 6am-2pm; New Haven   *Credit Cards* Visa, MC, AmEx
closed Sun. *Breakfast.*   (203) 562-9957   *Reservations* Not accepted

Roberto's is a classic no-frills diner, complete with seats at the counter and table service from a very friendly staff, although the booths and chairs in the two separate dining rooms don't quite have the standard diner feel. You might say that the atmosphere at Roberto's falls exactly halfway between the old-school diner and the quick, cookie-cutter office-furniture financial-district lunch counter. The lunchtime crowd is strictly local, enjoying each other's company in pleasant anonymity, and come noon during the week, in spite of the expansive space, you may have a hard time finding a seat.

The menu at Roberto's is unimaginative but extensive. For breakfast you can find dozens of familiar dishes, from a Western omelette to a "breakfast burrito wrap" to a soothing side of grits, which are remarkably hard to find in New Haven. The homemade muffins, shaped like mini-loaves, are an unexpected treat.

For lunch, try the Reuben. Its bread is nicely browned on the grill, the Swiss cheese has good flavor, and the meat is good, thickly cut (by New Haven standards) but tender. The tuna melt and BLT are also well executed. Perhaps the best dish on the menu, though, and one of its few surprises, is the sweet potato fries, served up piping hot, slightly salty, and thickly cut. A buffalo chicken salad is less impressive; the chicken isn't crispy enough and only thinly coated with sauce, and the blue cheese dressing is homogeneous and wimpy.

But if you don't expect culinary masterpieces, you won't be disappointed. When you order, you know what's going to be on your plate; you ask for something, and it shows up. And then you eat it. If you come in hungry, you're going to leave full.

Romeo & Cesare's

One of New Haven's most distinguished Italian
groceries, with great espresso and prepared foods

Italian   *East Rock/Grad Ghetto*

7.0 /10
Attitude

Specialty grocery   771 Orange St.
Mon-Sat. 7am-7pm; Sun. 8am-2pm.   New Haven   *Credit Cards* Visa, MC, AmEx
Breakfast. Outdoor dining.   (203) 776-1614
Vegetarian-friendly.

Romeo & Cesare's, which used to be known as Romeo & Giuseppe's
(Romeo & Joe's) before an unpleasant falling-out between Romeo and
Joe, is a wonderful Italian specialty grocery store located deep in the
Grad Ghetto out toward East Rock. The store qualifies to be reviewed
in *The Menu* by virtue of its great take-out sandwiches and "tavola
calda" mains, which are sold hot by the pound. In summer, it can all be
enjoyed on the spot, sitting outdoors at one of the little tables just off
the State Street sidewalk. But any time of year, it's one of New Haven's
best take-out meals.

The tavola calda selection rotates, but it might include artichokes
alla romana, which are big, slow-steamed, and stuffed with herbs,
bread crumbs, garlic, parsley, and olive oil. Pane cotto, another New
Haven Italian standby, is a delightful blend of escarole, beans, onions,
garlic, and olive oil on toasted hard-crust bread, soaked in chicken
broth with parmesan cheese sprinkled on top.

The selection of sandwiches is more standard, with a classic array of
Italian-style deli meats (sandwiches are not the grilled-pressed variety)
and such ingredients as chicken, sausage, and peppers. But all dishes
use top-quality ingredients; this is one of the best places in town for
imported prosciutto and specialty cheeses, for example.

A quick look around the store, where almost everything is imported
from Italy—not to mention the Italian staff—or a sip of the excellent
espresso, which is available to drink on the spot or at one of the
outdoor tables, should make it clear that you're getting one of New
Haven's best efforts at the real deal.

Roomba

9.0
10

A hip, subterranean Nuevo Latino hotspot that
remains one of New Haven's best restaurants

Latin American $**52**   *Theater District*

9.5 /10   **10** /10   **3.0** /10   **7.5** /10
Food   *Atmosphere*   *Attitude*   *Value*

Upmarket restaurant   1044 Chapel St.,   *Bar* Full
Tues. 5:30pm-9:30pm; Wed.-Thurs.   Sherman's Alley   *Credit Cards* Visa, MC, AmEx
noon-2:30pm, 5:30pm-9:30pm;   New Haven   *Reservations* Essential
Fri. noon-2:30pm, 5:30pm-   (203) 562-7666
10:30pm; Sat. 5:30pm-10:30pm;
Sun. 5:30pm-8:30pm; closed Mon. *Date-friendly. Good wine list. Outdoor dining.*

The opening of this glimmering temple to Nuevo Latino fusion
announced that after decades of crumbling into urban blight, New
Haven was back. Foodies and hipsters alike became so entranced by the
restaurant's cool cascades, ceviches, and caipirinhas that, years later, it's
still difficult to get a prime-time reservation. That said, there has been
some grumbling over the high-flying establishment's indifferent
attitude. In particular, there is absolutely no excuse for the imposition of
a two-hour limit on dinner, especially given how much you're spending.
We have received numerous letters from former regulars just to tell us
they're so insulted by this policy that they no longer patronize the
establishment.

Happily, though, the superb food is still worth all the fuss. The
atmosphere is trendy but refreshing; big plants and rushing water add
life to the room. The vivacious human buzz is mostly just conversation,
not see-and-be-seen plumage. And the food is top-notch. Fish ceviches
are reliably excellent. The three-ceviche sampler, when available, is great
for variation and enough for two. A portobello mushroom appetizer
with goat cheese blows away the bland preparations elsewhere.
Artistically presented main courses are ambitious, with mixed success.
We prefer meat to fish here; barbecued pork dishes, for example, are
tender and subtle, with lots of flavor and lots of attitude.

Portions are universally large, but you should save room for the tres
leches dessert, the best version we've ever had; it's a moist cake with
an unforgettable milky sweetness, and accompanied with fresh
bananas and banana ice cream. Even the mojito has modernist flair,
served with a stick of real sugar cane to chew on; some come just for a
mojito at the bar. If you haven't yet tried Roomba, it's money well
spent. Don't expect to linger over dessert, but the food is still reason
enough to cheer.

Roomba Burrito Cart

7.6
10

A conveniently located cart with quick, cheap, and delicious burritos, rain or shine

Tex-Mex   **$ 6**   *Broadway Area, Medical Area*

7.4 /10   **8.0** /10   **9.9** /10
Food   *Attitude*   *Value*

Take-out   Corner of York St.   *Bar* None
Mon.-Fri. 11am-7pm;   and Elm St.   *Credit Cards* None
Sat. 11am-5pm; closed Sun. New Haven   *Reservations* Not accepted
Vegetarian-friendly.   (203) 562-7666

Medical Area branch: Near York St. and
Mon.-Fri. 11am-4:30pm;   Cedar St., New Haven
closed Sat.-Sun.   (203) 562-7666

Even before the first snowfall, West Coast transplants to New Haven begin to long for a decent burrito. For years, their only option was to suffer through one of those stiff, bland wraps that the Yankee gringos mistakenly call burritos. The unannounced arrival of the Roomba Burrito Carts on the New Haven streets marked the end of the drought (now there's Bulldog Burritos nearby, but it's not nearly as good).

The first trick is to hunt down these amusing little contraptions. There's one on the corner of York Street and Broadway, and another in the Med School agglomeration; unlike many others, these carts and their cheerful attendants seem weather-proof—they're out there even on the coldest days of winter. Once you make it to the front of the line, you are invited to participate in an interactive culinary performance. It all starts with the same swift motion: a tortilla is whisked from a mysterious steaming chamber, slapped down on a cutting board, and topped with flavorful rice and saucy black beans.

But the rest is up to you. Vegetarians will be delighted by their grilled vegetable mélange, complete with thick slices of portobello mushroom. For the more carnivorous, the cart offers a never-ending supply of tender grilled steak and chicken. The latest version, and our favorite, is the pulled pork; at first it was just a periodic special, but now it seems to be available all the time—or at least until they run out. It's a mild flavor, but a good one, and it goes well with the inventive slaw of crunchy cabbage.

Among your other options for customization (some of which they now charge an extra 50 cents for): fresh-cut salsa, smooth guacamole, homemade hot sauce, and sweet corn. Create and take away. New Haven is your dining room.

Roseland Apizza

8.2
10

An old-time pizzeria with lots of charm and thin-crust pies that compete with New Haven's best

Pizza $**32** *Derby*

8.4 /10   **8.0** /10   **8.0** /10   **7.4** /10
Food   *Atmosphere*   *Attitude*   *Value*

Casual restaurant   350 Hawthorne Ave.   ***Bar*** Wine and beer only
Tues.-Fri. 4pm-10pm; Sat. 3pm-   Derby   ***Credit Cards*** Visa, MC, AmEx
10pm; Sun. 3pm-9pm.   (203) 735-0494   ***Reservations*** Not accepted
Vegetarian-friendly.

Derby is on the border of our jurisdiction, and it takes almost a half hour to get to Roseland Apizza from downtown New Haven. It's out of the way from almost anywhere, and it's worth it. Every pore of this 1936 pizzeria oozes with tradition, from the old-school glowing sign out front to the pies that compete with apizza contemporaries like Sally's and Pepe's. However, Roseland's atmosphere easily beats that of either competitor. The multifaceted division of the space into smaller rooms also makes Roseland more intimate than your average pizzeria. The daily specials are charmingly scrawled across a chalkboard; servers are just as informal and old-school as their counterparts on Wooster Street, but with less of an attitude and more of an open-armed warmth.

As for the pizza, Roseland's thin, delicate crust is legendary, and deservedly so. Likewise for the copious toppings: a shrimp Casino pizza, for example, features lots of garlic, bacon, and a fleet of giant shrimp whose collective weight must exceed that of the crust. In the mid $30s, it also has to be the most expensive single pie we've ever seen, but it is delicious—the best thing we've had here, and unique with respect to the competition. Simpler ared pid much cheaper pies like mozzarella and sausage are also quite good. A simple white clam pie—a New Haven classic—was, at our last visit, not as successful; the clams were fresh, but the pizza needed salt (we shook a lot of parmesan cheese on the top, which helped matters).

As a starter, a cheesy, garlicky bread might sport prosciutto and roasted red peppers, and there are also well-executed Italian-American comfort-food mains like spaghetti and meatballs, eggplant parm, and so on. Whatever happens, you'll go home full and satisfied—if you can find your way back.

Royal India

A cozy Indian restaurant, popular with students, that serves solid preparations at reasonable prices

Indian $**18**   *Broadway Area*

6.5 /10	**8.0** /10	**8.0** /10	**7.0** /10
Food	*Atmosphere*	*Attitude*	*Value*

Casual restaurant
Sun.-Thurs. 11:30am-3pm, 5pm-
10:30pm; Fri.-Sat. 11:30am-3pm,
5pm-11pm. *Brunch. Date-friendly. Delivery. Vegetarian-friendly.*

140 Howe St.
New Haven
(203) 787-9493

Bar Wine and beer only
Credit Cards Visa, MC, AmEx
Reservations Accepted

This comfortable, reliably tasty Indian restaurant is situated in a cute old house at the end of Howe Street, right across from Broadway and the Holiday Inn, a quick hop from Yale's law school, gymnasium, or bookstore, yet it's often overlooked. The space is worn around the edges, with chipped paneling and fake flowers, but it still feels cozy and welcoming. The food is as good as ever, and the prices make it the best-value Indian in the area, especially the all-you-can-eat lunch buffet, for which you should try to sit at the front of the room to avoid bumping into the queue.

You'll feel right at home as you dig into hearty, classic Indian fare that puts its Howe Street competitors to shame. Stick with the basics like saag paneer, which you just want to eat, eat, and eat, and the lamb vindaloo, with deep heat and a rich flavor, accented by the fresh bite of cilantro. There's an underlying sweetness to the vindaloo, whose potatoes sit at that magical meeting place of soft and firm. To top it off, an exquisite tamarind sauce is irresistibly tangy. We have also been convinced by the eggplant with peas, creamy and mild, with a sweet burst of pea flavor, and an extremely delicate dal.

Chicken tikka masala is not too rich, but it's often undersalted, and the chicken pieces can be dry; this dish is better elsewhere. So are sautéed mushrooms, which are bland at Royal India. The place also does a great take-out business, and it's one of the best choices in town for catering, which includes delivery. We salute Royal India for its devotion to a simple recipe for success: a good attitude, a warm and attractive space, and food that is satisfying, reliable, and easy on the wallet.

Royal Palace

Downtown's best full-service Chinese, with
interesting dishes like the legendary Water Beef

Chinese $**22** *Ninth Square*

7.8 /10   **4.0** /10   **8.0** /10   **6.3** /10
Food   *Atmosphere*   *Attitude*   *Value*

Upmarket restaurant   32 Orange St.   *Bar* Full
Mon.-Thurs. 11am-10pm; Fri.-Sat.   New Haven   *Credit Cards* Visa, MC, AmEx
11am-11pm; Sun. noon-10pm.   (203) 776-6663   *Reservations* Accepted
Delivery. Vegetarian-friendly.   www.ctmenusonline.com/rp.htm

Royal Palace is a cavernous Hong Kong-style Chinese restaurant, the
kind every serious city should have. In the category of sit-down, family-
style Chinese-American cuisine, Royal Palace has no competition in
town. The fresh and interesting options here will please both the fried-
rice dilettante and the diehard pig's-feet enthusiast.

Sadly, the décor is just as you'd expect. Calligraphy scrolls adorn the
walls, and the expansive dining room has more than its share of round
tables and high-backed, cushioned banquet chairs. Even more
disconcerting is the empirical truth that a restaurant of this size, in a
city this small, must always be under-filled. You'll waffle between the
pleasure of knowing that you are the center of attention and the
feeling of extreme loneliness, which isn't helped by the bright,
ruthlessly unromantic lighting.

One rule of thumb is to stick steadfastly to the Cantonese menu, a
short, folded, laminated document that is now translated into English
(it wasn't always), and to shun the large bound version, which is filled
with the usual Americanized parodies of Chinese cuisine (although the
hot and sour soup is good). The best things here, hands down, are the
"water" dishes—water beef, for instance—which have a unique
emulsion of flavor, with fresh and interesting vegetables, plus some
kick.

If you are with a group, you should not pass up the Peking duck, a
crispy whole duck sliced and individually wrapped with fresh scallions in
delicate pancakes before your eyes. Royal Palace is the only place in
town where you'll find this Chinatown-style treat. Among the sautéed
greens (which are, after all, a Cantonese specialty), follow advice from
the waitstaff about what's seasonal, though a good default is Chinese
broccoli greens with garlic.

Rudy's Restaurant

6.7
10

A delightfully dark, dingy bar which serves some of
the best Belgian frites this side of the Atlantic

Light American   **$ 8**   *Broadway Area*

6.3 /10   **8.0** /10   **5.0** /10   **7.9** /10
Food   *Atmosphere*   *Attitude*   *Value*

Bar and grill   372 Elm St.   *Bar* Full
Sun.-Thurs. 4pm-1am;   New Haven   *Credit Cards* Visa, MC, AmEx
Fri.-Sat. 4pm-2am.   (203) 865-1242   *Reservations* Accepted
Date-friendly.   www.rudysnewhaven.com

Rudy's is everything that's still right about old New Haven. Crude
epithets from Yalies past are scrawled into the soft wooden walls,
taking their place amidst crew-team posters and Ivy League football
headlines from fifty years ago. Everything is dark, dingy, and
downmarket. Shots of liquor are twice the size and half the price. One
of the good beers on tap always costs less than three dollars. Rudy's is
also a rightfully proud champion of local alternative rock acts, which
take the stage on many nights (usually resulting in a cover charge of a
few bucks). It may be called "Rudy's Restaurant," but it's a bar and
music spot, pure and simple.

And yet out of nowhere, Rudy's also serves some of the best and
freshest Belgian french fries anywhere in North America. The fries are
cheap, and they're available from early evening until last call. The entire
stainless-steel fryer just off the end of the bar, and even many of the
mayonnaise and curry sauces (mayonnaise is taken very seriously here),
are actually imported from Belgium by the bar's resident mad frites
genius, who hails from Antwerp. So belly up to the bar for some fries,
and dive into the wonderland of Belgian mayo. We also recommend
the sauce andalouse and the curry mayo. Aside from the fries, there's a
lineup of simple sandwiches, but they're less notable.

This is not the place for a squeamish blind date or dinner with the
parents, unless you have some perverse point to make. Go with school
buddies. Go to drink good beer, cheap. Go to listen to music, to down
double shots of Johnnie Red, and to eat the fantastic fries late into the
evening. Go to zone out, to be human, to live in New Haven.

Rusty Scupper

5.9
10

Come just for cocktails, and take in the water view without suffering through the overpriced fish

Seafood $37   Long Wharf

4.1/10   **9.0**/10   **7.0**/10   **3.7**/10
Food   Atmosphere   Attitude   Value

Upmarket restaurant   501 Long Wharf Dr.   *Bar* Full
Mon. 11:30am-9pm;   New Haven   *Credit Cards* Visa, MC, AmEx
Tues.-Sat. 11:30am-10pm;   (203) 777-5711   *Reservations* Accepted
Sun. 10:30am-2pm, 3pm-9pm.   www.selectrestaurants.com
Brunch. Outdoor dining.

The Rusty Scupper chain has the elite distinction of owning a waterfront restaurant that is actually within New Haven proper, which puts it in short company (with Sage). The views of the industrial port of New Haven are a pleasant change of pace from downtown—and a sad reminder of this city's dearth of establishments by the Sound, and of the even sadder way that the interstate cuts off most of the city from the water. Inexplicably, Rusty Scupper gets accolades from regional magazines and such, who declare that it has some of the best seafood around. Maybe they were intoxicated by the view.

To begin with, steer clear of the Dynamite Sticks, a deeply misguided riff on a tortilla wrap; these enormous deep-fried cigars are served with a cheesy bacon dipping sauce whose texture is deeply questionable. The deep fryer does double duty for dessert; an "apple strudel" is actually deep-fried pastry triangles, more reminiscent of old school Mickey D's pies than of delicate German pastry. Between Dynamite and dessert, you'll find fish such as salmon, almost uniformly overcooked (if you must, try the trout); mixed vegetables, overcooked and undersalted; or perhaps a cloyingly sweet miso glaze that reminds us of Family Circle, circa 1965. Lobster mashed potatoes are tasty—that is, if you add extra butter at the table.

The good news here is that you don't have to eat. Come early for a cocktail and catch the sunset, or show up later for a nightcap and a romantic view, perhaps a bowl of ice cream—they serve Wentworth's. Whatever you do, skip the main courses. Oh, and even though it's often empty, the place actually requires reservations for parties of five or more. Don't flatter yourself, Rusty.

Sage American Bar & Grill

A restaurant right on the water where the
spectacular view overwhelms the decent food

Traditional American   **$37**   *Medical Area/The Hill*

6.7/10   **8.5**/10   **8.0**/10   **6.3**/10
Food   *Atmosphere*   *Attitude*   *Value*

Upmarket restaurant
Mon.-Thurs. 4pm-10pm; Fri.-Sat.
5pm-11pm; Sun. 11am-10pm.
Brunch. Date-friendly.
Good wine list. Outdoor dining.

100 S. Water St.
New Haven
(203) 785-8086
www.sageamerican.com

Bar Full
Credit Cards Visa, MC, AmEx
Reservations Essential

At the terminus of Howard Avenue, this gracious restaurant is a great
place to soak up the atmosphere of the Long Island Sound from the
convenience of the New Haven waterfront. Formerly the Chart House,
the place became Sage when new owners took over.

Needless to say, the view is the same—and thank goodness, because
this is the best thing about a night out at Sage, especially on a balmy
evening, with boats batting around in the little harbor and the sun
setting over the Sound. There are wonderful plate-glass windows
inside, but in fine weather, the best seats in the house (even if they are
made of flimsy plastic) are on the outdoor balcony overlooking the
wharf. The weekday happy hour might be the best option—the drinks
are cheaper, there's a spread of free food, and views are at their peak.
The service is great, with an accommodating, treat-you-like-royalty
attitude.

The food, though, is very average American cuisine with some high
points. Oysters on the half shell are above average, as are the mini
lobster rolls (Connecticut-style, warm with melted butter over succulent
meat). An iceberg wedge salad is excellent, beautifully presented with
well-integrated dressing. Brunch mains like "Scottish eggs"
(underseasoned, with poorly integrated melted Gouda and chicken
sausage) are severely overpriced, although we love the blueberry
muffins and the rich, crispy "potato cake," which is like a peppery,
oniony gallette served with sour cream.

Fish mains fare less well. At our last visit, an $18 plate of salmon
was woefully overcooked and too bready and buttery to enjoy, with a
sweet-potato side with brown sugar that was sweet like pie. Steaks are
memorably overpriced. In the end, we prefer to come just to slurp
oysters, sip Bloodies, and take in the sea air.

Sahara

6.5
10

A downtown Middle Eastern restaurant with fresh ingredients, excellent falafel, and pleasant décor

Middle Eastern $ **9**   *Theater District*

6.5 /10   **6.5** /10   **6.0** /10   **7.4** /10
Food   *Atmosphere*   *Attitude*   *Value*

Counter service   170 Temple St.   *Bar* None
Sun.-Thurs. 11am-1am; Fri.-Sat.   New Haven   *Credit Cards* Visa, MC, AmEx
11am-3am. Kitchen closes Sun.-   (203) 773-3306   *Reservations* Accepted
Thurs. midnight; Fri.-Sat. 1am. *Delivery. Vegetarian-friendly.*

Rising like an oasis out of the desert of New Haven falafel quality, Sahara is not a mirage: it's for real. It has established itself next to Lalibela, Quattro's, and the Omni, a block of Temple Street that, in spite of its relative centrality, has been a historically difficult place for restaurants. But Sahara delivers in a way you don't expect from the font painted on the window, or from the category of fare on offer. Falafel is flavorful, crispy on the outside, smooth on the inside. It definitely rivals Mediterranea for the title of best falafel in town. Vegetables are fresh, and almost everything's made completely to order. We're impressed.

Perhaps most impressive of all (vis-à-vis one's expectations for a quick, largely take-out falafel joint), the atmosphere, once you step inside, is actually pleasant, almost hip—not too bright, with a colorful, vaguely Persian theme. Service is a bit slow, so why not sit down, enjoy yourself, and savor the Middle Eastern kitsch, complete with fake oil lanterns. In fact, it's worth sitting down just to enjoy the videos of belly dancers and other generally female entertainers shimmying beguilingly on the TV in the corner. Sahara is open quite late, and they'll deliver the falafel to your table, à la Mamoun's. But we think the food is better here than it is at Mamoun's. And we hope that Sahara can continue to defeat the Curse of Temple Street. Only time will tell.

Sally's Apizza

One of the best pizzas in America, period

Pizza $14   *Wooster Square Area*

9.6 /10   **7.0** /10   **4.0** /10   **9.2** /10
Food   *Atmosphere*   *Attitude*   *Value*

Casual restaurant   237 Wooster St.   **Bar** Wine and beer only
Tues.-Thurs. 5pm-10:30pm;   New Haven   **Credit Cards** None
Fri.-Sat. 5pm-midnight;   (203) 624-5271   **Reservations** Not accepted
Sun. 5pm-10pm; closed Mon. *Vegetarian-friendly.*

One of the two original, famed thin-crust Neapolitan "apizza" joints that put New Haven on the culinary map, Sally's is the current champion, easily surpassing Pepe's in this Second Edition and vaulting to #2 in the city for food. The choice between Sally's and Pepe's may be as much about family tradition and political leanings as it is about taste, but we're just food critics, and we're unsentimental about the decision. Visit our bulletin board at www.newhavenmenu.com and voice your own opinion.

The small room feels less like a historic venue and more like a standard, if lively, suburban pizzeria. Unless you're a friend of the house, the service is more rude, distracted, and frustrating than endearingly brusque. And the queue of hungry people mulling about outside is formidable. Customers arrive from miles around to sample one of the most famous pizzas in the country. They're rarely disappointed. (But what pizza wouldn't taste good after an hour freezing outside in line? In the words of Voltaire, hunger is the best sauce.)

But a pie with fresh tomatoes, garlic, and bacon, available only during tomato season, doesn't need any sauce. The thin crust, flaky, delicate, and gently oily, spotted with dark brown, oven-blown bubbles, is a thing of beauty. The red sauce also demonstrates absolute mastery of the medium, as does the famous combination of sausage and hot peppers. At this moment, Sally's is the only pizza in New Haven that's really in the running for best pizza in America (even if Pepe's still holds the edge for a white clam pie).

Don't take our word for any of this. Decide for yourself which is the fairest pizza of them all. After all, every self-respecting New Havener must have an opinion, and a well-founded one at that. Apple or Microsoft, Harvard or Yale, Sox or Yankees, Sally's or Pepe's.

Apple. Yale. Sox. Sally's.

Choose

 **your**

side.

Argue about pizza on our relentlessly opinionated discussion board.

Samurai

A Japanese restaurant that relies on College Street traffic to do well in spite of its bad, expensive food

Japanese $ **26**   *Theater District*

3.1 /10   **5.5**/10   **6.0** /10   **2.8**/10
Food   *Atmosphere*   *Attitude*   *Value*

Upmarket restaurant   230 College St.   *Bar* Full
Mon.-Thurs. 10:30am-3pm,   New Haven   *Credit Cards* Visa, MC, AmEx
4:30pm-10pm; Fri.-Sat. 10:30am- (203) 562-6766   *Reservations* Accepted
3pm, 4:30pm-11pm;
Sun. 4:30pm-10pm.

Samurai is operating on the theory that there are only three secrets to good sushi: location, location, and location. Just steps from the Shubert Theater in the heart of downtown, the place does a swimming business. But generally, the fish tastes to us like it hasn't been swimming for quite some time. Unless you like leathery toro.... On some nights, you might get lucky and have a piece of salmon or yellowtail that's quite good.

But the quality is, above all, unpredictable. Venture beyond the basic standbys at your peril, unless you are sitting at the pleasant sushi bar in back and spot something that looks particularly good. Regardless, be sure to ask the sushi chef what is fresh. Maki might be a better choice than nigiri much of the time. Spicy tuna rolls are the kind we prefer— soft chopped tuna blended with spicy mayo. But this is no place for the urban sushi aficionado.

The non-sushi standards, on the other hand, are fine; miso soup and edamame are characteristically inoffensive, and anything with udon is satisfying. Katsu isn't bad either; it's properly fried. Everything cooked is far preferable to the sushi, yet for some reason, most customers seem to choose the latter.

The atmosphere at Samurai is hushed and bland, with the requisite sushi bar and a standard layout of tables dressed in cotton-polyester. The chairs are vintage college library. The ideal location drives every aspect of the business: in spite of the mediocre quality and lack of character, the restaurant still reliably draws in the pre- and post-theater crowd of suburbanites. Listen up if you're a Taftian with a sushi craving—you know who you are. You lazy bastard, put on a coat and walk to Miso.

Sandra's

Authentic Southern comfort food served up in two
different sleek, trendy spaces

Southern   **$21**   *Arts District, The Hill*

7.6 /10   **8.5** /10   **6.0** /10   **7.5** /10
Food   *Atmosphere*   *Attitude*   *Value*

Casual restaurant   46 Whitney Ave.   *Bar* Full
Mon.-Wed. 11am-9pm; Thurs.-   New Haven   *Credit Cards* Visa and MC
Fri. 11am-10pm; Sat. 9am-10pm;   (203) 787-4123   *Reservations* Recommended
Sun. 9am-9pm. *Date-friendly. Brunch.* www.sandrasplace.com

Congress Ave. branch: 636 Congress Ave.
Wed.-Fri. 3pm-9pm;   New Haven
Sat. 1pm-9pm; Sun. 1pm-6pm;   (203) 787-5303
closed Mon.-Tues.

Sandra's, a modern showcase of Southern comfort food, made an
excellent choice in opening a downtown branch. Congress Avenue was
(and still is) home to the original Sandra's, but whether due to laziness
or ignorance, few Yalies or downtown denizens ever made the trek out
there. So Sandra's came to them, in a trendy room full of unexpected
angles, shapes, woods, and metals; in short, this is a space clearly
designed by new-school decorators. The menu is inexplicably clad in
bamboo. And yet the Whitney Avenue satellite serves the same reliably
tasty menu of North Carolina cooking at a spot convenient to Yale and
the New Haven Green. If you're a purist, though, you'll still want to
head out to Congress for the real thing.

The fare is soul food through and through. The meal starts with
cornbread and corn fritters. Both are delights: the cornbread buttery yet
delicate, the fritters a crispy indulgence. Then comes the main course
(although on weekdays, there's a lunch buffet, and on Sundays, a
brunch), for which you'll choose a plate that includes a main dish and a
couple of sides. Shante's plate (one small main with two sides) should
be plenty for most, though there are larger sizes. Barbecued ribs and
fried pork chops are good choices and authentic representations of
Southern cooking. The chopped barbecue, in particular, reveals the
kitchen's North Carolina roots—it's done in the vinegary NC style. We
don't particularly recommend the baked chicken, though.

Among sides, macaroni and cheese, collard greens, and black-eyed
peas are outstanding. Fried okra also gets high marks. Try a pitcher of
the legit sweet tea with copious dissolved sugar, or BYO for a very
reasonable corkage fee (they also serve wine here). You'll go home
satiated and satisfied, and at a reasonable price.

SBC

6.1
10

A strip-mall brewpub chain that's more fake than
real—in Branford, the tanks are just for show

Bar food   **$23**   *Branford*

5.6 /10   **7.5** /10   **5.0** /10   **5.5** /10
Food   *Atmosphere*   *Attitude*   *Value*

Bar and grill   850 W. Main St.   *Bar* Full
Sun.-Thurs. 11:30am-12:30am; Fri.-   Branford   *Credit Cards* Visa, MC, AmEx
Sat. 11:30am-1:30am. Kitchen   (203) 481-2739   *Reservations* Accepted
closes Mon.-Thurs. 10pm; Fri.-Sat.   www.sbcrestaurants.com
11pm; Sun. 9pm. *Outdoor dining.*

It can be hard to see SBC, which stands for Southport Brewing
Company, as anything more than just an inferior Branford version of
Bar, New Haven's legendary brewpub-pizzeria. In fact, SBC is even a
knock-off of itself: this is the third in a growing chain of southern
Connecticut brewpubs, the first being in (surprise, surprise) Southport,
the second in Stamford. We're told that a Milford branch (in the old
Amberjacks space) is also in the works.

We're immediately skeptical of a brewpub chain that gives each of
its beers different names for each franchise outlet, but we're even more
skeptical of a brewpub whose tanks are just for show (the beer is
actually brewed elsewhere). Most of the beer is serviceable, no better.
Our favorites are the hoppy but austere "Branford" Red and the
Saltonstall English Pale Ale.

The brewpub décor is fairly well executed, with a lineup of big,
gleaming beer tanks—some of them perched on a platform right above
the bar in the wide open space—and a long, open kitchen that covers
one full end of the space, where the brick ovens come into full view.

SBC's pizza is popular, and while it may not be up to New Haven
apizza standards, it's at least as thin as any pizza around—the crust is
more like toasted pita bread, or flatbread, than pizza crust. The smallish
pies have too much cheese, but their tomato sauce is chunky and
delicious, and with that great crust, it's the best choice on the menu.
Other offerings, from burgers to bar food, toe the brewpub party line,
and they're generally no better than average. Steaks and seafood aren't
SBC's best work. It's a brewpub, after all. Sort of.

Scarpellino's

7.0
/10

A popular and tasty Italian-American lunch
mainstay that's much more than it first appears

Italian   **$ 6**   *Theater District*

7.0 /10   **7.0** /10   **8.9** /10
Food   *Attitude*   *Value*

Take-out   204 College St.   *Bar* None
Mon.-Fri. 6am-2:30pm;   New Haven   *Credit Cards* Visa, MC, AmEx
closed Sat.-Sun. *Breakfast.* (203) 624-6000 *Reservations* Not accepted

At first glance, Scarpellino's, in a very central College Street location a
few steps from Crown, looks like a simple, garden-variety take-out deli.
But the fast-moving queue for weekday lunch—which can sometimes
stretch almost to the door—will likely be your first clue that this place
might be something more than that. It's worth it for the well-above-
average Italian and American prepared dishes that are served here.

The food, which rotates daily, might include well-executed
preparations of sausages and peppers, potato and egg, meatballs,
chicken cutlets, and so on. The best things here are the prepared daily
specials. Eggplant parmigiana is soft, cheesy, and good, whether
ordered as a sub, on a roll, or as a platter. There's sometimes a lobster
bisque, which is redolent of liquor, and a popular macaroni and cheese.

Some of the more deli-ish dishes are just okay, like "tuna mac"—
macaroni and tuna salad—and the basic cold-cut sandwiches aren't
much different from what you'd get anywhere else. A fried fish fillet,
though, in spite of being pre-cooked, is much better than you'd expect,
and it's hard to go really wrong with the daily specials. Keep an eye on
which dishes seem to be moving out the fastest; these are often the
best. Prices are quite reasonable, and portions are large.

Do make sure that you know what you want by the time you arrive
in the front of the queue; while the service is extraordinarily cordial and
helpful, holding things up is a big no-no. Scarpellino's provides clear
and convincing evidence—as if we needed any more—that the most
crowded places to eat are often the best.

Scoozzi

7.3
/10

An Italian restaurant with a wonderful garden, but the ambitious menu fails to fulfill its promise

Italian $**37**   *Upper Chapel Area*

6.7 /10   **9.0**/10   **6.0** /10   **6.2**/10
Food   Atmosphere   Attitude   Value

Upmarket restaurant   1104 Chapel St.   *Bar* Full
Mon.-Thurs. noon-2:30pm, 5pm-   New Haven   *Credit Cards* Visa, MC, AmEx
9pm; Fri. noon-2:30pm, 5pm-10pm; (203) 776-8268   *Reservations* Recommended
Sat. noon-10pm; Sun. noon-3pm,   www.scoozzi.com
5pm-10pm. *Brunch. Date-friendly. Good wine list. Outdoor dining. Vegetarian-friendly.*

Scoozzi is an ambitious and admirable project: to bring a big-city attitude, a big-city Northern Italian menu, big-city creative grilled pizzas, and a big-city wine list to New Haven. Certainly there's a market for all that. And Scoozzi succeeds along certain axes. The grilled pizza (offered as an appetizer, but also okay for a meal) is good—even in a town known for its pizza, Scoozzi differentiates itself with such superstar ingredients as truffle oil and arugula. Still, the last time we tried it, the dough was too chewy—it had lost its trademark snap.

Scoozzi's outdoor garden, set into a deep Chapel Street indentation and clad with trees, vines, and candles in warm weather, is downright beautiful. Pizza and a bottle of crisp white wine at an outdoor table make for a great summer evening, and the Italian wine list is good, including a solid selection by the glass. Things get even better on half-price-wine-list Mondays. The rest of the menu is as variable as the pizzas. Pasta is not overcooked, especially if you request it al dente—a welcome change from what we have come to expect. Prices are uncontained, though; we would set the bar quite high for a $20 plate of noodles.

We salute Scoozzi for serving dishes like sweet potato, walnut, and raisin ravioli with sautéed red onions and spinach in a sage-butter sauce, which are positively Northern Italian. Casereccia pasta with wild boar ragù is a traditional Italian recipe rarely seen on this side of the Atlantic. The problem lies in the uneven execution; however ambitious these dishes are, they underwhelm more than they overwhelm. And at these prices, that shouldn't be the case.

Scribner's

A famous Milford seafood stop with fresh fish—but
questionably worth the trip from elsewhere

Seafood, Traditional American   **$32**   *Milford*

7.0 /10   **7.0** /10   **8.0** /10   **6.2** /10
Food   *Atmosphere*   *Attitude*   *Value*

Upmarket restaurant   31 Village Rd.   *Bar* Full
Winter, 5pm-9pm daily.   Milford   *Credit Cards* Visa, MC, AmEx
Summer, Sun.-Thurs. 5pm-9:30pm;   (203) 878-7019   *Reservations* Recommended
Fri.-Sat. 5pm-10:30pm.   www.scribnersrestaurant.com

Scribner's is quite well known in the Milford area, a 30-year veteran
with accolades galore. The web site might advertise that the place is
"Consistently recognized as the Best Seafood Restaurant in
Connecticut," but the staff still tends to act a bit surprised when they
encounter a customer from outside Milford. The wood-paneled room is
cozy, and rather than being on a strip mall (as are many of the better-
known Milford restaurants), it's on an unassuming corner of a
residential block—a good start.

So are the reliable oysters on the half shell, and the Calamari
Alfonso, which at our last visit was recommended to us by the house;
they're deep-fried calamari with gorgonzola marinara sauce, tossed
with pine nuts and capers, and at $12, the price point is justified only if
you're hungry (the portion is enormous). Gorgonzola and the fried
batter might be a heavy pairing, but it's also a satisfying one. Throw in
the pine nuts—an interesting texture counterpoint—and suddenly
you've got an appetizer so filling that it's difficult to proceed to the
main event.

Fish mains, in spite of their renown, meet with mixed success.
Gorgonzola makes a repeat appearance on a grilled swordfish steak
that also features roasted red onions and chopped tomatoes. The
gorgonzola sauce isn't bad, but the swordfish is tough and reveals little
flavor. We prefer the bouillabaisse, made with mussels, clams, oysters,
chunks of fish, steamed with sweet onions, andouille sausage, fennel,
and tomato, with a Pernod-and-white-wine broth. The sausage is an
interesting addition, adding some much-needed flavor to the broth;
still, upon tasting it, we felt the need to add salt. The take-home
message: Scribner's is a bit above average for seafood, but we find it
difficult to make sense of the statewide recognition.

Seoul Yokocho

6.8
/10

Downtown's only Korean food, satisfying even if
the food is overpriced and and the décor drab

Korean   **$27**   *Upper Chapel Area*

7.6 /10   **5.0** /10   **7.0** /10   **6.1** /10
Food   *Atmosphere*   *Attitude*   *Value*

Upmarket restaurant	343 Crown St.	*Bar* Wine and beer only
Tues.-Thurs. 11:30am-10pm; Fri.-	New Haven	*Credit Cards* Visa, MC, AmEx
Sat. noon-10:30pm; Sun. noon-	(203) 497-9634	*Reservations* Accepted
9:30pm; closed Mon. *Vegetarian-friendly.*		

This is New Haven's only stab at Korean, so it gets some points right off
the bat for that. They also do sushi, which is actually good, though
pricey: it's fresh, and the spicy tuna rolls are the best in town—or out of
town for that matter, with the good kind of smooth, melt-in-your-
mouth, pre-chopped tuna well blended with spicy mayo.

The Korean food at Seoul is a controversial topic. Our Korean friends
seem united in their disdain for Seoul's cooking. We're told that it's
inauthentic, overpriced, and disappointing. But this is New Haven, after
all, and we swear that we've eaten well here at times. The stone pot bi
bim bap, their most popular dish, is a satisfying hodge-podge of mixed
rice with beef and cooked bean sprouts, Chinese cabbage, seaweed,
fiddleheads, carrots, and bamboo shoots, served with Korean hot sauce
over rice and topped with an egg. It's the best stone pot in town. We
also like the spicier soups, some of which might even activate the
cathartic runny-nose reflex. Tableside barbecue is less impressive, but
we've had kalbi (short ribs) that didn't disappoint. We don't
recommend any of the fish stews, however.

The service is friendly, if sometimes uninformed. The atmosphere,
though, is bright and impersonal; booths are boring and antiseptic,
tables worse. A little bit of atmosphere would go a long way at this
downtown spot, which is on a sadly desolate block in the shadow of
Crown Towers. And it's really in view of the bland, cheap atmosphere
that we, like others, are shocked by the high prices. When you're
paying $20 for many main courses, you expect something a bit more
romantic, a bit less brightly lit, a bit more polished.

Still, lunch is a better deal, and Seoul remains the only downtown
place at which to satisfy a Korean food craving.

Sidebar

5.7
/10

A popular after-work bar for downtowners, with excellent cocktails but mostly uneventful food

Bar food, Italian   **$22** *Financial District*

5.8 /10   **5.5** /10   **6.0** /10   **5.1** /10
Food   *Atmosphere*   *Attitude*   *Value*

Casual restaurant   259 Orange St.   *Bar* Full
Mon.-Thurs. 11:30am-1am; Fri. New Haven   *Credit Cards* Visa, MC, AmEx
11:30am-2am; Sat. 5pm-2am;   (203) 624-7333   *Reservations* Accepted
closed Sun. Kitchen closes at 10pm.

It's American to the core, this simple, clean, modern little sports bar and after-work happy-hour hotspot that does double duty as a lunch place, and triple duty as an Italian-American restaurant. Sidebar's sign is like something out of a skateboard commercial, and design touches inside are amusing, from the festive mosaic tile to the geometric lines on the wall that remind us of the '80s. The bar scene is definitely town, not gown, and they do drinks quite well, from a decent Bloody Mary to a well-balanced espresso martini, not too sweet, enough alcohol, the taste not overwhelmed by the coffee. During happy hour, there's a free fried-food buffet, but it's subpar.

If you do choose to dine, you should start with the buffalo tenders, which are the best thing we've had at Sidebar. In a nod to Japan, the tenders are coated with panko bread crumbs—a nice touch—and they're well fried and pre-dressed with a careful mix of gorgonzola and blue cheese along with plenty of strong buffalo sauce. Not subtle, but just right. The fried calamari, although tender on the inside, aren't as good; they're over-breaded for a clumpy, doughy effect, and made soggy by the sauce.

Pasta, which is available in half portions for lunch (a good idea), tends toward the overcooked—not as overcooked, however, as one burger that we ordered rare and arrived very well done. The fried onions and bacon were okay, and the cheddar cheese wasn't bad by itself, but it had melted a bit past the congealing point as the burger was being cooked to tasteless oblivion. Even the name reminds you that you would do best to think of Sidebar as just that—a bar.

Skappo

7.0 /10

A feel-good Umbrian wine bar and restaurant where everything—and everyone—is beautiful

Italian   **$29**   *Ninth Square*

5.2 /10   **9.5** /10   **10** /10   **6.2** /10
Food   *Atmosphere*   *Attitude*   *Value*

Upmarket restaurant   59 Crown St.   ***Bar*** Wine and beer only
Wed.-Sun. 4:30pm-11:30pm;   New Haven   ***Credit Cards*** Visa, MC, AmEx
closed Tues.   (203) 773-1394   ***Reservations*** Not accepted
Date-friendly. Good wine list.   www.skappo.com

With a small, warmly lit, rustic room and bold, lion-themed graphic design, Skappo is immediately likeable. Beauty is a defining quality here; one customer commented to us that the entire staff is good-looking. It's hard to disagree. And from the youthful waitstaff to their endlessly gregarious mama, Signora Anna, a local legend in the making, the folks at Skappo will greet you like family on your first visit. On many nights, you'll be serenaded by song. On Saturday mornings, the Signora gives Italian lessons.

The poetic menu is a refreshing regional departure from the norm, and the small (if pricey) portions are meant to compliment the excellent wine list, which features bottles from lesser-known regions. Expect a host of intriguing Umbrian specialties on the rotating menu. We've loved salsiccie con uvetta, served with a grape and raisin sauce that tends towards syrupy sweetness, yet comes together well (it's hard to go wrong with sausage). Other good choices include the succulent grilled prosciutto-wrapped shrimp, and a plate of regional Italian cured meats. Lyrical promise and good intentions aren't always enough, however; on one visit, peposo, a peppery beef stew with tomatoes, was chewy and dry, while a plate of beautiful homemade linguine lost much of its celebrated texture to overcooking.

Many people come just to sample the dessert list, which follows through better than the savory choices. A rum cake (brustengolo) offers an interesting counterpoint between a dense, nutty corn flour base and a sweet compote of apples and apricots, for a rustic and wholesome effect. Even better are the brutti ma buoni cookies. And the dessert wine list offers some very appealing options. Try the raisiny Passito di Pantelleria, which tastes like liquid honey with apricots—yet another reason why you will definitely leave Skappo feeling good.

Som Siam

7.7
/10

Som Siam's reasonably-priced food is the best Thai around, more than making up for the bland décor

Thai $**22** *Guilford*

8.2/10   **6.0**/10   **10** /10   **7.5**/10
Food   *Atmosphere*   *Attitude*   *Value*

Casual restaurant   63R Whitfield St.   *Bar* Wine and beer only
Sun.-Thurs. 11:30am-9:30pm; Guilford   *Credit Cards* Visa and MC
Fri.-Sat. 11:30am-10pm.   (203) 458 0228   *Reservations* Accepted
Vegetarian-friendly.

Easily the best Thai restaurant in the area (*The Menu*'s #1 for Thai for the second straight edition), Som Siam is held back only by its relatively remote location and uninspiring, fanciful décor. This was formerly Thai Inter, on State Street in New Haven—that restaurant was bought by new management, and the real thing is now out in the 'burbs. The new incarnation lies on the town green in quaint Guilford, but it's worth the trek out there from New Haven to sample the wonderful and unusual Thai fare. Som Siam's menu is far more interesting than any other Thai around, including some lesser-known Thai specialties that are often some of the best choices on the menu. The service is famously fantastic; the deferential and attentive waitstaff is nothing but genuinely friendly.

Prices are very reasonable at any time, but for the fiscally responsible, lunch specials are the best deal. Some of our favorites, most of them unique to Som Siam, include the som tum, a papaya salad with chilis, tomato, crushed peanuts, and lime juice; the spicy barbecued pork from the grill; and the choo chee fish, a deep-fried whole fish with coconut milk and curry sauce. Also excellent is the spicier, tangier pla-rad prik, another deep-fried fish. The only difficult thing is keeping yourself from overeating. We hope that more New Haveners will discover the unique charms of Som Siam, make their way out to Guilford, and help to populate its too-often-deserted dining room.

Soul de Cuba

8.3
/10

A hip new hangout with good, creative Cuban food, mojitos, and even cigars and vintage rums

Latin American   **$22**   *Theater District*

7.9/10   **9.5**/10   **7.0**/10   **8.2**/10
Food   *Atmosphere*   *Attitude*   *Value*

Upmarket restaurant   283 Crown St.   *Bar* Full
Tues.-Sat. 11:30am-2pm, 6pm-   New Haven   *Credit Cards* Visa, MC, AmEx
10pm; Sun. 6pm-10pm; closed Mon. (203) 498-2822   *Reservations* Not accepted
Date-friendly.   www.souldecuba.com

Stylish and cozy, Soul de Cuba brings a bold, urban aesthetic to New Haven, capturing the feel of the hipper parts of New York's outer boroughs. At the same time, this Cuban restaurant is a relaxing respite from the nearby Crown Street club antics, a laid-back, grown-up place to eat along the strip. The vibe is warm and sophisticated, with mellow jazz music in the background; and with most entrees under $15, there is scarcely a better atmosphere-to-price ratio anywhere in town.

To start, try papa rellena, a deep-fried ball of mashed potato stuffed with ground beef, or the slightly droopy yuca frita, a starchy fried indulgence that eats like a bar snack, with a crispy coating and a dense, almost creamy, center. You can have the yuca topped with black bean chili, a full-flavored and hearty version in which green olives make an appearance. An appetizer of shrimp in a martini glass is less notable and more overpriced.

Among mains, the Pollo Soul de Cuba, which the menu calls "Cuban-Chinois style," is a juicy, well-pounded breaded chicken cutlet covered by a sweet fruit salsa. An inspired sprinkling of cilantro harmonizes with the dish unexpectedly well. The rabo encendido is an admirable rendition of oxtail, soft and meaty, especially satisfying if you aren't too shy to gnaw on the bone a little. Plantain sides are fantastic. One of the few disappointments has been pargo, a dry filet of red snapper that has arrived seriously over-broiled. For dessert, try the apple caramel cheesecake; it's like a cheesecake stuffed inside an extremely sweet apple crisp.

The bar scene hops too. Tasty, cheap mojitos and good sangria both hit the spot; and there are even vintage rums and great (take-out) cigars. The concept is well thought out, the vibe alluring to passers-by. We are clearly not alone in our delight with this new arrival.

Southern Hospitality

6.6
10

A serviceable barbecue and soul food purveyor up
Whalley that's best for take-out

Southern

$10 *Whalley*

6.4/10
Food

7.0/10
Attitude

7.4/10
Value

Take-out
Mon.-Wed. 11am-10pm; Thurs.-
Sat. 11am-11pm; Sun. noon-9pm.
Delivery.

127 Whalley Ave.
New Haven
(203) 785-1575

Bar None
Credit Cards None
Reservations Not accepted

This place dubs itself a "Soul Food Restaurant," and its simple menu
fits the bill exactly: enormous dinners of fried chicken, ribs, pork chops,
chopped barbecue, chitterlings, shrimp, and the like are served with
two classic Southern sides, such as yams, collards, and so on. Every
meal also comes with a piece of reasonably good cornbread. There's
nothing in the bright white space other than a big, long counter and a
few tables; the atmosphere isn't conducive to eating in, and almost
everyone orders take-out. In fact, the aesthetic and menu at Southern
Hospitality remind us a lot of the old Jarman's, a dearly missed BBQ and
soul food purveyor whose Dixwell Avenue locale was not so far away
from where this place now sits.

Our favorite thing at Southern Hospitality is their rendition of oxtail,
which is tender and fatty. We know it's sacrilege, but the chopped
barbecue, while competent, is better with the addition of extra
barbecue sauce (plus some hot sauce). Deep-fried whole porgies, a
seasonal dish, can be wonderful, but the last time we tried them, the
bones, which should be soft, were too big and sharp to eat, causing
endless logistical problems. Mac and cheese is well executed, cheesy
and satisfying; collard greens, meanwhile, absorb a lot of flavor from
the big pork hocks they're cooked with, but are a bit sweet for our
taste.

Service is adequate, and the prices are cheap, if you keep in mind
that a 10-dollar dinner here easily serves two people. With Jaylyn's and
Jarman's gone, it's good to have an easy Whalley Avenue option
available for when the soul food craving hits—and, oh, it will.

Starbucks

7.1
10

An enormously popular downtown branch of the
infamous coffee chain—good luck trying for seat

Baked goods, Light American   *Theater District*

7.5/10   **6.0**/10
Atmosphere   *Attitude*

Café
Mon.-Thurs. 6am-11:30pm; Fri.
6am-midnight; Sat. 6:30am-
midnight; Sun. 7am-10:30pm.
Breakfast. Vegetarian-friendly.

1070 Chapel St.
New Haven
(203) 624-3361
www.starbucks.com

Bar None
Credit Cards Visa, MC, AmEx
Reservations Not accepted

What can we really say about Dr. Evil's coffee empire? You know the
drill. At least the coffee is pretty good and the lighting's not too bright.
The downtown New Haven franchise is an academic hotbed. As might
be expected anywhere, this Starbucks is infinitely popular. It's packed to
overflowing with Yalies, morning, noon, and night. Though it has
become fashionable to hate Starbucks, it's also next to impossible to
get a seat these days—even in a city with lots of other great choices for
coffee. This suggests that they're doing something right. Ah, the
contradictions of a chain America.

    Seating is an even more special challenge if you're angling for one
of the two comfy couches by the window; most of the time they're
inhabited by chess-playing authors who look as though they've been
working on their manuscripts in those seats since before Old Eli fled the
moral depravity of Harvard Square to found a better place. Starbucks is
one of the most comfortable places in town to flip open a laptop and
get to work. It also happens to be one of the most active singles scenes
in a neighborhood of student-singles-scene bookstore-cafés.

    We recommend that you stick to a cup of coffee—the Coffee of the
Day, as they call it—rather than wasting five dollars and five hundred
calories on some ridiculous Italian-sounding concoction that's basically
just milk, hot or cold, liberally adulterated with sugary syrup (although
we do have a soft spot for the thick and indulgent new Chantico hot
chocolate). But come for a decent cup of coffee, especially if it's a cup
of coffee to go, and for the love of God, fight the good fight and
steadfastly refuse to use their preposterous faux-Italian nomenclature
for the cup sizes. Nonviolent protest, grande into medium, swords into
plowshares.

Stella's European Bakery

5.0
/10

One of the only kosher places in town, with a light, airy vibe

Baked goods, Light American   **$ 9**   *Whalley*

4.5 /10
Food

6.0 /10
Attitude

5.3 /10
Value

Take-out
Sun.-Thurs. 8am-6pm;
Fri. 8am-sunset; closed Sat.
Breakfast. Brunch. Vegetarian-friendly.

372 Whalley Ave.
New Haven
(203) 772-4779

Bar None
Credit Cards Visa, MC, AmEx
Reservations Not accepted

Stella's is one of the only Kosher places in the area. (The nearby Edge of the Woods, Jewish Community Center in Woodbridge, Fox's in Westville, Claire's downtown, and Yale's Slifka Center are the others.) Stella's sits in a rather unlikely location on Whalley Avenue. The owners, who are of Polish origin, have put together a menu that has a mix of traditional Polish and traditional Jewish food.

As such, there are pierogies and whitefish sandwiches, blintzes, bagels, lox, and classic sugar cookies. Such fare is not so common in these parts, so we're delighted to find it here. The babka has a devoted following—it's sweet and fluffy, like bread and cheesecake put together. There's a light citrus taste too. Good also is the challah, although the tough day-old rye underperforms. (The price is right, though, and toasted, it's fine.)

A "special iced coffee," which comes with flavors such as almond, is frothy, watery, and cloyingly sweet. It's not their best work. Unless you're limited to kosher food, we wouldn't earmark Stella's as a place for a full meal, and regardless, they close before dinnertime (unless you're the sort that finishes dinner by 6). Stella's also serves a brunch on Sundays (not Saturdays, needless to say). One frequent problem here is the extremely slow service, even if the place is empty. It's not the sort of place you'd want to stop by for a quick bite on your way somewhere. But the bright, airy space has a very lunchy (or brunchy) vibe that's a pleasant escape from the chaos of Whalley Avenue.

Stillwater American Bistro

8.2
10

A brand-new restaurant right on the Q river, with outdoor seating and a romantic fireplace—amen

New American $31   *Fair Haven*

7.4 /10	**9.5** /10	**9.0** /10	**7.5** /10
Food	*Atmosphere*	*Attitude*	*Value*

Upmarket restaurant
Mon. 5pm-10pm; Tues.-Thurs.
11:30am-2pm, 5pm-10pm; Fri.
11:30am-2pm, 4pm-10pm; Sat.
4pm-10pm; Sun. 11am-9pm.
Brunch. Date-friendly. Outdoor dining.

3 Clifton St.
New Haven
(203) 466-2200

Bar Full
Credit Cards Visa, MC, AmEx
Reservations Recommended

Stillwater American Bistro is the newest resident of the impossibly romantic Fair Haven space that sits right on the Quinnipiac River, next to Kiraku. It's where Stuzy's, one of our old favorites, spent a brief time before sadly closing. This time around, the "American Bistro" designation name describes the menu pretty well: simple, upscale American preparations of steaks, chicken, and seafood. The new restaurant boasts a granite fireplace and a great river view; we think that the best seats in the house are in the back right corner of the restaurant, which combines the best of the fire and the view.

Although the muted furnishings and bar are typical of the genre, it's those windows that really make the place. Outdoor seats and an outdoor bar, when the weather is warm, add yet another level of atmosphere. As for dinner, it absolutely must begin with the fried calamari, a dish that vies for the title of best in town—and that's no small accomplishment. These squid rings are unbelievably tender within, and unbelievably crispy and delicate without; the marinara and tartar sauces are both excellent, and in an as-yet-unparalleled move, the hot cherry peppers, too, are fried with the calamari. Wow.

Moving on, the most impressive main course thus far (and it's still early) has been the London broil. It's like a postmodern interpretation, with the thin slices of appropriately rare steak sitting in an irresistible bowl of jus. We've also been mightily impressed by the tender lamb— like little lollipops—crusted with bread crumbs and also served appropriately rare. Less remarkable have been the New York strip steak and underseasoned fish dishes, but we reserve final judgment on brand-new restaurants until they've settled into their stride. Sunday brunch is served, too. It's a great start, and a much-needed addition to a beautiful and underutilized riverfront property.

Stone House

8.6
10

Not just another seafooder—this one's impeccable,
with spectacular pot pie and gracious marina views

Seafood, Traditional American   **$38**   *Guilford*

8.8 /10
Food

8.0 /10
Atmosphere

9.0 /10
Attitude

7.6 /10
Value

Upmarket restaurant
Tue.-Thurs. 11:30am-9pm (winter),
11:30am-10pm (summer) ; Fri.-Sat.
11:30am-10pm; Sun. noon-9pm;
closed Mon. Kitchen closes Fri.-Sat. 11pm. *Brunch. Date-friendly.*

506 Whitfield St.
Guilford
(203) 458-3700

Bar Full
Credit Cards Visa, MC, AmEx
Reservations Recommended

The Stone House, opposite the Guilford marina, is a charming, rambling
restaurant whose windows have lovely views, some of which look out
on boats bobbing around in the water. At first glance, the venue looks
too large-group-oriented, the dining room too "fine," and the bar too
well adorned with nautical artifacts for anyone possibly to suspect that
a first-class kitchen could lurk in the background.

Dubious on our first visit, we ordered the swordfish skewers
recommended by the house, expecting the usual overcooked, dry,
flavorless rendition of swordfish. Instead, we were treated to some of
the best in the area—meltingly tender, succulent, and well seasoned,
nicely balanced by a fresh mango salsa. On another visit, we were even
more reluctant to order seafood pot pie, which had also been
recommended to us, but when we tasted the Stone House's
deconstructed version of this dish, we really felt like idiots for having
thought twice about it. Large morsels of fish and shellfish bathe in a
decadent, creamy mussel soup, topped with a square pillow of ethereal,
golden brown puff pastry. This dish is a triumph.

But we *really* never thought that an upscale waterfront restaurant in
Guilford could compete in the New Haven pizza arena. Now we
believe. The flaky crust is thin and wonderfully oiled, toppings offer a
good garlicky kick, and combinations are an inspiration: for instance,
fresh tomato, bacon, and sweet baby scallops on a white pie. Other
notables include good, spicy Bloody Marys prepared with a generous
dose of horseradish, as well as fresh oysters that are everything they
should be in this part of the country—fresh, meaty, and delicately briny,
shucked well and free of grit. We're still somewhat dumbfounded by it
all—and happy as clams.

Stony Creek Market

8.0
10

A cozy spot packed with locals for breakfast, lunch, and sometimes pizza, with a superlative water view

Light American, Pizza   **$12**   *Branford*

7.6/10   **9.0**/10   **7.0**/10   **9.0**/10
Food   *Atmosphere*   *Attitude*   *Value*

Counter service   178 Thimble Islands Rd. *Bar* BYO
Market, Mon.-Fri. 6:30am-3pm;   Branford   *Credit Cards* None
Sat.-Sun. 8am-3pm. Pizza, Thurs.- (203) 488-0145   *Reservations* Not accepted
Sun. 5pm-9pm (summers only).
Breakfast. Brunch. Date-friendly. Outdoor dining. Vegetarian-friendly.

Stony Creek Market and Pizza is one of the only places around where you can eat pizza outdoors—and, better yet, it's one of the most vacation-like settings to eat in the entire New Haven area. Tables out on the porch overlook the Thimble Islands and the boats bobbing around in Branford's Stony Creek harbor.

The atmosphere inside the room, too, is charming, with a very cozy neighborhood feel—and it's no surprise, since the crowd is so incredibly local. You'll see people reading the paper, discussing local news with each other, or catching up on Stony Creek gossip. Folks who have discovered this little corner of the Shoreline are a unique and tight-knit bunch, but neither they nor the staff here will make you feel like you're an outsider if you're from out of town (and that might mean New Haven).

The breakfast and lunch food is uniformly good. A chicken curry croissant, in particular, approaches perfection; the salad is creamy, with a well-developed curry flavor and tender chicken, while the croissant into which it's stuffed is delicate, buttery, and very French, positively one of the best in the area. Eggplant and meatball subs are the other major standby choices here. They're enormous, in need of a bit of salt but otherwise quite well executed. Bread is fresh and the sauce has good flavor.

Pizza is available, but only in summer, and only in the evening, when the place turns into Stony Creek Pizza. The pies are good if not a revelation; the tasty crust, we're told, is made with sweet potatoes. Try the version with sliced tomatoes, fresh basil, onion, garlic, Romano, and mozzarella—although it may be hard to focus on the taste with such a view to distract you.

Su Casa

7.7
/10

Your Tex-Mex dream come true (or is it just we that have Tex-Mex dreams?)

Tex-Mex $ **22**   *Branford*

7.3 /10   **9.0** /10   **6.0** /10   **7.5** /10
Food   *Atmosphere*   *Attitude*   *Value*

Casual restaurant   400 East Main St.   *Bar* Full
Mon.-Thurs. 11:30am-10pm; Fri.-   Branford   *Credit Cards* Visa, MC, AmEx
Sat. noon-11pm; Sun. 4pm-10pm.   (203) 481-5001   *Reservations* Not accepted
Date-friendly. Outdoor dining.

Hidden along a highway in Branford, Su Casa is all that's good about Tex-Mex-themed environments. Multiple rooms conceal jovial diners out for the evening, downing margaritas and enjoying great guacamole and cheesy burritos slathered with enchilada sauce and piled with rice and beans.

There are some disappointments. Some main courses try to do too much: shrimp Acapulco are cooked Creole-style with roasted peppers, tomatoes, and spices, served over a bed of Spanish rice, for example. We recommend sticking with the standard but good antojito fare—enchiladas, chiles rellenos, and so on—and dishes like the steak fajita quesadilla, a grilled flour tortilla filled with marinated steak, sautéed mushrooms, onions, tomatoes, and melted cheese. We recommend most highly the Mexican combination plates; their prices are also eminently reasonable. There is certainly nothing subtle or sublime about the food, but it's surprisingly well executed. Probably, though, it's Su Casa's feisty atmosphere that keeps people coming back. Keep in mind that the wait can be long on weekends, as locals flock in from towns all around to partake of the suburban fiesta.

Su Casa is the perennial recipient of Best Mexican titles from press near and far. This is more than a bit misleading. While we do love the atmosphere, it's not because it serves the "best," or "most authentic," anything. But Su Casa has elevated the art of creating the Tex-Mex atmosphere to a science. That's what the place does best. Murals of Pancho Villa and his henchmen, hanging sombreros, and piñatas playfully watch over as you dig into your combination plate, while locals toast you with matching frozen margaritas from across the room. Toast, sit back, succumb to sensation, and devour your enchilada.

Subway

A fast-food chain whose homogeneous, tasteless
subs fail to live up to the advertising hype

Light American $ **6**   *Arts District, Whalley*

3.5 /10   **1.0** /10   **5.0** /10   **4.1** /10
Food   *Atmosphere*   *Attitude*   *Value*

Fast-food chain
Hours vary by location. Most
branches open daily at 9am and
close between 9pm and 11pm;
193 Whalley Ave. branch open
until midnight. *Breakfast.*

9 branches in
New Haven
(203) 787-0400
(Whitney Ave. branch)
www.subway.com

Bar None
Credit Cards None
Reservations Not accepted

Founded in 1965 in nearby Bridgeport, Subway has more recently
positioned itself as the fast-food restaurant that's not: according to the
television, this chain is healthier than others and serves food with
fresher ingredients, tasting more homemade. This is partly true and
partly false. While the store-baked bread is better than standard fast-
food hamburger buns, other ingredients are industrial specimens,
peeled out of plastic wrappers, and everything hot is microwaved
(although nowadays they're toasting the subs to keep up with the
rapidly spreading Quiznos). So much for "the fresh way—my way."

As for taste, Subway does offer a welcome dose of raw vegetables,
but subs are missing the elemental goodness of a cheeseburger. And
the formula—the same set of toppings with every meat, plus salt and
pepper, oil and vinegar—makes every sub taste more or less the same.
Among condiments, we recommend the Southwest and horseradish
sauces.

But Subway's implied claim of wholesomeness above and beyond
the fast-food competition rings false. Sodium stearoyl-2-lactylate,
mono- and diglycerides, and free glutamates all make appearances. This
is fast food, folks—nothing more. And as for the "7 under 6" menu—
seven subs with fewer than six grams of fat each—well, with apologies
to the spectacled everyman-dieter-cult hero Jared, they're six of the
most uninteresting subs on the menu (the roasted chicken breast is the
one exception), and the "under 6" measurement doesn't include basics
like cheese and oil, making them all the blander. Meanwhile, a footlong
meatball sub has 1,060 calories and 52 grams of fat. As for
atmosphere, don't eat in. Perhaps sit out on the Green. While a six-inch
should be enough for most appetites, a Yale ID gets $1 off footlong
subs at the branch on Whitney.

Sullivan's

An extremely basic Irish pub with extremely mediocre food—but outdoor seating

Bar food, Irish   **$17**   *Upper Chapel Area*

3.5 /10   **6.0** /10   **5.0** /10   **3.9** /10
Food   *Atmosphere*   *Attitude*   *Value*

Bar and grill	1166 Chapel St.	*Bar* Full
Sun.-Thurs. 11am-1am; Fri.-Sat.	New Haven	*Credit Cards* Visa, MC, AmEx
11am-2am. Kitchen closes at 10pm.	(203) 777-4367	*Reservations* Accepted
Outdoor dining.		

This used to be Kavanagh's. The name has changed, and the menu has added more vaguely Irish selections to the bar food options, but the place is ultimately not much different than it was: your basic neighborhood pub, Sullivan's appeals to a crowd of haphazard wandering grad students, after-work locals, a surprisingly consistent contingent of old men, and occasionally the women who love them. Oh, and don't forget about the Yale Architecture students ducking out from 18 straight hours in the nearby studio, here to bathe their sorrows in blended whiskey. The tone gets louder and bouncier as the night rolls along, especially on weekends, when things positively rage. The place is dark and uninviting during the day, though. The tables out on the sidewalk are the best option.

Standard bar food is served, including below-average, overcooked bacon cheeseburgers, and there are simple, not very good American classics like baked meatloaf with potatoes, gravy, and a vegetable on the side. French fries are soggy; wings don't have enough kick; more Irish dishes fare even more poorly.

The beer and drink selections are also standard (happily, a Harp tastes more or less the same anywhere), and they're offered at decent prices. It's worth noting that the tables are unusually big, especially a few of them; it's a good place to come with a large group, but not exactly intimate for a one-on-one, unless you go on a slow night and happen to score a booth. We should also note that the service seems to have improved since the switch-over to Sullivan's. Baby steps.

Swagat

A delicious little South Indian specialist that's
stunningly vegetarian-friendly and amazingly cheap

Indian   **$ 7**   *West Haven*

8.5/10   **7.0**/10   **9.0**/10   **9.8**/10
Food   *Atmosphere*   *Attitude*   *Value*

Casual restaurant   215 Boston Post Rd.   **Bar** Wine and beer only
Mon.-Sat. 11am-3pm, 5pm-10pm;   West Haven   **Credit Cards** Visa, MC, AmEx
closed Sun. Kitchen closes 30-45   (203) 931-0108   **Reservations** Not accepted
min. earlier; call in advance and
staff will accommodate arrivals
closer to 10pm. *Vegetarian-friendly.*

This little South Indian gem was recommended to us on *The Menu*
bulletin board (www.newhavenmenu.com/discuss) by a wise contributor
named DAFeder. Thanks, DA: for starters, Swagat, which opened in
2002, serves some of the best-value Indian food in the area,
underselling the downtown competition by two, three, even four or
five dollars.

Although standard northern Indian dishes like samosas and lamb
curry are unremarkable here, the real deal here is the authentic south
Indian cuisine that you will find nowhere else in the area. The
centerpiece is the dosa—something like a large, thinly rolled crepe
made from rice batter. There are seven variations on the dosa; the
wonderful uttapam, for instance, is a bit thicker, more like a pancake
with onions and cilantro. A delicious masala dosa comes stuffed with
potatoes. All come with a delectable assortment of condiments, from a
sweet coconut chutney to an interesting pink tomato sauce redolent of
ginger, to a soupy lentil sambar with tumeric and other spices. And a
full lunch or dinner of these southern specialties will cost three or four
dollars. Not as bargain-priced, but also nice, is the Chicken 65
appetizer, with well seasoned breast meat that gets a real kick from red
pepper flakes.

There's not much to say about the room—a few little tables and
tacky wall decorations—not to mention severe climate-control problems
(freezing in winter, boiling in summer). It's not the spot for a romantic
night out (many choose take-out), but in terms of food and value,
Swagat is a dream come true, especially for vegetarians: more than half
of the dishes on the dinner menu, including *every single South Indian
dish*, are strictly vegetarian. What a spectacular and rare find in West
Haven.

Sweet Relief

3.4
10

A small, dark, easily-missed shop just off Whitney
whose smoothies are better than their wraps

Light American, Sweets $ 7   *Arts District*

3.9 /10   **2.0** /10   **5.0** /10   **4.6** /10
Food   *Atmosphere*   *Attitude*   *Value*

Counter service   99 Audubon St.   *Bar* None
Winter, daily 8am-4pm; summer,   New Haven   *Credit Cards* Visa, MC, AmEx
daily 8am-7pm. *Breakfast. Delivery.*   (203) 789-9800   *Reservations* Not accepted
Outdoor dining. Vegetarian-friendly.   www.sweetreliefcafe.com

The Audubon Street nook where Sweet Relief is located is easy to miss,
even if you're walking down the thoroughfare that is Whitney Avenue.
It's a little take-out place with a few tables and chairs that never really
seem to be used. It's best during the summer months, when you can sit
at one of the tables out on the sidewalk rather than suffering through
time spent in the hushed interior of Sweet Relief. And on a good day, it
is a really nice place to sit, on a corner of New Haven's diminutive Arts
District, away from the heavy traffic of downtown, yet with a
somewhat urban feel.

That room is dark and strange, with an overarching silence, which
dominates while the smoothies and wraps are prepared to order,
creating a bit of an uncomfortable dynamic between you and your
underworked server. Something is seriously missing from the
environment.

Smoothies are generally great, however, especially those with berries
and honey. They're made exclusively with fresh fruit. Wraps are more
variable. Although many of them are healthy, they are also less exciting
than one might hope. The Santa Fe wrap combines chicken, cheddar
cheese, fat-free yogurt, baby greens, and homemade black-bean corn
salsa on a jalapeño cheddar tortilla. Some combinations are more
jarring, like the dream sandwich, which implausibly fuses chicken, fresh
strawberries, cheddar cheese, baby greens, honey mustard, and walnuts
on a tomato tortilla. Yowza. Ultimately, though, it's the fruit smoothies
and midday traffic from local lunch-breakers that keep this place in
business.

Tandoor

6.3
/10

A standard Indian restaurant distinguished by its bizarre but delightful location in an old diner

Indian   **$20**   *Upper Chapel Area*

5.8/10   **7.5**/10   **6.0**/10   **5.9**/10
Food   *Atmosphere*   *Attitude*   *Value*

Casual restaurant   1226 Chapel St.   ***Bar*** Wine and beer only
Daily 11:30am-10:30pm.   New Haven   ***Credit Cards*** Visa, MC, AmEx
Brunch. Delivery. Vegetarian-friendly. (203) 776-6620 ***Reservations*** Accepted
                                 www.campusfood.com (delivery only)

Actually set inside a diner, Tandoor certainly breaks new ground for Indian-restaurant packaging. It was once the Elm City Diner, the real thing, complete with the old ersatz train-car style. It's an amusing sign of the times that the most authentic-looking diner in this old-school American town serves Indian food. Incongruities abound. The fare is solid, but certainly not inventive, Indian cuisine. It's your standard Indian menu, with all the basics you'd expect—tandoori chicken, which is marinated in masala and yogurt for 24 hours and barbecued in a clay oven; rogan josh (lamb cooked in an onion sauce with yogurt, almonds, cream, and spices), and the rest of the standard Indian repertoire.

As you might expect for New Haven Indian, there's also a $7.95 all-you-can-eat weekend lunch buffet. Tandoor is open later at night than most downtown restaurants, a definite plus. It's also the only real, non-fast food, non-pizza restaurant (and certainly the only Indian restaurant) in New Haven that works with campusfood.com, a delivery service that makes students infinitely happy.

It's your basic, satisfying Indian; you've probably seen it all before. Aside from the décor, Tandoor has little to distinguish it from the competition, although the food is a notch above India Palace down the street. Do keep in mind that the entertainment value of eating Indian food inside an old diner is quite significant. You should see it for yourself.

Taquería Mexicana #2

7.1/10

A simple little grocery and lunch spot with the best and most authentic tacos in the New Haven area

Mexican $ **6**   *West Haven*

8.6/10   **4.0**/10   **7.0**/10   **9.2**/10
Food   *Atmosphere*   *Attitude*   *Value*

Counter service   702 Boston Post Rd.   *Bar* None
Daily 8am-10pm.   West Haven   *Credit Cards* None
                           (203) 931-8534   *Reservations* Not accepted

They even import their bottles of Coca-Cola from Mexico. If you don't believe us, look for the "Hecho en Mexico" printed on the bottles in the little fridge next to the Jarritos, the Fanta, the sweetened juices of mango and tamarind, the Squirt, and the most popular choice of all, that legendary Mexican soft drink to end all Mexican soft drinks—Boing. For us, though, the authentic Mexican Coke (it's fizzier and more concentrated in Mexico) is the sort of logistics-be-damned commitment to authenticity that separates the true culinary legends from the impostors. Well done, Taquería Mexicana #2.

Only such a hilariously authentic touch, in fact, could possibly push the first mention of the ridiculously good tacos served up at this little West Haven strip-mall joint near the University of New Haven into the second paragraph of this review. The tacos truly transport you to Mexico, from the delicious doubled-up corn tortillas to the meat itself. Best might be the barbacoa de chivo, whose deep, throbbing goatiness is craved by *Advocate* Managing Editor Tom Gogola; the tender goat meat's soft strands of fat play off the onions, cilantro, and fresh lime (you squeeze it on). Delicious also is the saltier and spicier adobado, little red pieces of pork with a remarkably well-developed flavor. The salsas are all worth trying; our favorite is a chunky salsa with onions and tomatoes that is impeccably fresh.

The room is so authentic in its downmarket simplicity—just a few tables and bare concrete walls—that you might want to take out. The menu also includes burritos, tostadas, tortas (Mexican sandwiches), and so on. You can order rice and beans as a side, though it's not on the menu. Know also that you should try everything, the more uncommon the better: al pastor (spiced, marinated, shaved pork), cabeza (head), and lengua (tongue). Trust us. Try it all.

Tasti D-Lite

5.3
10

A popular chain serving something like ice cream—
not good enough to be real, but it could be worse

Sweets   *Theater District*

4.5 /10   **7.0** /10
Food   *Attitude*

Take-out   45 High St.   *Bar* None
Daily noon-10pm.   New Haven   *Credit Cards* None
Vegetarian-friendly. (203) 503-0717   *Reservations* Not accepted
                        www.tastidlite.com

Everything about this 75-store chain seems too good to be true. The
company advertises their frozen dessert product as low-calorie,
cholesterol-free, 99% fat free, 100% all natural, creamy, and delicious.
Whatever it is, it's not ice cream, although they also scoop a handful of
delicious Ciao Bella gelato flavors at this store. Tasti D-Lite, on the other
hand, has a sixth of the calories of the real thing and a third those of
frozen yogurt. It's no wonder that this New York City invention
"perfected in a lab" has become a smash hit among urbanites that
strive to have it all while having none of it.

The space-age frozen confection can taste pretty good, especially
considering what's not in it. We're happy to say that there is guar gum,
there's no sorbitol, saccharin, or other scary sugar substitute involved—
just a little sugar. We can actually spell all of the ingredients. The final
result is sweet, but not too sweet (with 40 calories per serving, that's
no shock). The texture is best right out of machine, when it is freshly
"overrun," a technical term for whipping air into a product. At 75%
overrun, Tasti D-Lite right out of the machine tastes fresh and
unsurprisingly light, and offers a pleasing consistency.

But leave it untouched for more than 10 minutes, and this treat
starts to look decidedly less appetizing. Case in point: a "cake" that
people devour because it visually resembles ice cream cake—it tastes
like what might happen if you lived on a space station and you had
access only to dry ice, canned cool whip, and a small sachet of
evaporated milk. So stick to the flagship soft serve product, eat up
fast—the ingredients in the soft-serve will begin to dissociate—and
don't worry about your waist, because 75% of what you're eating is
nothing at all.

Temple Grill

7.2
10

Solid comfort food at a central downtown spot—
come for the meatloaf and stay for the game

Traditional American $ **26**   *Theater District*

7.1 /10   **7.0** /10   **8.0** /10   **6.6** /10
Food   *Atmosphere*   *Attitude*   *Value*

Bar and grill   152 Temple St.   *Bar* Full
Sun.-Thurs. 11:30am-1am; Fri.-Sat.   New Haven   *Credit Cards* Visa, MC, AmEx
11:30am-2am. Kitchen closes   (203) 773-1111   *Reservations* Not accepted
Sun.-Thurs. 10pm; Fri.-Sat. 11pm.

Temple Grill is vastly more user-friendly than its short-lived predecessor,
Diva. The theme is jazzy industrial chic, executed with welcome
restraint. Careful lighting endows the space with a flattering yellowish
hue. Still, the gleaming bar, with its two flat-panel televisions, takes
center stage, especially at game time.

Here we favor comfort food—the more comforting, the better. A
bacon cheeseburger with sautéed onions is simply excellent, with the
beef rich and well textured, the jack cheese melted correctly, and a
highly recommended chipotle mayo adding a creamy, homemade dose
of smoky heat. Crab cakes are moist, with crispy breading and a perky
lemon aioli. Meat in a lobster croissant is plump and resilient. But the
menu's crown jewel is a spectacular meatloaf, first baked and then
seared on the grill. The tender beef bursts with flavor, herbs, and
welcome spiciness, and it's drizzled with a heady demi-glace that
honors the chef's prestigious Culinary Institute of America pedigree.

The kitchen's more ambitious offerings are less successful. Tuna
tartare seriously lacks flavor; salt and oil help. A flank steak is chewy
and unappealing. Perhaps even more disturbingly, for a grill, the waffle
fries are consistently undersalted. This can't really be corrected with a
salt shaker; there's no substitute for salting just out of the fryer.

There's a cookie-cutter wine list, but cocktails are better. With a vibe
that's less collegiate than Richter's and less aloof than Hot Tomato's,
and outdoor seating in summer, Temple Grill is a good choice for an
after-work or pre-Shubert libation, made even more affable by friendly,
low-key service. As for the food, do keep in mind the word "grill"
when ordering. Stick with the basics—wings, burgers, meatloaf—and,
as the chef-owner says of his do-it-yourself salads, you're not going to
hit anything that you didn't want.

Templeton's

4.9
/10

A mediocre, mind-bendingly overpriced hotel restaurant that fits every stereotype of the genre

Traditional American   **$36**   *Theater District*

4.7 /10
Food

5.5 /10
Atmosphere

4.0 /10
Attitude

2.8 /10
Value

Upmarket restaurant
Daily 6:30am-10pm.
Breakfast. Brunch.

229 George St.
New Haven
(203) 498-3222
newhavenhotel.com/dining.html

Bar Full
Credit Cards Visa, MC, AmEx
Reservations Accepted

A hotel restaurant is a hotel restaurant is a hotel restaurant. Why are they all the same? Are the hotel management programs at institutions of higher learning across the country in cahoots, teaching a common curriculum of overcooked vegetables, tinny fake chandeliers, overdressed tables with cheap silverware, and service that is patronizingly effusive ("Oh yes, you are more than welcome, sir!") without being at all professional?

Templeton's, at the New Haven Hotel, is just such a place. The kitchen prepares consistently mediocre versions of boring American classics at prices that are so high they almost seem satirical. The other amusing thing about Templeton's is its acrophobia-inducing position, balanced high above the hotel lobby.

Our last visit went as follows: 2:00pm: We call ahead to Templeton's to see how late their lunch menu will be available that day. "Until 2:30," we are assured. 2:15pm: We arrive, to be greeted only with the afternoon "Lighter Fare" menu. 2:18pm: Debating with the staff quickly proves fruitless. "Don't worry, it's similar to our lunch menu," we are assured. 2:20pm: From the few available options, we choose the crab cake sandwich, as it is touted on the menu as "the best broiled lump crab cake in Connecticut." 2:25pm: We wait for our food, listen to the staff loudly discuss how to divide up the day's tips, and hum along to the horrible piano music that's piped in. 2:29pm: As we sample our $13.25 dish—mushy, underseasoned crabmeat on a dry, powdery Portuguese roll with mustard and strong red onions cut too thick to eat—our thoughts drift to the warm and elegant Union League Café three blocks away, where the same thirteen-plus bucks or so would have gotten us a sirloin steak with house-made fries and haricots verts.

Do these hoteliers ever wonder why there's never anyone in their restaurants?

Tenderloin's

8.0
10

A warm, inviting, and generally tasty steak-and-chop house serving a local Branford crowd

Steakhouse, Traditional American $**39**   *Branford*

8.0 /10
Food

8.0 /10
Atmosphere

8.0 /10
Attitude

6.9 /10
Value

Upmarket restaurant
Mon.-Thurs. 11:30am-2:30pm,
5pm-10pm; Fri. 11:30am-2:30pm,
5pm-11pm; Sat. 5pm-11pm; Sun.
1pm-9pm. *Date-friendly. Outdoor dining.*

2 East Main St.
Branford
(203) 481-1414

Bar Full
Credit Cards Visa, MC, AmEx
Reservations Accepted

Tenderloin's is a reliable steak, chop, and seafood specialist situated on the edge of picturesque downtown Branford, where the restaurant is like a beacon, straddling a fork in the road. Within, the atmosphere is inviting, casually elegant, vaguely hip. UFOish lights are set at a good level and pair well with the yellow walls. The office-style ceilings are curiously inoffensive; not so for the muzak, but still, the vibe survives. Even better, you can gaze out onto the quiet Branford street and what must be one of the only serif-font stop signs in North America. Now *there* is an affluent suburb.

For starters, fried calamari, that classic standby, have a thin, almost ethereal batter that is nonetheless crispy, and the squid isn't the least bit chewy. The accompanying marinara with red pepper flakes is just fine. An included dinner salad reveals Tenderloin's suburban roots, but at least it's not iceberg lettuce—this one has field greens, radicchio, and a somewhat gummy balsamic vinegar dressing.

As you might gather from the name of the place, steaks are one of the main attractions here, and they're good. Although we have had a steak ordered black and blue come medium rare—really two notches more cooked than we ordered it—the flavor still shone through. Mashed potatoes, too, are above average, and a juicy Cornish game hen, paired with asparagus and tomato, is well executed. Servers are friendly and helpful; the staff at Tenderloin's seems to understand, among many other things, that free alcohol is the gift that pays back, and as such, you may just be treated to a sparkling glass of moscato.

Thai Inter

6.4 / 10

A decent, if unremarkable, Thai place on a quiet stretch of State Street

Thai $18   *East Rock/Grad Ghetto*

6.7 /10   **5.0** /10   **9.0** /10   **6.2** /10
Food   *Atmosphere*   *Attitude*   *Value*

Casual restaurant   1027 State St.   ***Bar*** Wine and beer only
Mon.-Thurs. 11:30am-3pm, 5pm-   New Haven   ***Credit Cards*** Visa, MC, AmEx
9pm; Fri. 11:30am-3pm, 5pm-   (203) 752-1853   ***Reservations*** Accepted
10pm; Sat. 3pm-10pm; Sun. 3pm-9pm.

The Ship of Theseus problem has been well known to philosophers since the days of Plutarch: "The ship wherein Theseus and the youth of Athens returned [from Crete] had thirty oars, and was preserved by the Athenians…they took away the old planks as they decayed, putting in new and stronger timber in their place." The identity dilemma is this: once all of the original, decayed planks have been replaced by new wood, is it still the same ship? If you say it is, then you're faced with another, even more difficult, dilemma: let's say you now take the old, decayed planks, which you've kept around, and use them to reconstruct another ship. Which, then, is the real Ship of Theseus?

For a long time, Thai Inter was known as one of the best Thai places in the New Haven area, a place with a spectacular all-you-can-eat lunch buffet with unusual specialties, and an out-of-the-ordinary regional menu so good that it embarrassed the Chapel Street competition. But then, Thai Inter moved, deserting its State Street neighborhood for the greener, more suburban pastures of Guilford, keeping its menu and kitchen staff completely intact but renaming itself Som Siam (which is currently the #1 Thai restaurant in the *The Menu*).

But then, a little while later, the Som Siam folks turned their empty building, kitchen, and even the name of their old State Street restaurant over to new management, who promptly re-opened it as Thai Inter, with a similar menu, look, and feel as the old joint. The food at the new Thai Inter, though not quite in Som Siam's league, isn't bad—it's still above the level of Chapel Street Thai, with decent curries, noodle dishes, soups, and a still-more-interesting-than-average assortment of dishes like crispy fish. The service is still extremely deferential, the space still quiet to the point of awkwardness, the prices still unreasonably cheap. We're glad it's there—but deeply troubled by the philosophical dilemma that it has created.

Which is the real Thai Inter?

Thai Pan Asian

3.4
10

A strange, dark Southeast Asian restaurant that tries do too much—and accomplishes far too little

Thai

$19 *Upper Chapel Area*

2.0 /10
Food

5.0 /10
Atmosphere

7.0 /10
Attitude

2.7 /10
Value

Casual restaurant
Mon.-Thurs. 11:30am-3pm, 5pm-
10pm; Fri.-Sat. 11:30am-3pm,
5pm-10:30pm; Sun. noon-10pm.
Delivery. Outdoor dining. Vegetarian-friendly.

1150 Chapel St.
New Haven
(203) 624-9689

Bar Full
Credit Cards Visa, MC, AmEx
Reservations Accepted

Bravely offering a panoply of cuisine inspired by islands—and mainlands—all over the Pacific Rim, Thai Pan Asian has bitten off more than we can chew. A two-storied establishment with a strangely dark interior at the epicenter of the proliferation of Chapel Street Thai, this place combines Chinese, Thai, Japanese and, yes, even sushi, none of which is particularly inspiring. If you find yourself eating here, Thai is probably the best bet, although you may be frustrated to know that just a few paces in any direction are Thai restaurants that know how to stick to their knitting.

The inexpensive brunch buffet is to be avoided. It's a selection of some of the less interesting dishes on the menu, sitting out for a while and taking in some air. Every now and then we give it another chance and try it again, and every single time, the buffet is just as bad. Under-flavored dishes. Greasy dishes. Soggy dishes. Bland soups. Though it's a good deal in terms of amount of food, there are better Thai lunch specials for similar prices nearby on Chapel Street—and elsewhere generally.

As for the menu, some dishes, like deep-fried frog with garlic sauce, pineapple chunks, and romaine lettuce, sound interesting but are over-ambitious. Would you eat deep-fried frog at a place that serves sushi? And other selections are simply less inspired versions of the same Thai classics served elsewhere. We do like the outdoor seating, in good weather. But perhaps Thai Pan Asian would do better to focus on a more unique theme—like reinventing itself as a hip Pacific Rim cocktail bar—rather than trying to do everything, food-wise, and falling short on all fronts.

Thai Taste

A popular restaurant in the thick of Chapel's Thai row whose only advantage is its old beer-hall space

Thai $**21**   *Upper Chapel Area*

3.7 /10   **9.0** /10   **7.0** /10   **5.0** /10
Food   *Atmosphere*   *Attitude*   *Value*

Casual restaurant   1151 Chapel St.   **Bar** Full
Mon.-Thurs. 11:30am-3pm, 5pm-   New Haven   **Credit Cards** Visa and MC
10pm; Fri.-Sat. 11:30am-10:30pm; (203) 776-9802   **Reservations** Accepted
Sun. noon-10pm. *Vegetarian-friendly.*

This subterranean restaurant on Chapel Street is perhaps the best-known of the parade of options for Thai food in this part of town. It is, however, the only such place where you will be able to sit in a booth. Located in the basement of the Hotel Duncan, Thai Taste has décor that feels like an old-school bar—in fact, it is one, occupying a space that used to be a German beer hall called Old Heidelberg. It's rather dark and now well worn, with graftings of Thai paraphernalia, all presided over by framed photographs of the Thai royal family, which proudly take their places in the entrance and foyer. One unsettling aspect of this restaurant's location is the fishbowl effect of windows at knee height to passing foot traffic; on the other hand, this may be a boon to potential customers who have the opportunity to see for themselves just what existing patrons are eating.

The menu offers nothing more than standard fare, somewhat worse than the competition: multicolored curries and sautés featuring lemongrass, basil, peanut-based sauces, and fresh vegetables. Of these standards, it is the sauté style that Thai Taste does best. The "sizzling steak" comes from kitchen to table with memorable sound effects, emitting pungent aromas of ginger and garlic that will have fellow diners setting aside the printed menus and straining to peer over banquettes in search of inspiration. And then there's the chicken volcano, a marinated whole Cornish hen, flame-grilled and served with fish sauce, garlic, crushed coriander roots, crushed pepper seed, and sweet chili sauce. You certainly won't find it many other places in town.

But in general, the food here is subpar, even if the service is deferential and competent. Ultimately, it's just the unique atmosphere that distinguishes Thai Taste from the competition on Chapel Street.

Thai Taste Food Cart

5.5
/10

A food cart with three locations that are cheaper,
but often blander, than the competition

Thai   **$ 4**   *Broadway Area, Medical Area*

4.2 /10   **8.0** /10   **7.1** /10
Food   *Attitude*   *Value*

Take-out   Corner of York St.   *Bar* None
Mon.-Fri. 11am-2:30pm and   and Elm St.   *Credit Cards* None
5pm-8pm; closed Sat.-Sun.   New Haven   *Reservations* Not accepted
Vegetarian-friendly.   (203) 776-9802

Medical Area branch: Near York St. and
Mon.-Fri. 11am-2:30pm;   Cedar St., New Haven
closed Sat.-Sun.   (203) 776-9802

SOM branch: Near Prospect St. and
Mon.-Fri. 11am-2:30pm;   Sachem St., New Haven
closed Sat.-Sun.   (203) 776-9802

There are three locations of this portable version of the Chapel Street
Thai standby, although hours can be totally unpredictable. One parks
steps away from the Yale Medical School in the Hill district; a second is
on the corner of York and Elm; and yet another is inches from the
School of Management, near the hockey rink—a great place to pick up
some dinner on the way home if you're a Grad Ghetto resident. At
each cart, the Thai menu is limited to a few of the standard classics,
and combinations of two or three items are accommodated. In any
case, it's hard to spend more than about five dollars here, even with a
drink; in a city of low-priced food carts, this is one of the cheapest.

Even so, at the York and Elm branch, the unexciting versions of Thai
preparations have a hard time competing with the nearby Roomba
Burrito Cart, which does far more business even while charging a buck
or two more. The vegetable drunken noodle, one of the dishes that
cycles through the Thai Taste Food Cart, is made up of spicy noodles
sautéed with vegetables, purple basil, onion, and scallion. Chicken
massaman curry, with coconut milk, onion, peanut and potato, is a
popular choice, but it's a below-average version, with mealy potatoes.
Better might be the vegetable yellow curry, simmered with coconut
milk, pineapple, zucchini, onion, baby corn, and tofu. Barbecued garlic
chicken skewers are good, when they aren't overly dry. Pineapple fried
rice is our favorite thing here. Pad Thai is a staple.

Keep in mind that Thai Taste's fair-weather carts can be more elusive
than some others, and don't be shocked if they're not where you saw
them last.

TK's American Café

5.7/10

Sports, wings, sports, wings

Bar food   **$13**   *Theater District*

5.7/10   **6.0**/10   **5.0**/10   **5.8**/10
Food   *Atmosphere* *Attitude*   *Value*

Bar and grill
Sun.-Thurs. 11:30am-1am; Fri.-Sat.
11:30am-2am. Kitchen closes Sun.-
Thurs. 11:30pm; Fri.-Sat. midnight.
Outdoor dining.

285 George St.
New Haven
(203) 789-1776
www.tksamericancafe.com

Bar Full
Credit Cards Visa, MC, AmEx
Reservations Not accepted

Here's a true American joint, an extreme version of the sports bar for the truly devoted: 30 flavors of wings, 30 satellite TV screens, and generous happy hour specials on pitchers of beer. At TK's, sports bardom is taken to a level rarely approached elsewhere: even the cozy booths have their own little TV screens built into the wall; there are more screens on the outdoor deck, and there's one in each loo, too. But if TK's is a true homage to sports media, it's also a supremely local joint, far more town than gown, a place where it's easy to strike up an informed conversation about the fate of the XFL, the genius of Bill Belichick, or the complex psyche of Mark McGwire.

You've got to order wings when you're here: the spicier, the better. We recommend the basic hot buffalo, and honey barbecue, but why not come on "Wing Nite" and work your way down the list? So many, and so complex, are the wings specials that, after a couple of pitchers, you may chuck the menu altogether and take to ordering in pre-school parlance: "Wings. More wings."

If you're anxious about catching the NCAA playoffs (or mid-season games, for that matter), relax; your search has ended. TK's takes its mission seriously, so if there's a game on, it's going to be on here. (If you hate televised sports and yet you're here, perhaps you did something terrible in a past life and are now being punished.) Come the Super Bowl, the NCAA title game, or the Sox and the Yanks, don't expect to find a seat unless you arrive well before game time. But standing or sitting, the beer flows freely from taps all around the enormous, winding bar. And if it's just wings you crave, but not the sports-media frenzy, TK's does a sound take-out business as well.

Tony & Lucille's

7.0
/10

Sopranos kitsch in its finest Wooster Street form

Italian

$29 *Wooster Square Area*

5.8 /10
Food

9.0 /10
Atmosphere

8.0 /10
Attitude

6.2 /10
Value

Casual restaurant
Tues.-Fri. noon-3pm, 5pm-10pm;
Sat. 4pm-10:30pm; Sun. 1pm-9pm;
closed Mon. *Date-friendly. Outdoor dining. Vegetarian-friendly.*

150 Wooster St.
New Haven
(203) 787-1621

Bar Full
Credit Cards Visa, MC, AmEx
Reservations Accepted

We're well known among friends as Italian food snobs, so you'll have to take our advice about Italian restaurants with a grain of salt. Suffice it to say that, throughout this book, we tend to be critical of the culinary sensibilities of the Italian-American restaurants on offer in New Haven. But there's something about Tony & Lucille's that renders it immune from such dogged criticism, something to be said for the whole experience here that elevates it to another plane. Maybe it's the open arms of the wise and experienced waitstaff; maybe it's the warm feeling you get from beginning to end. The place has been around since 1953 (it first gained fame as a purveyor of calzones).

The best thing about Tony & Lucille's is that unlike much of the competition, the place has a lot of Sopranos-style kitschy charm. It's a dimly lit, fanciful room with canteens of Chianti hanging around, opera music piped in, and all the rest. Portions, needless to say, are mind-bogglingly enormous, and the food is true, competent, indigenous Italian-American. Fried calamari, clams casino, and fried mozzarella. Veal, eggplant, and chicken parmesan that come with another giant plate of somewhat overcooked spaghetti (share one between two people or you'll stumble home). There's even fettuccine Alfredo. There are a few more daring ventures, such as a grilled veal chop with a Portobello gorgonzola cream sauce, and chicken sorrentino, sautéed in butter, garlic, and white wine, layered with ham and eggplant, and topped with mozzarella. It's over the top.

And you can guess the rest. In any case, we recommend sticking with the true classics. You'll get what you came for: an Italian-American night out at one of the true survivors. A night from another era.

Town Pizza

3.4
10

A downtown pizza place serving up unremarkable
slices in an unremarkable cafeteria environment

Pizza, Light American   **$ 8**   *Arts District*

3.2 /10	**3.0** /10	**6.0** /10	**4.4** /10
Food	*Atmosphere*	*Attitude*	*Value*

Casual restaurant	25 Whitney Ave.	*Bar* Wine and beer only
Mon.-Sat. 11am-10pm; closed Sun.	New Haven	*Credit Cards* Visa and MC
Vegetarian-friendly.	(203) 865-6065	*Reservations* Not accepted

This pizzeria and Italian sub shop is quite well located on Whitney
Avenue. Perhaps that's why it still attracts such mobs at lunchtime, in
spite of the subpar food. Mobs come to gorge themselves on the very
standard all-you-can-eat soup-and-salad bar upstairs for just over $6.
But mediocre food is never a good deal, and this buffet is filled with
iceberg lettuce, standard cafeteria-style trimmings—tuna fish and so
on—and insipid soups such as pasta e fagioli drowned in a tomato
base. Many of the patrons also seem to be tackling implausibly filling
lunch plates with huge piles of french fries, mediocre mozzarella sticks,
and enormous iceberg-lettuce salads topped with, say, buffalo chicken.
Other options include veal parmigiana subs, and the various turkey and
chicken wraps—but they fare scarcely better, though the properly
toasted sub rolls are one high point.

  As per the name, there's also pizza, but it's problematic pizza. While
it's not so bad if it's very hot and you're very hungry, beware as your
slice cools, when the copious cheese topping forms a separate peel-off
layer, along with topping and grease, that quickly begins to congeal.
The sauce, meanwhile, is more like the thick red sauce you'd expect for
Italian-American pasta, not pizza. Among the available pizza options,
we recommend the sausage (which actually has hints of fennel) to
distract you from the taste of the pizza itself. At least the slices are big,
if you consider that a good thing in this case.

  Then there's the depressing, plasticky décor—Formica tables in
bright orange, and plastic booths in a slightly darker shade of the same
color, just different enough to clash, and the white walls with fake
bricks, which look yet another relic out of New Haven's checkered
urban-planning past.

Tre Scalini

7.7
/10

An above-average Italian-American restaurant with
a nice atmosphere and a lot of fanfare

Italian   **$32**   *Wooster Square Area*

7.5/10   **8.0**/10   **8.0**/10   **6.8**/10
Food   *Atmosphere*   *Attitude*   *Value*

Upmarket restaurant   100 Wooster St.   *Bar* Full
Mon.-Thurs. 11:30am-2:30pm,   New Haven   *Credit Cards* Visa, MC, AmEx
5pm-9:30pm; Fri. 11:30am-2:30pm, (203) 777-3373   *Reservations* Recommended
5pm-10:30pm; Sat. 5pm-10:30pm; www.trescalinirestaurant.com
Sun. 4pm-8pm. *Date-friendly. Good wine list. Vegetarian-friendly.*

Tre Scalini might be the best of New Haven's less-than-stellar Italian
restaurant lineup. Still, it might not be; L'Orcio, Adriana's, and the new
Avellino's make strong cases too. But Tre Scalini is good at what it does,
which is traditional Italian-American, even if it doesn't necessarily
deserve all the praise and accolades that are routinely showered upon it
by area media.

The memorable house special hot antipasto, an appetizer sampler
served only for parties of six or more, combines four of Tre Scalini's
hallmarks, including good pane cotto (escarole and beans sautéed with
peasant bread, topped with Parmigiano, and broiled) and appropriately
crispy fried calamari. Try also the melanzane alla Napoletana (eggplant
layered with fresh mozzarella, tomatoes, and herb olive oil). Mains are
more of a crapshoot; stick to the simpler sautéed veal dishes or a pasta
with some variety of red sauce. Cream sauces drift toward the
impossibly rich, whether over pasta or meat. Pasta, though, is
refreshingly not overcooked, particularly if you make a point of asking
that it be prepared al dente.

The two-tiered room is pleasant and elegant, if overdone. Happily,
it's not too bright, and service is friendly and conscientious. Prices are
also not unreasonably high, especially when compared with some of
the high-end Italian-American competition in New Haven.

However, if it's real, regional Italian cuisine you're after, you'll be
disappointed. For example, if you're an Italian speaker, you'll have to
search a bit to find any item with correct spelling, grammar, and
phrasing, anywhere on the entire menu (and every item is labeled in
Italian). It's silly to nitpick about spelling, but this should clue you in
somewhat to Tre Scalini's considerable distance from authenticity. But
Tre Scalini still stands as a temple to the Italian-American culinary
movement that dominated the latter twentieth century.

Trevethan's

The décor is understated; the adjectival menu of
mostly tasty Pacific Rim-influenced fusion is not

New American $**36**   *East Rock/Grad Ghetto*

8.3/10   **8.0**/10   **9.0**/10   **7.3**/10
Food   *Atmosphere*   *Attitude*   *Value*

Upmarket restaurant   758 State St.   ***Bar*** Full
Tues-Sat. 5:30pm-10pm;   New Haven   ***Credit Cards*** Visa, MC, AmEx
closed Sun.-Mon.   (203) 772-3415   ***Reservations*** Accepted
Date-friendly. Vegetarian-friendly.   www.trevethans.net

The menu at Trevethan's, an ambitious new restaurant on State Street,
reads like a satire of New American ingrediental snobbery. You may find
it difficult not to giggle when you come across such pomposities as
"lime-pressed sunchokes," "ash-brushed goat cheese," and "pea scoop
vegetables." We were fairly sure that, at 27 words, Trevethan's "Black
and White Sesame Seed-Crusted Sushi-Grade Tuna over wasabi-laced
whipped potatoes, orange-ginger spiked Asian greens and a five-
vegetable seaweed salad stuffed spring roll drizzled with soy-lime
glaze" would take the crown for longest dish name in New Haven.

Fairly sure, that is, until we noticed the "Yuca Fritter stacked with
warm chèvre infused with fresh herbs and grilled portabella shingles
topped with baby microgreens and drizzled with sweet basil oil and
aged balsamic glaze," which wins with 28. Portabella shingles? We're
food critics, and we don't understand half the menu.

But the good news is that most of it is tasty, especially dishes with
an Asian angle. We like the roasted chicken spring rolls, which are
crispy with an interesting sweetness. Salads, such as greens with
roasted pecans that have a hint of ginger, gorgonzola, and a mango
papaya vinaigrette, boast fresh ingredients and crisp flavors. Plantain-
crusted mahi mahi is excellent; we love the Thai "two-curry" coconut
sauce, whatever they mean by "two-curry." We are less convinced by
the salt-crusted grouper. Grouper can be a difficult fish to keep moist,
and here it's dry without enough flavor, although the passion fruit on
top is a good idea.

Décor is pleasant and simple almost to a fault, exhibiting a restraint
not seen on the menu. So whether or not you actually harbor a craving
for "crispy onion grass," "guava drops," or "baby drumstick squash,"
Trevethan's is an excellent addition to the restaurant scene.

Tropical Delights

A cheap neighborhood Jamaican take-out counter
with reliable stews and excellent beef patties

Jamaican $ **8**   *Westville*

7.8 /10   **6.0** /10   **8.7** /10
Food   *Attitude*   *Value*

Take-out   141 Fitch St.   *Bar* None
Mon.-Fri. 10am-9pm;   New Haven   *Credit Cards* None
closed Sat.-Sun.   (203) 389-5618   *Reservations* Not accepted

Perhaps because of its low-profile location—in the Beaver Hill Shopping
Center, a little row of stores on the corner of Fitch and Blake Streets—
this is probably the least known of New Haven's distinguished lineup of
Jamaican take-out places, even though it is fairly close to the Southern
campus and downtown Westville. Tropical Delights is nothing more
than a little storefront, and virtually everyone orders take-out, although
you can eat at a little counter if you can't wait to get home—which
might well be the case if you order one of the beef patties.

The staff is efficient but accommodating, in a neighborly sort of way.
The menu is extremely simple, which is a good thing—the matronly
chef in back cooks up an enormous pot of each dish in the little kitchen
in back each day, spooning out delicious, inexpensive portions until they
run out. The oxtail is tender and meaty, with an unusually high meat-
to-bones ratio. The sauce, which is helped along by a bit of additional
sauce, is dark and well reduced, with a nice sheen. Jerk chicken, one of
the most popular choices, is great but tends to run out unless you get
there early. Curry goat, another one of our Jamaican favorites, is fully
flavored but a bit dry, with less sauce than we would've liked; the only
other disappointment has been the leathery plantains (unless you
happen to catch them straight out of the fryer).

Rice and peas (that's Jamaican for red kidney beans) are top-notch,
as is the sweet cabbage. The beef patties, meanwhile, may be the best
in town; their rich, wonderfully seasoned, and gently spicy filling is soft,
almost like a paste, and it pairs absolutely deliciously with the flaky
yellow crust. It's the ultimate Caribbean comfort food.

Uncle Willie's BBQ

7.0
10

An ambitious and much-needed addition to the area ribs and pulled-pork scene

Southern $**16**   *Orange*

6.9 /10   **7.0** /10   **8.0** /10   **7.1** /10
Food   *Atmosphere*   *Attitude*   *Value*

Casual restaurant   89 Boston Post Rd.   *Bar* BYO
Sun.-Thurs. 8am-9pm, Fri.-Sat. Orange   *Credit Cards* Visa and MC
8am-9:30pm or later, depending (203) 799-0880   *Reservations* Not accepted
on the crowd. *Breakfast.*

A new barbecue place is always an exciting thing—especially now. Barbecue is America's greatest original culinary tradition, but a gaping hole had been left on the New Haven-area barbecue scene after Jarman's and Joe Grate's both, sadly, closed. Actually, Uncle Willie's "Real Down Home Pit BBQ"—that's the full name—isn't strictly new. It's a longstanding Waterbury institution that has entered our jurisdiction with a new Orange branch, a big, open room with bright yellow walls decked out with Americana and lined with basic plastic diner-style booths.

The St. Louis pork ribs are certainly more authentic than anything else in the area. The outside of the meat is as it should be: deeply imparted with smoke flavors and spices from an intense rub. Beneath that, some bites are magically tender, laced with delicious pockets of fat; but some bites aren't.

Now, some aficionados swear that truly great barbecue needs no sauce, but in this case, it's an absolute necessity (we prefer the hot version to the sweet, but ask for both). Not only is Uncle Willie's barbecue sauce quite good, it also adds a needed dose of salt and moisture to the meat; this is especially true for the pulled pork, some of whose large chunks are unusually lean and slightly dry. Nonetheless, the overall effect really hits the spot.

By no means does the menu end with the BBQ, although that's why we go to Uncle Willie's. There's also proper Southern breakfast (cornmeal cakes, grits, and biscuits and gravy are among the lineup), which is a rare treat in the area; plus some highly touted fried chicken, a long list of burgers and dogs, and other classics like smothered pork chops, meatloaf, and fried fish. Ambitious, perhaps, but we salute this restaurant's admirable effort to bring back the barbecue. Thanks, Uncle Willie.

Union League Café

The only proper way to dine, *n'est-ce pas?*

French $46   *Theater District*

9.3 /10
Food

9.0 /10
Atmosphere

9.0 /10
Attitude

7.9 /10
Value

Upmarket restaurant
Mon.-Thurs. 11:30am-2:30pm,
5:30pm-9:30pm; Fri. 11:30am-
2:30pm, 5:30pm-10pm; Sat.
5:30pm-10pm; closed Sun. *Date-friendly. Good wine list.*

1032 Chapel St.
New Haven
(203) 562-4299
www.unionleaguecafe.com

Bar Full
Credit Cards Visa, MC, AmEx
Reservations Essential

In many smaller American cities, for many years, the best meal in town—reliably, perennially—has been found at the fancy French place. Orthodoxy deems it the only proper choice. Happily, time and urban renewal have eroded that belief in New Haven. But Union League Café, housed in the Sherman Building—which has long served as an elite epicenter of local WASP culture—still fulfills its duties with grace. Its dining room boasts stately, generous proportions and wood paneling that gleams in buttery yellow light, making everything—and everyone—a little more lovely. We like it most in winter, when a well-tended fireplace roars.

Union League (#6 in *The Menu* for food, #3 overall) is always full of hotshot academics, visiting dignitaries, and perhaps the odd undergraduate with parents (and parents' wallet) in tow. Service can be slightly stuffy, but it's rarely pretentious. Neither is the menu of brasserie dishes, though they are tricked out with the occasional nouvelle or haute ingredient. You'll find grapefruit marmalade, truffle butter, and cucumber gazpacho elbowing their way in among such brasserie classics as entrecôte au poivre and pommes Anna.

Such preparations are reliably correct, as they might say in France, and equally reliable are the clean, fresh oysters. Even better is tender duck confit, sandwiched between pleasingly crispy potato slices, with porcini mushrooms adding an earthy note, and watercress salad bearing a delightful emulsified vinaigrette. Union League also has a way with game meats like wonderfully rare venison. Competent but not as impressive, recently, have been a slightly dry roasted pheasant and wild striped bass.

Prices are high but completely reasonable, especially at lunch. There is almost nowhere else in town where you can eat this consistently well—even if this grande dame no longer has the rest of the town flailing in her wake.

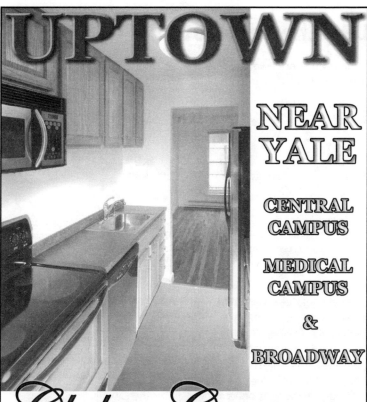

USS Chowder Pot III

5.9
10

It may win every award under the sun, but it's just a
suburban family chain with okay seafood

Seafood $ **30**   *Branford*

5.3 /10   **7.0** /10   **6.0** /10   **4.9** /10
Food   *Atmosphere*   *Attitude*   *Value*

Casual restaurant   560 East Main St.   *Bar* Full
Mon.-Thurs. 11:30am-9pm;   Branford   *Credit Cards* Visa, MC, AmEx
Fri.-Sat. 11:30am-10pm;   (203) 481-2356   *Reservations* Not accepted
Sun. noon-8pm. *Outdoor dining.* www.chowderpotiii.com

"Best Seafood - Statewide Runner-up (Connecticut Magazine, 2003).
Best Seafood - New Haven County (Connecticut Magazine, 2003). Best
Seafood - Statewide (Connecticut Magazine, 2002). Best Seafood -
Statewide Runner-up (Connecticut Magazine, 2001). Best Seafood -
New Haven County 1994, 1995, 1996, 1997, 1999, 2000. Best Happy
Hour 1998 (New Haven Advocate Reader's Choice). Best Rhode Island
Chowder (Water's Edge Chowder Festival)."

These are the sorts of accolades that greet you when you land on
the Web Site for USS Chowder Pot III. It's funny that the perennial
winners of such accolades are not just bland and unremarkable, but
always so hopelessly *predictable*. Is this what most of upper-middle-
class Connecticut really wants? Is everyone that uninterested in
something a bit more fresh and local?

At the Chowder Pot, just like at Connecticut Magazine darlings like
China Pavilion in Orange, you'll find everything you'd expect from a
suburban family restaurant, and little more. It's immensely popular with
families, so prime time might mean a wait (but it's near Su Casa, a
comparably suburban Mexican restaurant with comparable weekend
queues—you can hedge your bets and play the waits against each
other). The marine theme is overwhelming. Boat paraphernalia hanging
from the rafters. Nets, fish, glass bottles everywhere. You're almost
afraid of drowning. There's a bar that actually swings into action if you
catch it at the right time—they even do karaoke.

And then there's the seafood. Steamed lobster is a good way to go,
a bit dear, but that's true most everywhere. The chowder itself is
appropriately creamy in the New England style. But the fish here is
nothing more than standard. Not that you'd expect much more. While
the Chowder Pot is no mystery, the real mystery is this: Who is really
voting in these Connecticut Magazine polls?

Villa Del Sol

5.9
___
10

An often-empty Mexican restaurant that isn't interesting enough to justify the high prices

Tex-Mex $**27** *Theater District*

6.2/10   **5.5**/10   **5.0**/10   **5.1**/10
Food   *Atmosphere*   *Attitude*   *Value*

Upmarket restaurant   236 Crown St.   ***Bar*** Full
Daily 11:30am-11pm.   New Haven   ***Credit Cards*** Visa, MC, AmEx
                           (203) 785-0674   ***Reservations*** Accepted

Part of a four-restaurant chain, Villa del Sol is one of the true mysteries of the New Haven dining scene. The downtown location couldn't be more choice: it's right at the intersection of Crown and Chapel streets. And yet, evening after evening, the restaurant sits largely empty, the painted suns on the backs of its wooden chairs smiling sadly at nobody, and its lonely piñatas hanging from the ceiling in idle fiesta, while its staff watches TV, or looks forlornly out the windows at the nonstop bustle of one of New Haven's busiest street corners.

Where are all the people?

We think the problem is that neither the food nor the atmosphere can possibly justify the jarringly high prices that reflect the neighborhood's astronomical rent. New Haven has never been a hotbed of authentic Mexican food, and Villa del Sol's menu is mostly just competent Tex-Mex. Decent enchiladas, for instance, sport a good red sauce and soft, tamale-like corn tortillas. We like the chicken enchilada with green sauce, but the sauce is too sparse on the mole version. Cheese fillings are too stringy; stick to moist chicken or beef. Guacamole is expensive and undersalted. A simple chicken soup with lime, however, is comforting and surprisingly cheap.

The dinner menu does conceal some surprises. Puerco a la pipian (chunks of pork in pumpkin-seed sauce) has a definite tang, but the meat is dry; even such regional specialties aren't as interesting or flavorful as they promise to be. Best are the fresh salsas and the extraordinary homemade hot sauce. But condiments only go so far at a restaurant with neither notable food nor an exciting atmosphere. At this price point, it's not clear where this one fits into the downtown-dining equation.

Vito's Deli

7.1
/10

A quick downtown lunch option with a great talent for fresh, well-filled sandwiches

Light American $ **6**   *Ninth Square*

7.2 /10   **7.0** /10   **9.2** /10
Food   *Attitude*   *Value*

Take-out   35 Center St.   *Bar* None
Mon.-Fri. 6am-4:30pm;   New Haven   *Credit Cards* None
closed Sat.-Sun. *Breakfast.* (203) 624-1533   *Reservations* Not accepted

Vito's Deli takes sandwiches seriously. This impeccable deli has been a boon to the downtown lunch crowd for decades, serving up enormous sandwiches at very reasonable prices. It's a reminder that not all downtown New Haven lunch spots are created equal, and the same sum in the same four-block radius can be spent very wisely or very poorly. At Vito's, an average appetite could be sated with half a sandwich; split one with a friend and lunch comes in at under $3. At these prices, you can surely spring for a side of cole slaw, a slice of pie, or some old-fashioned rice pudding. The friendly cashier will assure that you really do need dessert.

There is a definite method to ordering at Vito's. Approach the sandwich counter with deference, and if there's a line, respect it. The masters behind the counter will ask you for your order only when they are ready to take it, and you will be expected to specify one of six kinds of bread. The standard sub roll is adequate; it's fresh, but it's nothing special. Focus on what's in the middle. Hot subs are satisfying, and cold subs are truly exemplary.

You can either name your toppings a la carte, or call one of the suggested combos. The "Vito's Combo" is a paragon of cold-cut decadence: ham, pastrami, bologna, and salami with just enough heat to add brightness. Fillings are purposefully layered, and if your order includes American cheese, you'll find it as the creamy core of a well-structured sandwich. For a more exciting sandwich, try one of the more flavorful cheeses. The overall effect is fresh and tasty—thank you, Vito.

Viva Zapata

3.2
10

A dark, loud, raucous college bar that's fine as long as you avoid the "Mexican" "food"

Tex-Mex, Bar food $18 *Upper Chapel Area*

1.2/10   **7.0**/10   **4.0**/10   **2.5**/10
Food   *Atmosphere*   *Attitude*   *Value*

Bar and grill   161 Park St.   *Bar* Full
Mon.-Tues. 4pm-1am; Wed.-Thurs   New Haven   *Credit Cards* Visa, MC, AmEx
11:30am-1am; Fri.-Sat. 11:30am-   (203) 562-2499   *Reservations* Accepted
2am; Sun noon-1am. Kitchen closes
at midnight. Appetizers only 11pm-midnight.

Viva Zapata fills nightly with itinerant bands of revelers whose primary project is to get completely and utterly soused. The young patrons, many from the suburbs, come to pound so-so margaritas, perhaps to munch on Tex-Mex food, certainly to check each other out with increasingly blurry admiration—and to display their plumage with decreasing selectivity. It's a strange town-gown mix, made stranger by the fact that town and gown seem to remain segmented once inside. (Once we're all drunk, why can't we be friends?)

We doubt that many of them come for the food, which reminds us of Old El Paso microwave TV dinners with the instructions followed haphazardly. It all begins with stale-tasting tortilla chips and awful salsa, and goes downhill from there. This is the worst Mexican food in the city. It's even worse than El Amigo Felix, and El Amigo Felix is *bad*. In fact, Viva Zapata takes the crown, this year, of lowest food rating in the entire book.

Viva's does have a certain dusty-cantina sort of charm, especially in the main back room, which has a few dimly lit, appealing little nooks. There's Tex-Mex paraphernalia hanging here and there. It's fake, but it's good fake. Viva's is a fun place to slurp down some tequila in any of its incarnations; we prefer to do so on a weeknight, when you can focus on the aromas of agave cactus, instead of cologne. Ultimately, Viva's fulfills its local role as a fratty scene. The drinks flow freely and the customers are happy. Beware the resulting condition of the bathroom floor. As a bar, the place meets its mandate. For a dining experience, run far, far away.

Warong Selera

7.2
10

A virtually unknown Malaysian strip-mall joint with tasty, interesting food that's best taken out

Malaysian $**11**   *West Haven*

7.9/10   **5.5**/10   **8.0**/10   **8.1**/10
Food   *Atmosphere*   *Attitude*   *Value*

Counter service   702B Boston Post Rd.   *Bar* None
Mon.-Thurs. 11:30am-10pm; Fri.   West Haven   *Credit Cards* None
2:30pm-10pm; Sat. 11:30am-10pm; (203) 937-0614   *Reservations* Accepted
closed Sun. *Vegetarian-friendly.* www.warongselera.com

We were delighted to stumble upon this little West Haven gem. In Malay, "Warong" means an outdoor food stall, a place that is known for good, cheap food, usually served to go. Although it's not outdoors, this is a pretty apt description of Warong Selera, which is the latest of a surprising number of Malaysian restaurants in New Haven and its suburbs.

As the place is geared more toward taking out than eating in, it does not have much in the way of atmosphere. It feels something like an abandoned basement rec room, with a large, outdated stereo system and 1980s TV dominating the middle of the bright white room. The walls are adorned with tourism posters, and the piles of brochures about the country's regions make the place seem more like an outpost of a Malaysian airline than a restaurant.

The menu offers a wide variety of noodle and rice dishes in combinations with beef, chicken, seafood, shrimp, and vegetables as well as a smaller number of chef's specials. As an appetizer, roti canai—fried bread served with curry gravy—is slightly greasy but flaky and delicious. Even better is the mee bandung with chicken, a satisfyingly rich and sweet broth with noodles, tofu, egg, and Chinese greens that add a welcome crunch. Masak pedas—beef cooked with fried potato and onions—is less successful. While shrimp paste adds an interesting, unfamiliar flavor and the potato has a delightful texture, the beef itself is tasteless and tough to the point of unpleasantness. Don't miss the chance to sample the Indonesian boxed drinks, like the very sweet guava juice, or jasmine iced tea. The restaurant has also been experimenting with Saturday tasting brunches that are said to bring in members of the Malaysian community from as far away as Boston.
–Jamie Kaiser

Wentworth's

8.1
10

A little ice cream destination justly famous not just in Hamden, but all over Connecticut

Sweets   *Hamden*

8.1 /10
Food

8.0 /10
Attitude

Take-out   3697 Whitney Ave.   *Bar* None
Daily noon-9pm. *Outdoor dining.*   Hamden   *Credit Cards* None
Vegetarian-friendly.   (203) 281-7429   *Reservations* Not accepted

Summer days call for ice cream, and the ice cream you dream of is at Wentworth's. It's fresh, creamy and delicious, in a rainbow of flavors for every taste—there's even a flavor for dogs. The folks at Wentworth's understand that ice cream is not just dessert. It helps that we New Englanders are the nation's most enthusiastic, and exacting, ice cream eaters, eating more of the stuff per capita do the folks than any other region in the nation, and we lay claim to some of the best artisanal brands—to wit, Steve Herrell of Northampton, Massachusetts (who sold his first name and then opened another ice cream chain under his last), and of course, the legendary Vermonters, Messrs. Ben and Jerry.

Wentworth's does justice to its place among such company. The ice cream is just shy of too creamy, a delicate alchemy that should not be under-appreciated, because the result is a judicious combination of decadence and subtlety which will allow you to contemplate the blessings of dairy and taste the careful flavorings. We're ice cream purists when sampling high-quality versions, and so our favorite here is vanilla, but there are plenty of others to choose from. If you like your ice cream dressed up, consider one of the legendary sundaes, adorned with chocolate fudge, whipped cream, and a lot more. The shop also offers frozen yogurt, brownies, cookies, and coffee.

The charm of Wentworth's goes beyond the ice cream itself to the cute, shady wrap-around porch that encircles the building, and accommodation for the line which inevitably forms during peak hours. It is clear that the rest of southeastern Connecticut likes Wentworth's as much as we do.

The Whole Enchilada

A little Tex-Mex spot with satisfying—if sometimes bland and pricey—burritos, soups, and salads

Tex-Mex $ 8   *Arts District*

5.7 /10   **4.0** /10   **6.0** /10   **5.8** /10
Food   *Atmosphere*   *Attitude*   *Value*

Counter service   21 Whitney Ave.   *Bar* BYO
Mon.-Sat. 11:30am-8pm; closed   New Haven   *Credit Cards* None
Sun. *Vegetarian-friendly.*   (203) 772-4454   *Reservations* Not accepted

The Whole Enchilada is a little Tex-Mex counter tucked into a storefront next to Anna Liffey's on Whitney Avenue. The place specializes in take-out, but there are also a few little tables and chairs in the bright room, which is painted with scenes from rural Mexico but sullied by institutional touches, like massive drink refrigerators.

The service is amazingly quick—you're scarcely done paying before you're handed a hot burrito wrapped in foil. Watch the preparation behind the counter, which reveals impressive burrito dexterity. And don't forget to take some of the hot sauce that comes out of metal spouts built into the cafeteria-style garbage can-cum-condiment station. These sauces pep up the flavors; we prefer the green version, though, as the red is quite vinegary.

The burritos are on the expensive side, and their caliber varies. The original chicken and beef burritos are somewhat dry and boring, and the copious quantities of rice and beans inside further dilute the taste. The flour tortillas, though, have a great texture and a pleasant sweetness, and make a good medium for the moist chicken curry burrito, our favorite choice here; the addition of curry sauce to a mélange of carb-loaded ingredients is a winning idea. Add some of the hot sauce and you've definitely amassed something worth your while. Along the same nontraditional lines, we also like the buffalo chicken burrito, with buffalo sauce and blue cheese dressing.

A rotating selection of soups is reliably good and fresh, especially the various versions of chili and split pea soups, though they, like the burritos, are overpriced. In short, the Whole Enchilada is an okay choice for a quick take-out carb/protein fix, especially at lunch, but the value proposition is not what it might be.

Wild Ginger

8.3
/10

Nobu-meets-the-suburbs Japanese fusion tucked
into a strip mall, with top-notch specialty sushi

Japanese $**33**   *Orange*

8.7 /10   **7.5** /10   **8.0** /10   **7.5** /10
Food   *Atmosphere*   *Attitude*   *Value*

Upmarket restaurant   111 Boston Post Rd.   *Bar* Full
Mon.-Thurs. 11:45am-3pm,   Orange   *Credit Cards* Visa, MC, AmEx
5pm-10pm; Fri. 11:45am-3pm, (203) 799-8887   *Reservations* Accepted
5pm-11pm; Sat. noon-11pm;   www.wildgingerrestaurant.com
Sun. noon-10pm.

Although you may not know it from outside the building, Wild Ginger
is not just another lackluster restaurant of the suburban Asian strip-mall
variety. Inside, the dining room is well-appointed, with a sushi bar in
view upon arrival—always a good sign. Window coverings are designed
to obstruct the view of cars passing by on the highway a few yards
away. The menu offers a range of cooked mains, most of which are a
list of Japanese and New American classics, but there's also a $35-and-
up omakase (tasting menu) that's far more interesting. In addition to
sushi and sashimi for purists, Wild Ginger puts on a show for those
who love fusion, employing yuzu sauces, signature rolls, and other
Nobu-esque accoutrements. These work, but we suspect that the best
fish is reserved for more straightforward sushi preparations.

   Upon arrival, ask at the sushi bar for the best indication of what's
freshest and best. On a recent visit, toro (fatty tuna) was the
recommendation, and indeed, what arrived at our table had all in
paroxyms of pleasure. At its best, the fish here is in East's league, some
of the best in southern Connecticut. Uni (sea urchin), when available, is
excellent, with exquisite sweetness and an unctuous, custardy texture.
When uni is bad, it's very very bad, and so it's wonderful to find a place
where it's reliably good enough to be ordered routinely. Though at one
visit seared tuna was unimpressive, Wild Ginger definitely has a way
with yellowtail. What's more, with the breadth and diversity of the
menu, it's a precious find for sushi-lovers who dine with more timid
eaters. Here, those folks can have their chicken breast and eat it too,
while you dine on bounty of vigorous negotiation by Wild Ginger's
fanatical fish buyer.

Willoughby's

A New Haven classic for quality coffee drinks (and all the trimmings) in a welcoming, light-filled room

Baked goods   *Financial District*

8.0/10   **9.0**/10
Atmosphere   *Attitude*

Café   258 Church St.   *Bar* None
Mon.-Sat. 7am-7pm;   New Haven   *Credit Cards* Visa and MC
Sun. 8am-6pm.   (203) 777-7400   *Reservations* Not accepted
Breakfast. Outdoor dining. Vegetarian-friendly.

The original Chapel Street branch of the beloved Willoughby's, known and loved for its rich aromas and quirky baristas, closed in 2003, but its more dapper Grove Street cousin remains as perky as ever, and for that we're deeply thankful.

Willoughby's, a New Haven native since 1985, has long been known for its excellent coffee, and that coffee is what draws the crowds. The cafe prides itself in roasting top-quality Arabica beans, resulting in a dark roast that's one of the tastiest in New Haven. Coffee snobs will fare well here: Willoughby's is the best place in town to buy beans for your French press, bar none. The store also sells baked goods that appeal to the average sweet tooth.

Willoughby's location charms, too. It's nestled at the intersection of Church and Grove, where Church becomes Whitney; this is a prime corner on the edge of the Yale campus. Picture windows provide natural light to a half-dozen tables, and several more appear outside when the weather turns warm. The staff is remarkably warm and direct.

There are also two or three tables outside in good weather, and happily, the sidewalk still plays host to a hyper-hip alterna-sloucher scene just outside the front door, a loyal group that migrated here after the old York Street Willoughby's (another dearly departed branch) turned into "Koffee Too?" in 2001. The ambience inside is hip in a more yuppie way than is the punk scene outside: myriad teas and gourmet café snacks complement the trademark coffee. And for those who don't wish to linger, it can also serve as a quick walk-in, walk-out place, especially convenient on the way from the Grad Ghetto to Yale.

Woodland Coffee and Tea

5.8
10

A coffeeshop with a pleasant atmosphere, decent veggie-oriented sandwiches, and a bad attitude

Light American, Baked goods $ 8   *Ninth Square*

5.3 /10   **8.0** /10   **2.0** /10   **6.6** /10
Food   *Atmosphere*   *Attitude*   *Value*

Café   91 Orange St.   *Bar* None
Mon.-Fri. 7am-6pm;   New Haven   *Credit Cards* Visa, MC, AmEx
Sat. 8:30am-5pm;   (203) 773-1144   *Reservations* Not accepted
closed Sun.   www.woodlandcoffee.com
Vegetarian-friendly. Wireless Internet.

Woodland Coffee and Tea, along a gentrifying (okay, gentrified) stretch of Orange Street down around Ninth Square, has an attractive look. The sign is well-designed; the walls are warm and yellow; there's great coffee-and-tea-themed wall art, and relaxing music. Shiny blond wood gives the place a newish feel, but it doesn't take away from the laid-back vibe. Two comfy chairs, free Internet access, lots of flavored lattes, and an exotic tea selection all make for a cutting-edge study space for students.

Woodland also has a short, focused selection of light fare. The breakfast menu boasts of organic eggs and healthy-sounding cereals, while the lunch menu lists three salads and six sandwiches (two and four of which, respectively, are vegetarian). Ingredients are generally pretty typical for a modern American lunch joint—gorgonzola, mesclun greens, cranberries, and the like. The problem with the panini is that they don't hold together well; the cheese often isn't melted enough and slips out of the sandwich. At one point, we ordered a sandwich that was supposed to contain roasted red peppers, mozzarella, pesto, red onion, and tomatoes; it arrived filled only with the first three ingredients, with no sign of the latter two.

Such sloppy preparation seems part of a larger attitude problem at Woodland: the service ranges from indifferent to downright rude. At one point we were even sternly upbraided for writing in our notebooks while glancing up at the menu. "You need permission to do that," we were told, "because you could be a competitor. Without permission, it's illegal." We'd go toe to toe with him in court on that in any U.S. jurisdiction. But may we suggest that before getting too paranoid about having their closely guarded panini secrets stolen, Woodland Coffee and Tea should bone up a bit on their sandwich-making.

Xando Cosí

Pizzeria, coffeeshop, sandwich shop, bar: mediocre, mediocre, mediocre, mediocre

Light American, Pizza, Baked goods **$15** *Broadway Area*

4.9 /10
Food

7.0 /10
Atmosphere

2.0 /10
Attitude

5.0 /10
Value

Casual restaurant
Mon.-Thurs. 8am-1am; Fri.-Sat.
11am-2am; Sun. 9am-1am.
Kitchen closes 1 hr. earlier.
Breakfast. Outdoor dining. Vegetarian-friendly.

338 Elm St.
New Haven
(203) 495-9869
www.getcosi.com

Bar Full
Credit Cards Visa, MC, AmEx
Reservations Not accepted

Once upon a time, this was a firehouse. Then it was the much-loved Fitzwilly's restaurant. In 1995, it became the Xando coffeeshop and bar, boasting Starbucks knockoff drinks, sidewalk seating and an indoors with the second-most square-footage of any coffeeshop in America. In 1999, they launched a pizza business, and apparently lured away some Pepe's staff (though you wouldn't have known it from the taste).

Nowadays, because of the marriage of the Xando coffeeshop to the Cosí chain, it's also a high-priced sandwich shop known for its warm and alluring flatbread. It's the latest folly in a long succession of bizarre juxtapositions and sorry indecision. The pizzas, now made from Cosí's signature flatbread, are stranger than ever; the innovation is no improvement.

But that's not all: Xando Cosí, as it's now called, is also a trying-to-be-hip nightspot, with two floors of awkward, multipurpose space illuminated by dim, trendy lighting; under-the-staircase nooks and crannies for furtive flirting; and a small bar open until 1am, although the bartender there always seems surprised to actually be serving patrons.

But you want a chilled-out coffee shop to be a chilled-out coffee shop, not a contrived-hip pizzeria. And, especially in New Haven, you want a pizzeria to be dedicated to slinging pies, not trying to hawk vodka-tonics on the one hand and double-skinny-lattes on the other. But what you *really* don't want is for your evening out at a local bar to be overrun by indifferent waiters trying to get drinks to late-nighters with the munchies and stepping over caffeine-wired zombies toting organic chemistry textbooks, all amidst fonts and interior decorating that scream Palo Alto, 1999. And so, as with the restaurant's name itself—an inane fusion of the two independently amusing names of its joint venturers—Xando Cosí is less than the sum of its parts.

Yalie's Pizza

A hole-in-the-wall reliable for its below-average
slices, worse subs, and extended hours

Pizza, Italian   **$ 6**   *Upper Chapel Area*

3.6 /10   **4.0** /10   **5.1** /10
Food   *Attitude*   *Value*

Take-out   166 York St.   *Bar* None
Sun.-Wed. 10am-1am; Thurs.   New Haven   *Credit Cards* Visa and MC
10am-2am; Fri.-Sat. 10am-3am (203) 772-2200 *Reservations* Not accepted
Delivery. Vegetarian-friendly. www.campusfood.com

This semi-subterranean take-out pizza place satisfies the nearby art and
architecture students with cheap and quick slices into the wee hours.
It's easier to spot the place by the sign than the storefront, which is
somewhat recessed from York Street. The inside of Yalie's is nothing
more than a walk-in counter, and there is no eat-in operation to speak
of. It's a white stand-up room decked out with the occasional ratty
poster and a soda machine; in fact, the atmosphere is so bad that it's
depressing even to have to stand in the room while your slice is heated.

If you're starving and it's 3am, all slice joints can seem much the
same, but trust us, they're not. The pizza here is loosely New York-style,
but below average, with poor execution; it's sometimes only moderately
heated, there's too much greasy cheese, and the sauce has little taste.
At least the crust is appropriately crispy—but that's about it. Est Est Est,
a chief competitor nearby, easily beats Yalie's on the pizza merits, and
stays open as late as Yalie's too (3am on weekends—certainly a boon to
students). So why eat this, in a town with so much good pizza?

There are some other options on the Yalie's menu, but we don't
recommend them. The menu is ambitious enough to include a "spinach
and sun-dried tomato chicken" wrap with mushrooms and balsamic
vinegar, and an eggplant parmigiana sandwich that, at one visit, was so
tough it was unchewable— perhaps the worst we've ever tasted.
There's pasta with clams on the menu, and even fish and chips. But you
should know better than that. If, for whatever reason, you must come
here, we advise you to stick to the mediocre pizza.

The Next New Restaurant

What will it be? You might miss the scoop if you
don't keep up with www.newhavenmenu.com.

?
___
10

New Ugandan   **$?**   *Theater District*

? /10   **?** /10   **?** /10   **?** /10
Food   *Atmosphere*   *Attitude*   *Value*

Upmarket restaurant   PO Box 204205,   *Bar* Full
Daily 24 hrs.   New Haven, 06520   *Credit Cards* Visa, MC, AmEx
Date-friendly. Good wine list. (203) 286-1775   *Reservations* Essential
Outdoor dining. Vegetarian-friendly. www.newhavenmenu.com
You can't afford to miss out.

The Menu's new, redesigned web site at **www.newhavenmenu.com**
doesn't just give you access to **1,000-word, longer-format reviews** of
many of the top restaurants in New Haven, with more detailed
descriptions of the ups and downs of their latest menus.

It doesn't just offer you a chance to buy discounted books online,
direct from the publisher.

And it doesn't just feature a **relentlessly opinionated discussion
board** where you can discuss new restaurants or old classics with your
fellow readers, take part in the **great pizza debate**, exchange horror
stories of New Haven meals gone wrong, or **start a flame war with
the authors**—Robin and Clare participate in the online discussion, and
they're ready for you.

No, that's not all. What's perhaps most useful of all is that we'll also
be posting **free online reviews of new restaurants** as they open, and
keeping you abreast of all new developments with our **New Haven-
area restaurant news blog**, so you and your copy of *The Menu* will
never be out of date.

We'll see you there.

Yankee Doodle

8.0
10

American food in all its short-order, butter-laden glory, now and forever: thank you, Yankee Doodle

Short-order American   **$ 6**   *Broadway Area*

8.2/10   **7.5**/10   **8.0**/10   **9.9**/10
Food   *Atmosphere*   *Attitude*   *Value*

Diner   260 Elm St.   *Bar* None
Mon.-Sat. 6am-3:30pm; Sun. 7am-   New Haven   *Credit Cards* None
3.30pm during the school year.   (203) 865-1074   *Reservations* Not accepted
Closed Sun. in summer. *Breakfast.*   www.thedoodle.com

Representing New Haven at its historic best, Yankee Doodle is your short-order dream come true. It's worth the wait in line for a coveted seat at the narrow counter in this classic greasy spoon—which, given the turnover, will often be shorter than you think. At "the Doodle," you can experience a true piece of fast-disappearing Americana, a place where absolutely everything is slathered in butter and tossed on the grill.

That may sound dubious, but trust us: it's pure genius, and the result is tastier than what you get at many of New Haven's wannabe-genteel sit-down restaurants. The cheeseburgers are spectacular: small, tender slabs of meat melt in your mouth between buttered, grilled, old-school hamburger buns and American cheese; order regular, not barbecue, for the unadulterated taste experience. The burgers are small, so even those with dainty appetites will probably want two. We don't quite get it, but the pigs in blankets (hot dogs wrapped in bacon and grilled) have a serious following. The bacon, egg, and cheese sandwich on a roll is a classic breakfast combination that's quite therapeutic as a hangover remedy, but good any time of day. The egg is broken at just the right time, creating the ideal texture. Thank God for small mercies. This sandwich might even be cited by carnivores as proof, once and for all, that, with apologies to dieticians and vegetarians everywhere, animal fat is the key to human happiness.

With its superlative comfort food, the Doodle might make our short list of last meals before execution (or expedite our natural demise). And speaking of deadly encounters with grilled goodness, don't call it quits before you've tried one of Yankee Doodle's grilled doughnuts (yes, they're buttered too), the first and only way to actually improve on this traditional fried-dough staple.

Yorkside Pizza

5.9
10

A casual, convenient joint known for milkshakes
and late hours—but not the grease-loaded pizza

Pizza, Light American, Greek   **$14**   *Broadway Area*

5.9/10
Food

5.5/10
Atmosphere

7.0/10
Attitude

5.9/10
Value

Casual restaurant
Sun.-Thurs. 11am-1am;
Fri.-Sat. 11am-2am.
Outdoor dining. Vegetarian-friendly.

288 York St.
New Haven
(203) 787-7471

Bar Wine and beer only
Credit Cards Visa, MC, AmEx
Reservations Not accepted

Yorkside is only steps away from the Yale Law School, Broadway, and
the College. So it's not hard to see why a steady stream of customers—
including a sizeable contingent of Yale Law professors—keeps the place
going even though the pizza is well below average. They serve pitchers
of Sam Adams along with the standard pizza-and-sub fare, and they're
open until 2am on weekends, doing a brisk business with the post-
concert gaggles from nearby Toad's Place.

The ridiculously big Greek salad, enough for two people, is your best
choice. It's a standard version but it's done well, with lettuce, tomatoes,
olives, plenty of feta, and a good, tangy Greek dressing. There's a
cheap lunch special that pleases fans by pairing a slice of greasy pizza
with a smaller portion of Greek salad on the side. The hot tuna melt is
another of the few promising options: a rich, creamy (and enormous)
tuna salad covered with melted cheese. If you prefer your meal (and a
half) in a cup, Yorkside's milkshakes also have a devoted following: all
of the standard flavors are there, plus the perpetually winning
"Moosetraks" blend.

Pizza is available by the slice—cheese, pepperoni, and one rotating
topping. Slices and pies are not Yorkside's strongest suit: they're thick,
cheesy, and oily, with uninspired sauce. Cheese is probably the poorest
choice of all; at least pepperoni and mushrooms add some much-
needed flavor. Yorkside thrives in part on its take-out business, selling
pies and two-liter Coke bottles en masse for Law School and College
functions. But in this pizza town, you can do so much better elsewhere
if that's what you're after.

Zaroka

6.6
10

A regally appointed Indian restaurant with fanciful dinner renditions as well as the usual lunch buffet

Indian   **$24**   *Upper Chapel Area*

6.3/10   **7.0**/10   **7.0**/10   **6.0**/10
Food   *Atmosphere* *Attitude*   *Value*

Upmarket restaurant   148 York St.   **Bar** Full
Mon.-Thurs. 11:30am-2:30pm,   New Haven   **Credit Cards** Visa, MC, AmEx
5pm-10pm; Fri.-Sat. 11:30am-   (203) 776-8644   **Reservations** Recommended
2:30pm, 5pm-10:30pm; Sun.   www.zaroka.com
noon-3pm, 5pm-10pm. *Brunch. Vegetarian-friendly.*

Veterans will know this place as "Nirvana," which was its name until the restaurant reportedly underwent a trademark dispute. The sexier urban legend holds that the place was actually sued by representatives of Kurt Cobain's canonical grunge band. We doubt it. Legends aside, this place is back in business after a fire sadly put them under for a while, and it vies with Royal India for best Indian in town. Prices are a bit higher than the norm, but the all-you-can-eat lunch buffet is a good deal.

Zaroka offers competent interpretations of the classics of Indian cuisine, but the novel dishes are where the place truly shines, and this won't happen in the buffet. Lamb achari comes in pickle gravy, shrimp malabar is served with coconut. Goan fish masala features tamarind and coconut along with tomato and onion, and dahi wada, one of the many vegetarian delights, is a dish of lentil doughnuts in yogurt sauce served with a vegetable and lentil broth. Stay away from the frightening, bright orange Zaroka Delight dessert, however; it's a disgusting, whipped mix of yogurt and mango that tastes like marshmallow fluff gone horribly wrong.

Zaroka's two-floored structure is strange but amusing. You're not quite sure, upon first entering the restaurant, whether to go up or down. Upstairs, you might feel as if you're an abdicated Indian prince (really—it's a silver throne you're sitting in), sailing through the India section of Disney's "It's a Small World" ride. Or you might discover the more practical applications of the ornate décor—little diamond chips of mirror embedded in the walls provide a delightfully faithful (though miniature) reflection of tables and diners across the room. But when it comes to flavorful Indian cuisine in downtown New Haven, Zaroka sits on a throne of its own.

Zinc

A modern, smartly appointed, Asian-influenced
restaurant with nice food and big-city leanings

New American $**45**   *Theater District*

9.0 /10   **7.5** /10   **8.0** /10   **7.2** /10
Food   *Atmosphere*   *Attitude*   *Value*

Upmarket restaurant   964 Chapel St.   *Bar* Full
Mon. 5:30pm-9:30pm; Tues.-Thurs. New Haven   *Credit Cards* Visa, MC, AmEx
noon-2:30pm, 5:30pm-9:30pm;   (203) 624-0507   *Reservations* Essential
Fri. noon-2:30pm, 5:30pm-10:30pm; www.zincfood.com
Sat. noon-2:30pm, 5:30pm-1am;
Sun. 4:30pm-8:30pm. *Date-friendly. Good wine list.*

The façade of this self-consciously smart downtown restaurant boldly
proclaims the arrival of 1980s Wall Street chic to the Elm City. Happily,
the feisty, creative cross-continental food usually lives up to the prices
and the pretense. Grilled tamari tuna with wasabi oil, fried spinach, and
a vegetable spring roll might sound like the typical New American-Asian
fusion dish—it is, in fact—but it's also extremely well executed. Lamb is
delicately grilled and served with a nice "smokey Black bean and ham
hock ragoût." Smoked duck nachos are a surprisingly harmonious
ménage of three continents' cuisines, with pieces of smoked duck on
fried wonton skins and chipotle aioli. It's this sort of dish that this
restaurant does best.

   Zinc is a hard nut to crack. It's hard not to laugh at the restaurant's
overzealous minimalism or its hippest-restaurant-in-town logo and "Z"
door handle, and it's hard not to assume that you're going to overpay
for pretentious service, delusions of New York grandeur, and
construction-cuisine flights of folly from down-and-out Culinary
Institute of America graduates. But the excellent food will allay your
fears. If you can handle the silence, the muted neon track lighting, and
the audacity with which menu prices are printed as punctuation-free
numbers (and they tend toward "11" for appetizers or "25" for mains)
you can enjoy, on a good night, one of the very best meals in New
Haven.

   If you don't want to spend all that money, the cocktails are good,
and it's not a bad idea to come in the early evening just to savor a slice
of bond-trader life, circa 1989. There's even live jazz on Saturdays from
10pm-1am (the kitchen still closes at 10:30, but drinks continue). So
don't dismiss Zinc. Sit down, relax, suspend judgment, and enjoy the
ride.

Do you know what's on the *Menu* in Northampton, Amherst, and the five-college area of Western Massachusetts?

Northampton and Amherst, Massachusetts, the pride of the Pioneer Valley, boast some of the world's most beautiful fall foliage. The idyllic area, just an hour and ten minutes north of New Haven on I-91, is home to five prominent colleges: Amherst, Smith, Mount Holyoke, Hampshire, and UMass. It also happens to have one of the most exciting food scenes in New England.

The Menu: Northampton, Amherst, and the Five-College Area is the **relentlessly opinionated** restaurant guide by *Menu: New Haven* authors Robin Goldstein and Clare Murumba. Order direct, for a special publisher's discount, at **www.fivecollegemenu.com**, or from **amazon.com**.

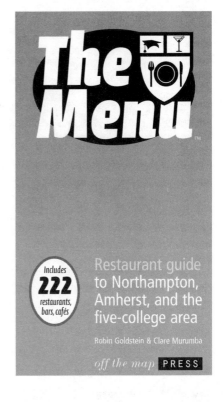

Includes **222** restaurants, bars, cafés

Restaurant guide to Northampton, Amherst, and the five-college area

Robin Goldstein & Clare Murumba

off the map PRESS

Zoi's on Orange

7.7
10

A cozy, informal, convenient joint whose American breakfasts and lunches are fresh and eclectic

Light American   **$ 8**   *Arts District*

7.4 /10   **8.0** /10   **9.0** /10   **9.4** /10
Food   *Atmosphere*   *Attitude*   *Value*

Counter service   338 Orange St.   *Bar* None
Mon.-Fri. 7am-3pm;   New Haven   *Credit Cards* Visa, MC, AmEx
closed Sat.-Sun.   (203) 777-6736   *Reservations* Not accepted
Breakfast. Vegetarian-friendly.

Zoi's is a cozy breakfast and lunch nook on State Street, at the corner of Grove, that is easily accessible from the very center of town and yet so petite that it is easily missed. The place is run by a husband-and-wife team whose husband left the corporate world in order to take over the space formerly inhabited by the popular Paula's. Zoi's has done an admirable job with the menu of creative standards plus the occasional Greek item. You order from the counter and can either take out or sit amidst the blond wood furniture and cutely evocative wall art in the airy, well-lit little room.

Deli sandwiches such as roast beef are simple and well executed, if not unusual, and their bread is extremely fresh. Our favorite sandwich creation has been the austerely named "Sandwich #8," which is piled with a chicken cutlet that's tender if not crisp, with bacon and smoked mozzarella—a good idea—but the beautifully conceived, ideally balanced chipotle mayo steals the sandwich show with a smoky kick that is just restrained enough not to dominate the flavors.

Zoi's also boasts H&H bagels and, generally speaking, a great vegetarian selection. A Greek salad is done by the book (what Greek salad isn't?) and enormous (what Greek salad isn't?), but the feta cheese is top-notch and the vegetables fresh. There's also the usual breakfast lineup, and there's something of a lunchtime grill lineup too—steak and cheese, pulled pork, and so on—the sort of items that make the cuisine difficult to categorize as anything other than, say, "eclectic American." Soft and delicious peanut-butter cookies lead the dessert parade.

INDEX

To look up food by category, neigbhorhood, or feature, please refer to the Lists section, which begins on page 19.

The Menu makes a tasteful gift.

Make somebody else—or yourself—happy, and order more copies of ***The Menu: New Haven*** or *The Menu: Northampton, Amherst, and the Five-College Area*, online, direct from the publisher at **www.newhavenmenu.com**. You can also order through amazon.com on our site.

Overnight shipping is available.

To order more than 10 copies at a special discount, or for information about using *The Menu* as a corporate gift, please call Off The Map Press at 203.286.1775.

WWW.OFFTHEMAPPRESS.COM

INFO@OFFTHEMAPPRESS.COM

off the map **PRESS**